Devotional experience and erotic knowledge in the literary culture of the English Reformation

Devotional experience and erotic knowledge in the literary culture of the English Reformation

Poetry, public worship, and popular divinity

RHEMA HOKAMA

Great Clarendon Street, Oxford, OX2 6DP,
United Kingdom

Oxford University Press is a department of the University of Oxford.
It furthers the University's objective of excellence in research, scholarship,
and education by publishing worldwide. Oxford is a registered trade mark of
Oxford University Press in the UK and in certain other countries

© Rhema Hokama 2023

The moral rights of the author have been asserted

All rights reserved. No part of this publication may be reproduced, stored in
a retrieval system, or transmitted, in any form or by any means, without the
prior permission in writing of Oxford University Press, or as expressly permitted
by law, by licence or under terms agreed with the appropriate reprographics
rights organization. Enquiries concerning reproduction outside the scope of the
above should be sent to the Rights Department, Oxford University Press, at the
address above

You must not circulate this work in any other form
and you must impose this same condition on any acquirer

Published in the United States of America by Oxford University Press
198 Madison Avenue, New York, NY 10016, United States of America

British Library Cataloguing in Publication Data

Data available

Library of Congress Control Number: 2022923615

ISBN 978–0–19–288655–2

DOI: 10.1093/oso/9780192886552.001.0001

Printed and bound in the UK by
Clays Ltd, Elcograf S.p.A.

Links to third party websites are provided by Oxford in good faith and
for information only. Oxford disclaims any responsibility for the materials
contained in any third party website referenced in this work.

For Bart

He nalu haki kākala

He nalu e ʻimi ana i ka ʻāina e hiki aku ai

Acknowledgments

In his *Occasional Meditations*, the English cleric Joseph Hall mused about how his visit to a great library filled with many books offered an occasion for intellectual wonder and delight. "What a world of wit is here packed up together?" he exclaimed. "There is no end of making many books; this sight verifies it. There is no end—indeed, it were pity there should." The writers of these books, Hall imagined, had "minds like unto so many candles," all of them "kindled by each other."[1] In a study about the ways in which communal and experiential devotional practices shaped individual thinking and affect, it is only fitting that I begin by acknowledging the many teachers, colleagues, and friends whose insight, guidance, support, and encouragement have helped to shape both my research and my thinking—the minds who "kindled" the ideas in this book.

My first debts are to my dissertation committee members. Stephen Greenblatt has been an exemplary adviser and mentor, who helped me see early modern texts and culture in new light. The most gratifying moments of the research process, and many of my best insights, have been the direct result of Stephen's capacious thinking and his ability to see the exchanges between disparate cultural domains. For these intellectual possibilities, I am eternally grateful to Stephen. James Simpson's fresh and original thinking about Reformation theology and intellectual life has left an indelible mark on my own research interests, and shaped this study's direction from the very outset. I am grateful to James for many years of personal encouragement and professional support in his role as both my adviser and teacher. Gordon Teskey's attentiveness to poetry's formal delights brought endless pleasure to my reading and rereading of Renaissance poetry. Gordon helped me understand that literary criticism is a necessary pursuit, one that affords the highest and best kind of gratification.

I am grateful to the members of Harvard's Renaissance Colloquium during my time in graduate school for providing me with invaluable support and encouragement when I was first beginning work on this book: Chris Barrett, Maria Devlin McNair, Rob Fox, Marjorie Garber, Jamey Graham, Stephen Greenblatt, Seth Herbst, the late Barbara Lewalski, David Nee, Katy Reedy, Craig Plunges, Will Porter, Luke Taylor, Misha Teramura, Gordon Teskey, Liz Weckhurst, Leah Whittington, and Benjamin Woodring offered generous feedback on several

---

[1] Joseph Hall, "Upon the sight of a Great library," in *Occasional Meditations* (London: Printed by M. F. for Nathaniel Butter, 1633 [1630]), 171–73. Copy from the Houghton Library, Harvard University.

ACKNOWLEDGMENTS vii

working manuscripts of my dissertation chapters. I have had the great fortune of arriving at Harvard along with a cohort of exceptionally gifted scholars and friends. For their camaraderie and support, I am thankful to Carra Glatt, Ari Hoffman, Calista McRae, David Nee, Len Neidorf, Misha Teramura, Stella Wang, and Annie Wyman.

In Singapore and at Singapore University of Technology and Design (SUTD), I am grateful to Sun Sun Lim, Pey Kin Leong, Phoon Kok Kwang, and Alan Kolata for their support for this project. For their enthusiasm, encouragement, and collegiality, I'm grateful to Nazry Bahrawi, Jeffrey Chan, Paolo Di Leo, Grace Dixon, Casey Hammond, Katherine Hindley, Andrew Hui, Jin Murakami, Olivia Nicol, Pang Yang Hui, Nina Raghunath, Michael Reid, Gordon Tan, Andrew Yee, Setsuko Yokoyama, Yow Wei Quin, and Zhenxing Zhao. I am especially grateful to Lyle Fearnley, Alastair Gornall, Samson Lim, Sandeep Ray, and Gabe Tusinski, who offered insightful comments on portions of this project in our faculty writing workshops at SUTD.

I am similarly grateful to the many professional colleagues who have provided me with vital suggestions and made critical interventions as I pursued my research. Audiences at Harvard University, Yale University, the University of Oxford, Northeastern University, the University of Toronto, Susquehanna University, Humboldt-Universität zu Berlin, the University of Cambridge, the University of Sydney, the University of Wellington, the National University of Singapore, the Singapore Ministry of Education, Tsinghua University, and the Indira Gandhi Centre for the Arts in New Delhi offered comments and feedback during presentations of earlier versions of this project. Additional conversations with the late David Bevington, Stephanie Burt, Bradin Cormack, Mimi Godfrey, the late Norman Hindley, Joseph Leo Koerner, Laura Lunger Knoppers, Barbara Lewalski, Kathleen Meyer, Edward P. Moore, John Pitcher, Martin Puchner, David Schalkwyk, Leah Whittington, and above all Richard Strier provided me with extremely helpful guidance, especially during the very early phases of my research and my thinking about Renaissance literature. In particular, Richard's intellectual generosity helped shaped my own thinking about Reformation religious culture when I first began thinking about many of the ideas that found their way into this project. At Oxford University Press, I owe much thanks to Ellie Collins, Karen Raith, Jacqueline Norton, and Aimee Wright for their enthusiasm and attention to this book during its various stages from manuscript to completion. I am also grateful to the readers at Oxford University Press for providing valuable suggestions about the argument and scope of this project.

A number of marvelous libraries and their expert curators made this project possible. I have benefited from the excellent collections at the Widener and Houghton Libraries at Harvard, the Regenstein Library at the University of Chicago, the Bodleian Library at the University of Oxford, the Cambridge University Library, the University of Pennsylvania Libraries, the Hesburgh

viii ACKNOWLEDGMENTS

Libraries at the University of Notre Dame, the Ghent University Library, and the National University of Singapore Library. I am especially grateful to Laura Farwell Blake and her colleagues at the Harvard University Libraries, who provided valuable research support as I worked on this study.

My dissertation research was supported by a Mellon Dissertation Fellowship from Harvard University, and facilitated by Dexter Fellowships and summer research grants from the Harvard English department. I am grateful to the Harvard English department and Harvard University for funding my project and research travel. I owe special thanks to the Harvard English department's administrative staff—and especially to Gwen Urdang-Brown, Shayna Cummings, Rebecca Cook, and Aubrey Everett—whose energy and support enriched my time at Harvard both academically and personally. In Singapore, a generous research grant from the Singapore Ministry of Education and from SUTD helped fund my work on this book project. At SUTD, I am also grateful for the expert administrative support of Christina Koek, Valeria Choo, Jane Zhang, and Angelina Law.

My Hawai'i *'ohana* provided me with much enthusiasm and *aloha. Mahalo nui loa* to Nathan Kyle Hokama, Frances Siu Kwan Yim Hokama, Patti Ann Hokama, Trinity Ann Schwartz, Chara Hokama, Nike Hokama, Pascha Hokama, Teddy Hokama, Michael Schwartz, Stephen Anson, Eddy Li, Kaishu Mason, as well as the Hokama, Chu, Wun, Yim, Ah See, Nordquist, Robison, Koorenhof, Nakano, and Creelman families. *Aloha wau iā 'oe.* I am grateful, too, to our worthy pioneers for all their *mālama* since small kid time. Sybil Wun Hokama, George Hokama, William Wun, Albert Wun, James Goon Jim Yim, and Woofgang Hokama, *a hui hou.*

My decades-long friendship with Leo Wong and his partner Samuel Wong has sustained, restored, and spirited me as I wrote this book. For many years now, Leo has listened enthusiastically as I talked about my work, always extending encouragement and support. Leo's home in New York offered me a respite from Boston when I needed to write—or to get away from writing—and the Wongs' home in Hong Kong has been a haven for me to think and revise during many much-needed trips away from Singapore. One supporter who has not read a word of my writing is Sybil Hi'iaka, who came into my life just as I was completing this book. During a time of pandemic, isolation, and international border closures, Sibby brought me immeasurable joy and delight. Above all, I am thankful to my husband Bart Van Wassenhove, who read and commented upon the entire manuscript many times over, and who sustained me and cheered me on from start to finish. As I worked on this book, Bart made our home conducive to creativity and intellectual flourishing. While I take full responsibility for any errors in this book, Bart surely deserves credit for many of my best insights. *Ik hou van jou.*

A portion of my Introduction has previously been published as "'Loves halowed temple': Erotic sacramentalism and reformed devotion in John Donne's 'To his Mistress going to bed,'" *Modern Philology* 119.2 (2021): 248–75.

Copyright © 2021, University of Chicago Press. Portions of Chapter 2 have previously been published as "Love's Rites: Performing Prayer in Shakespeare's Sonnets," *Shakespeare Quarterly* 63.2 (2012): 199–223. Copyright © 2012, The Johns Hopkins University Press. Portions of Chapter 6 have previously been published as "Praying in Paradise: Recasting Milton's Iconoclasm in Paradise Lost," *Milton Studies* 54 (2013): 161–80. Copyright © 2013, Duquesne University Press. I am grateful to these presses for permission to reprint portions of these publications in this book.

Contents

List of Illustrations	xi
Note on Early Modern Spelling and Editions	xii

Introduction
"Our senses do confirm our faith": Experience and
Devotional Certainty in *The Winter's Tale* and English
Reformation Culture — 1

1. Orthodoxy and Marginality: William Perkins, Richard
Hooker, and the English Experiential Tradition — 15

PART I. THEATER AND CEREMONY

2. Shakespeare's Sweet Boy: Love's Rites, Prayers Divine, and
Hallowed Name in the *Sonnets* — 47

3. Herrick's Players and Prayers: Ceremony, Theater, and
Extemporal Devotion in *Hesperides* and *His Noble Numbers* — 81

PART II. IMAGES, IDOLATRY, AND ICONOCLASM

4. Donne's Speaking, Weeping, Bleeding Images: Iconophobia
and Iconophilia in the *Holy Sonnets* and the Sermons — 121

5. Greville's Iconoclastic Desire: Reformed and Literary
Devotion in *Caelica* and *The Life of Sir Philip Sidney* — 159

6. Adam and Eve in Bed and at Prayer: Recasting Milton's
Iconoclasm in *Eikonoklastes* and *Paradise Lost* — 184

Bibliography	219
Primary Sources	219
Secondary Sources	224
Index	239

List of Illustrations

2.1. Frontispiece and title page of the 1609 edition of *Shake-speares Sonnets. Neuer before Imprinted*. At London: By G. Eld for T. T. and are to be solde by Iohn Wright, dwelling at Christ Church gate, 1609. Copy from the Folger Shakespeare Library.   52

3.1. Frontispiece and title page of Herrick's 1648 edition of *Hesperides*, containing the likeness of the poet. Printed in London for distribution at Thomas Hunt's Exeter bookshops. Copy from the Henry E. Huntington Library.   85

3.2. An unnamed shape poem from *His Noble Numbers*, formatted in the image of the Cross. London: Printed for John Williams and Francis Eglesfield, 1648. Copy from the Henry E. Huntington Library.   113

6.1. Frontispiece image of King Charles I at prayer from *Eikon basilike the pourtracture of His Sacred Majestie in his solitudes and sufferings*. London: Reprinted in R. M., Anno Dom. 1648 [1649]. Copy from the Houghton Library, Harvard University.   187

Note on Early Modern Spelling and Editions

I have worked from original editions whenever possible during my research for this study. These early editions of poetry, sermons, devotional tracts, and polemical treatises have supplied me with a trove of textual and material cues that even the best modern scholarly editions cannot provide. I have chosen to modernize the spelling of early modern prose, which often poses syntactical and orthographical challenges for contemporary readers. I make an exception for the titles of early modern prose works, retaining original spelling in my reference to all titles in this study. I have done so in order to help facilitate accurate retrieval of these works using online databases of early modern texts. Additionally, I quote the poetry as it appears in the original editions, since early modern orthographical flexibility often enables interpretive possibilities that remain overlooked when reading from modernized editions of the poems.

Introduction

"Our senses do confirm our faith": Experience and Devotional Certainty in *The Winter's Tale* and English Reformation Culture

The final act of *The Winter's Tale* stages a moment of epistemological uncertainty, one borne of a husband's sensory confusion as he gazes upon his long-lost wife. After an estrangement of sixteen years, King Leontes struggles to express a fitting devotion before the statue of Hermione, his absent queen. Of course, Hermione is merely participating in a ruse in order to test her husband's devotion: she poses as a statue of her own likeness, performing a miniature theatrical act on Shakespeare's stage as she stands stone-like before her husband and her daughter Perdita. The mastermind behind the queen's ruse is Hermione's lady Paulina, who has filled a chapel with a variety of art objects—one of these, she promises, is a statue that bears the likeness of the long-lost queen. When Paulina pulls back the curtain to reveal Hermione's form, Leontes is astonished by his wife's lifelike expression: "Her natural posture. / —Chide me, dear stone, that I may say indeed / Thou art Hermione; or, rather, thou art she."[1] For Shakespeare's early modern theatergoers, Leontes's attempts to look at the statue of his wife posed an interpretive quandary, one that was shared by the audience themselves: are we looking at a representation or at the queen in the flesh? What Leontes describes is a moment of sensory confusion, and he is uncertain as to how to interpret the statue before him. As Leontes looks on and observes, he notes oddities about his wife's representation: "But yet, Paulina, / Hermione was not so much wrinkled, nothing / So aged as this seems" (5.3.27–9). Hermione's wrinkles, which mark the passing of sixteen years, provoke an experiential conflict in Leontes: he is comforted to see his wife as she would have been now, even as this sight proves "piercing" to his soul (5.3.34).[2]

---

[1] 5.3.23–5. I have taken all citations of *The Winter's Tale* from *The Norton Shakespeare*, ed. Stephen Greenblatt et al. (New York: W. W. Norton, 2016). Hereafter I cite the play parenthetically in the text.

[2] Walter Lim and Richard Strier have argued that *The Winter's Tale* explores the question of how Reformation religious culture understood knowledge and belief. Lim argues that the reunion scene between Hermione and Leontes tracks a number of models of knowledge acquisition derived from post-Reformed literary culture—including the Calvinist claim that faith constituted a form of knowledge about one's salvation, Reformation anxieties about representation and figuration in both religious and theatrical contexts, and the play's status as a fictional "tale." Lim argues that the anxieties posed by the task of interpretation extend to the audience of *The Winter's Tale*, "who is then compelled to interpret and make sense of the play's apparent ideological contradictions and the meanings toward which

---

Devotional experience and erotic knowledge in the literary culture of the English Reformation. Rhema Hokama,
Oxford University Press. © Rhema Hokama (2023). DOI: 10.1093/oso/9780192886552.003.0001

2 DEVOTIONAL EXPERIENCE IN THE REFORMATION

In his confusion as to how to make sense visually and interpretively of the statue before him, Leontes experiences a moment of emotional paralysis, finding himself "Standing stone like" (5.2.42) before his wife: "I am ashamed. Does not the stone rebuke me / For being more stone than it?" (5.3.37–8). Here Leontes's line contains biblical echoes of Jesus's defense of the crowds who cry out in praise as he passes at the Mount of Olives: "if these should holde their peace, the stones would immediately cry out!"[3] A public, emotionally charged response to Christ's appearance is nothing less than a devotional requirement, and Leontes feels that he ought to give an equally powerful performance of praise upon the unveiling of his wife's statue.[4] Yet the sight of the statue and the memory of his wife render him stony, and he finds himself tormented by his sense of devotional inadequacy, one borne of his sensory and interpretive confusion. Leontes is not alone in his interpretive paralysis, and Perdita too is temporarily incapacitated by the sight of her mother's lifelike form: "So long could I / Stand by, a looker-on" (5.3.83–4).[5]

Perdita's self-characterization as a "looker-on" would have piqued the Reformed sensibilities of an early modern Protestant audience, who would have immediately understood that this characterization made her and her father extremely vulnerable to charges of devotional impropriety. Readers of this scene have long noted the sacramental resonances of the reunification, with takes place in a chapel.[6]

---

they gesture" in the play's confluence of Catholic and Reformation models of knowledge. See Walter S. H. Lim, "Knowledge and Belief in *The Winter's Tale*," *SEL Studies in English Literature, 1500–1900* 41, no. 2 (2001): 317–34. See p. 330 for Lim's quotation. Strier has argued that *The Winter's Tale* raises the fraught tensions between fact and opinion, arguing that the play demonstrates the way in which "the realm of belief is not necessarily and wholly determined by the realm of reality." See Richard Strier, "Mind, Nature, Heterodoxy, and Iconoclasm," *Religion & Literature* 47, no. 1 (2015): 31–59. See p. 31 for Strier's quotation.

[3] Luke 19:40. *The Holy Bible, Conteyning the Old Testament and the New* (London: Imprinted by Robert Barker, 1611). (*EEBO*, STC (2nd ed.) / 2217.)

[4] Strier has argued that Leontes's line contains an allusion to Habakkuk 2:11, in which the stones and beams of a home cry out in protest against the forced Israelite labor that built the structure. While Strier is correct in that Jesus's rebuke in Luke 19:40 is most likely an allusion to Habakkuk, it is undeniable that Leontes's lines makes more sense in light of a direct reference to the Gospel's commentary about the propriety of public devotional expression. For the discussion of the line's resonance with Habakkuk, see Strier, "Mind, Nature, Heterodoxy, and Iconoclasm," 43. Strier has noted that other readers of this scene, including Jennifer Waldron, have also noted resonances between Leontes's line and Ezekiel 11:19. See Jennifer Waldron, *Reformations of the Body: Idolatry, Sacrifice, and Early Modern Theater* (New York: Palgrave Macmillan, 2013), 81; and Jennifer Waldron, "Of Stones and Stony Hearts: Desdemona, Hermione, and Post-Reformation Theater," in *The Indistinct Human in Renaissance Literature*, eds. Jean E. Feerick and Vin Nardizzi (New York: Palgrave Macmillan, 2012), 205–27.

[5] James R. Siemon has also noted the scene's description of numbness and passivity. See James R. Siemon, *Shakespearean Iconoclasm* (Berkeley: University of California Press, 1985), 297.

[6] For the Eucharistic overtones of *The Winter's Tale*, see Louis Montrose, "The Purpose of Playing: Reflections on a Shakespearean Anthropology," *Helios* 7, no. 2 (1980): 51–74; Julia Reinhard Lupton, "*The Winter's Tale* and the Gods: Iconographies of Idolatry," in *Afterlives of the Saints: Hagiography, Typology, and Renaissance Literature* (Stanford: Stanford University Press, 1996), 175–218; T. G. Bishop, "*The Winter's Tale*; or, Filling Up the Graves," chap. 5 in *Shakespeare and the Theater of Wonder* (New York: Cambridge University Press, 1996), 125–75; Anthony Gash, "Shakespeare, Carnival, and the Sacred: *The Winter's Tale* and *Measure for Measure*," in *Shakespeare and the Carnival: After Bakhtin*, ed. Ronald Knowles (Basingstoke: Macmillan Press, 1998), 177–210, esp. 189–99; Michael O'Connell, *The Idolatrous Eye: Iconoclasm and Theater in Early-Modern England* (Oxford:

INTRODUCTION 3

A number of these readers have also noted that the reunification engaged with
Reformation anxieties about idolatry, considering that Leontes and Perdita's adoration of a statue made them liable to charges of idol worship.[7] But while the scene
registers a cultural anxiety about the nature of proper devotion, that anxiety was
not centered on the threat of idolatry, as past readers have maintained. While these
critics are right to note the scene's anxiety around proper devotional practice, those
anxieties center on Leontes and Perdita's own experiential engagement with the
statue and less on the statue's potentially imagistic nature. According to the *Book of
Common Prayer*'s sermon for the Holy Communion, written by John Jewel for the
Church of England's Reformed worship services, there were right and wrong ways
to partake in the sacrament. Most offensive to God, the sermon insists, are those
worshippers who stand aside as passive spectators during the performance of the
rites: "*if ye stand by as gazers and lookers on* them that do Communicate, and be
no partakers of the same yourselves," you are guilty of "contempt and unkindness
unto God."[8] Perdita's description of herself as a "looker-on" serves to position her

---

Oxford University Press, 2000), 138–44; Peter G. Platt, *Shakespeare and the Culture of Paradox* (Farnham: Ashgate, 2009), 198–201; Phebe Jensen, "Singing Psalms to Horn-Pipes: Festivity, Iconoclasm,
and Catholicism in *The Winter's Tale*," *Shakespeare Quarterly* 55, no. 3 (2004): 279–306; and Jensen's
expanded chapter of the same name, chap. 5 in *Religion and Revelry in Shakespeare's World* (Cambridge: Cambridge University Press, 2008), 194–233; and Jennifer Waldron, "Sacrament and Theater:
Shakespeare's Lawful Magic," chap. 2 in *Reformations of the Body: Idolatry, Sacrifice, and Early Modern
Theater* (New York: Palgrave Macmillan, 2013), 55–84.

[7] In his reading of the reunion scene, Michael O'Connell has argued that Shakespeare draws intentional parallels between idol worship and theatrical performance, making the audience complicit in
Leontes's act of idol worship: "If the scene for the moment fully associates theatricality with idolatry, Shakespeare does not counter, but embraces the charge." See O'Connell, *Idolatrous Eye*, 141. In
response to O'Connell, Jennifer Waldron has attempted to show the continuities between Catholic
and Reformed views of image-based worship, which both rely on the real body of the actor who plays
Hermione to demonstrate the legitimacy of Reformation sacramental worship based on Hermione's
embodied action and live performance. In drawing "attention not only to the lively medium of theatrical
bodies but also to the religious resonances of audience participation," Waldron argues that the reunion
scene complicates "the boundaries between the lawful and the unlawful in the Protestant imagination."
See Waldron, *Reformations of the Body*, 15–16, 82–3. For Waldron's quotation, see p. 82. In contrast to
O'Connell and Waldron, Richard Strier and Huston Diehl have argued that the play's reunion scene
did not appropriate or embrace modes of Catholic worship, nor did it frame lawful worship by renegotiating the boundaries of an existing Catholic sacramentalism. Strier and Diehl maintain Shakespeare
relied on Pauline claims about the legitimacy of ordinary bodily functions and actions in putting forth
a distinctly Reformed argument for the lawfulness of Leontes's and Perdita's adoration of Hermione.
See Strier, "Mind, Nature, Heterodoxy, and Iconoclasm," 31–60, esp. 43–7; and Huston Diehl, "'Does
Not the Stone Rebuke Me?': The Pauline Rebuke and Paulina's Lawful Magic in *The Winter's Tale*," in
Shakespeare and the Cultures of Performance, eds. Paul Yachnin and Patricia Badir (Burlington, VT:
Ashgate, 2008), 69–82, esp. 77–8. Others who have discussed the scene's engagement with the problem
of idolatry include Lupton, "*The Winter's Tale*," esp. 177–8; and Jensen, "Singing Psalms to Horn-Pipes"
(2004), 279–87.

[8] John Jewel, "The order of the administration of the Lordes Supper, or holy Communion," in
Thomas Cranmer and John Jewel, *The booke of common praier, and administration of the Sacramentes,
and other rites and ceremonies in the Churche of Englande* (London: In officina Richardi Iugge, &
Iohannis Cawode, 1559), sig. M5r (emphasis added). (EEBO, STC (2nd ed.) / 16292). For my previous argument about the threat of idol worship and the prayer book homily's references to "gazers
and lookers" in Shakespeare's literary output, see Rhema Hokama, "Love's Rites: Performing Prayer in
Shakespeare's *Sonnets*," *Shakespeare Quarterly* 62, no. 2 (2012): 199–223. For my discussion of Jewel's

4 DEVOTIONAL EXPERIENCE IN THE REFORMATION

devotion as passive, just like the communicants who show contempt before God. What is clear, then, is that the Reformed English church regarded passive participation in the Communion sacrament as the true devotional danger for Protestant worshippers. Paulina's admonition seems to capture the prayer book's injunction against passive gazing and looking: "It is required / You do awake your faith. Then all stand still. / On! Those that think it unlawful business / I am about, let them depart" (5.3.94–7). The lawfulness of what Paulina is about to reveal hinges on the active involvement of her onlookers, and the prerequisite that they first awaken their faith—which must come before the statue's transformation, not after.[9]

This book explores a Calvinist understanding of experiential devotion as a framework for ascertaining surety and truth in the religious and literary cultures of the English Reformation. For English Protestants, devotional experience melded the sensory and cognitive aspects of worship. In the case of Leontes, his sensory confusion leads to an interpretive quandary, which renders him devotionally inert—a passive "looker-on." In this book, I study the ways in which Reformed devotional culture shaped how early modern English poets understood what it meant to establish certainty in matters of devotional intention and effect. Like the exchange between Leontes and Hermione at the close of *The Winter's Tale*, these moments of devotional expression in early modern literature often straddle the realms of the spiritual and the worldly, and of the religious and the erotic. As such, one of the goals of this project is to track the ways that an early modern culture of religious devotion helped to change wider cultural perceptions about what it meant to ascertain devotional truth by means of cognitive and bodily experience—not only within contexts of religious devotion but also in a variety of erotic devotional encounters as they are treated in the literary output of the period.

This book makes a case for a distinctly Reformed epistemology of devotion and desire, one that has roots in an English interpretation of Calvin's experientialism. In doing so, this book explores the Reformed attention to the role of experience in the devotional practices of both official and popular English devotional culture during the decades bracketed by the lives of Shakespeare and Milton.

---

homily, see pp. 214–28; for my suggestion that the reunion scene of *The Winter's Tale* offered a response to the problem posed by idolatry in Cranmer, Jewel, and Hooker's Reformed Communion, see p. 211.

[9] Other readers have discussed the scene's allusions to the homilies of the *Book of Common Prayer*, including O'Connell, *Idolatrous Eye*, 141, and 57–8; and Strier, "Mind, Nature, Heterodoxy, and Iconoclasm," 44. Jay Zysk and Jennifer Waldron discuss the Reformed homily on the Communion sacrament in the argument that the scene mobilizes the homily's claim that lawful worship required participatory engagement on the part of the communicant. Zysk and Waldron's readings of the scene differ from mine, in that Zysk sees the homily renegotiating the figurative capacities of the late medieval sacrament, while Waldron focuses her energies on the way in which the body of the actor demonstrated the cultural exchange between the scene's engagement with sacramental theory and the theatrical process. See Jay Zysk, *Shadows and Substance: Eucharistic Controversy and English Drama across the Reformation Divide* (Notre Dame: University of Notre Dame Press, 2017), 221; and Waldron, *Reformations of the Body*, 70.

INTRODUCTION 5

These include devotional performances that took place as a part of state church worship—most significantly, the Communion and baptism sacraments, and the performance of the public liturgy. But this study also explores the role of experiential devotion in the popular devotional practices of the period, in the modes of worship and religious practices that took place outside of the contexts of the state church's services. In both official church ecclesiology and informal devotional practice, what the Reformation introduced to English religious and literary culture was the idea that an individual's experience of devotion did not entail only feeling, but also thought. For early modern English people, bodily experience offered a means of corroborating and verifying devotional truth, making the invisible visible and knowable. I maintain that these religious developments gave early modern thinkers and poets a new epistemological framework for imagining and interpreting devotional intention and access. Moreover, these Reformed models for devotion not only shaped how people experienced their encounters with God; the changing religious landscape of post-Reformation England also held profound implications for how English poets described sexual longing and access to earthly beloveds in the literary production of the period, as Leontes's desire for his long-lost wife makes clear.

The confluence of the sacramental and the sexual is apparent in Leontes's devotion to and desire for his wife in the final act of *The Winter's Tale*. Upon first touching the statue's form, its lifelike fleshiness astonishes the king. "O, she's warm!" Leontes cries. "If this be magic, let it be an art / Lawful as eating" (5.3.109–11). As Richard Strier has argued, Leontes's argument that his adoration of the statue is as "Lawful as eating" removes "the whole process from the realm of art (magic, of course, was an art) into the realm of ordinary natural behavior, and he taps into the Pauline (and Protestant) theme of the liberation of eating from restrictive laws."[10] For Leontes, this devotional experience offered the possibility of interpretive surety, enabling the king to establish the legitimacy of his desire and his awakened faith. For Leontes, to feel Hermiones's warmth, and to gaze upon her wrinkles and furrows with an interpretive intention, serves to remove his devotion from the realm of "magic" by making his desire for her as ordinary as the act of eating. In the sacramental overtones of the line's apparent reference to ingestion and digestion, Shakespeare severs the act of eating the sacramental bread and wine from the realm of "magic," recasting the reference to the Catholic Real Presence by reframing it in terms of Calvinist experientialism.[11] Leontes legitimizes his act of devotion to the queen by appealing to the experiential logic of Jewel's prayer book

---

[10] Strier, "Mind, Nature, Heterodoxy, and Iconoclasm," 46. For others who have discussed the lawfulness of eating in this line, see also Lupton, *"The Winter's Tale,"* 216; Diehl, "'Does Not the Stone Rebuke Me?,'" 78; Waldron, *Reformations of the Body*, 55, 70; and Zysk, *Shadows and Substance*, 214, 216–17.

[11] For an argument that frames the scene in terms of its engagement with a late medieval model of the Real Presence, see Zysk, *Shadows and Substance*, 217.

6   DEVOTIONAL EXPERIENCE IN THE REFORMATION

Communion homily, in his insistence that he is no passive "gazer" or "looker-on" but an active participant in the devotional process. In doing so, he makes a case for the way in which the intellect, senses, and bodily experience might serve as evidentiary proof of an awakened faith, and for the legitimacy of his adoration of his wife. In grasping at the statue in order to feel its warmth, Leontes acts out in a literal way a distinctly Reformed understanding of the Communion rites, one that rejected the Real Presence of Christ in favor of knowledge derived from sensory experience. In Thomas Cranmer's account of the Reformed Communion, the senses provide a means of establishing certainty in matters of faith, teaching us to believe the things that "we see daily with our eyes, and hear with our ears, and grope with our hands." For Cranmer, the senses did not just entail passive feeling, but constitute an active means of intellectual confirmation: "our senses do confirm our faith."[12] In his looking upon the queen and grasping her with his hands, Leontes's devotional experiences confirm his awakened faith.

The final scene from *The Winter's Tale* registers Leontes's anxiety about how to effectively interpret his own devotional experience, and how that experience can be presented to others in order to demonstrate the legitimacy of his desire. But that anxiety does not lie in the fact that the scene indicates an insurgent Catholic attachment to ceremony, as readers such as Julia Reinhard Lupton, Phebe Jensen, Elizabeth Williamson, and Jay Zysk have maintained.[13] As Lupton asserts, the play

---

[12] Thomas Cranmer, *A defence of the true and catholike doctrine of the sacrament of the body and bloud of our sauiour Christ.* (London: In Poules churcheyarde, at the signe of the Brasen serpent, by Reginald Wolfe. Cum priuilegio ad imprimendum solum, 1550.) (*EEBO.* STC (2nd ed.) / 6000, 22.) The prayer book's homily on the Communion rites entered use in the Reformed English state church with the publication of the 1549 *Book of Common Prayer*, which was written and compiled by Thomas Cranmer, Archbishop of Canterbury, during the reigns of Henry VIII and Edward VI. The year after the publication of this first edition, Cranmer published a curious argument about sensory engagement in his defense of the church's position on the Communion sacrament. Although Cranmer insisted that the sacrament offered communicants literal access to the presence of Christ, he nevertheless rejected the Catholic tenet that Christ's body and blood materially inhered in the sacramental bread and wine. Communicants know that the bread and wine are merely accidentals in the sacramental rites, Cranmer insisted, simply because our senses tell us so. In drawing an unprecedented distinction between the Reformed and Catholic Communion rites, Cranmer made the astonishing assertion that it was Protestants—and not Catholics—who had full access to the sensory experience of sacramental worship: "But to conclude in few words this process of our senses, let all the Papists lay their heads together, and they shall never be able to show one article of our faith, so directly contrary to our senses, that all our senses by daily experience shall affirm a thing to be, and yet our faith shall teach us the contrary thereunto." See Cranmer, *Defence*, 22–3.

[13] Lupton argues that the reunion scene of *The Winter's Tale* holds resonance with medieval hagiography and the cult of saints, Jensen proposes that the scene is suggestive of banned Catholic festivals, Elizabeth Williamson likens Hermione's performance to the medieval mystery cycles, and Zysk argues that the reunion scene models a semiotics of the Eucharist, one that sought to describe how "bodies are reconnected to their outward signs" in Reformation reimaginations of Catholic transubstantiation and the Catholic Real Presence. See Lupton, *"The Winter's Tale,"* 175–218; Jensen, "Singing Psalms to Horn-Pipes" (2004): 279–303; Jensen, "Singing Psalms to Hornpipes" (2008): 194–233; O'Connell, *Idolatrous Eye*, 138–44; Elizabeth Williamson, "'Things Newly Performed': Tomb Properties and the Survival of the Dramatic Tradition," chap. 2 in *The Materiality of Religion in Early Modern English Drama* (Farnham: Ashgate, 2009), 37–69; and Zysk, *Shadows and Substance*, 213–23. Others who have identified Catholic resonances in the final act of *The Winter's Tale* include Darryll Grantley,

INTRODUCTION 7

"picks out the paganism residual in Catholicism and the Catholicism residual in reformed England."[14] But what is clear is that Leontes's anxiety in the reunion scene is not indicative of cultural nostalgia so much as it captures the logic of Reformed experiential devotion itself. Like the prayer book's "gazers" and "lookers," Leontes fears his own ability to experience and feel devotion commensurate to the long-awaited reunion. For Leontes, that experience was of paramount importance, in that it offered a means of "confirming" his faith. In contrast to readers who have noted Catholic cultural resonances in the reunion scene's references to the liturgy, I maintain that Hermione's "magical" resurrection resonates less with the Real Presence of the Catholic Eucharist than it tracks the logic of a distinctly Reformed argument that experiential devotion could offer a framework not only for ascertaining truth and surety, but also a means to devotional access and intimacy with Christ.[15]

In the *Institutio*, Calvin describes the outcome of justification in terms of bodily transfusion and indwelling: "You see that our righteousness is not in us but in Christ, and that it belongeth to us only by this title, because we be partakers of Christ, because we possess all his richess with him ... [H]e meaneth no other fulfilling, but that which we obtain by imputation. For the Lord Christ doth in such sort communicate his righteousness with us, that after a certain marvelous manner, he pourest the force thereof into us."[16] As Susan Schreiner has argued, Calvin understood the devotional relationship between the believer and Christ in terms of bodily and spiritual exchange. Calvin's soteriology, Schreiner asserts, recognized "the nearness of or 'in-dwelling' of Christ within the believer." Schreiner maintains that throughout the *Institutio*, Calvin uses the language of bodily unification

---

"*The Winter's Tale* and Early Religious Drama," *Comparative Drama* 20, no. 1 (1986): 17–37, who argues that Hermione functions as a Virgin Mary figure as she commonly appears in the medieval Resurrection plays; Lim, "Knowledge and Belief," 317–34, who argues that the play complicates the boundaries between Catholic and Protestant models of knowledge; Maurice Hunt, *Shakespeare's Religious Allusiveness: Its Play and Tolerance* (Aldershot: Ashgate, 2004), 128–9, who reads Hermione's "iconicity" as an allusion to former Catholic devotional practice; Alice Dailey, "Easter Scenes from an Unholy Tomb: Christian Parody in *The Widow's Tears*," in *Marian Moments in Early Modern British Drama*, eds. Regina Buccola and Lisa Hopkins (Aldershot: Ashgate, 2007), 127–40, esp. 134–5, who argues that Hermione's unveiling is informed by the Catholic liturgy and belief in transubstantiation; and Sarah Beckwith, "Shakespeare's Resurrections: *The Winter's Tale*," chap. 6 in *Shakespeare and the Grammar of Forgiveness* (Ithaca, NY: Cornell University Press, 2011), 127–46, who notes the resonances between the portrayal of the Resurrection in the medieval cycle plays and Hermione's ultimate reawakening.

For a critique of Catholic approaches to the play, see Huston Diehl, "'Strike All that Look Upon With Marvel': Theatrical and Theological Wonder in *The Winter's Tale*," in *Rematerializing Shakespeare: Authority and Representation on the Early Modern English Stage*, eds. Bryan Reynolds and William N. West (New York: Palgrave Macmillan, 2005), 19–34; and Diehl, "'Does Not the Stone Rebuke Me?,'" 80.

[14] Lupton, "*The Winter's Tale*," 177.

[15] For a discussion of English Calvinism and the quest for devotional certitude in the erotics of John Donne's elegies, see Rhema Hokama, "'Loves halowed temple': Erotic Sacramentalism and Reformed Devotion in John Donne's 'To his Mistress going to bed,'" *Modern Philology* 119, no. 2 (2021): 248–75.

[16] John Calvin, *Institutes of the Christian Religion: 1536 Edition*, trans. Ford Lewis Battles (Grand Rapids, MI: Eerdmans, 1986 [1975]), 3.11.23.

to describe this relationship between the believer and Christ: "This oneness with Christ creates the experiential certainty of faith in the soul of the believer. Language about 'oneness,' 'indwelling,' 'engrafting,' 'imparting,' 'engraving,' 'interiority,' 'partaking,' and 'penetrating' describe the true depth of the certitude of faith."[17] In a similar fashion, Michelle Chaplin Sanchez argues that the sensing body and the material world provide the foundation for Calvin's providentialism. According to Sanchez, "Calvin's providence locates the world's meaning in God's deliberate and affirming relationship to the created world as such—the world of *physis* rather than *nomos*."[18] Sanchez contends that Calvin's theology emerges from the crossroads of scriptural interpretation and bodily experience: "The Divine Word does not just exist in isolation; it creates. Scripture needs a body to address and shape in order to do its work."[19] For Calvin and his English acolytes, ideas of what it meant to ascertain the realness of one's relationship to Christ's body hinged upon a devotional practice centered on experience. As Leontes's argument for the legitimacy of his faith makes clear, this view of devotional certitude offered a means of knowing and verifying truth. Equally important, the king is making a case for the legitimacy of his desire for his wife; his experience of nearness and oneness with his wife is an argument in itself for the validity of his devotion. As much as the scene offers a resolution to the problem of devotional experience and interpretation in Reformed doctrine, it also raises the possibility that sexual longing partook of the epistemological and interpretive capacities of Calvin's soteriology. As Strier argues, the opening act of *The Winter's Tale* raises the question of legitimate sexual desire; he maintains that "Hermione does not accept the view that adult sexuality is fundamentally sinful."[20] In the reunion between husband and wife, the scene supports the view of happy sexuality that Strier ascribes to Hermione in Act 1. In celebrating the legitimacy of a Calvinist experiential devotion, the reunion scene also asserts that reciprocal sexual desire between Leontes and Hermione offers a form of devotional "confirmation"—one that was as powerful as the forms of intellectual and spiritual assurance offered by the Reformed sacraments. In the final scene of *The Winter's Tale*, the king's devotional experience provides Shakespeare's audience with evidentiary proof of the legitimacy of his devotion and the embodied realness of his queen, proffering a distinctly Calvinist epistemology of desire.

In my argument about *The Winter's Tale* and in my literary readings of five early modern poets, I posit that English Calvinism provided not only a theology but an epistemology—one that articulated a sensory and experiential model

---

[17] Susan Schreiner, *Are You Alone Wise?: The Search for Certainty in the Early Modern Era* (Oxford: Oxford University Press, 2010), 69.

[18] Michelle Chaplin Sanchez, *Calvin and the Resignification of the World* (Cambridge: Cambridge University Press, 2019), 116.

[19] Sanchez, *Calvin and the Resignification of the World*, 8.

[20] Strier, "Mind, Nature, Heterodoxy, and Iconoclasm," 35.

INTRODUCTION 9

for ascertaining knowledge and truth. For Calvin, epistemological certainty was not based solely on intellectual apprehension. In the *Institutio*, Calvin asserted that devotional certainty was not something that could be guaranteed by either scriptural exegesis or theological study. It was, on the contrary, firmly rooted in experience and participatory engagement. According to Calvin, faith "requires full and fixed certainty such as men are wont to have from things *experienced and proved*."[21] Certainty, for Calvin, entailed firsthand experience. The Latin verb *experiri* captures both the active and passive meanings of experience; it means to test, examine, and demonstrate as well as to be affected by a particular condition. Calvin uses the terms *experientia* and *experimentum* interchangeably in his theological writings, and English Reformed Protestantism reflects these dual meanings in its conception of what spiritual experience should entail.[22] While one could document and test the knowledge that came from experience, this knowledge was not axiomatic or scientific in nature and could not be derived by those means. In Calvin's doctrine, T. H. L. Parker writes, "The knowledge of God cannot be regarded as one of the branches of epistemology, but differs fundamentally from all other forms of knowing."[23] Assurance of election took the form of experiential knowledge, fully grounded in the certainty that comes from cognitive and sensory experience.

R. T. Kendall has argued that Calvin's emphasis on subjective experience affected English religious culture most profoundly through the introduction of what Kendall has termed "experimental predestinarianism." In Kendall's terminology, "experimental" essentially means something akin to "experiential"—rooted in bodily and sensual experience. Kendall explicitly chooses to use the term "experimental" rather than "experiential" to describe the predestinarian theology of Calvin's English followers for two reasons. First, this is the term that English Calvinists like William Perkins and his contemporaries themselves used to describe their particular variety of faith. Second, it encodes a punning potentiality: "the word 'experimental' contains a useful ambiguity since it refers to experience but also to testing a hypothesis by an experiment. The experimental predestinarians put this proposition to the test: 'whether a man be in the state of damnation or

---

[21] Calvin, *Institutes*, 3.2.15, emphasis added. For discussion of Calvin's experiential understanding of faith, see Schreiner, *Are You Alone Wise?*, 66–8.

[22] Willem Balke, "The Word of God and Experientia According to Calvin," in *Calvin Ecclesiae Doctor: International Congress on Calvin Research*, ed. Wilhelm H. Neuser (Kampen, Neth.: Kok, 1978), 19–31, see esp. 20–1.

[23] Thomas H. L. Parker, *Calvin's Doctrine of the Knowledge of God* (Grand Rapids, MI: Eerdmans, 1959 [1952]), 106. For discussions of Calvin's experience-based understanding of spiritual knowledge and faith, see Walter E. Stuermann, *A Critical Study of Calvin's Concept of Faith* (Ann Arbor: Edwards Brothers, 1952), 63–112; Joel R. Beeke, *Assurance of Faith: Calvin, English Protestantism, and the Dutch Second Reformation* (New York: Peter Lang, 1991), esp. 49–55; Susan E. Schreiner, "'The Spiritual Man Judges All Things': Calvin and the Exegetical Debates about Certainty in the Reformation," in *Biblical Interpretation in the Era of the Reformation: Essays Presented to David C. Steinmetz in Honor of His Sixtieth Birthday*, eds. Richard A. Muller and John L. Thompson (Grand Rapids, MI: Eerdmans, 1996), 189–215, esp. 208; and Schreiner, *Are You Alone Wise?*, 66–8.

10 DEVOTIONAL EXPERIENCE IN THE REFORMATION

in the state of grace.'"[24] Nevertheless, in spite of the historicity of Kendall's term, I have chosen to use the modernized term "experiential" to avoid confusion among contemporary readers of this book, due to the fact that the word "experimental" now usually means something more akin to newfangled or innovative—a meaning that does not reflect the original import of the term's usage. My terminology also keeps within current scholarly trends. Recent works on experiential religion, most prominently Schreiner's *Are You Alone Wise?*, use the term "experiential" where Kendall would have used "experimental."[25] Much like Jewel and Cranmer's understandings of the Reformed Communion, Perkins's model of experiential devotion emerged from a commitment to the idea that God reveals devotional truth to the believer "through the help of things perceived by the outward senses."[26] Perkins asserted that "God revealeth things, either by the inward inspiration of his spirit, or outwardly by his word: or both inwardly and outwardly, by inward and outward effects."[27]

In focusing on the shared Calvinist experientialism in the devotional performances of the state church and popular religious culture, my intention in this book is twofold: first, my aim is to expand the discussion of early modern religious literary culture to include modes of worship that were practiced beyond the confines of the state church's public worship services. In particular, I look at Perkins's variety of English Calvinism in order to demonstrate the way in which his practical divinity, popularized in bestselling devotional manuals, can help us understand Leontes's defense of his devotion in terms of Calvinist experientialism. While Perkins's contributions to English devotional practice have primarily been understood in terms of sign hunting, the anxious search for signs of salvation or damnation, this account of Perkins's experiential Calvinism traffics in narrow stereotypes about "puritanism" and ignores the broad cultural applications of Calvin's experiential soteriology in the English devotional and literary output of the period. In my attention to popular devotional manuals of those like Perkins, Samuel Hieron, Joseph Hall, and William Gouge, I demonstrate how the English Calvinist tradition attributed epistemological potential to a wide range of ordinary experience, including sexual experience. Second, in placing the Reformed liturgy and sacraments in conversation with this popular experiential tradition— one that placed new emphasis on sense-based experience as a form of knowledge and as a means to devotional certainty—my goal is to highlight aspects of English devotional culture that have too often been overlooked in the literary readings

[24] See R. T. Kendall, *Calvin and English Calvinism to 1649* (Oxford: Oxford University Press, 1979), 9.

[25] See in particular Schreiner, "Experientia: The Great Age of the Spirit," chap. 5 in *Are You Alone Wise?*, 209–60.

[26] William Perkins, *A Golden Chaine: or The description of theologie containing the order of the causes of saluation and damnation* (Cambridge: Printed by Iohn Legat, printer to the Vniuersitie of Cambridge, 1600), 6. (*EEBO*, STC (2nd ed.) / 19646, document image 5).

[27] William Perkins, *A case of conscience the greatest that ever was, how a man may know, whether he be the son of God or no* (Imprinted at London: By Thomas Orwin, for Thomas Man and Iohn Porter, 1592), 40. (*EEBO*, STC (2nd ed.) / 19666, document image 22). Copy from the Bodleian Library.

INTRODUCTION 11

of the period, in part because experiential Calvinism has been regarded by a number of historians and literary scholars as the domain of a Puritan fringe culture rather than part of mainstream English Protestant devotional practice. As a result, although literary scholars have offered readings of the reunion scene of *The Winter's Tale* in relation to the official worship of the state church, there has been little attention to the ways in which Leontes's devotional justification also rests upon aspects of the Calvinist experientialist tradition celebrated by popular devotional writers like Perkins. My aim in this project is to demonstrate the continuities between the forms of worship that took place within the official ceremonies of the Reformed English church and the forms of experientialist popular devotion that shaped English religious life outside of the confines of the official church services. In doing so, I maintain that the Reformed liturgy and Communion—as imagined in *The Winter's Tale* and the literary culture of the Reformation—subscribed to an epistemology inspired by Calvinist experientialism that was shared in common in the devotional manuals and treatises of popular devotional writers like Perkins.

This study explores the way Calvinist experientialism provided both a theology and an epistemology in the poetry of five early modern English poets: William Shakespeare, Robert Herrick, John Donne, Fulke Greville, and John Milton. This book uses Shakespeare's staged performance of embodied devotion in the final act of *The Winter's Tale* as a fulcrum for thinking about the role of experience and the interpretive quest for certitude in comparable displays of Renaissance devotion—enacted not on stage but in poetry.

In Chapter 1, I argue that a shared soteriological outlook shaped both the public ceremonialism of Richard Hooker's *Lawes of Ecclesiastical Polity* and the experiential devotional practices that were developed by Reformed theologians like William Perkins. Although the prevailing scholarship on early modern church history and literary studies has largely regarded the theologies of Hooker and Perkins as mutually opposed, I maintain that it was the continuities between these religious outlooks that shaped the way early modern English worshippers understood devotional expression in the years after the Reformation. The shared ways in which Hooker and Perkins thought about the role of participatory worship and bodily affect provided models for how English Protestants could intellectually and experientially confirm their devotion, and my discussion of these continuities provides the historical and intellectual framework for my subsequent readings of the poetry in Parts I and II of this book.

Part I of this book explores the convergence of the English secular stage tradition and experiential devotional practice. In Chapter 2, on Shakespeare's *Sonnets*, I argue that Shakespeare used a number of topoi from Reformed devotional culture to describe both stage performance and erotic performance in the sonnets addressed to the young man. Although previous readers of the *Sonnets* have regarded its religious import—the poet's rote performance and reiteration of praise from the public liturgy—as evidence of devotional hypocrisy, I argue that these interpretations stem from a misunderstanding of Cranmer and Jewel's Reformed

12 DEVOTIONAL EXPERIENCE IN THE REFORMATION

ceremonialism as well as a misunderstanding of the role of the *Book of Common Prayer* in English devotional culture. Liturgical devotion in early modern England operated within a nexus of social exchange, and straddled the divide between private and public worship. I maintain that for Shakespeare's poet to co-opt those modes of devotion in describing his erotic entreaties to his boyfriend would not have been regarded as evidence of hypocrisy, but as a means of defining the contours of a distinctly early modern sense of embodied selfhood that exists at the crossroads of public expression and experiential devotion.

In Chapter 3, I further my exploration of the porous relationship between religious and erotic devotional culture in my reading of Robert Herrick's *Hesperides* and *His Noble Numbers*. While the majority of recent readers of Herrick have portrayed him as a royalist poet and have interpreted his lyrics as purveyors of conservative Caroline orthodoxy, I argue that recent scholarship on the redating of Herrick's lyric output compels us to recognize Herrick as a poet of the 1610s and 1620s—rather than one of the 1640s. As is the case in Shakespeare's *Sonnets*, Herrick's vision of erotic devotion was illuminated by topoi from the English theaters as well as a distinctly reformist experiential devotional practice— in particular, the practical divinity popularized by the cleric Joseph Hall. Herrick's devotional expressions only seem dull or childish—as a number of critics have described them—when we read his poems in anachronistic Caroline religious and political contexts. In stripping the lyrics from those confines, my goal is to elevate the inherently materialist and embodied nature of Herrick's devotional expression—both in his love poems to his girlfriends and to his ultimate erotic interest: Christ.

Part II of this book explores the early modern anxiety about the threat of dangerous images in Reformed devotional culture. In Chapter 4, I explore Donne's tendency to be simultaneously fascinated with and repelled by images of Christ in the *Holy Sonnets*, which alternatively seem to support and reject Perkins's admonition about the dangers of images. I argue that Donne's paradoxical and often contradictory stance on devotional images—both as a poet and as a preacher— was not indicative of an idiosyncratic spiritual struggle so much as it is telling of a wider devotional confusion about what constituted idolatry in the English Reformed tradition. I maintain that this confessional confusion about devotional images had distinctive repercussions for the way in which Donne allowed himself to ascertain and verify devotional affect, not only in his relationship with Christ, but also in his erotic encounters. In describing spiritual access to Christ, I suggest that Donne reappropriated the logic of his sexual relationships with his various mistresses—as well as with his wife, Anne More. As in these sexual relationships, Donne believed that the affinity between believer and Christ could be established by means of visible and experiential impressions, and through material and bodily proximity.

In Chapter 5, I turn my attention to Fulke Greville and his iconoclastic lyric sequence *Caelica*. While Donne grappled with dangers posed by the idols of the

INTRODUCTION 13

mind and the threat of mental images, Greville turned his attention to more tangible idols: the temptations of the flesh and the burden posed by the literary legacy of his friend Philip Sidney. For much of the twentieth century, the scholarly tradition has described Greville narrowly—as orthodox in both his theology and his poetics, and of interest only in his capacity as a satellite figure within Sidney's orbit. This reputation is one for which Greville himself was partly responsible, due to his understated self-presentation in his biography of his friend. However, Greville's self-deprecation was more guise than reality, and his self-fashioning gave him license both to reimagine the boundaries of Reformed devotional culture and to critique aspects of Sidney's poetics. I argue that Greville's treatment of lost Paradise in his erotic lyrics (too often overlooked in favor of his devotional poems) provided ways for him to describe precarious devotion—to girlfriends, to the young man Cupid, to God, and to his friend Sidney.

The allure and horror of a lost Eden in Greville's *Caelica* anticipates Milton's own obsession with the Fall and its aftermath in *Paradise Lost*, the topic of Chapter 6. In his polemical tracts, Milton vehemently criticized the use of set prayers; in the case of Charles I, Milton likened the king's use of set forms—both scriptural and poetic—to a kind of devotional plagiarism. What is surprising, then, is that despite his polemical rejection of set forms, Milton made ample use of them in envisioning Adam and Eve's Edenic prayer and praise in *Paradise Lost*. I argue that Milton sought to reimagine set prayer as a form of experiential devotion in his retelling of the Fall. While these forms would have sounded and looked much like the state liturgy for *Paradise Lost*'s Caroline readers, I maintain that Milton intended to strip those prayers of their original political and theological contexts by creating an Edenic origin for these forms of worship. For Milton, what might have appeared like early modern set worship was in fact an extension of Paradisal experience—all of which was, before the Fall, a mode of commune with God. To this end, Milton saw bodily acts such as sex and digestion as having a devotional equivalency to prayer; to have sex and to eat in Eden was for Milton as good, if not better, than formal worship in the state church.

In poetry written after the Reformation, English Calvinist experientialism, in both official and popular contexts, shaped literary accounts of devotional intimacy and access—not only to God, but also to dead wives, standoffish mistresses, exes, prostitutes, homoerotic lovers, and even Satan. Reformation worship engendered new means by which early modern English people could outwardly demonstrate and corroborate things otherwise invisible, drawing the unseen and unknown firmly within the grasp of the senses.

***

In the reunion scene in *The Winter's Tale*, the bonds that link Hermione to both husband and daughter reach across the insurmountable chasm separating life from death, seemingly drawing the queen back into the present realm of the living. "[D]o not say 'tis superstition that / I kneel and then implore her blessing," Perdita

14 DEVOTIONAL EXPERIENCE IN THE REFORMATION

asserts. "Lady, / Dear Queen, that ended when I but began, / Give me that hand of yours to kiss" (5.3.44–7). A few moments later, Leontes re-enacts his daughter's expression of devotion: "Let no man mock me," he proclaims, "For I will kiss her" (5.3.78–9). Two kisses, imprinted on Hermione's warm and breathing body, two public performances of desire and devotion, effectively overcome the ruptures between husband and wife, parent and child, and the living and the dead. Leontes and Perdita desire a beloved wife and mother, long absent; yet they pine for her not as an idea or fragment of memory but as a bodily being with live desires of her own. Quite unlike Pygmalion's statuesque creation, content to remain the passive object of longing, Hermione's statue quickly reveals her own capacity to reciprocate desire with desire.[28] "She embraces him!" the onlookers exclaim. "She hangs about his neck!" (5.3.112–13). For the onlookers, this moment of mutual desire sparks in everyone present an awakened faith, one alert to the interpretive possibilities of Hermione's expressions of longing for her long-lost husband. In Shakespeare's rendering of Calvinist experientialism, desire offers a form of devotional knowledge and provides a mode of ascertaining Hermione's "real presence"—not in the Catholic sense but in a distinctly Calvinist one—as embodied mother and wife.

As Paulina invites her audience to awaken their faith, Shakespeare, at the conclusion of the play, invites his own audience offstage to engage with the scene's epistemological uncertainty, and like Leontes, to rely on their own experiential encounter to ascertain the legitimacy of the final revelation. As Peter G. Platt has noted, "Unlike the audience of even Shakespeare's other plays of wonder—*Pericles*, *Cymbeline*, and *The Tempest*—the external witnesses of *The Winter's Tale* are ignorant of many of the play's crucial details and share the astonishment at Hermione's being alive with most of the on-stage audience."[29] In transforming Leontes and Perdita's passive spectatorship into active devotional engagement within the scene, *The Winter's Tale* engages the audience not as passive gazers and lookers-on but as active interpreters in the devotional process. That devotional process is an experiential one, proving in real time Cranmer's assertion that "our senses do confirm our faith." At the end of the play, Shakespeare invites his audience to join in with Leontes and Perdita's devotion to the queen. In *The Winter's Tale*, Shakespeare insists—as Cranmer and Jewel do for the sacramental rites—upon audience participation as a required condition for effective devotional performance.

---

[28] For a reading of the play's classical sources, including its resonances with the Pygmalion story, see Leonard Barkan, "'Living Sculptures': Ovid, Michelangelo, and *The Winter's Tale*," *ELH* 48, no. 4 (1981): 639–67.

[29] Platt, *Shakespeare and the Culture of Paradox*, 201.

1
Orthodoxy and Marginality
William Perkins, Richard Hooker, and the English Experiential Tradition

In my Introduction, I proposed a reading of the reunion scene in *The Winter's Tale* rooted in Calvin's experientialist theology. I suggested that the scene poses an epistemological problem for Leontes, one arising from his confusion about how to interpretively make sense of the "statue" of his wife. In this book, I maintain that attention to the popular experientialist vein of English Calvinist devotional culture can help us place the period's literary output in conversation with a distinctly Reformed epistemology, one that posited devotional experience as a form of knowledge and offered a framework for ascertaining devotional intent and access.

Recent literary studies on the role of sense experience in the post-Reformation English tradition have explored the role of perception and bodily engagement in early modern devotional culture, especially with respect to the official liturgies and sacraments of the English church. Nonetheless, attention to popular devotional practices—those that took place outside of the official contexts of the state church services—have largely been overlooked in scholarly treatment of the literary culture of the English early modern period. As I have noted in my Introduction, arguments that works like *The Winter's Tale* might be understood primarily in terms of late medieval sacramental or liturgical contexts, or as Reformed versions of these earlier Catholic practices, have dominated literary approaches to the play. These predominant approaches to *The Winter's Tale* ignore the ways in which Leontes's awakened faith in fact demonstrates a distinctly Calvinist view of the sensory and cognitive aspects of devotional experience, one that resonated with the popular piety of reformers such as William Perkins.

The argument for the persistence of a late medieval understanding of bodily experience and sensory engagement in post-Reformation worship undergirds a number of recent scholarly works on the Reformation and the senses. For example, in his study on the role of the senses in the devotional culture of the English Reformation, Matthew Milner has argued that a fundamentally Catholic understanding of the senses, shaped by Augustinian and Thomist interpretations of Aristotle as well as a late medieval understanding of Galenic humoral theory, continued to determine how English worshippers understood the role of the senses in the Henrican and Elizabethan churches: "I contend the reform was

---

Devotional experience and erotic knowledge in the literary culture of the English Reformation. Rhema Hokama, Oxford University Press. © Rhema Hokama (2023). DOI: 10.1093/oso/9780192886552.003.0002

16 DEVOTIONAL EXPERIENCE IN THE REFORMATION

shaped by the persistence of medieval sensory culture, its ethics and physiological contours," Milner asserts, maintaining that "sensory physiology remained relatively stable from the late thirteenth to the seventeenth century."[1] While Milner rightfully argues against the view that the Reformation ushered in "asensual austerity" in devotional culture, he does not think that the Reformation proffered a fundamentally different view of the senses than the one that shaped late medieval Catholic religious culture: "the contours of English reform owe much to the maintenance and even intensification of late-medieval sensory ethics, and the retention of Aristotelian-Galenic affective sensory physiology."[2] He takes the position that "the fundamentals of traditional medieval sensory culture did not change over the course of the sixteenth century in England. If anything they intensified."[3]

Milner's application of Catholic devotional frameworks to explain the role of experience and the senses in post-Reformation devotional life resonates with similar arguments put forth by those such as Jay Zysk and Jennifer R. Rust, who propose Thomist frameworks for their arguments about the role of the bodily experience in post-Reformation England. In his readings of both late medieval and early modern English drama, Zysk argues for a continuous semiotic framework for signification shared among both the English Communion rites and its Catholic predecessor, positing a Thomist framework for the Eucharistic arguments made by Reformation church thinkers such as Thomas Cranmer and Richard Hooker.[4] In a similar vein, Rust argues for continued interest in the Catholic *corpus mysticum* in the literary cultures of the Reformation. In doing so, Rust posits late medieval political thought as a guiding framework for her understanding of the liturgy in post-Reformation England, across the full sweep of the Henrican era through the English Civil War.[5]

Milner's, Zysk's, and Rust's arguments for the persistence of Catholic devotional culture in the religious life of early modern England means that their cultural focus rests primarily on the official sacramental, liturgical cultures, and worship spaces of the Reformed English church.[6] These scholars make carefully documented and astute connections between late medieval Catholic piety and post-Reformed English devotion, but by focusing exclusively on the official liturgy and sacraments

---

[1] Matthew Milner, *The Senses and the English Reformation* (New York: Routledge, 2011), 8 and 38. For Milner's argument for the persistence of late medieval Aristotelian views of the senses in Reformed worship, see also 14–21, 24–38, 53–92; for his treatment of the continued influence of late medieval Galenic humor theory, see 21–4.

[2] Milner, *Senses and the English Reformation*, 4, 146.

[3] Milner, *Senses and the English Reformation*, 4.

[4] Jay Zysk, *Shadows and Substance: Eucharistic Controversy and English Drama across the Reformation Divide* (Notre Dame: University of Notre Dame Press, 2017), 10.

[5] Jennifer R. Rust, *The Body in Mystery: The Political Theology of the* Corpus Mysticum *in the Literature of Reformation England* (Evanston, IL: Northwestern University Press, 2014), xi–28, 4–9, 18–19.

[6] For Milner's discussion of liturgical practice, see *Senses and the English Reformation*, 93–162, 241–342. For Milner's treatment of the role of the senses in the spatial layout of church spaces as places of worship, see *Senses and the English Reformation*, 163–206.

ORTHODOXY AND MARGINALITY   17

in their attention to the persistence of late medieval forms of piety, they overlook the ways in which Reformation theology reimagined the role of the senses in devotional life outside of the confines of the state church services. As I noted in my Introduction, Calvin's experientialist theology had a profound impact on popular devotional practice in Reformed England, disseminated in blockbuster devotional how-to manuals by English Calvinists such as William Perkins, Joseph Hall, and other devotional writers. In focusing exclusively on the devotional practices that took place in the official church services, Zysk and Rust overlook the powerful role that experience played in the popular devotional culture of post-Reformed England. Milner treats in brief the role of senses in perception and cognition in the popular experientialist tradition, noting that both those like Perkins (who Milner describes as a "Puritan") and Hooker (who Milner calls a "great apologist for conformity") saw the externals of worship as signs that could affect the senses of the believer.[7] However, Milner does not see this Calvinist view of the senses as the dominant one in Reformation religious culture, arguing that a Reformed attention to Calvin's ideas about election existed alongside "pre-reformation phenomenological principles," which continued to shape worshippers' "experience of English protestant culture."[8] He argues that in spite of the advent of English Calvinist thought, "sensation continued to be framed by Aristotelian perception" in the devotional cultures of Reformation England.[9] In fact, the influence that experiential Calvinism did have on Reformation devotional culture, Milner maintains, was disruptive. He argues that a Calvinist-inspired view of the senses led to a contradictory and anxiety-inducing understanding of the value of sensory perception—one that served to make religious experience and the senses sites of "blindness" and "deafness," rather than offering any clear interpretive framework for devotional understanding.[10] In doing so, Milner asserts that Calvin's experientialism had the effect of stripping the senses from their former place in a rationalist framework: "Protestant undermining of human rational capabilities was an also essential element of Calvin's theology."[11] In Milner's view, whatever new understanding of the senses was offered by Calvinist religious culture remained haphazardly developed, and led to devotional uncertainty rather than spiritual clarity.

While Milner, Zysk, and Rust are correct to argue that Reformation devotional culture should not be associated with a diminishment of sensory involvement in religious life, their claims that Reformed sensory engagement ought to be understood primarily in terms of late medieval Catholic contexts has the effect of ignoring the wide swath of devotional practice that had no official status in

---

[7] Milner, *Senses and the English Reformation*, 225–8. For Milner's description of Perkins, see 290; for his treatment of Hooker, see 205.
[8] Milner, *Senses and the English Reformation*, 236.
[9] Milner, *Senses and the English Reformation*, 229.
[10] Milner, *Senses and the English Reformation*, 229.
[11] Milner, *Senses and the English Reformation*, 202.

18   DEVOTIONAL EXPERIENCE IN THE REFORMATION

the English state church, in that these practices took place outside of the authorized church services. Additionally, by situating Hooker as an apologist for late medieval piety, Milner overlooks the ways in which ecclesiastical Reformers remained indebted to an English variety of Calvinistic doctrine. And by describing Perkins as a "Puritan" whose theology sat in opposition to the ecclesiology of those like Hooker and Cranmer, Milner ignores the continuities between the ecclesiology of the Reformed church and the informal devotional practices popularized by Perkins and his acolytes, in that both devotional domains were deeply informed by an experience-based understanding of devotion rooted in a Calvinist epistemology.

***

Like Milner, Zysk, and Rust, Jennifer Waldron has made a well-documented case for the important role that the senses have played in post-Reformation devotional life. In exploring the continuities between the ritual worship of post-Reformation England and secular theatrical performance, Waldron maintains that the body offered a shared means of tracking post-Reformation culture's attention to sensory affect. "Rather than associating the rise of commercial public theater with either the marginalization or the internalization of religious belief," Waldron argues that "playwrights such as Shakespeare exploited particular trends in Reformation thinking that had shifted the location of the sacred toward the horizontal plane of everyday life."[12] Waldron's argument builds upon foundational New Historicist arguments such as those put forth by Louis Montrose and Stephen Greenblatt for the continuity between late medieval devotional rites and secular stage performance.[13] But in a departure from her predecessors, Waldron attempts to nuance claims that present the theater as a secular repository for the latent worship practices of the late medieval church, arguing that Protestant devotional culture itself continued to maintain a lively interest in the body: "Instead of ceding the body to the domain of the secular or the profane, many Protestants competed for it."[14] And in a departure from those such as Milner, Zysk, and Rust, Waldron has argued that attention to the body in Reformation devotional culture should not be regarded primarily in terms of the persistence of late medieval Catholic thought.

---

[12] Jennifer Waldron, *Reformations of the Body: Idolatry, Sacrifice, and Early Modern Theater* (New York: Palgrave Macmillan, 2013), 2.

[13] For arguments about the continuity between early modern religious culture and the popular theater see Louis Montrose, *The Purpose of Playing* (Chicago: University of Chicago Press, 1996); Stephen Greenblatt, *Shakespearean Negotiations* (Berkeley: University of California Press, 1988); and Stephen Greenblatt, *Hamlet in Purgatory* (Princeton: Princeton University Press, 2002). For others who have made similar claims between the cultural transfers between the secular stage and post-Reformation devotional culture in England, see also Jeffrey Knapp, *Shakespeare's Tribe: Church, Nation, and Theater in Renaissance England* (Chicago: University of Chicago Press, 2002); and Ramie Targoff, "The Performance of Prayer: Sincerity and Theatricality in Early Modern England," *Representations* 60 (1997): 49–69.

[14] Waldron, *Reformations of the Body*, 8.

ORTHODOXY AND MARGINALITY   19

While acknowledging that Reformed religion allowed for the continuity of certain aspects of late medieval Catholic piety, Waldron also rightfully maintains that both the early modern divines and playwrights whose writings she explores held distinctly Reformed views of the body in their understanding of the ritual dimensions of idolatry, iconoclasm, and sacramental performance: "rather than presenting their embrace of the body as a compromise with Catholic doctrine or practice, a broad range of writers set out to reform the bodily experience of the worshipper and to reorient his or her sensory apparatus."[15]

In her study of the body, Waldron focuses her attention primarily on the ritual scaffolding of the English state church, focusing on sacramental reform, acts of iconoclasm against religious images, and the Reformed establishment's anxieties about idol worship.[16] Waldron's work successfully demonstrates that Reformation devotional culture should not be regarded as antithetical to the body or sensory engagement; in doing so, she builds upon arguments made by those like Milner who maintain that Reformation worship should not be regarded as ushering in "asensual austerity" in the ritual and performative devotion of the period. But unlike Milner, Waldron treats Reformed ritual worship in ways that distinguish these practices from their late medieval predecessors. While acknowledging the persistence of late medieval forms of piety, she also maintains that early modern secular theater and Reformed religious practices reflected distinctly post-Reformed ideas about the role of the body in their shared "dramatic medium."[17]

Waldron offers an argument about the role of the senses in Reformation culture rooted in Reformation theology itself, rather than relying solely on arguments about the persistence of late medieval Catholic piety in early modern forms of worship. Waldron demonstrates the theological exchanges between Protestant thinkers from a range of theological backgrounds, showing how mainstream church reformers as well as nonconformist critics of the theater were equally committed to the importance of bodily engagement in religious and secular performances. But like the scholarship of Milner, Rust, and Zysk, Waldron's study centers on the official ceremonies of the state church to the exclusion of the popular forms of piety that shaped post-Reformation English devotional and literary culture.[18] In "sketching a historical phenomenology of Protestant sacramental

---

[15] Waldron, *Reformations of the Body*, 8.
[16] Waldron, *Reformations of the Body*, 4.
[17] Waldron, *Reformations of the Body*, 4.
[18] For example, Waldron's attention to antitheatrical critics of the secular theater like William Rankins demonstrates Rankins's investments in bodily performance on stage, even as he continued to denigrate the body and stage acting in his cultural critique of the theater. Nonetheless, Rankins was not a theologian or a reformer so much as he was a cultural critic. In her attention to the "Puritans" of the period, Waldron tends to focus on those like Rankins, Stephen Gosson, and William Prynne who had vested interests in critiquing the theater, rather than on theological reformers and clerics such as Perkins, whose contributions are largely overlooked in Waldron's research on the theater.

20 DEVOTIONAL EXPERIENCE IN THE REFORMATION

participation as it was configured both against Catholic transubstantiation and against the more radical spiritualizing tendencies on the Protestant left," Waldron overlooks some of the most popular champions of sensory engagement in the post-Reformation devotional tradition.[19] In doing so, Waldron also presents popular forms of divinity in theological opposition to the sacramental practices that she highlights in her study. In her insightful reading of Marlowe's *Doctor Faustus*, for example, Waldron suggests that the Reformed practice of sign hunting, which she attributes to the theology of those like Perkins, might be read as offering a theological grounding for Faustus's anxious failures of faith. For Waldron, Perkins's theology, while rooted in the body and its senses, presents his variety of popular experiential Calvinism as obfuscating rather than illuminating devotional knowledge.[20] In Waldron's account, popular forms of experiential Calvinism are given only partial treatment, overshadowed by her more thorough work on Reformation ritual practice. By focusing primarily on the sacramental forms of worship practiced in the official services of the state church, as well as the church's position on idol worship and idolatry, Waldron ignores the wide range of experiential devotional practices that took place outside of the confines of the services of the state church. In her attention to the sacramental theory of those like Richard Hooker (who Waldron describes as "the inventor of 'Anglicanism'" and a "conformist" English divine), she overlooks the ways in which Hooker's sacramentalism partook in a wider culture of experiential devotion that had little to do with formal ritual worship.[21]

Nonetheless, Waldron's argument that English ritual worship owed a debt to Calvin's sacramental theory rightfully demonstrates that sensual and embodied experience played a role in the Reformed sacraments—in ways that often differed substantially from how late medieval forms of worship framed the mystical body in the sacred rites. In her reading of Calvin's *Institutio*, Kristen Poole likewise argues that the human body figured centrally in Calvin's cosmology, and argues that the body functioned as a "microcosm" that one could map, navigate, and explore in pursuit of higher knowledge about God and about one's place in the world.[22] Poole demonstrates that the theology of Calvin's *Institutio* remained deeply indebted to developments in early modern scientific knowledge, and especially to the burgeoning early modern interests in cosmology and cartography. Poole maintains that new attention to the natural world as the focus of scientific study influenced how Reformation thinkers like Calvin and his English followers saw the human body, which they regarded as a "microcosmic" world that was available for empirical study: "If God is in the world and the world is in man, then

---

[19] Waldron, *Reformations of the Body*, 63.

[20] Waldron, *Reformations of the Body*, 107–8.

[21] For her characterizations of Hooker, see Waldron, *Reformations of the Body*, 64 and 47.

[22] Kristen Poole, *Supernatural Environments in Shakespeare's England: Spaces of Demonism, Divinity, and Drama* (Cambridge: Cambridge University Press, 2011), 16.

ORTHODOXY AND MARGINALITY   21

both man's body and the world's must be exhaustively read and analyzed if man is to grasp God. For these interpreters, the body may be a mere container of all the world's constituent parts."[23] Poole offers a valuable contribution to early modern English views of devotion, furthering a distinctly Reformed understanding of the experience, the body, and sensory perception in post-Reformed devotional life. However, in her discussion of Calvin and his English interpreters, Poole misses an opportunity to explore the impact that popular theologians such as those like Perkins had in extending Calvin's experientialist approach to knowledge. Poole maintains that Perkins's popular divinity constituted "a distortion of [Calvin's] theology," in that it marked a movement away from the rationalist and empiricist foundations of Calvin's *Institutio*.[24] Poole frames Perkins's popular divinity, as those such as Milner and Waldron have done, in opposition to the sacramental theology of Reformers like Richard Hooker, who Poole argues shares and even extends Calvin's vision of a rational God and an ordered world: "Hooker's description of God's law rings true with Calvin's opening depiction of a structuralist God. ... Hooker's structuralist sensibility remains firm throughout the Lawes."[25] In her characterization of Perkins's popular divinity in opposition to Hooker's ecclesiology, Poole lays the groundwork for her claim that Hooker's sacramentalism formed the basis for what she terms an "Anglican" theology that was a precursor to the orderly Laudianism of the Caroline world.[26] In doing so, Poole subscribes to the view that Perkins and Hooker existed at opposing sides of a theological spectrum, and furthers an anachronistic view of Hooker's sacramentalism by portraying it as a version of proto-Laudianism.

In her portrayal of Hooker as a forerunner to the High Church Anglicanism of the Caroline church, Poole overlooks the fact that Hooker's own Tudor contemporaries held a much more nuanced and even contradictory understanding of the reformer. During the lifetimes of Hooker and Perkins, the question of what constituted mainline Protestantism in post-Reformation England involved a contested set of doctrines and practices. Hooker, who is now commonly regarded as quintessentially "Anglican" in his theology, was in fact claimed as an avatar by a range of religious camps during the decades immediately after his death. The *Lawes of Ecclesiastical Polity's* ambiguous stance on ceremonies and external expressions of devotion meant that Hooker's authority was used throughout the first half of the seventeenth century, often by those affiliated with opposing religious camps, to both justify and delegitimize public religious performance.

---

[23] Poole, *Supernatural Environments*, 14.

[24] Poole, *Supernatural Environments*, 151.

[25] Poole, *Supernatural Environments*, 153. See also Poole's argument that Calvin's God could be understood by rationalist approaches: "Calvin's language of measurement—of 'magnitude,' 'distance,' 'degrees'—creates an impression of an ordered universe, and thus a God, that is accessible through reason and calculation. ... This is a universe, and thus a God, whose beauty lies in its order and rationality. Calvin's God, it appears, is a structuralist." See Poole, *Supernatural Environments*, 143.

[26] Poole, *Supernatural Environments*, 156.

22   DEVOTIONAL EXPERIENCE IN THE REFORMATION

Hooker's contemporary reputation as an advocate of an Anglican *via media* is the result of successful efforts to appropriate his clerical authority roughly sixty years after his death. By the 1660s, supporters of William Laud's vision of church ceremonialism had succeeded in establishing Hooker as a mouthpiece for High Church Anglicanism, with its emphasis on liturgy and ritual as the foundation for communal religious practice.[27] But while the Laudians may have been the most successful in their efforts to mobilize Hooker's authority, they were hardly alone in their attempts to do so. In fact, Laud's opponents—even those with decidedly reformist affiliations—sought to appropriate Hooker's authority as justification for their nonconformist doctrine. Most prominently, the noted antitheatricalist William Prynne appealed to the authority of the *Lawes* to argue that Hooker believed that common prayer and public worship were in fact unnecessary for proper devotional practice.[28] What is clear, then, is that Hooker's association with robust ceremonial practice—to the exclusion of other kinds of devotional modes—is in some sense the result of the Caroline church's successful historical appropriation of Hooker for its own ecclesiastical and political policies.[29] But to retroactively apply these definitions of Anglican orthodoxy to sixteenth- and early seventeenth-century conceptions of proper devotion and performance is to overlook the alternative modes of performative worship that engaged seventeenth-century worshippers, and shaped the way post-Reformation English worshippers conceptualized expressions of intimacy and devotion.

Scholarly accounts of Perkins as an avatar for a peculiar variety of disordered or distorted thinking, brought about by the Reformation's darker cultural developments, are not unique to Milner, Waldron, and Poole. These scholars echo earlier arguments made by those like John Stachniewski and P. M. Oliver, who argue that Perkins's variety of Protestant predestinarian theology led to an anxious, paranoid,

---

[27] Michael Brydon, "The Establishment of Anglican Triumphalism," in *The Evolving Reputation of Richard Hooker: An Examination of Responses, 1600–1714* (Oxford: Oxford University Press, 2006), 81–122.

[28] Brydon, *Evolving Reputation of Richard Hooker*, 98; and Nigel Voak, *Richard Hooker and Reformed Theology: A Study of Reason, Will, and Grace* (Oxford: Oxford University Press, 2003), 321. Voak notes that the Laudian cleric Richard Montagu and his Reformed opponents both cited Hooker's authority to support their theological ideals.

[29] Elsewhere, Poole has studied the figure of the Puritan in early modern literary culture, arguing that Puritan bodies were portrayed as monstrous or deviant in the literary imagination of early modern England. In doing so, Poole is less interested in real nonconformists than she is in a socially constructed fiction of the "Puritan," one that captured prevailing anxieties about social and ecclesiological transformation in post-Reformation England. See Kristen Poole, *Radical Religion from Shakespeare to Milton: Figures of Nonconformity in Early Modern England* (Cambridge: Cambridge University Press, 2006), 14. Using Poole's distinction between real nonconformists and popular ideas about what nonconformity entailed, it is possible to argue that the predominant view of Perkins's theology as either fringe or a "distortion" of Calvinism might be counted among the ways in which the dominant religious establishment has tried to reimagine Perkins's theological legacy. These accounts of Perkins's theology have often bypassed historical representation in favor of portraying him as a cultural avatar for a collective notion of what "puritanism" entailed, one that subsumed the array of devotional life that could not be captured or explained by scholarly attention to the English church's official services.

ORTHODOXY AND MARGINALITY   23

or even "persecutory" mode of thought (to use Stachniewski's term) in the literary output of the period.[30] While these are valid accounts of the obfuscatory implications of a Reformed tradition of sign hunting, Perkins's own contributions to popular divinity were much more varied than the way he has been understood by these readers of early modern literary culture. These accounts of Perkins overlook the fact that he remained, during his lifetime and in the decades that followed, a highly regarded theologian—one who held a position in the state church alongside those like Hooker. To associate Perkins's popular divinity primarily with the development of sign hunting, as many readers have done, is to overlook the fact that he explored topics as wide-ranging as sex within marriage, household management, sacramental theology, intellectual and bodily experience, and the epistemological question of what it means to know.

Scholars of early modern literary culture who have regarded the theologies of Hooker and Perkins in terms of theological opposition in some sense echo the view of Protestant sectarianism articulated by the historian Peter Lake. In his landmark *Anglicans and Puritans?*, Lake describes an early modern Protestant culture as comprising a state-sanctioned "Anglican" ceremonialism situated in opposition to a marginal "Puritan" religious sensibility held by self-proclaimed detractors of the state church. As such, Lake argued for an inherent opposition between Richard Hooker's sacramentalism and the Reformed emphasis on experiential spirituality: "Hooker himself directly contrasted his own sacrament-centered view of the Christian community with the experimental predestinarianism of the Puritans," he argues. "Certainly, the style of piety being developed by Hooker in reaction against Presbyterianism was no more compatible with Perkins's experimental predestinarianism than it was with the discipline."[31] Lake treats the developmental trajectories of English ceremonialism and the predestinarian emphasis on visible, documentable evidence of salvation as if they were the theological outgrowths of disparate, even oppositional, religious factions. In Lake's account, state-sanctioned worship practices—the sacraments and the public liturgy—are the domain and preoccupation of the church, conceived of and championed by "proto-Anglicans" like Hooker. In contrast, the growing popular emphasis on experimental spirituality has been associated strictly with Puritan factionalists and detractors of the state church, those relegated to the peripheries. In his more recent work,

---

[30] See John Stachniewski, "John Donne: The Despair of the 'Holy Sonnets,'" *ELH* 48, no. 4 (1981): 677–705, reprinted in John Stachniewski, *The Persecutory Imagination: English Puritanism and the Literature of Religious Despair* (Oxford: Clarendon Press, 1991), 254–91; and Paul M. Oliver, *Donne's Religious Writing: A Discourse of Feigned Devotion* (New York: Longman, 1997). I discuss both Stachniewski and Oliver at length in my treatment of Donne's *Holy Sonnets* in Chapter 4. In a similar vein, James Simpson has argued that the theologies of Perkins's Lutheran forebears such as William Tyndale resulted in similar obfuscatory modes of thought. See James Simpson, *Burning to Read: English Fundamentalism and Its Reformation Opponents* (Cambridge, MA: Harvard University Press, 2007).

[31] Peter Lake, *Anglicans and Puritans? Presbyterianism and English Conformist Thought from Whitgift to Hooker* (London: Unwin Hyman, 1988), 179, 178.

24   DEVOTIONAL EXPERIENCE IN THE REFORMATION

written with input from Michael Questier, Lake has offered a revisionist account of the stark separations between state-sanctioned, mainstream Protestantism—what Lake terms "perfect" Protestantism—and its nonconformist Puritan or recusant Catholic counterparts. This revisionist account allows for "distinctions, where necessary, between the popular and the perfect protestant or the puritan, without ... envisaging the two categories as being utterly separate, mutually exclusive, inevitably opposed, indeed, incommensurable the one with the other."[32] Lake and Questier acknowledge that "relations between the 'popular' and not merely protestant but even puritan and 'Calvinist' canons of orthodoxy are not best conceived as straightforwardly adversarial, the result of a simple polarity or opposition, but rather as a series of exchanges and negotiations."[33]

Despite Lake's revisionist account of the cultural and religious separations between "Anglicans" (or "perfect" Protestants in his revisionist accounts) and their "Puritan" or nonconformist counterparts, versions of Lake's original view of a Protestant mainline versus a Puritan fringe continue to be echoed in historical and theological accounts of early modern English ecclesiology and religious culture—even in accounts like those of Milner, Waldron, and Poole that do much to demonstrate the continuities among Catholic and Reformed religious cultures, and among the varieties of Protestantism within the post-Reformed period. This view persists not only among readers of early modern literature, but also among those in religious and theology departments who continue to treat the official services of the English church and the popular piety of the period as separate cultural developments.[34] Daniel Eppley's suggestion, for example, that the theology underpinning official church ecclesiology should be regarded as distinct from developments in English popular divinity, might explain in part why so much of the attention to the convergence of the devotional and literary cultures of the early modern period prioritize the official liturgies and sacraments of the state church while largely ignoring how developments in popular divinity shaped the literary output of the period. Over the past three decades, literary scholars have written a number of superb works on the cultural exchanges between the devotional and literary cultures of post-Reformation England. Michael Schoenfeldt, Ramie Targoff,

---

[32] Peter Lake, with Michael Questier, *The Antichrist's Lewd Hat: Protestants, Papists, and Players in Post-Reformation England* (New Haven: Yale University Press, 2002), 318.

[33] Lake, with Questier, *Antichrist's Lewd Hat*, 331.

[34] Daniel Eppley has asserted that "the sacramental focus of worship in England meant that as conditional predestinarianism took root there it emerged with an additional, sacramental dimension that was not essential to its nature. Hooker's *Lawes* seems to be a parallel case in which the liturgy of the English church gave rise to an equally sacrament-centred unconditional predestinarian view of salvation." According to Eppley, we should not try to locate doctrinal overlaps or oppositions between these two separate arenas of English spiritual life. And yet Eppley's view that formal ecclesiastical worship and practical divinity must be regarded as entirely distinct cultural practices overlooks the fact that the vast majority of worshippers would have availed themselves of both forms of devotional expression in post-Reformation England. Daniel Eppley, "Richard Hooker on the Un-Conditionality of Predestination," in *Richard Hooker and the English Reformation*, ed. W. J. Torrance Kirby (Dordrecht: Kluwer Academic Publishers, 2003), 63–77. See p. 73 for Eppley's quotation.

ORTHODOXY AND MARGINALITY   25

Jeffery Knapp, and Timothy Rosendale have successfully demonstrated the extent to which the public liturgy shaped English literary culture.[35] In a similar vein, literary scholars such as Barbara Kiefer Lewalski, Richard Strier, Regina Schwartz, Theresa DiPasquale, Robert Whalen, Ryan Netzley, and Kimberly Johnson have written valuable studies that illuminate the influence of the state church's sacraments on the period's literary output.[36] While these studies focus primarily on the formal devotional performances that were officially endorsed by the state church—the baptism rites, the Protestant Communion, and the liturgies of the *Book of Common Prayer*—they largely overlook the role that popular devotional practices played in the lives and literary culture of early modern English people.

The scholarly tendency to "silo" official and popular forms of worship has also meant that the theological contributions of those like Perkins have not been presented as a part of mainstream Protestant devotional culture. In my Introduction, I discuss R. T. Kendall's landmark work on Calvinism's experiential focus in the popular divinity of English theologians like Perkins. Kendall effectively demonstrates that Perkins's practical divinity succeeded in popularizing experiential devotional practices among his English readership, and yet limits his study of Perkins and his influence solely to early modern theologians who scholars might have traditionally classified as nonconformist Puritans—including the Reformed English theologians Paul Baynes and Richard Sibbes, as well as American colonial ministers such as John Cotton of the Massachusetts Bay Colony and Thomas Hooker, a founder of Connecticut Colony. In focusing his research on English experiential devotion solely on Perkins and his reformist acolytes, Kendall overlooks the fact that the experiential emphasis of English Calvinism not only shaped the popular devotional practices of the period but also the ecclesiology of the English church itself. As a result, while Kendall places Perkins's theology in conversation with peripheral forms of puritanism, he overlooks the shared experiential preoccupation of both popular divinity and official church ecclesiology.

The stark demarcations between Anglican and Puritan, and between official and popular worship, do not account for the porous boundaries that demarcated the

---

[35] Michael Schoenfeldt, *Prayer and Power: George Herbert and Renaissance Courtship* (Chicago: University of Chicago Press, 1991); Ramie Targoff, *Common Prayer: The Language of Public Devotion in Early Modern England* (Chicago: University of Chicago Press, 2001); Jeffrey Knapp, *Shakespeare's Tribe*; and Timothy Rosendale, *Liturgy and Literature in the Making of Protestant England* (Cambridge: Cambridge University Press, 2007).

[36] Barbara Kiefer Lewalski, *Protestant Poetics and the Seventeenth-Century Religious Lyric* (Princeton: Princeton University Press, 1974); Richard Strier, *Love Known: Theology and Experience in George Herbert's Poetry* (Chicago: University of Chicago Press, 1986); Regina M. Schwartz, *Remembering and Repeating: On Milton's Theology and Poetics* (Chicago: University of Chicago Press, 1993 [1988]); Theresa M. DiPasquale, *Literature and Sacrament: The Sacred and the Secular in John Donne* (Pittsburgh: Duquesne University Press, 1999); Robert Whalen, *The Poetry of Immanence: Sacrament in Donne and Herbert* (Toronto: University of Toronto Press, 2002); Ryan Netzley, *Reading, Desire, and the Eucharist in Early Modern Religious Poetry* (Toronto: University of Toronto Press, 2011); and Kimberly Johnson, *Made Flesh: Sacramental Poetics in Post-Reformation England* (Philadelphia: University of Pennsylvania Press, 2014).

confessional categories of post-Reformation English identity and culture. Indeed, as Brian Cummings has rightfully pointed out, religious identity in early modern England was "not constructed around fixed points of doctrine."[37] Similarly, Michael Questier has noted that it is historically inaccurate to divide "the religious and ecclesiastical spectrum" of early modern English religious identities "into zealots and conformists."[38] And as Alexandra Walsham has maintained, "To assume that early modern people were as aware of theological distinctions as modern scholars who spend hours studying, dissecting and categorizing them in books is to do violence to the unstable and amorphous nature of religious affliction at this time." Walsham notes that assumptions about the neatness of early modern confession identity "accord too little importance to the genuine confusion of individuals entangled in a bewildering series of institutional and intellectual adjustments and it runs the risk of investing groups on the outer fringes, but nevertheless within the broad embrace of the established Church, with an artificial coherence."[39] Likewise, with respect to the devotional practices of the majority of English worshippers, Alec Ryrie has demonstrated that "[a]gain and again, on the questions which are supposed to define them, we find individuals straying heedlessly across the boundaries [of confessional identity]."[40] Ryrie asserts that early modern English people availed themselves of a range of models for proper devotion and prayer: "[Early modern] divines explicitly presented them with an expansive menu of gesture and posture, and encouraged them to sample it at will. There is every reason to think that ... individual Protestants' experience of prayer was more diverse than we might think."[41]

By focusing on the Calvinistic roots of Reformation devotional experience, my own project aims to draw attention to the continuities between official church worship practices and the forms of popular divinity that became fashionable beginning in the late sixteenth-century through the circulation of popular devotional handbooks published by those such as Perkins. In doing so, my goal is to shed new light on aspects of Reformation devotional culture that has been too often overlooked by literary critics. In arguing that Calvin's *Institutio* provided a shared epistemology both for popular reformers like Perkins and church ecclesiologists like Hooker, my aim is to broaden the archive of devotional practices

---

[37] Brian Cummings, *The Literary Culture of the Reformation: Grammar and Grace* (Oxford: Oxford University Press, 2002), 369.

[38] Michael C. Questier, *Conversion, Politics and Religion in England, 1580–1625* (Cambridge: Cambridge University Press, 1996), 3.

[39] Alexandra Walsham, *Charitable Hatred: Tolerance and Intolerance in England, 1500–1700* (Manchester: Manchester University Press, 2006), 20. For a similar argument, see also Alexandra Walsham, "The Parochial Roots of Laudianism Revisited: Catholics, Anti-Calvinists and 'Parish Anglicans' in Early Stuart England," *Journal of Ecclesiastical History* 49, no. 4 (1998): 620–51, esp. 636–7.

[40] Alec Ryrie, *Being Protestant in Reformation Britain* (Oxford: Oxford University Press, 2013), 471–2.

[41] Ryrie, *Being Protestant*, 171.

ORTHODOXY AND MARGINALITY 27

and the set of reformers through which we can approach the topic of devotional experience in the literary culture of the period.

William Perkins and popular Protestantism

The Calvinist emphasis on the experiential aspects of devotional life, while associated with Perkins's doctrine, was not unique to his practical divinity or especially exceptional in the religious thought of the first decades of seventeenth-century England.[42] Indeed, participatory predestinarianism would continue to hold powerful sway over the English people's spiritual imagination for the next sixty years, and dominate the official policies of the state church.[43] Nevertheless, these experiential overtones of English worship practices have been overlooked in scholarly treatments, in part because Perkins's reputation has suffered due to his purported Puritan commitments. Yet Perkins himself would have balked at the suggestion that his religious innovations and teachings were in any way "Puritan" or contrarian. In fact, he argued that the "vile term" should be reserved for extreme radicals—not used as a descriptor for those who subscribed to his own variety of Reformed theology.[44]

Perkins's present reputation rests on an anachronistic understanding of the circulation of religious ideas during his own lifetime. Despite the fact that Hooker is

[42] Kendall counts religious writers like Richard Rogers, Miles Moss, George Webbe, Paul Baynes, and Richard Sibbes among the theologians writing during the first three decades of the seventeenth century who were inspired by Perkins's variety of experiential spirituality. See R. T. Kendall, *Calvin and English Calvinism to 1649* (Oxford: Oxford University Press, 1979), 81–3. Ian Breward writes that many English Reformed preachers and theologians advocated a practical divinity "strongly marked by an experimental emphasis. ... This tendency was well established before Perkins attracted any public notice." See Ian Breward, Introduction to *The Work of William Perkins*, ed. Ian Breward (Abingdon: Sutton Courtenay Press, 1970), 29. Similarly, Lake counts this experiential emphasis among the contributions of moderate Reformed theologians to popular English religious life. It was this *"religious experience* that structured their priorities and shaped their attitudes" toward social life, "while they themselves yet remained wedded to those conventional forms and categories" sanctioned by the state church. See Peter Lake, *Moderate Puritans and the Elizabethan Church* (Cambridge: Cambridge University Press, 1982), 141.

[43] Kenneth Fincham and Nicholas Tyacke, *Altars Restored: The Changing Face of English Religious Worship, c. 1547–1700* (Oxford: Oxford University Press, 2007), 109. In fact, from roughly 1590 until the late 1640s, the Church of England was largely predestinarian in its official outlook on the role individual agency played in the process of securing salvation. "Only a fool," Peter Lake has asserted, "would seek to deny the importance of the Genevan example of the direct influence like Calvin and Beza" on religious life in early modern England. See Lake, *Anglicans and Puritans?*, 3–4. For supporting arguments about the powerful influence Reformed theology—and specifically predestinarian soteriology—had on establishment religion in England during the first decades of the seventeenth century, see also Voak, *Richard Hooker and Reformed Theology*, 3; Nicholas Tyacke, "Puritanism, Arminianism and Counter-Revolution," in *Origins of the Civil War*, ed. Conrad Russell (London: Palgrave Macmillan, 1978 [1973]), 119–43, esp. 120; Nicholas Tyacke, *Anti-Calvinists: The Rise of English Arminianism, c. 1590–1640* (Oxford: Oxford University Press, 1987); and Kendall, *Calvin and English Calvinism*, 79.

[44] William Perkins, *A godly and learned exposition of Christs Sermon in the Mount* (Cambridge: Printed by Thomas Brooke and Cantrell Legge, printers to the Vniversitie of Cambridge, 1608), 30. (*EEBO*, STC (2nd ed.) / 19722, document image 20.)

28 DEVOTIONAL EXPERIENCE IN THE REFORMATION

now regarded as among the most influential theologians of the Elizabethan and Jacobean church, this characterization does not accurately describe his influence during his own lifetime. Indeed, sales of Hooker's works were consistently dwarfed by sales of works by his contemporary Perkins—a trend that persisted throughout their lifetimes and for nearly six decades after their deaths.[45] Astonishingly, editions of Perkins's works sold more copies than those of any other writer in England between 1590 and 1620. In total, English and continental presses produced 372 editions of his work prior to 1700.[46] During that time, Perkins's devotional writing was published, circulated, and read in places as far away as Russia.[47] "If contemporary influence be the criterion," Philip Benedict writes, "Perkins was easily the most prominent English churchman and theologian of his remarkable generation."[48]

Despite the tendency to associate Perkins with "Puritan" or nonconformist thought, his handbooks and treatises enjoyed widespread popularity in the print and reading cultures of the seventeenth century—well into the Caroline era, the English Civil War, and the Interregnum. After 1590 and up through the 1660s, religious works like Perkins's devotional how-to manuals, tracts on practical divinity, and works on conversion consistently outsold the combined printed output of *belles lettres*, plays, and poems by nearly two to one in England.[49] During the first six decades of the seventeenth century, those who were literate were more likely to have been reading religious works than literary ones. Printed works by Perkins steadily outsold Shakespeare's by a ratio of two to one in the early decades of the seventeenth century.[50] One could easily claim that the late sixteenth and early

---

[45] Arthur Stephen McGrade, ed., *On the Laws of Ecclesiastical Polity* (Oxford: Oxford University Press, 2013), 2:ix; Kari Konkola, "'People of the Book': The Production of Theological Texts in Early Modern England," *The Papers of the Bibliographical Society of America* 94 (2000): 5–34; and Bryan D. Spinks, *Two Faces of Elizabethan Anglican Theology: Sacraments and Salvation in the Thought of William Perkins and Richard Hooker* (Lanham, MD: Scarecrow Press, 1999), 3. Breward writes that at the time of Perkins's death, the preacher was "far more influential than Richard Hooker who has since been regarded as *the* theologian of the Elizabethan Church." See Ian Breward, "The Significance of William Perkins," *The Journal of Religious History* 4, no. 2 (1966): 113–28, esp. 113. For discussions of Perkins's widespread popularity as a religious writer and preacher during his own lifetime, see also Spinks, *Two Faces of Elizabethan Anglican Theology*, 2–3; Kendall, *Calvin and English Calvinism*, 52–3; and W. B. Patterson, *William Perkins and the Making of a Protestant England* (Oxford: Oxford University Press, 2014), 3, 41–2, 195–6, 215.

[46] Philip Benedict, *Christ's Churches Purely Reformed: A Social History of Calvinism* (New Haven: Yale University Press, 2002), 318–19.

[47] Leif Dixon, *Practical Predestinarians in England, c. 1590–1640* (Farnham: Ashgate, 2014), 62.

[48] Benedict, *Christ's Churches Purely Reformed*, 319. For an overview of how the English print industry helped give rise to Perkins's widespread popularity, see Ian M. Green, *Print and Protestantism* (Oxford: Oxford University Press, 2000), esp. chap. 1, "The Rise of Print and Its Public," 1–41, and the list of Perkins's print titles in Appendix I, 591–647. Green notes that sales from Perkins's works were so lucrative that his printer John Legate sought to gain sole ownership of his titles after the preacher's death, and many other printers produced works that were very similar in style to those by Perkins using author names such as "W. Perkins" that were meant to evoke the great Cambridge theologian. See Green, *Print and Protestantism*, 17–18, 478, 479–87.

[49] Sales of printed works on the Continent similarly indicate reading publics that were galvanized by the circulation of printed religious works. See Konkola, "'People of the Book,'" 25, 28.

[50] Konkola, "'People of the Book,'" 26.

ORTHODOXY AND MARGINALITY   29

seventeenth centuries were the age of Perkins, rather than the age of Shakespeare. Against the strength of Perkins's print sales, the literary works that we now define as *the* iconic works of the Renaissance—the poetry of Shakespeare, Donne, Milton, and their contemporaries—seem an almost decidedly "minor" literature, one that would have been and should now be read within these larger reading and religious trends.[51]

What is clear, then, is that Perkins was by no means an ideological outlier, nor was he a detractor of the state-sanctioned religious orthodoxy. His theology was neither marginal nor opposed to the central teachings of the English religious establishment during the first decades of the seventeenth century. Yet the fact that Perkins has been branded a "Puritan" means that his contributions to English practical divinity have been treated as marginal in the critical discourse about what constituted mainline English devotional practice and experience. This has resulted in an unfortunate oversight in the critical conversation about how early modern people understood the wide range of devotional experiences in both the literary and theological currents of the period. On the contrary, the theology of Perkins and those like him had wide appeal and great popular influence during the decades between Shakespeare's and Milton's lifetimes, and the literary output of those decades must be understood within this religious context.

The lacunae in the existing conversation about early modern poetic expressions of devotion stems from the marginalization of popular forms of devotional practice—forms of worship that were equally if not more widely practiced than what modern scholars have deemed the official policies of the religious establishment. It is limiting and inaccurate to suppose that an early modern layperson, or even a member of the clergy in the Church of England, could not simultaneously uphold elements of both the church's official stance on ceremonies and the popular emphasis on experiential spirituality. Such a view would fail to acknowledge the breadth of what constituted official church theology and accepted devotional practice in early seventeenth-century England.[52] Rather than being conceptualized as antagonistic or fundamentally unrelated religious developments, the

---

[51] While one could argue that Shakespeare's primary medium, the secular theater, was not inherently directed toward print publication, the same argument could be made about Perkins's craft: pulpit preaching. Perkins's devotional print publications were, in some sense, a byproduct of his sermons.

[52] Both Perkins and Hooker should be regarded as "Anglican" theologians, in that their theologies were sanctioned by the Church of England. This is especially the case in light of the fact that the doctrines and practices that constituted English religious orthodoxy were still in flux during the late sixteenth and early seventeenth centuries. Prior to the establishment of any consensus of what Anglicanism ought to entail, both proponents of ecclesiastical ceremonialism and those who have been classified as moderate Puritans by later historians had equal claim to Anglicanism. Perkins, Peter Iver Kaufman notes, defied religious classification: "his career confounds those working with the familiar names and classifications, 'Puritan,' 'Anglican,' and the like." See Peter Iver Kaufman, *Prayer, Despair, and Drama: Elizabethan Introspection* (Urbana, IL: University of Illinois Press, 1996), 6. "In his day," Spinks argues, "[Perkins] was regarded as authentically 'Anglican' as Hooker, insofar as that term had any meaning in the Elizabethan Church." See Spinks, *Two Faces of Elizabethan Anglican Theology,* 1. Perkins was "an apologist, perhaps the chief apologist, for the Church of England" during the late

30   DEVOTIONAL EXPERIENCE IN THE REFORMATION

ceremonialism of the state church and popular experiential theology should be read as having complementary effects upon the way early modern people understood the role of experience in both devotional and literary contexts.

The enduring popularity of Perkins's devotional manuals for a period of more than seventy years demonstrates that Calvinist popular divinity was not relegated to the religious margins of early modern English life, but was rather key to a widespread post-Reformation understanding that experience constituted a form of devotional knowledge. Attention to Perkins's popular divinity demonstrates the coextensiveness between the experientialism of Perkin's devotional manuals and the way in which church reformers like John Jewel, Thomas Cranmer, and Richard Hooker turned to Calvin's experientialism in their attempts to describe a Reformed liturgy that may have looked like its Catholic predecessor but offered a vastly different doctrinal account of experience, cognition, and interpretation. In imagining a distinctly Protestant liturgy and sacrament for the English church, church clerics like Cranmer and Hooker imparted Calvin's attention to devotional experience and feeling to their vision of official state worship and prayer.

"Remembrancers" of devotion:
Perkins, Hooker, and experiential Calvinism

In a sermon delivered at St. Paul's Cross in May 1627, John Donne made a striking case for the value of outward forms of worship in the state church—one which captured the paradoxical position that the body and the senses assumed in post-Reformation devotional culture. Donne maintained that the sacraments

---

sixteenth and early seventeenth centuries, Patterson asserts. "Perkins was not a Puritan or even a moderate Puritan, terms that suggest opposition to the established Church. He was a mainstream English Protestant." See Patterson, *William Perkins*, 40, 218.

Similar claims can be made for Hooker's ambiguous religious associations and commitments. Spinks, for example, goes on to suggest that "Richard Hooker's version of Anglicanism, now considered the standard definition of it, was only in the process of achieving widespread acceptance and diffusion in the early seventeenth century." See Spinks, *Two Faces of Elizabethan Anglican Theology*, 5. The fact that Hooker has been claimed by both Reformed theologians like Joseph Hall and by those who were inspired by the High Church Anglicanism of William Laud is testament to the inconsistent views of Hooker's authority in the seventeenth century. "If Hooker was seen as a figure of the mainstream Church of England," Voak maintains, "much depended upon how that mainstream was defined by the interested parties concerned." He goes on to say, "Given the authority with which Hooker has become invested in the English Church, it is little wonder that he has been rewritten so often in the past as either thoroughly 'Anglican' or as thoroughly Reformed. Hooker should be taken on his own terms, in all his complexity, as a major if somewhat enigmatic contributor" to English church orthodoxy. See Voak, *Richard Hooker and Reformed Theology*, 2, 324. Peter Lake argues that Hooker's contemporaries would not have seen him as "either Anglican or Reformed business as usual. ... On the contrary, they took him to be departing from existing modes of argument." If Hooker deserves commemoration as an Anglican theologian, this is not because he "personified or expressed existing 'anglican' attitudes and values but because he, more than anyone, invented them." See Peter Lake, "Business as Usual? The Immediate Reception of Hooker's Ecclesiastical Polity," *The Journal of Ecclesiastical History* 3 (2001): 484; and Lake, *Anglicans and Puritans?*, 230.

ORTHODOXY AND MARGINALITY 31

were useful devotional aids not because they had the power to change the mind of God, but because they could change those who worship: "Ritual, and ceremonial things move not God, but they exalt that devotion, and they conserve that order, which does move him."[53] Donne was adamant that while rituals and ceremonies themselves remained devoid of sacramental power, they retained their value in the Reformed church as sensible and visible supports for devotion. These material, visual, and sensible things, Donne maintained, offered witness as what he called "remembrancers" of scriptural truth and of pulpit preaching.[54] In Donne's argument, these experiential aspects of devotion were things recalled, pondered, and ultimately apprehended. As Donne understood them, these *remembrancers* were nothing less than vehicles for devotional engagement and intellectual thought.

Donne's stance on the interpretive value of externals in worship should not be regarded as especially unusual within the Reformed church. It is no coincidence that his sermon articulates the same logic of experiential devotion enacted in the final act of *The Winter's Tale*, which presents Leontes's gazing and Perdita's participation as a "looker-on" as legitimate acts of devotion—precisely because these acts serve cognitive purposes in the king and princess's quest for knowledge about Hermione's true form. As such, neither Donne's sermon nor the culmination of Shakespeare's comedy should be interpreted as indicative of nostalgia for a former Catholic ritual practice; nor should they be read anachronistically as precursors to the ceremonialism of William Laud and the Caroline church. On the contrary, both Donne and Shakespeare describe a mainstream Reformed conviction that the outward and sensible aspects of devotion made one's devotional intent knowable—not only to spectators but also to oneself. What Donne articulates in his sermon reflected a distinctly Reformed understanding of worship and devotion, one firmly rooted in Calvin's experiential theology.

For Calvin, the sensible aspects of devotion were vital in that they supported the cognitive aspects of performed worship: "we do not here condemn speaking and singing provided that they are associated with the heart's affection and serve it. For thus do they exercise the mind in thinking of God and keep it attentive which (as it is slippery) is easily relaxed and diverted in different directions." In addition to helping the mind grasp spiritual truth and certainty, the body at prayer also helped make God's otherwise invisible qualities physically manifest by means of the sensible qualities of the worshippers themselves, allowing the glory of God "to shine in the several parts of our bodies" and especially in the tongue, which God has "assigned and destined for this task, both through singing and through speaking."[55] Calvin makes a similar argument for the role of the body in the performance

---

[53] John Donne, Sermon 17, in *Sermons*, ed. Evelyn Mary Spearing Simpson and George Reuben Potter, 10 vols. (Berkeley: University of California Press, 1953–62), 7:430.

[54] Donne, *Sermons*, 7:431–2.

[55] John Calvin, *Institutes of the Christian Religion: 1536 edition*, trans. Ford Lewis Battles (Grand Rapids, MI: Eerdmans, 1986 [1975]), 3.20.31.

of the sacraments, which he describes as a public "symbol and proof" of spiritual renewal.[56] In sacramental worship, "not only do our hearts breathe the praise of God, but our tongues also and all members of our body sound his praise in every way they can. For thus, as is fitting, all our faculties are employed to serve God's glory, which ought to lack nothing."[57] Calvin's vision of sacramental practice not only posited the body as a means of visually verifying and proving otherwise imperceptible spiritual truth; he also saw it as an extension of the forms of knowing that provided the foundation for surety in matters of faith.

Bodily proof of devotional truth was, for Calvin, as powerful as argumentative exhortation. By giving bodily and outward testament to one's devotional affect, Calvin argued that a public worshipper could go so far as to enhance an onlooker's own devotional surety, arousing the viewer to participate in both the sacramental rites and the granting of certainty that they afford. "[B]y our example others are aroused to the same efforts," he insisted. "We ought to deem it certain and proved that it is God who speaks to us through the sign [of the sacrament]."[58]

Calvin endorsed bodily gestures in performed worship as a form of knowledge, one that was especially suited to helping us ascertain inner devotional truth: "prayer itself is properly an emotion of the heart within."[59] As Brian Cummings has argued, Calvin followed the German reformer Martin Bucer in justifying the use of performed worship in the Reformed church and acknowledging the usefulness of bodily signs of devotion by means of "a theory of mental assent and of implied meaning."[60] For Calvin, "physical expression can be corroborated with interior meaning or intentionality," Cummings asserts. "Physical acts of worship support established prayers by confirming the feelings that underly them and by engaging the mind in assenting to them willingly."[61] According to Calvin, the efficacy of devotional performances remained contingent upon the fact that they required cognitive and interpretive participation on the part of the worshipper. His understanding of performed worship posited Reformed devotional practice as part of a larger epistemology—as a method for ascertaining and verifying devotional truths.

In her revisionist account of the role of the body and the senses in Reformed sacramental practice, Jennifer Waldron has demonstrated that mainstream Reformed sacramental theology, as described by Hooker's ecclesiology, was shaped by Calvin's insistence upon the importance of the material world and bodily experience in performed worship. Waldron notes that the Calvin and Hooker's ecclesiologies were aligned in "their shared assumption that the visible church

---

[56] Calvin, *Institutes*, 4.15.1.

[57] Calvin, *Institutes*, 4.15.13.

[58] Calvin, *Institutes*, 4.15.13 and 4.15.14.

[59] Calvin, *Institutes*, 3.20.29.

[60] Brian Cummings, "Prayer, Bodily Ritual and Performative Utterance: Bucer, Calvin and the *Book of Common Prayer*," in *Prayer and Performance in Early Modern English Literature*, ed. Joseph William Sterrett (Cambridge: Cambridge University Press, 2018), 16–36, esp. 35.

[61] Cummings, "Bucer, Calvin, and the *Book of Common Prayer*," 35.

could and should edify the worshippers, along with their similar justifications for the role of the human body in the process of edification."[62] Waldron maintains that while Hooker's argument is meant to be figurative rather than literal, the importance that he ascribes to the body of Christ in his sacramental theology draws connecting links between "both mystical and bodily dimensions."[63] In focusing on the importance of Christ's body in both Calvin and Hooker's visions of sacramental theology, Waldron notes that the human body retained its central role in Reformed performed worship: "Even as they denied the magic of transubstantiation, both Calvin and Hooker tied their models of sacramental participation to the miracle of Christ's incarnation in human flesh."[64]

In my treatment of Hooker's sacramental theory as follows, I want to build upon Waldron's argument for the continuities between Calvin and Hooker by suggesting that Hooker's ultimate attention to the human body in fact did not rest primarily on the figurative body of Christ, but upon the real bodies of his human communicants. I aim to demonstrate that Hooker's sacramentalism partook of the same epistemological framework undergirding the popular experiential piety of those like William Perkins and his peers. While Hooker primarily understood Christ's human form in figurative terms, he saw the sacraments engaging with the bodies of Christ's communicants in very literal and demonstrable ways: "The real presence of Christ's most blessed body and blood is not therefore to be sought for in the sacrament," Hooker writes, "but in the *worthy receiver* of the sacrament."[65] Hooker saw the figurative presence of Christ in the Communion sacrament as assuming a secondary place relative to the experiences of the communicants in the sacramental rites. In their discussion of the Reformed Communion in their treatment of the sacramental theology of Cranmer, Stephen Greenblatt and Joe Moshenska have argued that Cranmer's treatment of the Real Presence of Christ hovers uncertainly between both figural and literal representations of Christ's body and blood.[66] I

---

[62] Waldron, *Reformations of the Body*, 65.

[63] Waldron, *Reformations of the Body*, 65.

[64] Waldron, *Reformations of the Body*, 66.

[65] Richard Hooker, *Of the Lawes of Ecclesiasticall Politie. The Fift Booke* (London: Printed by John Windet dvvelling at Povvles wharfe at the signe of the Crosse Keyes and are there to be solde, 1597), 5.67.176, emphasis added. (*EEBO*, STC (2nd ed.) / 13712.5.) Hooker printed the first four books of the *Lawes* in 1594 [1593], and the fifth book in 1597. I refer to both printed editions throughout this chapter.

[66] In Cranmer's understanding of the Reformed Communion, Greenblatt notes "an uneasy meeting" between "the conjunction of gross physicality and pure, abstracted spirituality." See Stephen Greenblatt, "Remnants of the Sacred in Early Modern England," in *Subject and Object in Renaissance Culture*, eds. Margreta de Grazia, Maureen Quilligan, and Peter Stallybrass (Cambridge: Cambridge University Press, 1996), 337–45. See p. 344 for quotation. In a similar vein, although Moshenska takes issue with Greenblatt's claim that Cranmer prioritizes the figurative over the literal in his understanding of the Communion sacrament, Moshenska acknowledges ambiguity between actual and metaphoric access in Cranmer's Reformed sacrament: "Cranmer makes a calculated attempt to obscure and obviate the very distinction between literal and figurative in his description of sacramental touch. This allows him simultaneously to proclaim the believer's direct sensory relation to God through the sacraments, and to disown, if challenged, the physicality of the ritualised liturgical forms in which such

34   DEVOTIONAL EXPERIENCE IN THE REFORMATION

maintain that Hooker resolved some of the tensions between the figurative and the literal that proved vexing in the sacramental theologies of earlier reformers such as Cranmer by shifting the attention from Christ's Real Presence to the embodied and cognitive experiences of the communicants themselves. In other words, Hooker was more interested in the "real presence" of the communicants than he was in the figurative body of Christ. In Hooker's sacramentalism, devotional access to Christ depended less on the realness of his flesh and blood than in the cognitive and sensory experiences of those who worship him. Although one could no longer eat Christ's body in the bread or drink his blood in the chalice of wine, in the rites and ceremonies of the English church the participant's own material body and participatory engagement ensured access to God: "Participation is that *mutual inward hold* which Christ hath of us and we of him," Hooker writes in his explication of the power of the sacraments, "in such sort that *each possesseth other* by way of special interest, property, and *inherent copulation*."[67] In Hooker's sacramentalism, Christ's figurative body is wrested into the realm of human experience by means of the inherent copulation between the communicant and Christ. For Hooker, God is knowable—both bodily and cognitively—by means of this copulatory exchange between the communicant and Christ. The material and bodily import of Hooker's

contact occurs." According to Moshenska, Cranmer at once acknowledges "that the sacraments allow this 'sensible touching, feeling and groping'," only to simultaneously assert that "this language is only an approximation of the truth: there is some relation between the washing with the baptismal water and this manner of direct sensory engagement with Christ, but the exact nature of this relation is left studiously unclear." See Joe Moshenska, "'A Sensible Touching, Feeling and Groping': Metaphor and Sensory Experience in the English Reformation," in *Passions and Subjectivity in Early Modern Culture*, eds. Brian Cummings and Freya Sierhuis (Farnham: Ashgate, 2013), 184–99. For an expanded version of Moshenska's argument, see also Joe Moshenska, *Feeling Pleasures: The Sense of Touch in Renaissance England* (Oxford: Oxford University Press, 2014), esp. 15–46. In Cranmer's attempt to situate the Reformed sacrament at the crossroads of the figurative and the literal, Greenblatt and Moshenska point to a troubling inexactness in Cranmer's understanding of devotional access to Christ; Cranmer disavows literal access to Christ's body and blood even as he continues to imagine Christ's presence in the sacrament in bodily and material terms. But if Cranmer's reformist assessment of the sacrament ushered in the problem of material access to Christ, his vision of the sacrament also suggested a potential solution to the nature of Eucharistic materiality. In positing that the communicant's senses could verify and establish certain devotional truths, what is clear is that Cranmer's experientialism sowed the theological and conceptual groundwork that would enable later Reformed thinkers like Hooker and Perkins to shift the material focus from the sacramental bread and wine to the physical body of the communicants.

[67] Hooker, *Lawes*, 5.56.120, emphasis added. In his defense of Hooker's *Lawes of Ecclesiastical Polity* from the writers of the anonymous *A Christian Letter*, the majority of which was written by the moderate Reformed theologian Andrew Willet, William Covell reiterates Hooker's claim about the power of the sacraments to help us locate God's body—not in the material externals of the sacrament, but within ourselves: "The whole benefit which the church hath is from Christ and this by no other means but by participation. For Christ to be what he is, is not to be what he is to the church, but only by a participation of all that he is (as a mediator) betwixt him and us. This we call the *mutual, inward hold which Christ hath of us and we of him*, in such sort that each possesseth other by way of special interest, properly, and *inherent copulation*." See William Covell, *A iust and temperate defence of the fiue books of ecclesiastical policie: written by M. Richard Hooker* (London: Printed by P. Short for Clement Knight, dwelling at the signe of the holy Lambe in Paules church-yard, 1603), 113, emphasis added. (*EEBO*, STC (2nd ed.) / 5881, document image 61.) See Lake, "Business as Usual?," 456–86, for a discussion of Covell's role in the immediate reception of Hooker's *Lawes*.

ORTHODOXY AND MARGINALITY 35

description of the relationship between Christ and the believer is amplified by Erasmus's strikingly similar description of the "wonderful copulation" of God's nature into ours—which Erasmus likened to the miracle of Christ's incarnation.[68] But while Erasmus saw bodily access to God as contingent upon Christ's time as an embodied man on earth, on the contrary, Hooker attributed that physical connection to a worshipper's devotional experience of the rites. In Hooker's account of experiential worship, no longer could the devout rely on God's incarnation as the basis for devotional intimacy; it was only through direct participation that the worshipper could hope to restore a bodily connection to God.[69]

This fusional, copulatory access to God's bodily being was not limited to early modern conceptions of the Communion, however, and Perkins makes a similar claim about the role of the body in securing access to Christ during the sacrament of baptism: "[F]or as certainly as the body is washed with water, so certainly are they that believe *engrafted* into Christ." Perkins writes, "For in the right and lawful use of baptism, God according to his own promise *engrafts* them into Christ that believe: and the inward washing is conferred with the outward washing."[70] In Perkins's sacramental vision, the act of performing the outward rite functions as an impetus for spiritual and bodily metamorphosis—the creation of a new being birthed from the engrafted parts of both the worshipper and Christ. In describing spiritual and bodily oneness with Christ, Perkins adopts the language and imagery of Calvin's theology. The *Institutio* is replete with language that describes the relationship between the true believer and Christ in terms of corporeal unity. According to Calvin, the benefits of sacramental and outward forms of worship do not come from without; they simply reveal a prior inward bond with Christ: "For we await salvation from him not because he appears to us as far away but because he makes us, *engrafted into his body, participants not only in all his benefits but also in himself*," Calvin maintained. "Christ is not outside us but dwells within us. Not only does he cleave to us by an indivisible bond of fellowship but with a wonderful communion, day by day, he grows more and more into one body

[68] See Desiderius Erasmus, Preface to "The paraphrase of Erasmus vpon the gospell of sainct Iohn," in *The first tome or volume of the Paraphrase of Erasmus vpon the Newe Testamente*, trans. Nicholas Udall (London: Enprinted at London in Fletestrete at the signe of the Sunne by Edwarde Whitchurche, the last daie of Januarie, 1546), iii. (*EEBO*, STC (2nd ed.) / 2854.5, document image 444.)

[69] W. Speed Hill has noted that the sensory and subjective elements of Hooker's theology have been largely overlooked by historians who have focused exclusively on the political implications of Hooker's *Lawes*: "because the *Laws* have been appropriated largely by ecclesiastical historians and political theorists, the inward and intuitive element at the base of Hooker's thought has not always been sufficiently recognized." Unfortunately, within literary studies, the critical tendency that Hill noted half a century ago still dominates literary scholarship on Hooker, as the majority of studies on literature and religion continue to focus on the role Hooker's theology played in fostering communal affect rather than individual devotional experience. See W. Speed Hill, "The Evolution of Hooker's Laws of Ecclesiastical Polity," in *Studies in Richard Hooker: Essays Preliminary to an Edition of His Works*, ed. W. Speed Hill (Cleveland, OH: Press of Case Western Reserve University, 1972), 117–58, esp. 151.

[70] William Perkins, *A commentarie or exposition, vpon the fiue first chapters of the Epistle to the Galatians* (Cambridge: Printed by Iohn Legat, printer to the Vniuersitie of Cambridge, 1604), 240, emphasis added. (*EEBO*, STC (2nd ed.) / 19680, document image 130.)

36   DEVOTIONAL EXPERIENCE IN THE REFORMATION

with us, until he comes completely one with us."[71] It was Calvin's understanding of the spiritual certainty that comes with bodily perception and oneness that Perkins appropriated in his popular devotional writing and preaching.

Hooker, too, used the same language to describe the assurance that comes from firsthand experience of Christ's promises: "I know in whom I have believed; I am not ignorant whose precious blood hath been shed for me; I have a shepherd full of kindness, full of care, and full of power: unto him I commit my self; *his own finger hath engraved this sentence into the tables of my heart.*"[72] Hooker co-opts a language of spiritual assurance that is linked directly to Calvin's soteriology. According to Calvin, Schreiner writes, "The Spirit of God is, for the elect, the 'sure guarantee and seal' of their salvation. This seal of certainty is 'engraved' upon the heart in such a way that it cannot be erased."[73] For Calvin and the English Reformed tradition, the movements of the spirit were neither invisible nor ineffable. On the contrary, they were perceptible by means of careful attention to bodily and cognitive experience. According to Calvin, the body and the heart were like engraving tablets—to be written upon and read as evidence of devotional assurance.[74]

I have sought to demonstrate that public worship in the English Reformed church shared in the experiential theology most associated with popular pre-destinarianism. My argument poses a corrective to recent assessments of early modern English public worship, which have maintained that state worship practices sought to liberate the individual from the vicissitudes of spontaneous worship and devotional practice. These studies argue that Hooker's set forms of prayer and models for public religious engagement were designed to free the individual worshipper from the limitations posed by spiritual fickleness. "Far from imagining liturgical spontaneity as a liberation," Ramie Targoff writes, "Hooker offers a novel

---

[71] Calvin, *Institutes*, 3.2.24, emphasis added. Cited in Susan E. Schreiner, *Are You Alone Wise?, The Search for Certainty in the Early Modern Era* (Oxford: Oxford University Press, 2010), 69.

[72] Richard Hooker, *A learned and comfortable sermon of the certaintie and perpetuitie of faith in the elect especially of the prophet Habakkuks faith* (At Oxford: Printed by Ioseph Barnes, and are to be sold by John Barnes dwelling neere Holborne Conduit, 1612), 17, emphasis added. (*EEBO*, STC (2nd ed.) / 13707.) For a brief but useful discussion of the Calvinist resonances in Hooker's theological treatment of the body, see Waldron, *Reformations of the Body*, 65–6.

[73] Schreiner, *Are You Alone Wise?*, 69.

[74] Although Debora Kuller Shuger stops short of identifying Hooker as a Reformed theologian, she notes that there are substantial similarities between Hooker's doctrine of assurance and that of the English Calvinists of the period: "Among English Calvinists, one finds passages closely resembling Hooker's sermon in the pastoral writings of [Richard] Greenham and Perkins. ... The similarities are partial, yet they are also significant and extensive enough to make it clear that *The Certaintie* is part of the considerable body of Protestant literature dealing with the interior vicissitudes of belief." And: "[Hooker's] sermons focus on the same issues of faith and assurance that stand at the centre of Reformed pastoral theology. They speak to the same spiritual anxieties with which Reformed divines grappled, and offer much the same consolation. Hooker rejects too large a swathe of Calvinist doctrine to be meaningfully considered a Reformed thinker, yet he writes about faith and assurance from within the Reformed tradition." See Deborah K. Shuger, "Faith and Assurance," in *A Companion to Richard Hooker*, ed. Torrance Kirby (Leiden: Brill, 2008), 221–50, esp. 223, 235–6.

account of devotional freedom as an enormous burden upon the individual's psychic well-being; formalized language becomes in this account a crucial safeguard against the natural weakness of human devotion."[75] In his study on the sociopolitical implications of the English liturgy, Timothy Rosendale corroborates Targoff's argument that state-controlled worship provided the only foolproof method for the cultivation of devotional affect: "In [Hooker's] ecclesiastical polity, public worship under royal power must leave no room for the chaos of individuality or improvisation; as the textual form of order, the [Book of Common Prayer] is the ideal and only proper expression of the commonwealth at worship."[76] This view has been echoed by others, such as Milner, who saw the knowledge-based approach to affect advocated by those such as Perkins as counter to the experience of corporate worship. Perkin's approach to knowledge, what Milner describes as "interior affectivity," was "problematic when it came to public collective worship whose common denominator was external sense experience, not comprehension."[77]

Yet considering the state church's insistence, from Cranmer and Jewel onward, on the necessity of the sensual and interpretive aspects of experience in ascertaining devotional truth, what becomes clear is that these prior assessments of the purposes and function of state worship offer only partial accounts of how early English reformers understood the purposes of public worship. Indeed, what these accounts of English state-controlled worship do not consider are the fissures that allowed individual experience and interpretation to seep into even the state church's attempts to regulate spiritual life. The sacraments and the liturgy could bolster an already existing devotion, Hooker maintained, but these external rites could not ultimately effect salvation: "they contain *in themselves* no vital force or efficacy, they are not physical but *moral instruments* of salvation, duties of service and worship, which unless we perform as the author of grace requires, they are unprofitable."[78] In his insistence that devotional externals possess no inherent effectiveness, Hooker argued that spiritual grace must be found elsewhere, beyond the accidental materiality of the rites and prayers themselves. Indeed, their value

---

[75] Targoff, *Common Prayer*, 5.

[76] Rosendale, *Liturgy and Literature*, 59. In their accounts of Hooker's rigid conformity to outward forms of worship, Rosendale and Targoff subscribe to a view of Hooker's ceremonialism that gained support in the aftermath of Peter Lake's 1988 book *Anglicans and Puritans?* In his monumental study of English ecclesiastical reform, Lake argued that Hooker regarded corporate prayer and the sacraments as devotionally superior and more effective than preaching or private modes of spontaneous worship. More recently, James F. Turrell has characterized Hooker's applied theology in a much similar vein, arguing that Hooker was primarily interested in fostering Anglican conformity. See James F. Turrell, "Richard Hooker on Uniformity and Common Prayer," in Kirby, *Companion to Richard Hooker*, 337–66; and Lake, *Anglicans and Puritans?*, esp. 166–70.

[77] Milner, *Senses and the English Reformation*, 232.

[78] Hooker, *Lawes*, 5.57.127–8. For a discussion of how Hooker justified the sacraments as devotionally valuable despite acknowledging their lack of inherent spiritual effectiveness, see Spinks, *Two Faces of Elizabethan Anglican Theology*, 109–58; and W. David Neelands, "Christology and the Sacraments," in Kirby, *Companion to Richard Hooker*, 369–402.

38   DEVOTIONAL EXPERIENCE IN THE REFORMATION

lay not in their ability to suppress individual variance in devotional experience, but in the fact that they allowed for precisely this variance in experience and interpretation. The sacraments, Hooker asserted, are valuable only insofar as they operate as outward, sensible, and interpretable representations of spiritual truth: "Sacraments are those which are *signs* and tokens of some general promised grace, which always really descends from god unto the soul that duly receives them."[79] Devotional performances help to remind worshippers of their existing spiritual commitments to God—but only if they have already secured grace.[80] While Hooker acknowledged that the sacraments and the liturgy might be useful devotional aids for those who already possessed spiritual grace, he also insisted that those external gestures of devotion lacked any inherent spiritual potency: they "really exhibit, but for ought we can gather out of that which is written of them they are not really nor do really contain in themselves that grace which with them or by them it pleases God to bestow."[81]

Despite outward resonances with its papal forebears, Hooker's ceremonialism owes its greatest debt to the logic of Calvin's experiential devotion. Indeed, while Christopher Haigh and Eamon Duffy have argued for the persistence of Catholic traditionalism in Reformed sacraments and liturgical practices, they overlook one fundamental difference between the two sacramental models: after the Reformation, outward ceremonial worship could no longer effect salvation.[82] Although

[79] Richard Hooker, *Of the Lavves of Ecclesiasticall Politie. Eyght books* [books 1–4] (Printed at London by Iohn Windet, dwelling at the signe of the Crosse keyes neare Powles Wharffe, and are there to be solde, [1593]), 4.1.169. (*EEBO*, STC (2nd ed.) / 13712).

[80] On Hooker's view of the sacraments as devotionally useful only for the elect, see Eppley, "Richard Hooker on the Un-Conditionality of Predestination," 73; Neelands, "Christology and the Sacraments," 369–402; W. David Neelands, "Hooker and Predestination," in Kirby, *Companion to Richard Hooker*, 185–219; W. David Neelands, "Richard Hooker and the Debates about Predestination, 1580–1600," in Kirby, *Richard Hooker and the English Reformation*, 43–61; Egil Grislis, "Reflections on Richard Hooker's Understanding of the Eucharist," in Kirby, *Richard Hooker and the English Reformation*, 207–23; Charles W. Irish, "'Participation of God Himselfe': Law, the Mediation of Christ, and Sacramental Participation in the Thought of Richard Hooker," in Kirby, *Richard Hooker and the English Reformation*, 165–84; Ranall Ingalls, "Hooker on Sin and Grace," in Kirby, *Companion to Richard Hooker*, 151–84; Voak, *Richard Hooker and Reformed Theology*, 267; and Spinks, *Two Faces of Elizabethan Anglican Theology*, 109–58.

[81] Hooker, *Lawes*, 5.67.176. Importantly, Hooker was not unique among Church of England clergy in his view that outward forms of worship had no inherent spiritual force—nor was this a distinctly "Calvinist" or "Puritan" view of the sacraments and the liturgy. Other church divines—including Thomas Cranmer, Robert Some, John Prime, and William Attersoll—subscribed to similar views that posit performed gestures of devotion as signs, but not causes, of grace. For an overview of the range of theologians who argued for this view of performed devotion, see Fincham and Tyacke, *Altars Restored*, 66–7.

[82] On this point, see Eamon Duffy, *The Stripping of the Altars: Traditional Religion in England c. 1400–c. 1580* (New Haven: Yale University Press, 1992), esp. 4, 566–89; and Christopher Haigh, *English Reformations: Religion, Politics, and Society under the Tudors* (Oxford: Clarendon Press, 1993), esp. 289–91. For similar arguments by Haigh, see also "The emergency of recusancy" and "Recusants and church-papists," chaps. 16 and 17 in *Reformation and Resistance in Tudor Lancashire* (Cambridge: Cambridge University Press, 1975), 247–68 and 269–94. For those who have argued against this view of Catholic persistence in Reformed devotional practice, see Judith Maltby, *Prayer Book and People in Elizabethan and Early Stuart England* (Cambridge: Cambridge University Press, 1998), *passim*; Patrick

ORTHODOXY AND MARGINALITY   39

the Reformed sacraments and liturgy outwardly *looked* like the former Catholic ceremonial practices, they now had radically different devotional purposes and effects. In his commitment to preserving elements of Catholic ceremonial worship for use in the English church, Hooker remained adamant that outward ceremonial practice, while not necessarily idolatrous, contained no intrinsic devotional power. The devotional utility of these externals lay solely in their role as sensible symbols and signs of an otherwise invisible inner grace.[83] Although accounts of Hooker's outward rites have sought to position his defense of ecclesiastical policies as a continuation of older papal ceremonies, Hooker's devotional performances had little functional overlap with these banned practices.[84] Devoid of any inherent spiritual power, Hooker's Reformed sacraments and public prayers could not, unlike their Catholic counterparts, provide direct means to spiritual grace. For Hooker, devotional performances could only operate as outward and bodily *signs* of inward devotional affect—but never as *causes* of spiritual renewal. The ceremonies merely offered another set of bodily and experiential tokens that one could read as probable evidence of spiritual grace.

Like Hooker, Perkins remained similarly adamant that although the church's ceremonies and rites were devotionally useful, they could not *effect* grace. At most, external worship could corroborate an existing grace that had been secured prior to the worshipper's engagement in the sacred performance: "It is not an instrument having the grace of God tied to it, or shut up in it: but an instrument to which grace is present by assistance in the right use thereof: because in and with the right use of the sacrament, God confers grace; and thus it is an instrument, and no otherwise, that is, a moral and not a physical instrument."[85] If the church's ceremonies held devotional value, this value was derived independently from the material form of the rites and sacraments themselves. For Perkins, the rites and rituals of the state church are merely *adiaphora*—matters indifferent with respect to salvation and faith but nonetheless permissible in devotional practice.[86]

In spite of his insistence that public devotion could not guarantee salvation, Perkins nonetheless saw no reason to condemn corporate prayer, and argued that communal worship should play a vital role in spiritual life: "Ministers in teaching are the mouth of God to the people: and in praying they are the mouth of the people to God, and therefore must the people in fervent affection lift up their hearts

---

Collinson, *The Religion of Protestants: The Church in English Society, 1559–1625* (Oxford: Clarendon Press, 1982), esp. 191–2; and Walsham, "Parochial Roots," 632, 636.

[83] Hooker, *Lavves*, 4.1.168–70.

[84] In matters of early modern confessional identity, Questier rightly notes that "Not everyone who acted outwardly in a similar way showed identical thought patterns." See Questier, *Conversion, Politics and Religion in England*, 2.

[85] Perkins, *Commentarie or exposition*, 254. (*EEBO*, document image 135.)

[86] William Perkins, *A cloud of faithful witnesses, leading to the heauenly Canaan, or, A commentary vpon the 11 chapter to the Hebrewes* (London: Printed by Humfrey Lownes, for Leo. Greene, 1607), 336. (*EEBO*, STC (2nd ed.) / 19677.5, document image 176.)

40 DEVOTIONAL EXPERIENCE IN THE REFORMATION

unto God, and in mind give assent to the prayers made in the name and behalf of the congregation by their teachers: and for this cause it is, that we are all to say, *amen.*[87] Clearly, Perkins did not perceive his popular divinity—with its emphasis on bodily and sensory experience—as inherently opposed to a robust communal worship practice, as those like Milner have maintained.[88] In fact, Perkins insisted that the strength of a worshipper's devotional affect would increase proportionally to the number of times he participated in these communal rites: "Therefore signs of graces are as it were an applying and binding of the promise of salvation to every particular believer: and by this means, the oftener they are received, the more they help out infirmity, and confirm our assurance of mercy."[89]

Although he did not ascribe any inherent devotional power to the church's ceremonies and rites, Perkins nonetheless saw epistemological and devotional value in communal worship practices. For Perkins, devotional performances were valuable not primarily as outward works, as they had been in the Catholic church, but as sensible "signs and pledges of God's mercy."[90] Perkins insisted that "A sacrament is that, whereby Christ and his saving graces, are by certain external rites, signified, exhibited, and sealed to a Christian man."[91] For Perkins, public worship in the state church offered one of the many interpretive signs and tokens of spiritual grace. For both Hooker and Perkins, the church's rituals of devotion were valuable not, as Targoff and Rosendale have maintained, because they diminished variance among individual devotion, but because they offered verifiable evidence that could help further an individual worshipper's intellectual certainty about matters of devotion and faith. In the Reformed church, the value of public devotion lay in its epistemological function as one of many external signs that an individual worshipper could study and interpret in the quest for devotional knowledge and certainty.

Hooker's and Perkins's distinctly Reformed accounts of the sacraments might be understood as extensions of a larger experiential predestinarianism, one that posited the bodily signs and symbols of devotion—whether formal or not—as outward indicators of one's intentions, desires, and spiritual standing. Indeed,

---

[87] William Perkins, *A warning against the idolatry of the last times* (Cambridge: Printed by Iohn Legat, Printer to the Vniuersitie of Cambridge, 1601), 263. (*EEBO*, STC (2nd ed.) / 19763.5, document image, 121.)

[88] Indeed, Lake has argued that the theologians whom historians have conventionally described as "moderate puritans" cannot be defined in terms of any doctrinal consensus, or by any unified resistance to the ceremonies and polity of the state church. Most of these moderate Puritans did not see themselves as upholding doctrines opposed to, or even distinct from, those of the state church. See Lake, *Moderate Puritans and the Elizabethan Church*, 282.

[89] William Perkins, *A reformed Catholike: or, A declaration shewing how neere we may come to the present Church of Rome in sundrie points of religion* (Cambridge: Printed by Iohn Legat, printer to the Vniuersitie of Cambridge, 1598), 290. (*EEBO*, STC (2nd ed.) / 19736, document image 156.)

[90] William Perkins, *A Golden Chaine: or The description of theologie containing the order of the causes of saluation and damnation.* Cambridge: Printed by Iohn Legat, printer to the Vniuersitie of Cambridge, 1600, 1001. (*EEBO,* STC (2nd ed.) / 19646, *document image 533.*)

[91] Perkins, *Golden Chaine*, 104. (*EEBO*, document image 58.)

ORTHODOXY AND MARGINALITY   41

Perkins's stance on the church's ceremonial performances bears striking resemblance to his applied divinity: his assessment of the devotional value of official worship practices might be understood as an extension of his position on the many unofficial devotional performances that unfolded on a continual basis even outside the parameters of the state worship services. According to Perkins, the official rites and ceremonies of the state church comprised only a few of the innumerable outward signs of inward grace; the worshipper did not need to rely on the official rites and ceremonies to determine his or her inward state. There were numerous means, apart from the official ceremonies of the church, through which an individual might discern his spiritual standing vis-à-vis God. Any number of unofficial bodily performances, Perkins maintained, could serve as equally powerful signifiers of one's devotional access to God. The devout could find God's presence and likeness "in every natural action, belonging to each living creature, as to nourish, to engender, to move, to perceive." Liberated from the need to rely wholly on formal worship for devotional proximity to God, it was now possible to find God's presence "in every humane action, that is, such as belong to all men."[92] Although it might be unlawful to create material images of God's likeness—and indeed, Perkins utterly forbade participation in "all such processions, plays, and such feasts, as are consecrated to the memorial and honor of idols"—he nevertheless insisted that the material, sensible world ought to play a vital role in the devotional process: "The more obscure manifestation, is the vision of God's majesty in *this life*, by the eyes of the mind, *through the help of things perceived by the outward senses*."[93] As the sacraments were devotionally valuable in their capacity to make God's grace "visible to the eye," similarly, human life and the natural world worked in concert to make God's presence perceptible by means of one's bodily senses.[94] Although Perkins cautioned against certain outward and performative aspects of devotion, he also insisted that the body and its senses must function like spiritual barometers of sorts—visible and perceptible indicators of a worshipper's devotional well-being. Despite their differences, the theologies of Perkins and Hooker reimagine the worshipper's body as an index of Reformed devotional experience.

Experiential Calvinist theology acknowledged the cognitive and interpretive nature of devotional practice, and invested sense and experience with evidentiary authority. As a result, experiential Calvinists like Perkins and Hooker were able to argue that the devotional value of the public sacraments and rites could be translated into any experience or encounter that could similarly bolster an individual's epistemological certainty in matters of devotion and faith. More importantly, post-Reformation worship culture imbued early modern English life with a new

---

[92] Perkins, *Cloud of faithful witnesses*, 19. (*EEBO*, document image 15.)
[93] Perkins, *Cloud of faithful witnesses*, 6, emphases added. (*EEBO*, document image 5.)
[94] Perkins, *Commentarie or exposition*, 254. (*EEBO*, document image 135.)

42   DEVOTIONAL EXPERIENCE IN THE REFORMATION

epistemological framework for assessing and verifying devotion and access. The porous boundary between official and popular worship now meant that how one could ascertain devotional access to Christ might equally serve to ascertain devotional access in an array of secular devotional contexts. Indeed, Perkins himself described sexual devotion in the same terms that he and the early church reformers used to describe the sacramental rites. In *Christian Oeconomie*, his 1609 manual for proper Christian household management, Perkins several times described marriage as a "sacrament"—despite the fact that the Reformed church no longer regarded holy matrimony as a sacrament in any formal sense.[95] Adopting the language of the Communion rite, he calls marriage a "communion" between spouses, one in which both partners "do mutually and willingly communicate, both their persons, and goods each to other."[96] For Perkins, spiritual communion between married lovers is aided by sexual communion. He describes sex—what he calls a "due benevolence" between married partners—using evidentiary and interpretive language seemingly lifted directly from early church descriptions of the sacraments. Spouses strengthen their commune with each other "by an holy kind of rejoicing and solacing themselves with each other, in a mutual declaration of the *signs and tokens* of love and kindness."[97] Here Perkins lifts the Reformed church's conception of devotional access to God to describe devotional access between married lovers. Just as the outward gestures of devotion could offer evidentiary support for ascertaining a worshipper's devotional access to God, Perkins argued that sex, when it was joyous and solacing, could be read evidentiarily—as a sign or token that could verify the depth of devotion between married communicants.

The cultural logic of experiential devotion granted English worshippers continual access to the effects of devotional performance in the church, in popular devotional practice, and even in the act of sex between loving partners. Both in and outside of the official services of the church, a Reformed Christian could partake in an ever-unfolding sequence of devotional experiences by which they could make their commitments knowable and certain. By uncoupling the official devotional performances from their original sacramental origins, the Reformed Christian was subsequently free to ascribe that sacramental power to a range of informal devotional performances—including Leontes's act of gazing upon his wife and his assessment of his own bodily comportment. As Perkins maintained

---

[95] William Perkins, *Christian Oeconomie, or a Short Survey of the Right Manner of erecting and ordering a Familie, according to the Scriptures* (London: Imprinted by Felix Kyngston, and are to be sold by Edmund Weauer, 1609), 112 and unnumbered pages from the dedicatory epistle. (*EEBO*, STC (2nd ed.) / 19677.)

[96] Perkins, *Christian Oeconomie*, 110.

[97] Perkins, *Christian Oeconomie*, 122, emphasis added. For an illuminating discussion of Perkins's treatment of due benevolence between spouses, as well as the way English reformers understood sexual fulfillment as an extension of their spiritual practice, see Tom Schwanda, *Soul Recreation: The Contemplative-Mystical Piety of Puritanism* (Eugene, OR: Pickwick Publications, 2012), 35–74, esp. 50–1 for Schwanda's discussion of Perkins.

ORTHODOXY AND MARGINALITY 43

in his argument about happily married sex, devotional power was no longer located in ceremonial accoutrements; that power was now vested in the bodily and intellectual experiences of the worshippers—even as they worshipped in the privacy of their marriage bed. English ceremonialism effectively promoted a practical theology that placed the sensing, material body at the center of Reformed devotional practice. Perkins's ceremonialism and practical devotion did not seek to diminish this sacramental impulse so much as he sought to locate that impulse in every facet of lived experience, including "sexual experience."[98]

The Reformed belief that regarded it a devotional obligation to bear witness to and actively interpret bodily signs of devotional affect was not limited to Puritan resistance factions; that devotional requirement was, on the contrary, central to Reformed English Protestant devotional practice during the late sixteenth and early seventeenth centuries. I have endeavored to show that the Reformed idea that experience could constitute a form of knowledge also gave rise to a wider cultural epistemology that made the sensing body central to the period's understanding of devotional certainty and access. The Reformed emphasis on sensual and bodily experience in early modern life not only had the effect of shaping the way the English people went about their devotional lives, but also held powerful implications for the way they interpreted and understood their own feelings and thoughts. As Perkins described ideal devotion, the perfect union with Christ required not only that the worshipper have access to Christ's mind, but the converse as well. Christ too must have free access to the worshipper's private impulses and intent: "Our salvation stands not so much in our apprehending of Christ, as in Christ's comprehending of us."[99] Unmediated access to Christ involved both corporeal and cognitive participation on the part of the believer. No longer was the penitent merely keen to know the mind of God; equally urgent was the requirement of making oneself spiritually knowable both to God and to oneself. Ultimately, in the Renaissance, the act of reading God and all others involved the task of reading oneself and one's own desires.

For Calvin and his English adherents, faith entailed an active way of thinking. Poems—much like Calvin's understanding of what might be described as a thinking faith—ask their readers to construct forms of knowledge that are neither axiomatic nor scientific; this thinking is subjective, and requires the reader to be open to affective encounters.[100] Walter Stuermann offers a succinct explanation

[98] For Hooker, to remove the sacraments from their original contexts within the state church did not entail a diminishing of their devotional force. Lake has argued that in the immediate aftermath of the publication of *Lawes of Ecclesiastical Polity*, Hooker faced a backlash for suggesting that an individual did not necessarily need to be an ordained member of the clergy in order to preach and that the laity—and even women—could privately conduct baptisms without diminishing the spiritual force of the sacrament. See Lake, "Business as Usual?," esp. 470–5.

[99] Quoted in Breward, Introduction, 32.

[100] For descriptions of early modern poetry as a mode of thought that requires affective contribution on the part of the reader, see Patrick Grant, "Augustinian Spirituality and the *Holy Sonnets* of

of how the Reformed understanding of knowledge diverges from other forms of cognition and thought: "In the case of mathematical or experimental knowledge, the perceiving subject tries to achieve an objectivity, a state of emotional isolation from the object of knowledge. ... To the extent that the subject is found to be *personally* pre-occupied with the object under analysis the suspicion arises that the knowledge he pretends is not really valid." On the contrary, the Reformation offered "a kind of knowledge which involves personal acquaintance with the object toward which the subject's attention is directed and in which affective elements seem to be integral to the knowledge."[101] This Reformed view of spiritual knowledge might equally be used to describe the kind of knowledge that comes from reading poems: the poetry written in the decades after the Reformation's arrival in England didn't just tell their readers how to think about devotion; these poems actively helped their readers *feel* these encounters as if through firsthand experience. The poetry of post-Reformation England captures the experiential logic of Reformed spirituality, making these poems particularly useful vehicles for thinking about how Reformed religion shaped devotional expressions of the period.

John Donne," *ELH* 38, no. 4 (1971): 542–61, esp. 543; on poetry's formal attributes, see Margaret Mauer, "The Circular Argument of Donne's *La Corona*," *Studies in English Literature, 1500–1900* 22, no. 1 (1982): 51–68, esp. 59; and David Marno, *Death Be Not Proud: The Art of Holy Attention* (Chicago: University of Chicago Press, 2016), esp. 3–4.

[101] Walter E. Stuermann, *A Critical Study of Calvin's Concept of Faith* (Ann Arbor: Edwards Brothers, 1952), 89.

PART I
THEATER AND CEREMONY

2

Shakespeare's Sweet Boy

Love's Rites, Prayers Divine, and Hallowed Name in the *Sonnets*

In several declarations of devotion addressed to the young man in the *Sonnets*, Shakespeare defends what seems like a penchant for rewriting the same poem over and over. Against the implicit accusations of his boyfriend, Shakespeare compares his apologia in Sonnet 108 to a kind of spoken prayer, a highly ritualized and publicly performed devotional gesture:

> like prayers diuine,
> I must each day say ore the very same,
> Counting no old thing old, thou mine, I thine
> Euen as when first I hallowed thy faire name.[1]

Echoing the young man's doubts, he asks whether repeated words have the capacity to express the depth of his love: "What's new to speake, what now to register, / That may expresse my loue, or thy deare merit?" (108.3–4).

These questions have not only bothered the young man to whom Shakespeare addresses his poems. Generations of readers of the *Sonnets* have shared the young man's concern over the repetitive nature of the sequence's devotional tropes, finding that the blandness of sentiment betrays a desire that expresses itself "monotheistically, monogamously, monosyllabically, and monotonously."[2] Moreover, the *Sonnets'* references to liturgical performance have come under fire for more than just aesthetic reasons. Readers who have discussed the *Sonnets'* peculiar use of devotional language have described the poem's performances of ritualized

---

[1] Sonnet 108, lines 5–8. I have taken all citations of the *Sonnets* from the 1609 quarto edition. See William Shakespeare, *Shake-speares Sonnets Neuer before imprinted* (At London: By G. Eld for T[homas] T[horpe] and are to be solde by William Aspley, 1609). (*EEBO*, STC (2nd ed.) / 22353.) Sonnet and line numbers are hereafter given parenthetically in the text.

[2] Joel Fineman, *Shakespeare's Perjured Eye: The Invention of Poetic Subjectivity in the Sonnets* (Berkeley: University of California Press, 1986), 141. Likewise, Joseph Peguigney detects a "whiff of boredom" on the poet's part in Sonnets 105 and 108, two poems that "proffer various rationalizations for laxity in sonneteering." See Joseph Peguigney, *Such Is My Love: A Study of Shakespeare's Sonnets* (Chicago: University of Chicago Press, 1985), 192, 193. In a similar vein, John Kerrigan concludes that the poet's celebration of that which has already been said, in the end conduces to an aesthetics of repetition and tautology, resulting in poems that are "scrupulously and Shakesperianly dull, but ... dull nonetheless." See John Kerrigan, (ed.), *The Sonnets and "A Lover's Complaint,"* by William Shakespeare (London: Penguin, 1986), 29.

Devotional experience and erotic knowledge in the literary culture of the English Reformation. Rhema Hokama,
Oxford University Press. © Rhema Hokama (2023). DOI: 10.1093/oso/9780192886552.003.0003

48   DEVOTIONAL EXPERIENCE IN THE REFORMATION

prayer as evidence of the poet's hypocrisy. For example, Stephen Booth makes this argument about the *Sonnets*, citing Christ's commandment to "use no vain repetitions as the heathen: for they think to be heard for their much babbling."[3] These readers have been consumed with the question of why Shakespeare commits the double offense of writing bad poetry and then of resorting to idolatry to defend his lack of craftsmanship. But readers who have maintained that the *Sonnets* are guilty of idolatry rely on anachronistic views of public worship that even now continue to be shaped by post-1660 Restoration attempts to reimagine the Reformation. These revisionist views invariably sought to define Caroline Anglicanism in opposition to non-conformist dissent. As such, the Caroline church sought to effectively eclipse the range of Elizabethan and Jacobean confessional outlooks and viewpoints that had regarded Cranmer's liturgy and Hooker's *Lawes* as cornerstones of their Reformed theology.[4]

What is clear is that, contrary to Booth, most readers of Shakespeare's *Sonnets* during the period in which they were written would not have regarded common prayer as either insincere or idolatrous. As Judith Maltby convincingly demonstrates, the prayer book liturgy gained widespread acceptance in post-Reformation England. Maltby has argued that the *Book of Common Prayer* had universal appeal in Elizabethan and Stuart England across genders, social classes, and confessional outlooks.[5] Maltby's case studies show that it is likely that many English people owned private copies of the *Book of Common Prayer*, considering that sales records reveal that prayer books were even cheaper to own than vernacular bibles.[6] This suggests that the liturgy shaped not just public devotion in England but also private worship at home. With the rise of literacy and the advent of print dissemination, the Reformed public liturgy sat at a crossroads between public and private devotion.

---

[3] Matthew 6:6–7. I have taken all references to the Bible in this chapter from Laurence Tomson's edition of the Geneva New Testament, *The Newe Testament of Ovr Lorde Iesvs Christ* (London: Christopher Barker, 1586 [1560]). (*EEBO*, STC 2887.) Noting the litany-like repetition in Sonnet 108 of the quatrain ("thou mine, I thine") and the direct reference to the Lord's Prayer ("hallowed thy faire name"), Booth reads the lines as the poet's "apparent obliviousness to the implication of his words." Booth notes that the Lord's Prayer is prefaced in the gospel of Matthew by Christ's Sermon on the Mount, in which Christ explicitly associates public, ritualized prayer with hypocrisy. See Stephen Booth, (ed.), *Shakespeare's Sonnets*, by William Shakespeare (New Haven: Yale University Press, 2000 [1977]), 349.

[4] Judith Maltby, *Prayer Book and People in Elizabethan and Early Stuart England* (Cambridge: Cambridge University Press, 1998), 236. Diarmaid MacCulloch has argued that both conformists and Puritan separatists regarded Cranmer as an authority in matters of theology and ecclesiology, and Debora Shuger has maintained that Hooker should not be regarded as a defender of a conservative religious establishment considering that his theology equally appealed to non-conformists like the Puritan Richard Baxter. See Diarmaid MacCulloch, "Cranmer, Thomas (1489–1556), Archbishop of Canterbury," in *Oxford Dictionary of National Biography* (Oxford: Oxford University Press, 2004; online ed., 2015); and Debora Shuger, "'Society Supernatural': The Imagined Community of Hooker's *Laws*," in *Religion and Culture in Renaissance England*, eds. Claire McEachern and Debora Shuger (Cambridge: Cambridge University Press, 1997), 116–41.

[5] Maltby, *Prayer Book and People*, *passim*, esp. 80 and 30.

[6] Maltby, *Prayer Book and People*, 29.

SHAKESPEARE'S SWEET BOY   49

The *Book of Common Prayer*'s broad appeal in Shakespeare's period effectively meant that it was less controversial than many readers of the *Sonnets* have assumed. Alec Ryrie has pointed out that prior to the Caroline reforms in the 1640s, outright resistance to the use of the public liturgy was the view of a fringe minority—"the province of a few separatists," and a "threat [that] remained more potential than real."[7] In Shakespeare's period, "virtually all British Protestants accepted set forms' legitimacy," Ryrie asserts.[8] This was the case even for the majority of British Protestants whom contemporary historians have described as non-conformists or separatists. Patrick Collinson has demonstrated that even among more radical Puritans, the Reformed liturgy and rites played a central and public role in their providentialism and soteriology.[9] In a similar vein, Alexandra Walsham has demonstrated that outward conformity to the Church of England's public liturgy and ceremonies encompassed a number of evolving and divergent confessional commitments. Up until the end of the Jacobean period, Walsham notes that English people's participation in outward worship "camouflaged a bewildering range of religious convictions and standpoints."[10] What the historical research makes clear is that the *Book of Common Prayer* was neither viewed with suspicion in Shakespeare's period nor forced upon English worshippers; instead, as Walsham notes, the Reformation succeeded in making "the Homilies and vernacular Protestant liturgy ... a familiar and much-loved part of the fabric of parochial life."[11]

This chapter challenges the longstanding critical tradition of viewing prayer in the *Sonnets* as either a cause for suspicion or a mere backdrop to what Shakespeare really wanted to say about something else entirely.[12] What does Shakespeare believe he is achieving—both poetically and erotically—when he insists upon extolling the young man through the use of repeated prayers and praise? To assume that the *Sonnets'* repetitions and reiterations function primarily as mimesis (of the

---

[7] Alec Ryrie, *Being Protestant in Reformation Britain* (Oxford: Oxford University Press, 2013), 215.

[8] Ryrie, *Being Protestant*, 217.

[9] Patrick Collinson, *The Elizabethan Puritan Movement* (Oxford: Oxford University Press, 1990 [1967]), 356.

[10] Alexandra Walsham, "The Parochial Roots of Laudianism Revisited: Catholics, Anti-Calvinists and 'Parish Anglicans' in Early Stuart England," *Journal of Ecclesiastical History* 49, no. 4 (1998): 620–51, esp. 637.

[11] Walsham, "Parochial Roots," 632.

[12] While Booth acknowledges the copious references to the Eucharist in his commentary on Sonnet 125, he nevertheless downplays the contribution the Eucharist makes either imagistically or as an analogy to gestures of erotic devotion: "None of the evidence is such as would lead a reader to think about the Eucharist while he reads the poem." Booth's comments on the sonnet's fundamental non-religiousness resonate with longstanding views of Shakespeare as an essentially theologically neutral playwright. Booth (ed.), *Shakespeare's Sonnets*, 430. Both David Bevington and Roland Mushat Frye have suggested that Shakespeare's plays are inherently "non-theological"—to use Bevington's term—with all reference to religion merely comprising the backdrop to dramatic coherency. See David Bevington, *Tudor Drama and Politics: A Critical Approach to Topical Meaning* (Cambridge, MA: Harvard University Press, 1968), 201–2; Roland Mushat Frye, *Shakespeare and Christian Doctrine* (Princeton: Princeton University Press, 1963), 265–71.

50   DEVOTIONAL EXPERIENCE IN THE REFORMATION

real world or of another poet's craft), as recollection (of a past event), or as information transmission (for example, a lyric account of a mood or an impulse) is to ignore the performative dimension of the poems. It is to ignore the fact that these prayers and praises are events that *happen*, that are done, and that take place in the world. According to Jonathan Culler, the lyric form is less a "fictional representation of an experience or an event so much as an attempt to be itself an event."[13] He continues, "A distinctive feature of lyric seems to be this attempt to create the impression of something happening now, in the present time of discourse."[14] Similarly, Susan Stewart describes our experience of lyric as "[s]omething that 'happens,' that 'occurs' as an event and can be continually called on, called to mind, in the unfolding present."[15] Shakespeare's cluster of religious sonnets—with their liturgical repetitions and rote prayers—are singular events unto themselves, ones that take place during each live performance. More than mimicry, memorial recollection, or narrowly prescribed acts of praise, the *Sonnets* serve as live arenas for erotic and devotional negotiation between the performer and his lover.

Culler and Stewart's theories about the function of lyric utterance, in the case of Shakespeare's religiously inflected *Sonnets*, can be corroborated by early modern historical conceptions of performance. It is impossible to understand the poems' reiterated, public expressions of devotion apart from wider early modern cultural practices in which reiterated utterance was elicited, or even required. In her discussion of Richard Hooker's efforts to broaden public participation in state-sanctioned worship practices, Ramie Targoff has argued that Hooker and the Church of England were less preoccupied with the task of cultivating private devotion than they were with ensuring public conformity: "Hooker's interest in broadening the scope of public participation as well as his distrust of men's 'private discretion' extend far beyond his polemical response to specific non-conformist proposals. Repeatedly throughout the *Lawes*, he demonstrates his overarching concern with forging an ecclesiastical polity in which sacrifices of personal voice are exacted in exchange for the collective good."[16] Hooker remained absolutely certain, Targoff insists, "that the liturgical practices of the public sphere are more devotionally effective than their private and spontaneous counterparts."[17] According to Targoff, Hooker conceived of communal forms of prayer as safeguards against the devotional weaknesses of individual parishioners.[18] While Targoff is not incorrect to emphasize the role of public worship in her account of Hooker's ecclesiology, she overstates his belief in the inherent devotional effectiveness of

[13] Jonathan Culler, *Theory of the Lyric* (Cambridge, MA: Harvard University Press, 2015), 16.
[14] Culler, *Theory of the Lyric*, 37.
[15] Susan Stewart, *Poetry and the Fate of the Senses* (Chicago: University of Chicago Press, 2002), 104. Cited in Culler, *Theory of the Lyric*, 353.
[16] Ramie Targoff, *Common Prayer: The Language of Public Devotion in Early Modern England* (Chicago: University of Chicago Press, 2001), 50.
[17] Targoff, *Common Prayer*, 51.
[18] Targoff, *Common Prayer*, 47–56.

SHAKESPEARE'S SWEET BOY   51

public worship. Although Hooker emphasized the importance of the sacraments in Reformed worship, he also made clear that no outward display of devotion could produce an inward state of grace in those not already in possession of it. At most, outward gestures could only corroborate or enhance a prior state of spiritual grace. Bryan D. Spinks captures this paradoxical understanding of public worship in his explication of Hooker's stance on the sacraments. The sacraments are "visible sign[s] indicating grace obtained for us. ... They are not themselves the cause of grace, but a visible means that God uses whereby we may know even if we cannot see the divine."[19] Devotion in the *Sonnets* is deeply informed by this paradoxical view of performance; public worship had the capacity to bolster the individual's devotional affect, yet could not single-handedly effect that devotion.

The *Sonnets'* preoccupation with the relationship between outward form and inward thought provides one lyric exploration of the early modern belief that common forms of prayer afforded a devotional effectiveness that spontaneous prayer did not. Like Hooker's vision of communal worship, the *Sonnets* reveal a lively enthusiasm for public displays of devotion while also seeming, at several points in the sequence, to recoil from this position. The *Sonnets* capture the state church's paradoxical emphasis on a sacraments-based worship practice that simultaneously prioritized the worshipper's individual devotional experience.[20] The *Sonnets* reflect this cultural anxiety about what intimate access looked and felt like—and about how one could confirm the legitimacy of that access. In response to this anxiety, Shakespeare develops a keenly materialist understanding of intimate access to interiors—not just to the intentions of another but also to one's own ineffable impulses and desires.

Contextualizing the *Sonnets* within early modern public worship practices enables us to move beyond readings of ritualized prayer as evidence of hypocrisy or feigned affection. On the contrary, devotion in the *Sonnets*, as in the secular theater houses and in the state church, is deeply informed by public performance. We can only perceive in full what critics have dismissed as either hypocrisy or aesthetic dullness within the context of early modern conceptions of both ecclesiastical and secular performance. In reading public gestures of devotion in the *Sonnets*, I start with historical conceptions of early modern performance in both the professional theater and the state church.

---

[19] Bryan D. Spinks, *Two Faces of Elizabethan Anglican Theology: Sacraments and Salvation in the Thought of William Perkins and Richard Hooker* (Lanham, MD: Scarecrow Press, 1999), 142–3.

[20] That Shakespeare's plays contain echoes of Hooker's ecclesiology is not a new proposition. Most recently, Daniel Eppley has argued for Shakespeare's probable familiarity with Hooker's ecclesiastical writing. See Daniel Eppley, *Reading the Bible with Richard Hooker* (Minneapolis: Augsburg Fortress, 2016), 69. Virgil Whitaker has identified passages in Shakespeare's play that "obviously came straight out of Hooker." See Virgil Whitaker, *Shakespeare's Use of Learning: An Inquiry into the Growth of His Mind and Art* (San Marino, CA: Huntington Library, 1953), 207 and esp. 198–9. Ken Jacobsen has observed similarities between the social vision of Hooker's *Lawes* and that of *The Taming of the Shrew*. See Ken Jacobsen, "'The Law of a Commonweal': The Social Vision of Hooker's *Of the Laws of Ecclesiastical Polity* and Shakespeare's *The Taming of the Shrew*," *Animus* 12 (2008): 15–38.

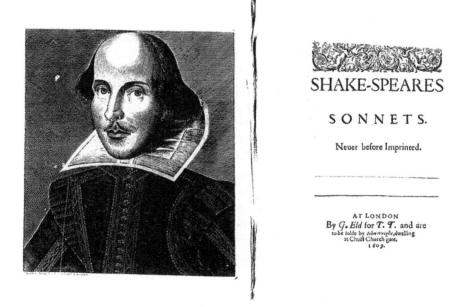

Figure 2.1 Frontispiece and title page of the 1609 edition of *Shake-speares Sonnets. Neuer before Imprinted*. At London: By G. Eld for T. T. and are to be solde by Iohn Wright, dwelling at Christ Church gate, 1609. Copy from the Folger Shakespeare Library.

Unperfect actor

A direct comparison between secular performance and religious liturgical rites comes early in the sequence in Sonnet 23, in which Shakespeare compares his inability to offer a public show of praise to a kind of stage fright, an inability to perform:

> As an vnperfect actor on the stage,
> Who with his feare is put besides his part,
> Or some fierce thing repleat with too much rage,
> Whose strengths abundance weakens his owne heart;
> So I, for feare of trust, forget to say,
> The perfect ceremony of loues right.
>
> (23.1–6)

Although readers such as Richard McCoy note oppositions between inward and outward devotion in their reading of religious ritual in the *Sonnets*,[21] it is clear that

---

[21] In a reading of the role of sacrament in the *Sonnets*, Richard C. McCoy argues that the poet "seems intent on moving past outward signs" to an inward space that might be more genuinely touched by

the display of devotion in Sonnet 23 blurs our ability to determine inward experience from outward gesture. Like a bad actor who fails to sustain a cohesive role for himself, Shakespeare fears that his inability to sustain outward gestures of devotion has caused "own loues strength ... to decay," becoming "Ore-charg'd with burthen of [his] owne loues might" (23.7–8). In the poem, the state of desiring encodes that desire's own undoing; a surplus of love prevents the proper outward expression of that love. The poem's anxiety is that the inability to outwardly *demonstrate* love has a corrosive effect upon that love itself. Desire's muteness threatens to corrode the very foundations of that desire before it can manifest itself, registering its realness in the visible, sensible world. Preoccupied with the state of his love, the poem draws a causal connection between Shakespeare's failure to perform the proper rites of love and his inability to feel commensurate love for the young man.

As a solution to his devotional shortcomings, Shakespeare urges his boyfriend to subscribe to a view of devotional affect that can be corroborated by performed gesture. He claims that his outward expressions—alternatively his "looks" or his "books," depending on who is editing Shakespeare—whether bodily performed or materially transcribed, provide a fair index of what transpires in his heart:

> O let my books [/looks] be then the eloquence,
> And domb presagers of my speaking brest,
> Who pleade for loue, and look for recompence,
> More then that tonge that more hath more exprest.
>
> (23.9–12)

While "books" is the subject in the 1609 quarto printing of the line, there is a long editorial tradition of emending the line to read "looks."[22] But whether the line emphasizes Shakespeare's looks or books, both editorial decisions produce similarly rich interpretive readings. In either case, Shakespeare asks his boyfriend to read for external signs of a deeply interior devotional state—whether by means of his bodily comportment or via a material transcription of his desires. In appealing to his outward looks, Shakespeare insists that inward experience is not opposed to outward gesture but is coexistent with it. The experience of being desired, like the experience of reading a book, is hardly a passive enterprise: "O learne to read what silent loue hath writ: / To heare wit eies belongs to loues fine wiht" (23.13–14). The sonnet is a celebration of the body's role in cultivating desire,

---

religious ritual. See Richard C. McCoy, "Love's Martyrs: Shakespeare's 'Phoenix and Turtle' and the Sacrificial Sonnets," in *Religion and Culture in Renaissance England*, eds. Claire McEachern and Debora Shuger (Cambridge: Cambridge University Press, 1997), 188–209, esp. 200. With respect to the early modern lyric more broadly, Louis Martz and Anne Ferry both posit conceptions of inwardness opposed to outward show. See Louis Martz, *The Poetry of Meditation: A Study in English Religious Literature of the Seventeenth Century* (New Haven: Yale University Press, 1954); and Anne Ferry, *The "Inward" Language: Sonnets of Wyatt, Sidney, Shakespeare, and Donne* (Chicago: University of Chicago Press, 1983).

[22] For a discussion of the two editorial decisions regarding this line, see Booth (ed.), *Shakespeare's Sonnets*, 172.

54   DEVOTIONAL EXPERIENCE IN THE REFORMATION

but it is the young man's sensual experience—his reading, hearing, and seeing—that most fascinates Shakespeare. In effect, the sonnet imagines a performance of devotion that is contingent less upon the actor than upon the witness's private experience of that erotic ceremony.

Sonnet 23 highlights the cultural resonances between the secular theater and the state liturgy; for a Puritan minority of early modern worshipers, these resonances would have been cause for alarm. For these extremists, Sonnet 23's melding of performances—both liturgical and theatrical—would have suggested evidence of the poet's devotional insincerity. Indeed, as Jonas Barish has noted, these attacks on both the English liturgy and on public stage performance charged that it was impossible to be sincere while relying on set forms and scripted roles:

> Not only the Puritan attack on the stage, but the Puritan attack on the liturgy, it may be suspected, drew strength from the belief in a total sincerity. Worship, to be genuine, could only be a direct translation of one's inner self. It could only be unique, spontaneous, an unpremeditated out-pouring from the grateful soul. To reduce it to set forms, to freeze it in ritual repetitions of word or gesture, to commit it to memory, to make it serve a variety of occasions or a diversity of worshippers, was to make the individual a mimic of sentiments not exactly, or not entirely, his own.[23]

These polemicists grounded their attacks on the stage and the liturgy on the alleged disjunct between a performer's outward form and inward affect. The reformist clerics John Field and Thomas Wilcox, for example, likened set prayer and recitation from the *Book of Common Prayer* to performing on stage: "bare reading of the word and single service saying ... is as evil as playing upon a stage, & worse too. For players yet learn their parts without book, and these, a many of them can scarcely read within book."[24] In their assessment of the relative dangers of set worship and playacting, Field and Wilcox assert that the Reformed liturgy is even more pernicious than the playhouses; while actors at least know their lines by heart and have

---

[23] Jonas Barish, *The Antitheatrical Prejudice* (Berkeley: University of California Press, 1981), 95. For an earlier version of this argument, see also Jonas Barish, "The Antitheatrical Prejudice," *Critical Quarterly* 8.4 (1966): 329–48, esp. 334. For other readers who have described the cultural overlap between early modern English theater and post-Reformation worship, see Maltby, *Prayer Book and People*, 3; Brian Morris, "Elizabethan and Jacobean Drama," in *English Drama to 1710*, ed. Christopher Ricks (London: Sphere, 1971), 65–117, esp. 65–6; Jeffrey Knapp, "Preachers and Players," chap. 4 in *Shakespeare's Tribe: Church, Nation, and Theater in Renaissance England* (Chicago: University of Chicago Press, 2002), 115–40; Targoff, *Common Prayer*; Huston Diehl, *Staging Reform, Reforming the Stage* (Ithaca, NY: Cornell University Press, 1997); Bryan Crockett, *The Play of Paradox: Stage and Sermon in Renaissance England* (Philadelphia: University of Pennsylvania Press, 1995); Louis Montrose, "Shakespeare, the Stage, and the State," *SubStance* 25, no. 2 (1996): 46–67; Louis Montrose, *The Purpose of Playing* (Chicago: University of Chicago Press, 1996); and Stephen Greenblatt, *Shakespearean Negotiations* (Berkeley: University of California Press, 1988), 94–198.

[24] John Field and Thomas Wilcox, *An Admonition to the Parliament* (Hemel Hempstead: Printed by J. Stroud, 1572), unpaginated. (*EEBO*, STC (2nd ed.) / 10848, document image 9.)

SHAKESPEARE'S SWEET BOY   55

internalized the affect that they perform on stage, by contrast, clerics and their parishioners must rely on the printed prayer books for their sermons and prayers. While the actors on stage have internalized their roles, Field and Wilcox maintain that preachers and parishioners in English churches have not—an indication of devotional insincerity.

Field and Wilcox derided set prayers as "stagelike songs," and regarded the preachers who relied on the public liturgy as "empty feeders, dark eyes, ill workmen ... blind guides, sleepy watchmen, untrusty dispensers of God's secretes, [and] evil dividers of the word."[25] The apologia offered by Sonnet 23 seems almost a direct response to the charges set forth by Field and Wilcox in their admonition. For them, to read from books is an indication of devotional insincerity; for Shakespeare, outward gestures—even clumsy ones—emanate from an inner devotional truth. As in the print history of the sonnet, the argument of the poem seems to conflate the function of books and looks in the poet's devotional entreaties to his boyfriend. For Shakespeare, there is no gap between inner devotion and its outward manifestations—whether printed on the page or revealed in his outward gestures of praise.

While few of Shakespeare's contemporary readers would have worried about the charges of insincerity that Field and Wilcox leveled against those who used the *Book of Common Prayer*, it appears that a great number of them likely worried about their ability to correctly perform those rites. In this sense, the poet's fear that he is unable to perform the "ceremony of loves rights" might have struck a chord with early modern readers of the *Sonnets*. As Ryrie has noted, anxieties about the inability to come up with the words for effectual prayer were rife in Shakespeare's period.[26] Indeed, the poet of the *Sonnets* is merely echoing the question posed by the Reformed cleric Robert Harris: "What if a man be so dumb and barren, that he can say nothing when he should pray?"[27] The devotional writer Robert Linaker posed this problem succinctly in a self-help treatise written to aid those afflicted with an inability to pray. During particularly difficult moments of devotion, Linaker lamented that his heart is sometimes "so narrow and barren in prayer, that many times I cannot pray at all." As a result, Linaker saw no choice but to rely on set prayers, which he had "been forced for the most part to use ... almost word for word." Without these set prayers, Linaker found his own spontaneous prayers inadequate—so much so that his unscripted devotion prompted spiritual anxiety: "[my spontaneous prayer] is such poor, dry, naked, and silly stuff, both for words and matter, that after I have prayed, I am a great while

---

[25] Field and Wilcox, *Admonition to the Parliament*, unpaginated. (*EEBO*, document images 9–10.)

[26] For a discussion of how Reformed clerics addressed the problem of being tongue-tied in prayer in Elizabethan and Stuart England, see Ryrie, *Being Protestant*, 102–4.

[27] Robert Harris, *Peters enlargement upon the praryers of the Church* (London: Printed by H[umphrey] L[owns] for John Bartlet, at the golden Cup, in the Gold-Smiths Row in Cheape-side, 1627), 24. (*EEBO*, STC (2nd ed.) / 12842.) Quoted in Ryrie, *Being Protestant*, 102.

56　DEVOTIONAL EXPERIENCE IN THE REFORMATION

marvelously tormented in conscience."[28] The anxieties articulated by Harris and Linaker suggest that many English Protestants often felt at a loss for words while crafting their prayers—even prayers in the vernacular. The challenge of speaking prayers aloud encompassed more than the problem of mere understanding, and vernacular comprehension alone was only a starting point but not a guarantee of effectual prayer.

In their assessment of the problems posed by being tongue-tied in prayer, both Linaker and Harris offer a comforting possibility: when it came to effectual prayer, devotional intent mattered as much as the words of the prayer itself. Linaker assured his readers that those who found themselves resorting to inarticulate sighs and groans, or who could speak no words at all, nevertheless offered up valid prayer to God, who "knows our meaning and thoughts before we speak, yea although we speak not at all." Linaker assured his readers that even "if you cannot pray in set words, and in fine order," their intention to pray nonetheless had powerful import. He insisted, "If you can sigh and groan, after this manner, be of good comfort. ... you pray very effectually."[29] Sonnet 23 captures the anxieties articulated by Harris and Linaker about the challenges of finding fit words for prayer, and seems to resolve the issue by deferring to something akin to their resolution to the problem of finding oneself tongue-tied in prayer. When the poet insists that his "dombe" performance gives credence to his devotion just as much as formal ceremonies do, he is, in effect, offering a secular version of Linaker's argument that the sighs and groans of a tongue-tied worshipper nonetheless hold devotional power. In insisting upon the legitimacy of his devotional entreaties—whether as reiterated language or affect ultimately left unspoken—the poet co-opts popular Reformation views of prayer in defending his own erotic expressions of praise. For the poet, the devotional legitimacy of his praises rests on his prior intentions—and not on his outward expressions. Just as the moderate Reformed preacher Richard Sibbes insisted that "God can pick sense out of a confused prayer,"[30] the *Sonnets* make an argument for the validity of devotional expression—even as "dombe" performance or simple set language—that has value in spite of its formal limitations.

Despite acknowledging the formal limitations of public devotional performance, importantly, the *Sonnets* do not reject the value that external performances play in the poet's devotional process. On the contrary, in Sonnet 23, Shakespeare celebrates outward rites as essential to the poet's private devotional process; his outward show of devotion serves as an accurate signpost for his

---

[28] Robert Linaker, *A comfortable treatise for the reliefe of such as are afflicted in conscience* (London: Valentine Simmes for R. Boyle, 1595), 46. (*EEBO*, STC (2nd ed.) / 15638.) Discussed in Ryrie, *Being Protestant*, 103.

[29] Linaker, *Comfortable treatise*, 47–8.

[30] Richard Sibbes, *The bruised reede, and smoaking flax* (London: Printed [by M. Flesher] for R. Dawlman, dwelling at the signe of the Brazen Serpent in Pauls Church-yard, 1630), 133. (*EEBO*, STC (2nd ed.) / 22479.) Quoted in Ryrie, *Being Protestant*, 103.

unarticulated affect. The poem closes by shifting the burden of the interpretation of the performance onto the young man himself: "O learne to read what silent loue hath writ: / To heare with eies belongs to loues fine wiht." In effect, Shakespeare is asking the young man to surmise his innermost desires—either via his bodily gestures ("looks") or in the written chronicle of his passion (his "books" of love poems). In the poem, Shakespeare describes the poet's erotic difficulties in terms of the devotional difficulties outlined by Harris, Linaker, and Sibbes. In fact, the poet seems to expect of his boyfriend an almost God-like omnipotence when he asks his boyfriend to do what has seemed to modern critics to be impossible: to read his mind simply by observing his external comportment.

Idolatrous amens

Shakespeare returns to the Reformation preoccupation with the relationship between inner devotional feeling and the perceptible expression of that feeling in Sonnet 108. Here, as in Sonnet 23, the poet finds himself struggling to perform, and the poem begins by anticipating the young man's doubts about the poet's devotional sincerity:

> What's in the braine that Inck may character,
> Which hath not figur'd to thee my true spirit,
> What's new to speake, what now to register,
> That may expresse my loue, or thy deare merit?
> Nothing sweet boy, but yet like prayers diuine,
> I must each day say ore the very same,
> Counting no old thing old, thou mine, I thine,
> Euen as when first I hallowed thy faire name.

(108.1–8)

The poet's inability to express his devotion in Sonnet 108 is a recapitulation of the problem of Cordelia's tongue-tiedness at the outset of *King Lear*. In response to his own preemptive hypotheticals—"What's in the brain?" and "What's new to speak?"—the poet can only offer a Cordelian reply: "Nothing, sweet boy." The poem anticipates Cordelia's own "Nothing, my Lord" (1.1.85), as she finds herself tongue-tied during Lear's love test in Act 1 of the tragedy. As we read the sonnet, we almost expect the poet to utter Cordelia's subsequent lines: "Unhappy that I am, I cannot heave / My heart into my mouth" (1.1.89–90).[31] In their explications of Cordelia's reticence, readers of *King Lear* have gone out of their way to defend Lear's youngest daughter—attributing her tongue-tiedness alternatively to

---

[31] I have cited Cordelia's lines from the combined text of *King Lear* from William Shakespeare, *The Norton Shakespeare*, eds. Stephen Greenblatt et al. (New York: W. W. Norton, 2015).

58 DEVOTIONAL EXPERIENCE IN THE REFORMATION

shyness, inarticulateness, coyness, or even a political artlessness.[32] But what they haven't called her—and rightfully so—is a hypocrite. And yet, for uttering nearly the same sentiment in a similar public forum, critics have been eager to attribute the poet's motives in Sonnet 108 to hypocrisy and devotional disingenuity. At the start of this chapter, I mentioned that Booth finds evidence of hypocrisy in the poem's language of devotion—the poet's ritual of "each day say[ing] oer the very same" laudatory tropes, like "prayers diuine." For Booth, the poet's reliance on set forms and repeated praise is indicative of spiritual insincerity. Likewise, in her reading of the sonnet, Helen Vendler presents public performance as antithetical to genuine devotional affect. Vendler identifies what she calls the poet's "inner 'rebellion'" against the "young man's enslavement to novelty," as if devotional intensity in the sonnet must necessarily emanate from something imperceptible to spectators observing from without.[33] Yet it is clear that the sonnet maintains precisely the opposite claim. Contrary to Booth and Vendler's interpretations, in repeating ancient forms of praise, Shakespeare finds "eternall loue in loues fresh case," a love weighed down neither by the "dust and iniury of age" nor one that succumbs to those "necessary wrinckles" that plague many another hackneyed phrase (108.9–11). In seeking eternal love in the antique panegyrics, Shakespeare finds "the first conceit of loue there bred, / Where time and outward forme would shew it dead" (108.13–14). Like Cordelia, Shakespeare's poet makes a case for devotional sentiment that exists prior to and indeed belies its outward expression. But unlike Cordelia, in Sonnet 108 the poet relies on set forms to help him articulate his devotional affect. As he did in Sonnet 23, the poet once more affords his boyfriend a God-like ability to discern "What's in his brain" via his outward, albeit imperfect, gestures of devotion. In presenting the poet of the *Sonnets* as too inarticulate to come up with his own expressions of praise, Shakespeare captures a concern about devotional expression that, as Ryrie has argued, was a distinctive concern that arose after the Reformation: in a devotional culture that demanded individual conviction, "some people found it hard to string words together to make a coherent prayer."[34] As Ryrie points out, set prayers offered a solution to devotional inarticulacy, and even the staunchest of Puritans prior to the Caroline reforms would not have thought that reliance on set forms of praise were in any way indicative of a worshipper's devotional insincerity.[35]

---

[32] In criticism and stage history, Cordelia has been conceived both by directors and critics as a shy, tongue-tied girl. Most prominently, Stanley Cavell imagines Cordelia "shuddering with confusion," as small and slight, young and least, a girl who, if she must speak, murmurs in her characteristically quiet voice. In Cavell's reading, Cordelia's unfamiliarity with the ways of the court stymies her ability to meet her father's demands. See Stanley Cavell, "The Avoidance of Love: A Reading of *King Lear*," chap. 10 in *Must We Mean What We Say?* (Cambridge: Cambridge University Press, 2003 [1967]), 267–353, p. 292.

[33] Helen Vendler, *The Art of Shakespeare's Sonnets* (Cambridge, MA: Harvard University Press, 1997), 460, 459.

[34] Ryrie, *Being Protestant*, 102–3.

[35] Ryrie, *Being Protestant*, 202–38.

SHAKESPEARE'S SWEET BOY   59

Sonnet 108 is a defense of the rites and ceremonies of love, one that ultimately rests upon the assumption that the outward form of these gestures, like the Reformed liturgies and sacraments, are *adiaphora*—things spiritually indifferent. Love's rites register a powerful desire—ancient and timeless, and prior to all ceremony itself. In its final lines, the sonnet straddles the divide between the performance and the audience's own interpretive participation in that performance. Shakespeare's rote performance is foundational to the devotional process, but it is the young man's participation in the performance that gives it its peculiar erotic power. Eternal love makes hoary antiquity his "page" (108.12)—his boy-servant, but also the material vehicle for literary transmission.[36] The sonnet reappropriates all of erotic and literary history as Shakespeare's creative source materials, revitalizing a long history of desire that exists prior to this moment's performance.

Shakespeare assumes the role of performer in Sonnet 108, but he undergoes a role reversal in Sonnet 85, in which he imagines himself not as a performer but as spectator to his rivals' utterances of praise. In Sonnet 108 he justifies his tendency to repeat himself over and over; but in Sonnet 85 he apologizes for what some might qualify as an even greater transgression—his mimicry of the words of others. Shakespeare, like an "vnlettered clarke still crie[s] Amen / To euery Himne that able spirit affords / In polisht forme of well refined pen" (85.6–8). He admits his penchant for freely assenting to unoriginal sentiment: "Hearing you praisd, I say 'tis so, 'tis true" (85.9).

These lines have elicited critical censure, not only of Shakespeare's efforts to praise his boyfriend using well-worn phrases, but of various early modern liturgical traditions that readers have associated with the sonnet's conceit. Booth has compared the unlettered clerk to a priest lacking knowledge of Latin, and consequently casts doubt upon the poet-parishioner's capacity for individual conviction. In short, Booth posits that the sonnet veers dangerously close to committing both spiritual and erotic falsity.[37] Booth takes his cue from the Pauline injunction against the practice of speaking in tongues—*glossolalia*—for its power to activate the spirit but not the mind: "Else, when thou blesses with the spirit, how shall he that occupieth the room of the unlearned, say, 'Amen,' at thy giving of thanks, seeing he knoweth not what thou sayest?"[38] Protestant denouncers of the Catholic liturgy leveled a similar argument against the Latin Mass. In their vision of Reformed public worship, vernacular comprehension and participation in the public rites were of paramount importance for early reformers. William Tyndale

---

[36] Shakespeare makes a similar argument in Sonnet 59: "Show me your image in some antique booke, / Since minde at first in carrecter was done, / That I might see what the old world could say / To this composed wonder of your frame" (59.7–10).

[37] Booth (ed.), *Shakespeare's Sonnets*, 287. Both Kerrigan and Hyder Edward Rollins have made similar claims about the unlettered clerk's spiritual hypocrisy for his reappropriation of his "amens." See Kerrigan (ed.), *Sonnets*, 280; and Hyder Edward Rollins (ed.), *A New Variorum Edition of Shakespeare*, 2 vols. (Philadelphia: Lippencott, 1971), 1: 216.

[38] 1 Corinthians 14:16.

60   DEVOTIONAL EXPERIENCE IN THE REFORMATION

insisted that sacraments performed in the Latin were "unfruitful," for the reason that the average English parishioner could not understand their import and consequently could not grasp the promises that they had come to symbolize.[39] Likewise, in his Preface to the 1559 *Book of Common Prayer*, Thomas Cranmer draws precisely this connection between Paul's caution against prayers in tongues and the Latin liturgy:

> Whereas Saint Paul would have such language spoken to the people in the church, as they might understand, and have profit by hearing the same: the service in this church of England (these many years) hath been read in Latin to the people, which they understand not: so that they have heard with their ears only and their hearts, spirit, and mind, have not been edified thereby.[40]

In a similar vein, John Jewel, Bishop of Salisbury, insisted that common prayer must be performed in the English vernacular: "We make our prayers in that tongue which all our people ... may understand."[41] But as the vernacular liturgy gained in popularity, early modern views regarding the challenge of effective prayer shifted. The Reformation introduced the necessity, in both public and private devotional life, of contributing one's individual assent to worship. Now that vernacular speech and literal understanding were prerequisite for effectual devotion, Reformed worshippers discovered new obligations in both public and private worship and prayer.

Readings of Sonnet 85 that draw comparisons between the poet's assent to the praises of others and either the Latin liturgy or the practice of speaking in tongues are problematic in one respect. Whether praying in Latin or in tongues, the lay parishioner cannot access the literal meaning of the words being uttered. However, in Sonnet 85, the "hymn that able spirit affords" (85.7) is ostensibly composed in the English vernacular; it is clear that the poem refers neither to the practice of the Latin Mass nor to *glossolalia* in describing Shakespeare's outward show of devotion for his boyfriend. The poet-parishioner is "unlettered" because he cannot compose his own original and spontaneous verse; he is literally devoid of the constituent letters and words that come together in his rivals' praises of his boyfriend. Nowhere does Shakespeare indicate that he cannot understand the literal meaning of those words when they are uttered by others. The dangerous schism between

---

[39] William Tyndale, *The Obedience of a Christian Man*, ed. David Daniell (London: Penguin Books, 2000), 130.

[40] Thomas Cranmer and John Jewel, Preface to *The booke of common praier, and administration of the Sacramentes, and other rites and ceremonies in the Churche of Englande* (London: In officina Richardi Iugge, & Iohannis Cawode, 1559), sig. A5r. (*EEBO*, STC 16292.)

[41] John Jewel, *An Apology of the Church of England (1564)*, ed. John E. Booty (Ithaca, NY: Cornell University Press, 1963), 37. Booty's edition is based on the second English translation of Jewel's original Latin. Due to significant variations among the earliest printed editions and copies of Jewel's treatise, I cite all reference to the *Apology* from Booty's definitive edition.

SHAKESPEARE'S SWEET BOY   61

the cognitive and spiritual faculties potentially introduced by the practices of either *glossolalia* or the Latin liturgy is irrelevant to the conceit of Sonnet 85. Indeed, the sonnet alludes to neither prayers in tongues nor the Latin Mass, but to cultural practices that lay closer to Shakespeare's own historical moment: the performance of the Protestant liturgy and common prayer in the English church.

That proper devotional sentiment must exist prior to the performance of public gesture is a modern critical assumption that has skewed readings of the *Sonnets'* religious references, leading readers to interpret the poem's amens as evidence of ignorance, unoriginal sentiment, or even hypocrisy. But there is evidence that there were other early modern lyric and liturgical occasions in which giving assent to public, reiterated forms of speech had the effect of deepening spiritual devotion for those who participated with their own amens. In 1608, a year before the quarto edition of the *Sonnets* appeared in print, a clergyman in the Church of England named Samuel Hieron penned what was to become a best-selling devotional handbook, *A Helpe unto Devotion*. Hieron's manual remained so popular that it appeared in a new edition nearly every year for the first decade after its initial printing. The title page of the tract promised to instruct lay parishioners in "certain molds or forms of prayer, fitted to several occasions; and penned for the furtherance of those, who have more desire then skill, to pour out their souls in petitions unto God."[42] In the dedicatory epistle to his devotional, Hieron outlined his motivations for providing lay worshippers with the prescribed "molds" and "forms" of common prayer, observing that a lack of artfulness in all too many lay worshippers had the debilitating effect of hindering sincere prayer: "For want of exercised wits, of knowledge in the Scriptures, and especially of experience in the power of godliness, and of a lively sense and distinct conceiving of their own personal necessities, they are not able to be their own messengers, not to do their own errand, in presenting the sacrifice of Prayer before the Lord."[43] In his note to the Christian reader at the outset of the volume, Hieron contends that outward show of devotion plays a necessary role in proper worship by preparing the supplicant's mental and emotional states. Prescribed prayer is "but a means rather of quickening and stirring up the spirit of him that prayeth ... his spiritual feeling shall increase, enlarge any particular request, if it bee not so full to his present case."[44]

Hieron published *A Helpe* a year after he clandestinely published his lengthy critique of the state liturgy, which he entitled *A defense of the ministers reasons for the refusal of subscription to the Book of Common Prayer, and of Conformitie* (1607).

---

[42] Samuel Hieron, *A helpe vnto deuotion containing certain moulds or forms of prayer, fitted to seuerall occasions* (London: by H[umphrey] L[ownes] for Samuel Macham, and are to be solde at his shop in Pauls Church-yard at the signe of the Bull-head, 1608), unpaginated. (*EEBO*, STC (2nd ed.) / 13406.3, document image 1.) With the exception of the year 1609, Hieron's *Helpe* underwent subsequent print editions each year between 1608 and 1618, and enjoyed wide popularity well into the middle of the century.

[43] Hieron, *Helpe vnto deuotion*, sig. A4v.

[44] Hieron, *Helpe vnto deuotion*, sig. A7v.

62   DEVOTIONAL EXPERIENCE IN THE REFORMATION

Across two volumes totaling nearly 400 pages of text, Hieron criticized the *Book of Common Prayer* on a range of issues—including its scriptural "mistranslations," its reliance on what he felt to be apocrypha, and its printing errors.[45] Yet despite his voluminous criticism of the state liturgy, what Hieron did not take issue with was the prayer book's use of set forms. Indeed, *A Helpe unto Devotion* was Hieron's attempt to write his own set prayers, for private use, given what he felt to be the doctrinal inaccuracies of the common prayers of the state church. In *A Helpe*, Hieron appropriates the devotional technique of the state liturgies and applies it to private devotional practice. The spiritual benefits that were formerly associated with state worship alone could now be had within the intimacy of one's private devotional life.

Much like Hieron, the clergyman Christopher Harvey emphasized the devotional effectiveness of common prayer in his collection of poems *The Synagogue* (1640), an imitation of George Herbert's *The Temple* (1633). In a poem entitled "The Book of Common Prayer," an addition of the 1647 edition of the collection, Harvey writes that those who join in the practice of common worship need not fear that they blaspheme by giving their assent and contributing their amens to the collective voice:

> They need not fear
> To tune their hearts unto his tongue, and say
> Amen; nor doubt they were betray'd
> To blaspheme, when they should have pray'd.[46]

Reminiscent of Hieron's belief that the proper practice of devotion has the power to hone devotional affect on the part of the one who prays, *The Synagogue* suggests that contemporary English worshippers saw nothing either shameful or hypocritical in giving assent—in saying "Amen"—to prayers performed by others. Artful forms of set prayer might even do for the parishioner what original, spontaneous worship could not. Harvey's poem alerts us to the early modern belief that proper external comportment during communal worship might be a prerequisite for, and not just a manifestation of, genuine devotion. In the final stanza of the poem, Harvey emphasizes how the proper practice of prayer betters the one who prays:

> Devotion will adde life unto the letter;
> And why should not
> That which Authority

---

[45] Samuel Hieron, *A defense of the ministers reasons for the refusal of subscription to the Book of Common Prayer, and of Conformitie against the seuerall ansvvers* ([S.I., and Amsterdam?]: Imprinted [by W. Jones's secret press, and J. Hondius?], 1607). (*EEBO*, STC (2nd ed.) / 13395.)

[46] Christopher Harvey, *The Synagogve, or, The Shadow of the Temple. Sacred Poems, and Private Ejacvlations. In Imitation of Mr. George Herbert*, 2nd ed. (London: Printed by J. L. for Philemon Stephens, 1647), sig. C3r. (*EEBO*, Wing H1045.)

> Prescribes esteemed be
> Advantage got?
> If the pray'r be good, the commoner the better.[47]

Harvey articulates precisely the early modern view that engagement with external gestures of devotion invigorates the practitioner, enabling his devotional commitment.

Like the devotional techniques of liturgy and set forms, desire in the *Sonnets* is animated by contemporary beliefs about the purposes—and power—of repeated utterances. In the *Sonnets*, Shakespeare harnesses the affective power of public performance—which Hieron recognized as an indispensable tool for cultivating devotional affect—and co-opts this performative technique in his efforts to describe a decidedly private desire. Shakespeare harnesses the transformative power of repeated utterances in his persistent yet distinctly abstract praise of his boyfriend. Unlike Petrarch's Laura, Sidney's Stella, Daniel's Delia, or Greville's Caelica, we never learn what Shakespeare's young man looks like, much less his name. As David Schalkwyk points out, rarely does the *Sonnets'* language of praise serve a descriptive function.[48] Indeed, Shakespeare denies his readers even a single blazon detailing his boyfriend's physical attributes. What is clear is that the primary purpose of Shakespeare's repeated praises of the young man is not to describe desire, but to demonstrate and cultivate devotional sincerity through each performance of praise.

The final couplet of Sonnet 85 alludes to precisely the forms of worship Harvey, and Hieron before him, believed were best suited to producing devotional conviction on the part of the parishioner: "Then others, for the breath of words respect, / Me for my dombe thoughts, speaking in effect" (85.13–14). The "effect" through which Shakespeare attests an observer might detect his unsung devotion to the young man could simply mean "in fact, in reality," which would juxtapose his actions against the mere "breath of words" spoken by his betters.[49] During the late sixteenth century, the word "effect" could also indicate outward manifestations, signs, tokens, or symptoms of otherwise undetectable phenomena.[50] The wit of the sonnet lies in its attempt to shift its readers' attitudes regarding the role of the perceptual faculties in the external expression of devotion. The poet's dumb show, the symbols and gestures that affect not only his own senses but those of his spectators,

---

[47] Harvey, *Synagogve*, sig. C3v.

[48] David Schalkwyk, *Speech and Performance in Shakespeare's Sonnets and Plays* (Cambridge: Cambridge University Press, 2002), 1–28, esp. 7–9.

[49] The *OED* defines "in effect" as "in fact, in reality (opposed to in show, in words)." See also 5b, "practical reality, fact, as opposed to name or appearance." *Oxford English Dictionary Online*, s.v. "effect (*n.*)" (Oxford: Oxford University Press, 2008; online ed., 2022).

[50] *OED Online*, s.v. "effect (*n.*)," 4a, "an outward manifestation, sign, token, symptom; an appearance or phenomenon in nature." Compare Shakespeare's use of the term in *Much Ado about Nothing* to describe Beatrice's alleged comportment as she falls in love with Benedick: "What effects of passion shewes she?" (2.3.107). Quoted in *OED Online*, s.v. "effect (*n.*)."

64 DEVOTIONAL EXPERIENCE IN THE REFORMATION

is the very reason for his esteem before his rivals and readers. As Schalkwyk has written, Sonnet 85 is testament to the fact that inwardness is not a state ultimately unknowable to observers looking from without, for it is the very performative force of the poet's language that makes intelligible his private thoughts.[51]

Shakespeare's defense of gestural tokens of his otherwise dumb thoughts, both mute and stupid, receives fuller attention in Sonnet 105, an apologia for his decision to express his devotion to his boyfriend in repeated, set prayers: "Faire, kinde, and true, is all my argument, / Faire kinde, and true varrying to other words" (105.9–10). Sonnet 105 is one in a cluster of sonnets that has drawn critical ire for its supposed enslavement to dull conceits and tautologous wit.[52] With respect to the latter, readers have pointed out that the poem provides an inadequate defense against implicit accusations of idolatry:

> Let not my loue be cal'd Idolatrie,
> Nor my beloued as an Idoll show,
> Since all alike my songs and praises be
> To one, of one, still such, and euer so.

> (105.1–4)

Booth has pointed out the sonnet's "studiously inadequate understanding of idolatry." According to Booth, that the object of Shakespeare's devotions is monotheistic does not exonerate him from the charge of idolatry. Citing the 1571 homily *Against Peril of Idolatry*, Booth contends that "although all polytheism is idolatrous, it does not therefore follow that any and all monotheisms are orthodox as the speaker here pretends."[53] Likewise, John Kerrigan has argued that Shakespeare's defense of his devotional gestures is "obvious sophistry" for the very reason that "idolatry is not necessarily polytheistic."[54] For Kerrigan, the tone of the sestet supports this, making it apparent that Shakespeare thinks his boyfriend is a "worldly god, an *idol*."[55]

Critical readings that detect an idolatrous import in the *Sonnets*' use of ceremonial language to describe erotic devotion misunderstand the formal and historical contexts of the poems' references to set prayer. First, the reasoning that Shakespeare's likening of his boyfriend to Christ constitutes a form of blasphemy seems to be a criticism less of his particular sonnets than of the sonnet form itself. It

---

[51] Schalkwyk, *Speech and Performance*, 114.

[52] In addition to his remarks on Shakespeare's use of religious tropes in the *Sonnets*, Kerrigan claims that Sonnet 105 "is not particularly complex. Almost bare of metaphor, with a chaste rhetorical 'colour' scheme, it exemplifies in verbal terms the flatness of *constancy*." See Kerrigan (ed.), *Sonnets*, 310.

[53] Booth (ed.), *Shakespeare's Sonnets*, 336. See also John Jewel, "An Homilie against *perill of idolatrie*, and *superfluous* decking of Churches," in *The second tome of homilees of such matters as were promised, and intituled in the former part of homilees* (Imprinted at London: In Poules Churchyarde, by Richarde Iugge, and Iohn Cawood, printers to the Queenes Maiestie, 1571), 98. (*EEBO*, STC 13669, document image 50.)

[54] Kerrigan (ed.), *Sonnets*, 309, 310.

[55] Kerrigan (ed.), *Sonnets*, 310.

was a common conceit among sonneteers to praise one's beloved by comparing her (or in Shakespeare's case, him) to a Christ-like figure.[56] Second, and more important, disputes about the alleged idolatrousness of Shakespeare's *Sonnets* fail to acknowledge the core of the poetry's assertions. Idolatry in post-Reformation England came to embody a range of belief systems and religious practices inherited from the medieval Catholic liturgical tradition. In sixteenth- and seventeenth-century England, idolatry not only referred to image worship but also included a broad set of religious and cultural practices deemed to be "superstitious" by the English church.[57] As a result, Reformation iconoclasm targeted not just physical images and icons but also allegedly superstitious ceremonies and rites.

The connection between idolatry and superstition was so powerfully intertwined in the minds of certain factions of the Reformed church that Hooker took it upon himself to dispel this misconception in his *Lawes of Ecclesiastical Polity*, which provided the first sustained and exhaustive justification of the church's practice of common prayer. Against those who proceed from the "strange conceit, that to serve God with any set form of common prayer is superstitious," Hooker replied that, on the contrary, common molds and forms of public liturgy afford a devotional efficacy that spontaneous prayer cannot.[58] Common prayer provides "a pattern whereby to frame all other prayers, with efficacy, yet without superfluity of words." Prayers only qualify as superstition, Hooker added, if it is the case that they "be actions which ought to waste away themselves in the making;

---

[56] Indeed, the topos is ubiquitous and assumes various conceits found in Petrarch's portrayal of Laura in *Il Canzoniere*, in which Sonnet 4 compares Laura's humble birth to Jesus's nativity at Nazareth, and Sonnet 16 positions Laura as the final instantiation of perfection—comparable to God himself. We can detect a similar argument inherent in the entire structure of Fulke Greville's *Caelica*. The sequence's opening poems reveal deep preoccupation with Caelica/Myra's refusal to reciprocate erotic love, yet as the sequences progresses, *eros* and Christ-like *agape* assume a fusional relationship through Greville's application of the metaphor of Christian worship to courtly love. Thom Gunn notes in *Caelica*'s later poems that "deprivation of the unkind absent mistress becomes deprivation of God's grace. The mistress had been an absolute, an ideal, an unchangeable, as contrasted to the flawed, fallen, and changeable particulars of creation: so is God." Simply to argue then that a sonnet is insincere or aesthetically unpleasing because it resorts to potentially blasphemous conceits fails to acknowledge the particular way in which an individual sonneteer chooses to engage with the widespread comparison between the beloved and Christ. See Thom Gunn, Introduction to *The Selected Poems of Fulke Greville*, ed. Thom Gunn (Chicago: University of Chicago Press, 2009 [1968]), 35. On the blasphemous implications of the association between Laura and Christ in *Il Canzoniere*, see Frederick J. Jones, *The Structure of Petrarch's "Canzoniere": A Chronological, Psychological, and Statistical Analysis* (Cambridge: D. S. Brewer, 1995), 57–8, 214. For a sustained treatment of the interplay between sexuality and spirituality in the sonnet tradition from Petrarch to Shakespeare, see Danijela Kambaskovic-Sawers, "Carved in Living Laurel: The Sonnet Sequence and Transformations of Idolatry," *Renaissance Studies* 21 (2007): 377–94.

[57] In *The Winter's Tale*, for instance, we see the interchangeability of the practice of idolatry and superstition in the play's final scene. Kneeling before what is ostensibly a painted statue of Hermione, Perdita sees it necessary to defend her behavior against charges of superstition: "And do not say 'tis superstition, that / I kneel, and then implore her blessing." See William Shakespeare, *The Norton Shakespeare*, eds. Stephen Greenblatt et al (New York: W. W. Norton, 2016), 5.3.43–8. On the connection between idolatry and superstition, see Helen C. White, *Tudor Books of Private Devotion* (Madison: University of Wisconsin Press, 1951), 73, 92–3.

[58] Richard Hooker, *The Fift Book of Ecclesiasticall Pollity*, 1597 [1594], 5.26.1, Bodleian MS Add. C.165, fol. 43v.

66 DEVOTIONAL EXPERIENCE IN THE REFORMATION

if being made to remain that they may be resumed and used again as prayers."[59] Yet Hooker concluded that, unlike material objects or human words, the original forms of prayer, derived from the scripture itself, never ceased to be as relevant and as fresh as they were when first spoken by the first believers.

It was against this culturally specific charge of idolatry, enmeshed with the early modern understanding of the performance of superstitious ceremonies and image worship, that Shakespeare crafts his defense of his devotional rites in Sonnet 105. The strength of the poem's wit derives from the fact that Shakespeare affirms that his rites conform to the standards of orthodox, and thus effective, worship: "Let not my love be cal'd Idolatrie, / Nor my beloved as an Idoll show, / Since all alike my songs and praises be" (105.1–3). If we read the poem's thesis as a causal clause—"My love is not idolatry *since* (or because) all of my gestures of devotion remain the same each time I extend praise"—then we see that it is precisely through the constant and measured uniformity of Shakespeare's praises (and not so much the monotheistic nature of his worship) that he hopes to redeem the value of his devotion before the eyes of his beloved.

Importantly, Shakespeare recognizes the value of his observable, outward gestures as evidence of his genuine devotion. Far from indicating something lesser than or even contrary to true devotion, Shakespeare's public gestures are commensurate with his purest love for his boyfriend:

> Kinde is my loue today, tomorrow kinde,
> Still constant in a wondrous excellence;
> Therefore my verse, to constancie confin'de,
> One thing expressing, leaues out difference.
>
> (105.5–8)

In loving *kindly*, Shakespeare stresses his affection toward his boyfriend, but more importantly, he points to the possibility that one day's love might be *kind*—as in kin—to another's.[60] Today's kind of love is kin to tomorrow's love, so that today's expressions of devotion, as Hooker contended, are just as suited to the present as they are to posterity.

Gazers and lookers

The *Sonnets* return again to the relationship between inner affect and public worship in Sonnet 125, which contains echoes of the language of the *Book of Common Prayer*'s Communion service. Sonnet 125 begins with an imagined public ritual

---

[59] Hooker, *Fift Book of Ecclesiasticall Pollity*, 5.26.2.
[60] *OED Online*, s.v. "kind (*adj.*)," 6, "Of persons, their actions, etc.: Affectionate, loving, fond; on intimate terms"; and 3d, "Related by kinship; of kin (*to*); one's own (people)."

SHAKESPEARE'S SWEET BOY   67

of devotion: "Wer't ought to me I bore the canopy, / With my extern the outward honoring"? (125.1–2). The public ceremony, in the case of the sonnet, is an erotic competition of sorts; the poet is keenly aware that his expressions of devotion are being compared to those of his rivals. Does it matter if I participate in the public rites, the poet asks, and in doing so outwardly pay devotion? The answer supplied by the poet is negative, and in defending his claim, he points to all of his rival poets whose outward performances have no bearing on their true devotion. The second quatrain provides two descriptions for these rivals—the types of worshippers he holds in disdain:

> Haue I not seene dwellers on forme and fauor
> Lose all, and more by paying too much rent
> For compound sweet; forgoing simple sauor,
> Pittifull thriuors in their gazing spent.
>
> (125.5–8)

Shakespeare's epithet for his rivals—those "dwellers on forme and fauor"— compounded with the sonnet's suffusion of Eucharistic language has led readers to conclude that the distinction he makes between his rivals' praise and his own devotion is contingent upon the opposition between outward form and inward essence, between the dissembled and the genuine. In the second descriptor, Shakespeare chastises the "pitiful thrivers" who seek to vicariously gain the devotional advantages of public praise by doing nothing more than "gazing" upon the performance. He faults his rivals not for their excess of theatricality, as Thomas M. Greene has maintained, but for the opposite offence.[61] According to the poem's logic, the rivals are gazers upon, but not participants in, the public performance of praise. The pitiful thrivers' refusal to participate in the panegyric rites suggests that any attempt on their part to worship will necessarily prove insufficient.

Two years before writing *The Winter's Tale*, Shakespeare was already pondering the problem posed by inadequate devotion in the *Sonnets*. Indeed, Sonnet 125 reads like a precursor to the comedy's reunification scene, and the poet articulates a devotional anxiety that anticipates Leontes's feelings of inadequacy as he gazes upon his wife's stony form. In the sonnet, the poet's criticism of the rival poets seems lifted almost directly from the *Book of Common Prayer*'s Communion service, which chastises communicants who watch the sacramental rites as mere gazers and onlookers rather than active participants. Admonishing those believers who either neglect or refuse to perform the Communion rites, the service exhorts such parishioners not to compound

---

[61] See Thomas M. Greene, "'Pitiful Thrivers': Failed Husbandry in the Sonnets," in *Shakespeare and the Question of Theory*, eds. Patricia Parker and Geoffrey Hartman (New York: Methuen, 1985), 230–44.

68   DEVOTIONAL EXPERIENCE IN THE REFORMATION

their affront to God with further insult by merely engaging as spectators of the holy rites:

> And whereas you offend God so sore in refusing this holy banquet, I admonish, exhort, and beseech you, that unto this unkindness ye will not add any more. Which thing ye shall do, *if ye stand by as gazers and lookers* on them that do Communicate, and be no partakers of the same yourselves. For what thing can this be accounted else, then a further contempt and unkindness unto God?[62]

The Communion service chastises these "gazers and lookers" precisely because they expect to receive the benefits of Communion as spectators, without performing the rites for themselves. Eamon Duffy has argued that the Reformation demoted communicants from active participants to mere spectators in the Eucharistic rites: "[The *Book of Common Prayer*] set itself to transform lay experience of the Mass, and in the process eliminated almost everything that had till then been central to lay Eucharistic piety. ... [T]he book clearly envisaged that in the foreseeable future, most of those present in the parish Mass would be onlookers, not communicants."[63] Yet contrary to Duffy's claims, the Communion service of the *Book of Common Prayer* makes absolutely clear that passive onlookers had no place in the Reformed sacrament. By adopting the language of the prayer book's Communion service, Shakespeare dismisses the erotic and poetic entreaties of his rivals as disingenuous praise rather than genuine devotional expression. They are, like the passive communicants, mere "gazers and lookers."

The poem's allusions to the Communion rites have prompted a number of anachronistic readings of the role of public worship in the poem's understanding of devotion. These readings—like the one put forth by Booth—have sought to conflate the poem's references to ritual worship with idolatry, despite the fact that Protestants of all confessional identities widely accepted the use of the public liturgy and sacraments prior to the Caroline reforms. Greene, for example, in his reading of Sonnet 125, regards the sonnet's allusion to the prayer book's Communion service as mere pomp and circumstance, presenting the practice of public prayer as an external accident opposed to inward essence. He contends that the poet's devotion "consists purely of uncalculated internal gestures and it leads to a genuine, unmediated exchange," while others display their love by external gestures.[64] Such readings of the sonnet's Eucharistic language associate the

---

[62] Cranmer, "The order of the administration of the Lordes Supper, or holy Communion," in *Booke of common praier* (1559), sig. M5r (emphasis added). The possible reference to the *Book of Common Prayer* has been noted by Booth, in *Shakespeare's Sonnets*, 429; and Colin Burrow, ed., *The Complete Sonnets and Poems*, The Oxford Shakespeare (Oxford: Oxford University Press, 2008), 630.

[63] Eamon Duffy, *The Stripping of the Altars: Traditional Religion in England c. 1400–c. 1580* (New Haven: Yale University Press, 1992), 464.

[64] See Greene, "'Pitiful Thrivers,'" 230. Similarly, Kerrigan maintains that the poet defends his love for his friend "by insisting that he recognizes the vanity of pomp and circumstance and has been

SHAKESPEARE'S SWEET BOY   69

performance of religious ritual with theatricality, and consequently, these interpretations of the sonnet commence from the assumption that engagement with
all ritual is contrary to devotional feeling.[65] However, a problem arises when we
attempt to associate the performance of all religious ritual in the sonnet with
hypocrisy, precisely because Shakespeare deploys the practice of public worship
as a shared metaphor for both his rivals' behavior and his own devotion to his
boyfriend. If the performance of prayer is a measure for his rivals' disingenuousness in the octet, it nevertheless doubles as a measure of the poet's real devotion
in the sestet.

The sonnet's most salient allusions to the *Book of Common Prayer* show that
religious ritual in the poem serves a more complicated function than what Greene
and others have attributed to it, namely, as evidence for the hypocrisy of Shakespeare's rivals. Greene's argument about the disingenuousness of public worship
was, in some sense, anticipated by Jewel. In 1562, the bishop defended the Communion rites against critics who equated the practice with popish idolatry. Jewel
concedes that there are indeed certain prescriptions pertaining to the Communion
(namely, the Catholic belief in transubstantiation) that degrade the sacrament to
the level of a "stage-play ... to the end that men's eyes should be fed with nothing else but with *mad gazing and foolish gauds.*"[66] Yet he salvages the Reformed
sacrament by demonstrating its participatory (as opposed to speculative) nature.
Against the practice of private mass, Jewel contends that from the primitive church
onward, if ever "there had been any which would be but a looker on, and abstain
from the holy Communion," that individual would have rightfully been excom-
municated "as a wicked person and as a pagan."[67] Never "was there any Christian
[during the time of the apostles], which did communicate alone, while others
looked on."[68] To assume the part of a spectator—a gazer—upon the holy rites was
tantamount in the Church of England, as it had been in the time of the apostles, to
sacrilege. To worship effectively and sincerely, one must aggressively participate in
the performance and cultivation of devotion; simply bearing witness to that performance was not a sufficient measure of spiritual privilege. For those who gazed,

---

impressed in the past by the folly of those seduced by appearances." See Kerrigan (ed.), *Sonnets*, 348.
Likewise, Booth sees in the sonnet's allusions to Holy Communion "the contrast between external
accidents and internal essence," and McCoy reads the poem's Eucharistic terminology as evidence that
the poet holds "nothing but scorn for those preoccupied with 'outward honoring.'" See Booth (ed.),
Shakespeare's Sonnets, 430; and McCoy, "Love's Martyrs," 199.

[65] Booth has noted that the sonnet commences with an allusion to formalized worship. A canopy was
often carried over the Host in religious processions. See Booth (ed.), *Shakespeare's Sonnets*, 429. That
the poet seems to initially reject formalized, public expressions of devotion by equating the canopy
procession to mere outward show—"my extern the outward honoring" (125.2)—has led some critics
to hold *all* public display of devotion as evidence of hypocrisy.

[66] Jewel, *Apology*, 35–6. On the Protestant comparison of the Catholic Eucharist and secular stage
plays, see Barish, *Antitheatrical Prejudice*, 155–90, esp. 159–65.

[67] Jewel, *Apology*, 32.

[68] Jewel, *Apology*, 32.

70   DEVOTIONAL EXPERIENCE IN THE REFORMATION

the Communion was merely ritual; for those who engaged with the holy rites, the sacrament enabled one to internalize and reenact Christ's Passion.[69]

Sonnet 125 does not abdicate all public ritual but rather appropriates it as a measure of the poet's desire. The sonnet's sestet appropriates the relationship between Christ and his believers outlined in the Holy Communion service in order to model the poet's own devotion to his boyfriend: "Noe, let me be obsequious in thy heart, / And take thou my oblation, poore but free" (125.9–10). Shakespeare conceptualizes his devotion by using the ritualized language of the common prayers performed in local Elizabethan parishes. His presentation of his devotion as a kind of oblation, a ritual offering, resonates with the Communion sermon, which likens Christ's Passion to an oblation presented to the community of Christian believers: "By his one oblation of hymself once offered," Jesus Christ successfully carried out "a full, perfect and sufficient sacrifice, oblation, and satisfaction for the sins of the whole world."[70] The sermon outlines how parishioners were to go about returning Christ's oblation, instructing them to offer up their prayers to God in conjunction with outward show of their devotion: "We humbly beseech thee most mercifully to accept our almose, and to receive these our prayers which we offer unto the divine Majesty."[71] As early as the mid-1400s, an oblation could mean simply the performance of the Holy Communion rites by presenting the bread and wine to God during the Eucharist.[72] The Church of England was committed to the spiritual value of a sacraments-based worship practice; indeed, the printed marginal note accompanying the prayer makes the straightforward observation that "if there be none alms or oblations, then shall the words be left out unsaid."[73] Here, the marginalium underscores the same belief that a worshipper must actively participate in the Communion rites if his prayers are to achieve maximum devotional effectiveness. As I have argued, the belief that the performance of prayer could

---

[69] In both the Reformed and Catholic traditions, the participatory nature of the holy rites produced states of devotion commensurate with the public performance of praise. Maltby has noted the parallels between the secular theater and Protestant common prayer, while Duffy suggests that the ritual prayers of the late medieval Catholic Candlemas celebration had "the tendency to turn liturgy into 'sacred performance.'" See Maltby, *Prayer Book and People*, 3–30; and Duffy, *Stripping of the Altars*, 26. In Anglo-Catholic orthodoxy, the performance of liturgical prayer had profound effects upon the parishioners, affecting equally those who prayed and those who were spectators to the holy rites. Margaret Spufford demonstrates that in the Anglo-Catholic tradition, parishioners' relationship with God was profoundly contingent upon the details—down to minute changes—of formal liturgical rites. See Spufford, *Contrasting Communities: English Villagers in the Sixteenth and Seventeenth Centuries* (Cambridge: Cambridge University Press, 1974), 239–40.

[70] Cranmer, *Booke of common praier* (1559), sig. M8v.

[71] Cranmer, *Booke of common praier* (1559), sig. M4r. In the 1662 *Book of Common Prayer*, the passage was amended, with "alms and oblations" replacing "almose," which by the late 1580s had become obsolete. See *OED Online*, s.v. "†almose (n)."

[72] *OED Online*, s.v. "oblation (n.)," 3.a, "*Christian Church.* The action of offering or presenting the elements of bread and wine to God in the Eucharist; the whole office of the Eucharist, esp. the Eucharist understood as offering or sacrifice."

[73] Cranmer, *Booke of common praier* (1559), sig. M4r. In addition, the printed marginalium in the 1559 edition reads, "If there be none a'mos given unto the pore, then shall the words of accepting our almes belefte out unsayd."

SHAKESPEARE'S SWEET BOY   71

enhance the devotional experience of the one who prays provides the basis for Shakespeare's chastisement of his rivals—those pitiful thrivers who deplete their devotional capacities by remaining mere gazers upon the holy rites instead of partaking in the performance of worship for themselves. By contrast, Shakespeare's oblations present him as an active participant in the rites of worship, one that draws his spectators—in this case, his boyfriend—into his performance of praise.

Erotic access to the young man is contingent upon the consistent and persistent performance of love's sacramental rites. But that performance alone is insufficient to bring about the desired intimacy between poet and beloved, and requires from both a prior state of something akin to erotic election. The sonnet's puzzling, paradoxical view of performance captures the church's own efforts to defend the public sacramental worship practices while simultaneously shifting the emphasis away from communal ritual to individual religious experience. As I have argued in my Introduction and Chapter 1, Richard Hooker—a staunch defender of sacramental worship in the English church—nonetheless acknowledged that outward devotion alone could corroborate, but not produce, an inner state of grace. Hooker maintained that the sacraments "contain *in themselves* no vital force or efficacy, they are not physical but *moral instruments* of salvation."[74] The sacraments "really exhibit, but ... they are not really nor do really contain in themselves that grace which with them or by them it pleases God to bestow."[75] Sonnet 125 captures this Reformed understanding of the role of the sacraments in the cultivation of private devotional experience. Shakespeare at once endorses love's rites as essential to erotic vitality while insisting—as Hooker did with respect to the sacred rites—that they possess no inherent devotional force. Like the sacraments—devotionally useful only for those who are already elected to salvation—the pitiful thrivers of the sonnet are excluded from the performative benefits of the poet's public praise of the sought-after young man. The poet's performance of praise is essential to his desire, but his singular access to the young man equally rests upon his "true soul" and his insistence that he "knows no art" (125.13, 11).

Shakespeare outlines his erotic commune with his boyfriend in distinctly liturgical terms. The Holy Communion sermon's intentional fashioning of the parishioners' prayers as a kind of oblation, one commensurate with the oblation Christ

---

[74] Richard Hooker, *Of the Lawes of Ecclesiasticall Politie. The Fift Booke* (London: Printed by John Windet dvvelling at Povvles wharfe at the signe of the Crosse Keyes and are there to be solde, 1597), 5.57.4. (*EEBO.* STC (2nd ed.) / 13712.5.) Hooker printed the first four books of the *Lawes* in 1594 [1593], and the fifth book in 1597. I refer to the 1597 printed version of the fifth book throughout this rest of this chapter.

[75] Hooker, *Lawes*, 5.67.6. Egil Grislis, Bryan D. Spinks, and W. David Neelands each support the position that Hooker advocated for a sacraments-based worship practice while also denying the inherent devotional efficacy of the sacraments themselves. See Egil Grislis, "Reflections on Richard Hooker's Understanding of the Eucharist," in *Richard Hooker and the English Reformation*, ed. W. J. Torrance Kirby (Dordrecht: Kluwer Academic Publishers, 2003), 207–23, esp. 213; Spinks, *Two Faces of Elizabethan Anglican Theology*, esp. 109; and W. David Neelands, "Christology and the Sacraments," in *A Companion to Richard Hooker*, ed. Torrance Kirby (Leiden: Brill, 2008), 369–402.

72 DEVOTIONAL EXPERIENCE IN THE REFORMATION

first bestowed upon his believers by sacrificing his life for their sins, hints at an equitable exchange that Shakespeare appropriates to describe his own devotion in line 12. As with Christ and the church, Shakespeare imagines that he and his boyfriend enter into a contractual relationship defined by equitable exchange; in extending his offering of praise, he insists that he "knows no art, / But mutuall render, onely me for thee" (125.11–12). Shakespeare frames his devotion to the young man as a form of "mutuall render"—an echo of the economic language of line 6, which compares the rivals' loss of devotional potency to the financial losses of tenants who squander their wealth "by paying too much rent" (125.6). Juxtaposing his own performance of praise with that of his rivals, Shakespeare insists that his public praise serves as an accurate gauge of his genuine devotional feeling for the young man. He neither indulges in extravagant worship, losing his devotional credibility by "paying too much rent," nor does he fail to engage sufficiently in the rites of praise, letting his capacity for praise wither like that of the pitiful thrivers who remain mere gazers upon the rites of worship. Shakespeare's performance of praise, ostensibly equitable, is oriented outward and directed toward his community of spectators—his boyfriend, his poetic rivals, and generations of readers yet unborn.

By pitting genuine devotion against ritualized praise, readers who harbor suspicions of the *Sonnets'* religious allusions fail to see that not only is the sestet of Sonnet 125 imbued with the language of communal prayer, but that Shakespeare nowhere extols the monadic sense of self they have read into the poem. On the contrary, the sonnet's wit lies precisely in its ability to resist an atomizing view of the individual worshipper. This is achieved by positing a "mutual" exchange between the poet and his boyfriend that assumes a peculiar quality of fusion; in the exchange of "me for thee," it is impossible to distinguish the separation between Shakespeare's gestures of devotion, the real conviction that these gestures denote, and the transformative power these gestures hold for those who take in their performance as spectators. Oddly, the poem's entreaty, "let me be obsequious in *thy* heart," imagines an engagement with the rites of worship conducive to particular states of devotion in others' hearts.[76] We expect Shakespeare to demand recognition for being obsequious in his *own* heart, which would ostensibly mean that he exonerates himself from the duty of publicly and physically engaging in the gestures of devotion, insisting that he can achieve superior devotional effectiveness merely by worshipping silently and privately in his heart. But the line's substitution of *thy* for the expected *my* suggests the "mutual exchange" that perfectly renders Shakespeare's *me* for his boyfriend's *thee*. By means of this exchange, he asserts what would in any other context seem absurd: that he can publicly perform gestures of devotion in the interior of his boyfriend's heart. The

---

[76] 125.9, emphasis added. Burrow notes that "obsequious" insinuates a formalized devotion on the part of the poet, and as a noun form, could mean "one who follows after [another in either] mourning or respect." See Burrow (ed.), *Complete Sonnets and Poems*, 630.

SHAKESPEARE'S SWEET BOY   73

pronoun substitution dissolves the distinctions between self and other, private and public, and inward and outward in its peculiar account of the poem's performance of praise. As a result, the witty knowledge of an intimacy—perhaps even a unity—with his boyfriend is one to which his rivals can never be privy. Importantly, it is precisely the language of common prayer that enables Shakespeare both to make his startlingly original proclamation about his own access to his boyfriend and to maintain the value of formal gestures of devotion as recourse to that deeply individual and private intimacy.

Sonnet 125 extends a vision of erotic selfhood in which the poet's personhood is intimately bound up—indeed, inseparable, both physically and grammatically—from that of his boyfriend. Nancy Selleck has posited an early modern conception of selfhood in which personal identity is inextricably linked to others and one's social environment, arguing against notions of a Renaissance sense of interiority that is distinct from an individual's external, physical, and social self.[77] Unlike modern ideas of selfhood, Selleck argues that early modern thinkers conceptualized individual identity around what she terms "other-oriented actions," as forms of "exchange, permeation, borrowing, anticipation."[78] Early modern ideas about the self are necessarily, Selleck maintains, ideas about "the self-in relation."[79] Using Cressida's line to Troilus as her central fulcrum—"I have a kind of self resides with you"—Selleck argues that early modern culture enabled individuals to describe themselves "not inwardly but in the minds of others."[80] "It is 'a kind of self *resides with*' some 'you,'" she writes.[81] While Selleck largely traces these experiential and corporeal configurations of early modern selfhood to the period's understanding of humoral theory, I suggest that the interpersonal and relational conceptions that certain early modern thinkers held about identity and selfhood can also be detected in the period's understanding of public devotion.[82] Both Sonnet 125 and Selleck's observations about early modern interpersonal identity present a vision of a permeable, other-oriented self that is striking in its parallels with Cranmer's description of the relationship between the communicant and Christ. In the Communion service of the *Book of Common Prayer*, Cranmer writes that when we spiritually eat Christ's flesh and drink his blood in the form of the sacramental bread and wine, "then we dwell in Christ and Christ in us, wee bee made one with Christ, and Christ with us."[83] In Cranmer's sacramentalism, the communicant's engagement with Christ is an engagement with a subjective self that cannot

---

[77] Nancy Selleck, *The Interpersonal Idiom in Shakespeare, Donne, and Early Modern Culture* (Basingstoke: Palgrave Macmillan, 2008), 30.
[78] Selleck, *Interpersonal Idiom*, 1.
[79] Selleck, *Interpersonal Idiom*, 18.
[80] Selleck, *Interpersonal Idiom*, 24.
[81] Selleck, *Interpersonal Idiom*, 9.
[82] For Selleck's treatment of early modern humoral theory, see especially *Interpersonal Idiom*, 56–88.
[83] Thomas Cranmer, "The Supper of the Lorde, and the holy Communion, commonly called the Mass" (1549), in *The Book of Common Prayer: The Texts of 1549, 1559, and 1662*, ed. Brian Cummings (Oxford: Oxford University Press, 2011), 22.

74 DEVOTIONAL EXPERIENCE IN THE REFORMATION

be consumed, literally, but can be subsumed and understood vis-à-vis a distinctly interpersonal exchange. As I have discussed in Chapter 1, both Stephen Greenblatt and Joe Moshenska have described the relationship between the communicant and Christ in the Reformed Communion as hovering between the literal and the figurative. Moshenska maintains that Cranmer, in his sacramental theology, manages to "avoid acknowledging that his language is metaphorical, or even having to draw a distinction between literal and figurative."[84] As in his *Defence of the True and Catholic Doctrine of the Sacrament of the Body and Blood of our Saviour Christ*, the language of Cranmer's Communion liturgy likewise seems to insist upon a literal inhering of the body of Christ within the bodies of the communicants— even as Cranmer acknowledges that Christ's presence is only ingested in a spiritual sense. In the Reformed sacrament and in Shakespeare's *Sonnets*, it is impossible to imagine the individual as separable from the presence of another subjective self. For both Cranmer and Shakespeare, those interpersonal engagements were neither figurative nor metaphorical, but understood in terms of corporeal and social exchange. Sonnet 125 captures, both poetically and grammatically, this distinctly early modern idea of the self that "resides" with and in the bodies of others.

Love sonnet as common prayer

For early modern English people, the distinction between individual and corporate worship was tenuous at best.[85] In the acts of erotic performance in the *Sonnets*, the poet finds himself transformed not only by his own repeated utterance of "faire, kinde, and true" in Sonnet 105, but by the performative utterances of others. He finds value in Sonnet 85 in his ability to cry "Amen" to his rivals' praises, enabling him to partake in and even add to the praises of others. Shakespeare holds similar expectations for how his own readers will react to his praises, imagining the future generations who will find echoes of their own erotic afflictions in the formal incantations of the poem's lines. C. S. Lewis noted this link between the devotional effectiveness of the *Sonnets* and performed prayer, writing that "a good

[84] Joe Moshenska, *Feeling Pleasures: The Sense of Touch in Renaissance England* (Oxford: Oxford University Press, 2014), 38.

[85] Maltby has demonstrated that corporate worship after the English Reformation was intended to engage not only the whole person—body and soul—but whole communities. See Maltby, *Prayer Book and People*, 117. When an individual worshipped alone in his own chambers, private prayer was virtually indistinct from its communal counterpart. Private prayer consisted simply of those forms of worship conducted in a solitary place, but did not indicate something more internal or otherwise different from public prayer. It was not uncommon for early modern believers to conduct solitary prayer aloud, such that it would have been possible for an observer to gauge a worshipper's conviction, "if not with the mouth," as Martin Luther observed, "yet with the hart and harty signs," or with "unspeakable gronings of the hart." See Luther, *A commentarie vpon the fiftene Psalmes, called Psalmi graduum, that is, Psalmes of degrees* (Imprinted at London by Thomas Vautroullier, 1577), 108, 67. (*EEBO*, STC (2nd ed.) / 16975.5.) Copy from Harvard University Library. For a discussion of the overlap between performance in private and public prayer, see Ferry, *The "Inward" Language*, 53–4.

SHAKESPEARE'S SWEET BOY 75

sonnet (*mutatis mutandis* and *salva reverentia*) was like a good public prayer." If the performance was good, the audiences in either case could join in on the performance and internalize its forms: "It does not matter who is speaking to whom in 'Since there's no help' any more than in 'Oh mistress mine.' Love poetry of this sort is transferable," and consequently, "the analogy of the public prayer holds good. The whole body of sonnet sequences is much more like an erotic liturgy than a series of erotic confidences."[86] The widely held belief in the effectiveness of erotic and liturgical performance affords Shakespeare a fusional relationship with his boyfriend through the mutual rendering of "me" for "thee" in Sonnet 125. This same belief in the effectiveness of communal praise lies at the core of his desire to secure immortal fame for himself and his boyfriend. Just as Shakespeare notes that he might be obsequious in the heart of another, so too does he imagine that his own acts of devotion become internalized in distinctly corporeal terms.

Sonnet 55 presents a vision of poetic immortality that rests upon the kind of fusional exchange that Cranmer described in the Reformed Communion rites—one that Shakespeare co-opts in Sonnet 125 when he imagines a devotional encounter conducive to a self that straddles the grammatical and material boundaries between "me" and "thee." Although readers such as Booth have focused on the immortalizing power—and fragility—of texts preserved on paper,[87] what is surprising is that written words and material documents are *not* Shakespeare's claim to immortality in the poem. Instead, what the *Sonnets* make clear is that the power of the poems lies not in their status as printed texts on a page, but as words that can be performed again and again.

Contra Booth, Sonnet 55 begins with an assertion by the poet that his poem will outlast even what one might consider the most durable of tributes—those carved in stone: "Not marble, not the guilded monument, / Of Princes shall out-liue this powrefull rime" (55.1–2). The poet goes on to list all the ways in which material forms of commemoration are vulnerable to physical destruction. Statues carved from stone are ravaged by "sluttish time" (55.4), "wastefull warre" (55.5), "broils" and tumult (55.6), and "warres quick fire" (55.7). Like the churches and icons razed by religious iconoclasts, material forms of devotion are not impervious to ruin. Thus when the poet promises his boyfriend that "you shall shine more bright in these contents / Then vnswept stone" (55.3–4), it is clear that these contents—the words of the poem—need preservation in modes that transcend the material limitations posed by monuments of stone.

Indeed, the poet acknowledges that the written record of his love alone cannot secure either his boyfriend's commemoration or his own poetic fame. The particular form of poetic immortality afforded by the poems is what the poet calls, at the

---

[86] C. S. Lewis, *English Literature in the Sixteenth Century, Excluding Drama* (Oxford: Clarendon Press, 1965 [1954]), 490.

[87] Booth suggests, "Even as [lines 7–8] assert the immortality of the poem these lines remind a reader of the flimsiness and vulnerability of anything written on paper." See Booth (ed.), *Shakespeare's Sonnets*, 229.

76 DEVOTIONAL EXPERIENCE IN THE REFORMATION

end of the octet, a "living record of your memory." As the sonnet goes on to make clear, this living record of the young man's memory is more than just the printed poem on the page; for the poem to be effective in its intention to immortalize, it must also be read and internalized in the bodies of its readers. The poem's sestet elaborates on what, precisely, Shakespeare meant when he equated "these contents" of the poem to a "living record" of memory: "Gainst death, and all obliuious enmity / Shall you pace forth, your praise shall still finde roome, / Euen in the eyes of all posterity" (55.9–11). Shakespeare imagines that this particular "content" is the type from which a long dead beloved might once again "pace forth," as if he were bodily resurrected from the grave. The strangeness of the conceit is compounded further by the promise that, upon pacing forth, the young man will find himself incorporated into the bodies, into the eyes, of others. Just as the *Sonnets* imagine a devotional vitality that demands—grammatically, materially, and socially—an intermingling of the poet's body and that of his boyfriend, so too does the sequence imagine a devotional strength that comes from the exchange among the voices and bodies of the readers—both now and in the future—who will read over and recite these poems.

In Sonnet 81, Shakespeare extends the corporeal conceit of Sonnet 55, imagining that when he is dead, his beloved will nevertheless remain "intombed in mens eyes" (81.8). He predicts that his unborn readers will respond in distinctly bodily ways to the formalism of his verse: "eyes not yet created shall ore-read, / And toungs to be your beeing shall rehearse" (81.10–11). His readers' acts of over-reading and rehearsing remain key to the poem's vision of poetic immortality. For the young man to become immortalized—both commemorated and resurrected—the "eyes not yet created" and the "toungs to be" must participate in acts of ritual repetition, *over*-reading and *re*hearsing the poet's praise. In performing these acts of repetition, the young man is both re-*hearsed* and re-*heard*, entombed and grieved anew, but also heard anew as if he were bodily resurrected from the grave. The conceits of Sonnets 55 and 81 are profoundly indebted to the conviction that oral reiteration of and repeated aural attention to words that are not strictly one's own are devotionally effective in ways that spontaneous prayers are not. It is precisely through the repeated performance of praise that Shakespeare secures immortality for his boyfriend: "When all the breathers of this world are dead, / You still shall liue (such virtue hath my Pen) / Where breath most breathes, euen in the mouths of men" (81.12–14). The young man's immortality rests not in the written poem but in reiterated praise; "intombed" in their eyes, Shakespeare promises his boyfriend an eternity of future readers whose "mouthed graues will giue thee memorie" (77.6).

As early as the sequence's opening procreation poems, Shakespeare imagines that set forms of praise—that is, the form of the sonnets themselves—have the power not only to memorialize the young man after his youthful beauty inevitably fades, but to physically recreate his beauty in the world. In Sonnet 15, for example,

SHAKESPEARE'S SWEET BOY 77

Shakespeare posits his poetry as an antidote to beauty's inconstancy: "all in war with Time for loue of you, / As he takes from you, I ingraft you new" (15.13–14). Importantly, poetry counterbalances the ravages of time not by preserving the young man as he is now, perfect as he is in this "little moment" (15.2), but rather by engrafting him anew. Here Shakespeare affords to poetry the fusional possibilities that reformers like Calvin, Cranmer, Perkins, and Hooker ascribe to sacramental practice. As I have argued in Chapter 1, William Perkins—like Calvin before him— saw the sacraments as a means whereby the bodies of believers become "*engrafted into Christ*."[88] Likewise, in the following poem, Sonnet 16, the poet insists that the ultimate goal of poetry is to "make you liue your selfe in eies of men" (16.12). What is clear from the *Sonnets* is that while poetry might be a prerequisite for the young man's promised immortality, it alone is not sufficient to ensure it. Even early in the sequence's procreation poems, Shakespeare is already hinting at the idea that poetry requires the bodily confirmation of a community of readers if it is to be devotionally effective. In Sonnets 55 and 81, the bodies of the readers themselves confirm the veracity of the poems. Here, the young man's qualities are engrafted into the bodies of future readers through their rereading, rehearing, and rehearsing of the poems. In doing so, generations of unborn lovers will engraft the young man's beauty into their own expression of devotion; so long as these lyric praises are reiterated, the young man's qualities will be engrafted into eyes not yet created and tongues to be. Set forms of praise—whether love sonnet or common prayer—are ineffectual if not performed by a living body of worshippers.

Much like Sonnet 125 imagined an inter-bodily exchange between the poetic me and thee, so too does Shakespeare imagine his beloved living anew—long after he is dead—resurrected in the eyes, mouths, and bodies of his readers. Like Perkins's and Cranmer's views of the Reformed sacraments, Shakespeare's vision of inter-bodily exchange is not purely metaphorical; this interpersonal and inter-material exchange is, as Selleck describes in her view of early modern subjectivity, essential to how early modern people understood the permeable boundaries that demarcated the self—and one that does not have a corresponding modern notion. In the *Sonnets*, the poet presents a desiring self that is permeable, drawn into focus via its relations to others—via the body of his boyfriend and those of his readers, both now and in the future.

In describing the performance of devotion as an interpersonal network of relations and of bodies, Shakespeare imagines that his own performances of praise have the devotional power to bolster the praises of others. To return to Lewis's analogy, like good common prayers, Sonnets 55 and 81 enable a whole host of

---

[88] William Perkins, *A commentarie or exposition, vpon the fiue first chapters of the Epistle to the Galatians* (Cambridge: Printed by Iohn Legat, printer to the Vniuersitie of Cambridge, 1604), 240, emphasis added. (*EEBO*, STC (2nd ed.) / 19680, document image 130.) For my discussion of how Reformation thinkers like Perkins and Hooker described the fusional relationship between the worshipper and Christ in the sacramental tradition, see Chapter 1, 33—36.

78   DEVOTIONAL EXPERIENCE IN THE REFORMATION

readers to add their own voices to the chorus of praise. As he assents to the praises of his rivals, crying "Amen" to his betters' hymns, so too does Shakespeare imagine that the form of his own acts of praise might in turn heighten devotional affect for his readers. Lewis succinctly captures the sonnet form's capacity to draw readers in through its use of a common language of devotion when he observes, "The sonneteers wrote not to tell their own love stories, not to express whatever in their own loves was local and peculiar, but to give us others, the inarticulate lovers, a voice."[89]

I return now to the critical concern over the chasm between inward and outward with which I opened this chapter. Booth's concern that Christ's Sermon on the Mount might be suggestive of the *Sonnets*' hypocrisy or devotional falsity was in fact already anticipated by certain early modern defenders of publicly performed prayer. In his 1533 *Exposition of Matthew*, William Tyndale offered an early Protestant justification for both the spiritual and cultural value of public worship. Tyndale emphasized the need to bolster the value of communal prayer over private worship by emphasizing the Protestant community's need for a public space to give thanks and praise for shared concerns:

Of entering into the chamber and shutting the door to, I say as above of that the left hand should not know what the right hand doeth, that the meaning is that we should avoid all worldly praise and profit, and pray with a single eye and true intent according to God's word, and is not forbidden thereby, to pray openly. For we must have a place to come to gather to pray in general, to thank and to cry to God for the common necessity.[90]

By interpreting Christ's commandment to pray behind shut doors in a strictly metaphorical sense, Tyndale paved the way for later Reformed thought on the value of communal liturgy. More than fifty years after Tyndale justified public worship in distinctly Protestant terms, Hooker found it necessary to continue the project of justifying public worship by arguing that liturgical practices had a place within state-sanctioned worship.[91] Only when we contextualize the public performance of prayer within early modern conceptions of communal worship can we understand the *Sonnets*' culturally specific treatment of ritualized acts of devotion. For Hooker, liturgical practices performed in communal settings countered moments of spiritual weakness that might inhibit a parishioner who prayed in private. Public devotion had a "force and efficacy ... to help that imbecility and

---

[89] Lewis, *English Literature*, 490.

[90] William Tyndale, *An exposycyon vpon the v.vi.vii. chapters of Mathewe* (London, 1536 [1533]), sig. H8v. (*EEBO*, STC / 24441.3)

[91] On Hooker's attempts to reclaim liturgical and public forms of worship for the English Church, see Peter Lake, *Anglicans and Puritans? Presbyterianism and English Conformist Thought from Whitgift to Hooker* (London: Unwin Hyman, 1988), 164–82.

SHAKESPEARE'S SWEET BOY   79

weakness in us, by means whereof we are otherwise of ourselves the less apt to perform unto God so heavenly a service, with such affection of heart, and disposition in the powers of our souls as is requisite."[92] Expanding on Tyndale, Hooker contended that when parishioners prayed amid a community of fellow believers, "thus much help and furtherance is more yielded" for their devotional efficacy: "if so be our zeal and devotion to Godward be slack, the alacrity and fervor of others serves as a present spur."[93]

The community of lyric voices to which the *Sonnets* allude derives its potency from the spiritual and political negotiations spawned by early modern debates over the value of public, ritualized worship—and the role that public worship ought to play in fostering the individual worshipper's singular spiritual experience. In constructing his vision of poetic immortality, Shakespeare co-opts the early modern belief that the collective nature of public forms of praise served as an impetus to devotion on the part of those who join in on the panegyric rites. But just as Hooker conceded that the sacraments alone were not inherently effectual, Shakespeare acknowledges that set praises of the young man cannot single-handedly guarantee an eternal poetic legacy or resurrect the beloved. For the young man to live again, and forever, his praises must be sung by those who join together to form a community of worshippers. Simply to over-read praise has the effect of repeating death, "intombing" the beloved "in men's eyes" (81.8). Shakespeare's bold assertion about his boyfriend's immortality—"You liue in this, and dwell in louers eies" (55.14)—rests upon the belief that the performance of praise has the capacity to confirm and enhance the desires of those who partake in the panegyric rites. If his beloved dwells in lovers' *eyes*, the poet's acts of devotion powerfully affect the way lovers perceive each other in their cultivation of intimacy. When lovers gaze into each other's eyes, Shakespeare imagines that they will see not their own reflection but rather the image of his young man reflected in their beloved's pupils. The *Sonnets'* acts of performed praise thus inform the innumerable loves of those who over-read and rehearse the panegyric rites. The punning potentialities of Sonnet 55 also enable us to hear in the line a suggestion of another way of understanding the devotional efficacy of communal praise. The performance of repeated praise deeply informs the lovers' *Is*, broadening not only their capacity to love, but shaping even their very access to their own deeply held impulses and desires.

In my reading of the *Sonnets*, I have argued that the sequence's vision of devotional expression reveals a particularly early modern view of the self, in which one's external comportment—and even the bodily performances of others—both animates and externally corroborates a parishioner's idiosyncratic devotional experience. Acts of public prayer reflect the relationships among a whole community of

---

[92] Hooker, *Lawes*, 5.15.1.
[93] Hooker, *Lawes*, 5.24.2.

worshippers. The performance of prayer in the *Sonnets* takes place within a nexus of interweaving social relationships involving the poet, his boyfriend, his rivals, and generations of as yet unborn readers. In the sonnets that I have discussed, the poet navigates between his roles as both performer of praise and participant in the praises of others. Prayer in these poems elucidates the interactions between oneself and others, revealing the capacity of both ecclesiastical and secular performance to shape a spectator's capacity to interpret bodily expressions of devotion as fair indicators of what transpires within. The expression of devotion in the *Sonnets* is an undeniably social act—one that requires the poet's bodily performance and a community of embodied witnesses to pay testament to love's rites. But at the same time, the *Sonnets* also offer a vision of private devotion—devotion that is legitimate even if it is inarticulately uttered or left unsaid. The sequence captures the tension between these competing early modern views of devotion: the poems offer a secular recapitulation of the Reformation's celebration of private devotional expression—however clumsy, crude, or tongue-tied—while simultaneously insisting on the value of devotion performed within a community of worshippers. In doing so, the *Sonnets* offer a distinctly early modern understanding of the "self in relation" that—like Cranmer's understanding of sacramental devotion—could only be understood within a wider nexus of social, material, and bodily communion.

3

Herrick's Players and Prayers

Ceremony, Theater, and Extemporal Devotion in *Hesperides* and *His Noble Numbers*

In "To Julia," one of the many erotic lyrics in his 1,130-poem collection *Hesperides*, a spiritually errant Herrick implores his girlfriend to help him learn to pray:

> Help me, *Julia,* for to pray,
> Mattens sing, or Mattens say:
> …
> Bring the Holy-water hither;
> Let us wash, and pray together.
> When our Beads are thus united,
> Then the Foe will fly affrighted.[1]

While Herrick woos in his quest to gain dominion over his girlfriend's body, it is Julia who holds authority over matters of the soul. She leads Herrick through the Mattens—referring either to the matins of the Catholic Latin liturgy, or the morning prayers that were sanctioned by the English church's *Book of Common Prayer*. The holy water cleanses both body and soul; it sanctifies Herrick's fantasy of a co-ed bathing rite in which he and Julia sop, souse, and pray. In the poem's closing couplet, the co-mingling of the couple's prayer beads suggests the union of sexual consummation itself.

"To Julia" is one of several lyrics in *Hesperides* that imagines erotic pursuit in terms of religious devotion. Herrick's tendency to imagine erotic desire as an extension of church ceremony has led the majority of his critics over the past few decades to read *Hesperides* as sympathetic to High Church Anglicanism, with its emphasis on the religious rites and rituals championed by Archbishop William Laud. According to these readings, Herrick imagined his *Hesperides* as a literary critique of the advancing tide of Puritan assaults on ceremonial worship that threatened

---

[1] Robert Herrick, "To Julia," in *Hesperides, or, The works both humane & divine* (London: Printed for John Williams and Francis Eglesfield, and are to be sold by Tho[mas] Hunt, 1648), H1069.1–2, 5–8. (*EEBO*, Wing / H1595.) I have taken all references to *Hesperides* from the 1648 edition. For ease of reference, I also cite poems from both *Hesperides* and *His Noble Numbers* using the numbering system devised by Herrick's most recent editors, Tom Cain and Ruth Connolly. See *The Complete Poetry of Robert Herrick*, eds. Tom Cain and Ruth Connolly, 2 vols. (Oxford: Oxford University Press, 2013). These poem numbers are denoted "H" and "N" respectively.

Devotional experience and erotic knowledge in the literary culture of the English Reformation. Rhema Hokama, Oxford University Press. © Rhema Hokama (2023). DOI: 10.1093/oso/9780192886552.003.0004

82   DEVOTIONAL EXPERIENCE IN THE REFORMATION

to undercut traditional religious devotional practices. For example, Achsah Guibbory claims that Herrick wrote his poetry as a reaction against the Puritans'
intensified attacks on ceremonial worship: "With its allusive, charged language,
Hesperides constitutes an elegant expression—at once defiant and elegiac—of a
generally ceremonialist, and probably specifically Laudian, mentality. ... Herrick's
effort parallels the Laudian attempt to reinvigorate a communal, ceremonial worship in the face of Puritan opposition."[2] Echoing Guibbory's argument for the
anti-puritanism of Herrick's poems, Leah S. Marcus likewise suggests that *Hesperides* ought to be read nostalgically, "as a celebration of vanishing political
and ecclesiastical ideals"—all of which had come under fire during the reign of
Charles I.[3]

---

[2] Achsah Guibbory, *Ceremony and Community from Herbert to Milton: Literature, Religion, and
Cultural Conflict in Seventeenth-Century England* (Cambridge: Cambridge University Press, 1998),
81–2. For her earlier account of Herrick's Laudian ceremonialism and anti-Puritan sentiment, see
also Achsah Guibbory, "The Temple of *Hesperides* and Anglican–Puritan Controversy," in *"The Muses
Common-Weale": Poetry and Politics in the Seventeenth Century*, eds. Claude J. Summers and Ted-Larry
Pebworth (Columbia, MO: University of Missouri Press, 1988), 135–47, esp. 146–7.

[3] Leah S. Marcus, "Afterword: Herrick and Historicism," in Ann Baynes Coiro, ed., special issue
on Robert Herrick, *George Herbert Journal* 14, nos. 1–2 (1990–91): 172–7, esp. 173. See also her
similar previous arguments about Herrick's Anglicanism and royalism in Leah S. Marcus, "Herrick's
'Hesperides' and the 'Proclamation Made for May,'" *Studies in Philology* 76, no.1 (1979): 489–74;
and Leah S. Marcus, "Churchman and the Maypoles: Herrick and the *Hesperides*," in *The Politics of
Mirth: Jonson, Herrick, Milton, Marvell, and the Defense of Old Holiday Pastimes* (Chicago: University
of Chicago Press, 1986), 140–68.

Arguments for Herrick's supposed sympathies with High Church Anglicanism have gone hand in
hand with arguments for his royalist allegiance. With few exceptions, his royalism has been taken for
granted over the last four decades of Herrick criticism. In 1978, Claude J. Summers wrote that the dominant political position in Herrick's collection is "extreme royalism"—that is, wholesale commitment
to both Charles I and the Church of England. See Claude J. Summers, "Herrick's Political Poetry: The
Strategies of His Art," in *"Trust to Good Verses": Herrick Tercentenary Essays*, eds. Roger B. Rollin and
J. Max Patrick (Pittsburgh: University of Pittsburgh Press, 1978), 171–83, esp. 173. Summers reiterates
this claim in a more recent essay in the 1990–91 special edition of the *George Herbert Journal*, argu-
ing that Herrick's collection—and *His Noble Numbers* in particular—"affirm its author's commitment
to the conservative Anglican ideal of the English as submissive children of their mother the church."
See Claude J. Summers, "Tears for Herrick's Church," in Coiro, ed., special issue on Herrick, *George
Herbert Journal* 14, nos. 1–2 (1990–91): 51–71, esp. 51. That position remains essentially uncontested.
For example, Syrithe Pugh, in her book-length study on Herrick, describes the politics of *Hesperides* as
fundamentally orthodox in its intentions: "the political views expressed in his poetry are thoroughly
consonant with ultra-royalism." See Syrithe Pugh, *Herrick, Fanshawe and the Politics of Intertextuality:
Classical Literature and Seventeenth-Century Royalism* (Farnham: Ashgate, 2010), 4.

In a similar vein, numerous critics have likewise argued for interpretations of *Hesperides* that fore-
ground Herrick's Anglican and royalist commitments, or argue that he wrote his poems as defensive
responses to the advancing tide of Puritan efforts to regulate social behavior, the arts, and worship. See
Thomas N. Corns, *Uncloistered Virtue: English Political Literature, 1640–1660* (Oxford: Clarendon
Press, 1992), 118; Nigel Smith, *Literature and Revolution in England, 1640–1660* (New Haven: Yale
University Press, 1994), 262; Roger Rollin, "Missing the Hock-Cart," *Seventeenth Century News* 24, no.
3 (1966): 39–40; Peter Stallybrass, "'Wee feaste in our Defense:' Patrician Carnival in Early Modern
England and Robert Herrick's 'Hesperides,'" *English Literary Renaissance* 16, no. 1 (1986): 234–52,
esp. 248; Miriam K. Starkman, "*Noble Numbers* and the Poetry of Devotion," in *Reason and the Imagination: Studies in the History of Ideas 1600–1800*, ed. J. A. Mazzeo (New York: Routledge and Kegan
Paul, 1962), 1–27, esp. 1; Edmund Gosse, "Robert Herrick," *The Cornhill Magazine* 32 (1875): 176–91,
esp. 186–7; Robert H. Deming, *Ceremony and Art: Robert Herrick's Poetry* (The Hague: Mouton, 1974),
10; Robert H. Deming, "Robert Herrick's Classical Ceremony," *ELH* 34, no. 3 (1967): 327–48, esp. 336;

HERRICK'S PLAYERS AND PRAYERS   83

The critical tendency to read Herrick's ceremonial poems as evidence of his
Laudian sympathies stems primarily from a misunderstanding about the dating
of the poems. Herrick published his mammoth *Hesperides* in 1648. The edition
was bound with his slimmer volume of 242 devotional poems *His Noble Numbers*,
which he had first published the previous year. The collection's 1648 publication
has led Herrick's readers to view him primarily as a poet of that decade, and his
book an artifact of the Laudian–Puritan controversies that destabilized the English
church during the 1630s and 1640s. Indeed, Guibbory maintains that *Hesperides*
constitutes Herrick's lyric response to the religious and political turmoil on the
eve of the English Civil War: "Published in 1648, soon after Herrick was ejected
from his parish as part of Parliament's program for removing clergy too closely
associated with the Laudian church, *Hesperides* demands to be read within the
context of the conflict over worship that was part of the Revolution."[4] In spite of
these views, to read Herrick primarily as a poet of the Revolution is anachronistic, and provides a distorted view of a prolific poetic career that spanned three
decades. While Herrick did not pursue printed publication prior to 1647, he had
been actively writing and circulating his poems in manuscript as early as the 1610s.
Tom Cain and Ruth Connolly, editors of the most recent edition of Herrick's
complete poems, date his earliest poem to 1611.[5] Based on the inclusion of Herrick's poems in manuscript miscellanies and literary exchanges among his peers,
Cain and Connolly, as well as John Creaser, have argued that many—if not the
majority—of Herrick's best known poems from *Hesperides* were likely written in
the 1610s and 1620s, and were widely read by those in Herrick's literary circles
at Cambridge and London before they appeared in print.[6] According to Cain and
Connolly, "Through [the 1620s], until well beyond the publication of *Hesperides*,
Herrick's popularity is attested not only by the number of surviving manuscript
witnesses—which though lower than for Donne, Carew, or Corbett is still in the
hundreds—but also by the variety of sources that supplied poems to copyists."[7]
Cain, Connolly, and Creaser's convincing arguments for the redating of the poems

and A. Leigh DeNeef, *"This Poetic Liturgie": Robert Herrick's Ceremonial Mode* (Durham, NC: Duke
University Press, 1974).

[4] Guibbory, *Ceremony and Community*, 80. Others who have read Herrick's poems as responses to
the parliamentary attacks on ceremony and worship of the 1640s include Pugh, *Herrick, Fanshawe and
the Politics of Intertextuality*, 22–3; Smith, *Literature and Revolution*, 262; Gerard Hammond, *Fleeting
Things: English Poets and Poems, 1616–1660* (Cambridge, MA: Harvard University Press, 1990), 246;
and William C. Johnson, *"In Vino—et in Amore—Veritas*: Transformational Animation in Herrick's
'Sack' Poems," *Papers on Language and Literature* 41, no. 1 (2005): 89–108, esp. 94.

[5] Tom Cain and Ruth Connolly, Introduction to *"Lords of Wine and Oile": Community and Conviviality in the Poetry of Robert Herrick*, eds. Cain and Connolly (Oxford: Oxford University Press,
2011), 1.

[6] Tom G. S. Cain, "Robert Herrick, Mildmay Fane, and Sir Simeon Steward," *English Literary Renais-
sance* 15, no. 2 (1985): 312–17; John Creaser, "'Jocond His Muse Was': Celebration and Virtuosity in
Herrick," in Cain and Connolly, *"Lords of Wine and Oile*," 39–62; John Creaser, "'Times trans-shifting':
Chronology and the Misshaping of Herrick," *English Literary Renaissance* 39, no. 1 (2009): 163–96;
Cain and Connolly, Introduction to *Complete Poetry of Robert Herrick*, 1:viii.

[7] Cain and Connolly, Introduction to *Complete Poetry of Robert Herrick*, 1:xl.

84 DEVOTIONAL EXPERIENCE IN THE REFORMATION

demonstrate that Herrick's literary output should not be interpreted primarily in terms of the Laudian controversies of the subsequent decades. Although it is now clear that Herrick's early literary output, written during the reign of James I, should not be read through the lens of Caroline conflict, no critic has thus far ventured to re-historicize Herrick's lyrics in terms of the religious trends of the 1610s and 1620s.[8]

In light of Cain, Connolly, and Creaser's arguments about the dating of Herrick's poems, it is likely that he wrote many of the lyrics of the *Hesperides* shortly after the time that Shakespeare was writing and revising his *Sonnets*. Like Shakespeare, Herrick's poems freely appropriate reference to the Communion rites and performed prayer, and his poems actively engage with the period's debates about the proper role of the body in outward gestures of devotion—both sacred and secular. Although Herrick published *Hesperides* after Laud's ecclesiastical reforms, he wrote the bulk of his poems in the decades prior, during a period when the English church subscribed to a broadly Genevan approach to sacramental and ceremonial worship. As a result, it makes sense that the contemporary circumstances surrounding Herrick's poetry would have had more in common with the Jacobean theological currents that shaped Shakespeare engagement with the Communion and liturgical rites, rather than with the Laudian church reforms and Caroline royalist politics that critics like Marcus and Guibbory have read into the poems.

Building on recent efforts to resituate Herrick's lyrics within the manuscript culture of the 1610s and 1620s, this chapter proposes two religious frameworks that might illuminate the devotional import of Herrick's lyric poems: the Reformed

---

[8] Creaser has argued that Herrick's lyrics resist historicizing: "Despite recent criticism, he is by no means an extreme royalist, or extreme in anything except his absorption in poetry. His moral and indeed political significance lies in his hedonism, and his readiness to embrace contradictions and to avoid commitment to aggressive certainties in decades of growing antagonism. Herrick's mind was too acute to become possessed by an idea and degenerate into propaganda." See Creaser, "'Jocond his Muse was,'" 64. See also John Creaser, "Herrick at Play," *Essays in Criticism* 56, no. 4 (2006): 324–50, esp. 325.

Other readers of Herrick's poetry have sought to nuance claims about the poet's political and religious orthodoxy, although none have questioned the fundamentally Anglican framework used to read the poetry. For Alexander B. Grosart, Herrick was a committed royalist who was also attuned to the flaws of the state and church: "underlying Herrick's Royalism and loyalty, there was open-eyed and sad-hearted insight into the high-handed procedure of his sovereign and his advisers, and a yearning for a way of escape and reconciliation." See Alexander B. Grosart, "Memorial-Introduction: Critical," in *The Complete Poems of Robert Herrick*, vol. 1, ed. Alexander B. Grosart (London: Chatto and Windus, 1876), clxxviii–iv. Daniel H. Woodward has argued that individual poems within *Hesperides* both satirize and celebrate the core tenets of Anglican worship, suggesting that Herrick assumes a parodic tone regarding *all* religious ceremonies—"Anglican as well as Roman Catholic." See Daniel H. Woodward, "Herrick's Oberon Poems," *Journal of English and Germanic Philology* 64, no. 2 (1965): 270–84, esp. 278. More recently, other critics have made similar arguments about the political ambiguities of Herrick's ceremonialism in *Hesperides*. Heather Dubrow argues that Herrick evokes Anglican ceremonies in order to "destabilize, not stabilize, the poems and the ceremonies themselves." See Heather Dubrow, *A Happier Eden: The Politics of Marriage in the Stuart Epithalamium* (Ithaca, NY: Cornell University Press, 1990), 248. In a similar vein, Ann Baynes Coiro writes that "Herrick's ceremonialism may serve the social order, but it does so with significant hesitations and undercurrents." See Ann Baynes Coiro, *Robert Herrick's "Hesperides" and the Epigram Book Tradition* (Baltimore: Johns Hopkins University Press, 1988), 160.

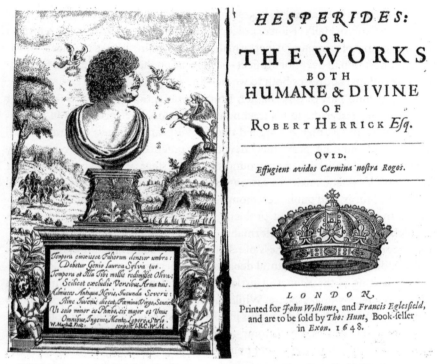

Figure 3.1 Frontispiece and title page of Herrick's 1648 edition of *Hesperides*, containing the likeness of the poet. Printed in London for distribution at Thomas Hunt's Exeter bookshops. Copy from the Henry E. Huntington Library.

ceremonial worship in the Elizabethan and Jacobean churches, and the experiential devotional practices championed by clerics like William Perkins. These two facets of Reformed devotion were synthesized and popularized by Joseph Hall, a colleague of Perkins at Cambridge who would eventually become presiding bishop of Herrick's Exeter vicarage.[9] Hall granted Herrick the vicarage at Dean Prior in 1629, and Herrick addresses the bishop as both a religious and literary authority in *Hesperides*.[10] I argue that, far from evidencing support for Laudian ceremonialism, Herrick's poems champion the Calvinist model of devotional affect and ceremonial practice envisioned by Hall—whom Laud would eventually

---

[9] I maintain that Hall's devotional technique should be regarded as a variation on Perkins's experiential devotional style in part because it sought to hone Perkins's methods of sign hunting for external indicators of election. As Richard A. McCabe puts it, an "inclination" toward Hall's devotional method "can easily be interpreted as a sign of election." He continues: "Like Perkins, Hall is fascinated by the psychology of salvation." See Richard A. McCabe, *Joseph Hall: A Study in Satire and Meditation* (Oxford: Oxford University Press, 1982), 151, 181.

[10] Herrick addresses Hall in his poem "To Jos: Lo: Bishop of Exeter" (H168).

86   DEVOTIONAL EXPERIENCE IN THE REFORMATION

count among his detractors.[11] I suggest that Herrick sought to present his poems as lyric equivalents of Hall's vision of practical devotion. Herrick's distinctly reformist understanding of ceremonial performance, I maintain, lies at the heart of his poetic conception of devotional affect—a conception that Herrick makes manifest in his devotional addresses both to women and to Christ.

In the second part of this chapter, I turn my attention from Herrick's secular poems in the *Hesperides* to his treatment of devotional performances in his religious poems. In Chapter 2, I argued that Shakespeare's *Sonnets* explore cultural anxieties surrounding performed devotional practice in religious contexts by engaging with parallel debates surrounding secular stage performance. In a similar way, Herrick's poetic anxieties surrounding religious performances—communal prayer, the liturgy, and public ceremony—are informed by his simultaneous attention to the culturally adjacent problems posed by stage performance. Herrick's skepticism regarding stage performance, most apparent in *His Noble Numbers*, underscores his parallel wariness of religious performance. But although Herrick is responding to the same cultural debates about performance that shaped Shakespeare's writing of the *Sonnets*, Herrick's poems offer a different resolution than the one offered by Shakespeare. While the *Sonnets* celebrate ceremony, common prayer, and secular theater as various means of bolstering a community of lovers—both now and in generations to come—Herrick's poems remain more conflicted in their treatment of these modes of public performance. In his devotional addresses to his girlfriends, to God, and to Christ, the performances that Herrick regards as unseemly for others nevertheless remain key to his own efforts to express devotion.

***

As I have argued in Chapter 1, when Herrick was born in 1591—the year when the Cambridge theologian Perkins published his best-selling devotional manual *A Golden Chaine*—the Elizabethan church was predominantly Calvinist in its outlook. Herrick would have gained familiarity with mainline Reformed sentiment early on, growing up in the household of his late father's brother and sister-in-law,

---

[11] On Hall's opposition to Laud on matters of ecclesiastical polity, see Creaser, "'Times transshifting,'" 168; and Nicholas Tyacke, *Anti-Calvinists: The Rise of English Arminianism, c.1590–1640* (Oxford: Oxford University Press, 1990), 209–13. Tyacke describes Hall as a committed Calvinist "beyond serious dispute" (212), but one who also had significant Arminian sympathies. Indeed, despite his Calvinist sympathies, Hall could hardly be considered Puritan with respect to his support of the ecclesiastical polity. In fact, his efforts to defend his order in 1640–1 made him the target of five leading Puritan thinkers who wrote under the *nom de plume* Smectymnuus. The group's excoriation of Hall inspired none other than John Milton to attack Hall in a series of five pamphlets, in an effort to lend support to Smectymnuus. See Smectymnuus [pseud.], *An answer to a booke entitvled An hvmble remonstrance in which the originall of liturgy, episcopacy is discussed* (London: Printed for I. Rothwell and to be sold by T. N., 1641). (*EEBO*, Wing / M748); and for an overview of Milton's involvement in the controversy, see Christopher Hill, *Milton and the English Revolution* (New York: Viking, 1978 [1977]), 49.

HERRICK'S PLAYERS AND PRAYERS   87

William and Joan Herrick.[12] When Herrick went off to earn his BA and MA at Cambridge, the university was an intellectual epicenter of Calvinist sentiment. While Herrick was a student at St. John's College—a stronghold of reformist learning and thought—his classmate Simonds D'Ewes wrote approvingly of the college's strong Calvinist ties:

> But yet no Anabaptistical or Pelagian [Arminian] heresies against God's grace and providence were then stirring, but the truth was in all public sermons and divinity acts asserted and maintained. None then dared to commit idolatry by bowing to, or towards, or adoring the altar, the communion table, or the bread and wine in the sacrament of the Lord's Supper.[13]

Remembering his final year at St. John's in 1620, D'Ewes described a wider rejection among the college fellows of the cultural practice of kneeling before the communion altar—but importantly, not an outright rejection of the Communion rites or public ceremony.[14] What is interesting is that D'Ewes presents his position as above all a form of ecclesiastical moderation in contrast to the Puritan and Arminian extremes. D'Ewes regarded the college's position on ecclesiology as a *via media* between Laudian ceremonialism and the branches of radical puritanism that rejected public worship altogether. Herrick's poetry, likely written during his school years in Cambridge and London, models a similar view of the sacraments and public performances of devotion. Like D'Ewes, Herrick's ecclesiology remained open to sacramental and ceremonial performance—so long as those performances could be undertaken in moderation and without recourse to idolatry. As I discussed in Chapter 1, revisionist historians such as Alexandra Walsham and Alec Ryrie have pointed out that the theological categories often labeled as "Puritan" or "Anglican" are anachronistic when applied to contexts prior to the 1630s, when confessional identity and practice were still in flux.[15]

---

[12] For Herrick's reformist upbringing and his early exposure to mainstream Calvinism, see Cain and Connolly, Introduction to *Complete Poetry of Robert Herrick*, 1:xxii; and Graham Parry, "His Noble Numbers," in Cain and Connolly, "*Lords of Wine and Oile*," 276–99, esp. 278–9.

[13] Simonds D'Ewes, *The Autobiography and Correspondence of Sir Simonds D'Ewes, Bart., During the Reigns of James I and Charles I*, ed. J. O. Halliwell (London: Richard Bentley, 1845), 1:142. Quoted in Cain and Connolly, Introduction to *Complete Poetry of Robert Herrick*, 1:xxxi.

[14] D'Ewes's position on kneeling during the communion sacrament points to the reformist leanings of the college, contrary to the 1618 Five Articles of Perth, which mandated kneeling during the Communion rites in an effort to bring the Church of Scotland into ecclesiastical alignment with the Church of England. As Alec Ryrie has noted, the practice of kneeling in Reformation England was not as controversial as the scholarship has made it out to be, and was only controversial within the specific context of Communion. "It was precisely because kneeling was such a universal symbol of worship that kneeling before a communion table was felt to be idolatrous," Ryrie writes. "Outside that setting, kneeling to pray was an expected and entirely uncontroversial norm." See Alec Ryrie, *Being Protestant in Reformation Britain* (Oxford: Oxford University Press, 2013), 172.

[15] See Alexandra Walsham, *Charitable Hatred: Tolerance and Intolerance in England, 1500-1700* (Manchester: Manchester University Press, 2006), 20. For a similar argument, see also Alexandra

88   DEVOTIONAL EXPERIENCE IN THE REFORMATION

Herrick matriculated at Cambridge about a decade after Joseph Hall completed his education at the university. Like D'Ewes, Hall saw himself as a moderate reformer, one who charted a middle ground between the extremes of radical puritanism and Arminianism.[16] At Cambridge, Hall moved within the same intellectual and theological circles as Perkins, who was a fellow at Christ's College while Hall was studying for his BA at Emmanuel College, another Cambridge stronghold of Calvinist thought.[17] At Emmanuel, both Perkins and Hall had been taught by Laurence Chatterton, a Reformed divine and a translator of the King James Bible.[18] It was at Emmanuel, too, where Hall gained exposure to what he would later term "experimental divinity," the experiential devotional practices developed by Perkins and his Cambridge colleagues.[19]

By the time Herrick had assumed his vicarage in Hall's Exeter diocese, the bishop had already established his own literary reputation with a series of satirical poems.[20] In a poem addressed to Hall, Herrick makes clear that he regarded the bishop not only as a spiritual mentor but as a literary one:

> Whom sho'd I feare to write to, if I can
> Stand before you, my learn'd *Diocesan*?
> And never shew blood-guiltinesse, or feare
> To see my Lines *Excathedrated* here.
> Since none so good are, but you may condemne;
> Or here so bad, but you may pardon them.
>
> ("*To* Jos: *Lo*: *Bishop of Exeter*," H168.1–6)

While critics have noted the influence of Hall's devotional innovations on the poetry and devotional writings of writers like Donne, his impact on Herrick's

---

Walsham, "The Parochial Roots of Laudianism Revisited: Catholics, Anti-Calvinists and 'Parish Anglicans' in Early Stuart England," *Journal of Ecclesiastical History* 49, no. 4 (1998): 620–51, esp. 636–7; and Ryrie, *Being Protestant*, 471–2.

[16] Hall left his Cambridge fellowship at Emmanuel College shortly after his ordination in 1600, and Herrick entered St. John's College in 1613—both colleges were centers of English Calvinist thought. See Richard A. McCabe, "Joseph Hall," in *Oxford Dictionary of National Biography* (Oxford: Oxford University Press, 2004; online ed., 2008). For an overview of Herrick's university years, see Cain and Connolly, Introduction to *Complete Poetry of Robert Herrick*, 1:xxx–xxxvi. On Herrick's political connections to Hall, see Cain and Connolly, Introduction to *Complete Poetry of Robert Herrick*, 1:xxiii, xlii; and Creaser, "'Jocond his Muse was,'" 41–2. See Parry, "His Noble Numbers," in Cain and Connolly, 280–3, for Herrick's political ties to other noteworthy Calvinist sympathizers such as Sir Edward Giles and Bishop John Williams—the latter to whom Herrick addressed two poems, H146 and MS41. For the latter, I use the manuscript numbering system devised by Cain and Connolly.

[17] For Hall's intellectual exchanges with Perkins while at Cambridge, see McCabe, *A Study in Satire*, 7.

[18] W. B. Patterson, *William Perkins and the Making of a Protestant England* (Oxford: Oxford University Press, 2014), 207.

[19] Joseph Hall, "Epistle 7 (To Mr. William Bedell)," in *The Works of the Right Reverend Joseph Hall*, ed. Philip Wynter (Oxford: Oxford University Press, 1863), 6:150.

[20] For Hall's literary reputation and a discussion of his Cambridge satirical poetry, see McCabe, *A Study in Satire*, 27–72.

HERRICK'S PLAYERS AND PRAYERS   89

poetry has been overlooked, despite the fact that both men received similar Cambridge educations and that Herrick counted Hall as one of his literary and ecclesiastical supporters.[21] It is likely that Herrick wrote many of the poems of *Hesperides* not only with the goal of impressing his Cambridge and London peers, but also to gain the attention and favors of his "learn'd *Diocesan*."

In 1606, Hall published *The Arte of Diuine Meditation*, which, along with Hall's five other devotional manuals, helped to establish his position as a major influence on English devotional poetry and thought during the first half of the seventeenth century.[22] In the manual, Hall provided generous scope for the forms of prayer and worship that were appropriate for a Reformed Christian's personal devotional practice. While Hall did not deny the devotional value of the ceremonies and liturgies of the state church, or of formal kneeling and bowing during prayer, he also insisted that those were not the only models of worship that could induce feelings of devotion.

For Hall, the body played a key role in cultivating and expressing devotion. But importantly, Hall was hesitant to offer a circumscribed view of what a proper expression of devotion entailed. On the contrary, he remained alert to the possibility that one could embody devotion using an array of external gestures, and in all kinds of places—all outside of the confines of the state church's official worship services:

> Neither is there less variety in the site and gesture of the body: the due composedness whereof is no little advantage to this exercise; even in our speech to God, we observe not always one and the same position; sometimes we fall groveling on our faces, sometimes we bow our knees, sometimes stand on our feet, sometimes we lift up our hands, sometimes cast down our eyes.[23]

Hall averred that God, being spirit himself, did not concern himself overly much with the particulars of devotional practice, being "not scrupulous for the body" and requiring less that these outward gestures "be uniform as reverent." As a result, Hall maintained that a number of theologians have all correctly put forth various models for their daily devotion, each "according to their disposition and practice."[24]

---

[21] See McCabe, *A Study in Satire*, 154–8, 165–6; Barbara Kiefer Lewalski, *Protestant Poetics and the Seventeenth-Century Religious Lyric* (Princeton, Princeton University Press, 1979), 227; Barbara Kiefer Lewalski, *Donne's "Anniversaries" and the Poetry of Praise: The Creation of a Symbolic Mode* (Princeton: Princeton University Press, 1973), 220, 73–107; and Louis L. Martz, *The Poetry of Meditation: A Study in English Religious Literature of the Seventeenth Century* (New Haven: Yale University Press, 1954), 2 (on Hall's influence on Donne) and 25, 113, 331–52 (on Hall's influence on devotional literature more generally).

[22] McCabe, *A Study in Satire*, 24–5.

[23] Joseph Hall, *The Arte of Diuine Meditation profitable for all Christians to knowe and practice; exemplified with a large meditation of eternall life* (Imprinted at London by *Humfrey Lowes*, for *Samuel Macham*, and *Mathew Cooke*: and are to bee sold in Pauls Church-yard at the signe of the Tigers head, 1605), 60–1. (STC (2nd ed.) / 12642.) Copy from the Houghton Library, Harvard University.

[24] Hall, *Arte of Diuine Meditation*, 61.

90 DEVOTIONAL EXPERIENCE IN THE REFORMATION

It was possible to perform devotion while sitting and resting, standing with eyes lifted to heaven, leaning at rest, or while walking. Regardless of an individual's preferred approach to devotion, Hall insisted that the body and external gestures were vital for the cultivation of devotional affect: "In this let every man be his own master; so be we use that frame of body that may both testify reverence, and in some cases help to stir up further devotion."[25]

Hall insisted that a worshipper would be devotionally correct to perform the formal ceremonial gestures of prayer—the bowing, kneeling, genuflection, the groveling, the lifting of hands—and equally devotionally correct if he chose not to make use of any of these gestures. Now that the ceremonies and rites of devotion were rendered *adiaphora*—practices spiritually indifferent in matters of soteriology—Hall gave Reformed worshippers license to use devotional ceremonies as they saw fit, both in and outside the formal services of the state church. Just as Hall refused to prescribe set bodily expressions for devotion, or to limit devotional practice to certain places, he also refused to limit devotional expression to preset times. Quite contrary to the *Book of Common Prayer*, with its prayers for matins and evensong as well as its recitations and lessons set according to the yearly calendar, Hall argued that proper prayer need not be limited to set times of the day:

> One time cannot be prescribed to all: For neither is God bound to hours; neither doeth the contrary disposition of men agree in one choice of opportunities: the golden hours of the morning some find fittest for meditation, when the body newly raised, is well calmed with his late rest, and the soul hath not as yet had from these outward things any motives of alienation: Others find it best to learn wisdom of their reins in the night hoping, with Job, that their bed will bring them comfort in their meditation; when both all other things are still; and themselves wearied with these earthly cares, doe out of a contempt of them, grow into greater liking and love of heavenly things: I have ever found Isaac's time fittest, who went out in the evening to meditate.[26]

Hall allowed for an individualized approach to devotion that need not follow the temporal or calendrical rhythm set by of the church's official prayers and worship. By arguing that there was never a wrong time or way to cultivate devotion, Hall's tract implied that there was never a time that was *not* suited to prayer and meditation. A Reformed Christian, Hall maintained, might say his prayers properly while going about his daily tasks and routine, while out for a stroll, or lying awake at night in the intimacy of his own bed, as most suited his inclination and needs. "No precept, no practice of others can prescribe to us in this circumstance:

[25] Hall, *Arte of Diuine Meditation*, 63.
[26] Hall, *Arte of Diuine Meditation*, 55–7.

HERRICK'S PLAYERS AND PRAYERS   91

It shall be enough, that first we set ourselves a time."[27] Hall's experiential meditative practice—which could take place in a worshipper's home, the fields, while he was out walking in the town—provided the model for Herrick's peculiar vision of ceremonial devotion, and gave him license, when he was first beginning to write seriously in the 1610s, to envision a ceremonial worship practice rooted in the world around him, properly suited to celebrating worldly occasions and longings.

In "To Julia," as is true of his other sacramental love poems, Herrick celebrates the devotional power of religious ceremony—but not within the rarefied world of the English church services. Liberated from the prayer book liturgies of the state church, the matins might be sung at any time or any place; in Herrick's poem, they elevate the poem's fantasy of the bathing rite to the stature of ecclesiastical ceremony itself. Indeed, Herrick rarely celebrates religious ceremony as religious ceremony *per se*. In "The Rosarie," another poem praising Julia's beauty, Herrick describes his girlfriend's attributes in familiar ceremonial terms:

> One Ask'ed me where the Roses grew?
> I bade him not goe seek
> But forthwith bade my *Julia* shew
> A bud in either cheek.
>
> (H45.1–4)

The poem's punning title presents Julia's incarnadine cheeks as a rose garden, and also as twinned beads in a red rosary by which he might learn to say his prayers. While harkening back to a former Catholic practice, the beads of Julia's cheek and the beads at the close of "To Julia" are hardly endorsements of the devotional device. By transforming Julia's cheeks into two prayer beads and imagining sexual consummation as a rosary prayer, Herrick effectively divests the Catholic rosary of any particular devotional power. "The Rosarie" and "To Julia" suggest that the same devotional experience might be occasioned by a passerby's question for directions, by the act of gazing upon his girlfriend, or by having sex with her.

There is little in Herrick's *Hesperides* that would have pleased either Laudian or Catholic proponents of formal rituals and rites. Indeed, Herrick's lyrics often make use of liturgical and ceremonial language to encode critiques of formal worship. This is the case in "Corinna's going a-Maying," which uses the Maying celebrations as a pretext for a *carpe diem* argument about the pursuit of sexual fulfilment. In the poem, Herrick uses ceremonial imagery to woo his girlfriend to join in on the Maying celebrations. Although "Corinna's going a-Maying" has been read as evidence of Herrick's attachment to ceremony, there is little in the poem about the secular May celebrations that could be construed as formal ceremonial worship.[28]

---

[27] Hall, *Arte of Diuine Meditation*, 57.
[28] For a Laudian reading of the poem, see Guibbory, *Ceremony and Community*, 84–5.

92 DEVOTIONAL EXPERIENCE IN THE REFORMATION

The only prayers in the poem are those that take place in the natural world, outside of church worship services:

> Nay! Not so much as out of bed?
> When all the Birds have Mattens seyd,
> And sung their thankfull Hymnes: 'tis a sin,
> Nay, profanation to keep in.

(H178.9–12)

Herrick's persona wants little to do with formal prayers and rites, which he seems to think distract from the day's desired outcome: "Wash, dress, be briefe in praying: / Few Beads are best, when once we goe a Maying" (H178.27–8). Yet Herrick's rejection of formal ceremony in the poem is not a rejection of the religious aspects of the May celebrations; in fact, the natural world itself provides the devotional aids that bolster the couple's sense of wonder in matters of faith and desire:

> Come, my *Corinna,* come; and coming, marke
> How each field turns a street; each street a Park
>   Made green, and trimm'd with trees: see how
>   Devotion gives each House a Bough,
>   Or Branch: each Porch, each doore, ere this,
>   An Arke a Tabernacle is
> Made up of white-thorn neatly enterwove;
> As if here were those cooler shades of love.

(H178.29–36)

For Herrick, open fields, streets, parks, boughs, branches, porches, and doors provide occasions for devotional awe, both religious and erotic: "Can such delights be in the street, / And open fields, and we not see't?" (H178.37–8). Importantly, Herrick's litany of places where he and Corinna pause to marvel upon devotion's delights would have been sanctioned by Hall as acceptable places to pray and meditate. What appears to be a celebration of ceremony in Herrick's poem very quickly morphs into a rejection of those ceremonies as sole markers of devotional expression; Corinna does not need her beads because simply to walk through a field studded with May tree boughs offers the same devotional effect as the formal prayers and rites. In the poem, Herrick harnesses the ceremonial power of rites and rituals, and transplants them onto the ordinary places and objects of his Devonshire world.

Like the birds who sing their matins in "Corinna's going a-Maying," the natural world provides many occasions to bolster Herrick's religious and erotic devotion in his poem "To the Lark." In the poem, the lark's songs serve a devotional function that replicates that of the formal matins of the *Book of Common Prayer*:

> Good speed, for I this day
> Betimes my Mattens say:

HERRICK'S PLAYERS AND PRAYERS   93

> Because I doe
> Begin to wooe:
> Sweet singing Lark,
> Be thou the Clark,
> And know thy when
> To say, *Amen.*

(H214.1–8)

As he exhorts Corinna to put aside her prayer beads in the poem on the May celebrations, Herrick now cuts short his own prayers. He hastens to finish his formal devotions so that he can begin the day's real purpose, which is to woo. He justifies his rushed prayers with an argument that seems almost lifted from Hall's devotional tracts. In a world where every occasion might give rise to prayer, Herrick never really stops praying. In the poem, the lark's song obviates the *Book of Common Prayer*, and the bird itself replaces the English priest, who—much like Shakespeare's unlettered clerk of Sonnet 85—leads his congregation in joining in the liturgy's amens. Despite the poem's attention to the features of ceremonial worship, what is clear is that Herrick is in fact refusing to join in on formal prayer of any sort. In "To the Lark," as in many of Herrick's erotic poems that reference ceremonial forms, the rites and rituals of formal church worship provide the scaffolding for a deeply private and individual erotic devotion.

For Herrick, the notion that a lark's song might constitute an appropriate occasion for devotion may have come from reading the devotions of his mentor Hall. Undoubtedly, Herrick would have been familiar with Hall's *Occasional Meditations*, which, according to Richard McCabe, "had a profound influence upon contemporary habits of private devotion," and garnered "almost instant recognition as one of Hall's most outstanding contributions to literature and devotion."[29] In one such meditation, the sight of a lark taking flight occasions Hall's reflection upon the upward journey of the soul to heaven.[30] Likewise, in Meditation 36, "*Vpon the singing of the Birds in a Spring morning*," Hall celebrates the birds' joyous calls as patterns for his perpetual prayers and praise: "How cheerfully do these little birds chirp and sing out of the natural joy they conceive at the approach of the sun, and entrance of the spring; as if their life had departed, and returned with those glorious and comfortable beams," he writes. For Hall, the joyful birds encapsulate the delight of the penitent, who relinquishes his spiritual affliction in the presence of God the Father: "No otherwise is the penitent and faithful soul affected to the true sun of righteousness, the Father of lights? ... Oh thou, who art

---

[29] McCabe, *A Study in Satire*, 25, 152.

[30] Joseph Hall, Meditation 35, "*Vpon the sight of a Lark flying up*," in *Occasional Meditations by Ios. Exon. Set forth by R. H. The third Edition: with the Addition of 49 Meditations not heretofore published* (London: Printed by M. F. for *Nathaniel Butter*, 1633 [1630]), 87–9. (STC/12689.) Copy from the Houghton Library, Harvard University.

94 DEVOTIONAL EXPERIENCE IN THE REFORMATION

the God of all consolation, make my heart sensible of the sweet comforts of thy gracious presence, and let my mouth ever show forth thy praise."[31] Much like Herrick's poetic reflection on the lark, here Hall's encounter with the warbling bird provides the external prompt for a profoundly private devotional occasion.

The bishop's *Occasional Meditations* outline devotional reflections prompted by an array of everyday, natural phenomena—the sights and sounds of the sensible, material world around him. Hall named these devotions "extemporal meditations"—not in the sense that he intended them to be practiced extemporaneously, but because they are "occasioned by outward occurrences offered to the mind."[32] Hall often based his devotional reflections on the lives of the smallest creatures—snails, worms, bees, wasps, dormice, and birds.[33] His meditations encourage the viewer to regard the divinity that inheres in the ordinary—in clouds, stars, and sundials.[34] He meditates upon the motes in a beam of light, upon a spider in a window, upon the tulips and marigolds in his garden, and upon the flowers that an unnamed mourner has placed atop a coffin.[35] According to Hall, each of these impressions presents an opportunity for a devotional occasion.

In poems like "To the Lark" and "Corinna's going a-Maying," Herrick seems to suggest that poetry might function as a lyric equivalent of the devotional practice conceived of by Hall. Much like the catalogue of scenes and objects from the natural world that comprises Hall's *Occasional Meditations*, the structure of the *Hesperides* itself reads like a behemoth register of the various parts of the world—profane and secular—all subsumed within the book's devotional scope. As in Hall's *Occasional Meditations*, Herrick's *Hesperides* celebrates the devotional possibilities that inhere in ordinary things. "I sing of Brooks, of Blossomes, Birds, and Bowers," he proclaims in the collection's opening poem. "Of April, May, of June, and July-Flowers. / ... I sing of Dewes, of Raines, and piece by piece / Of Balme, of Oyle, of Spice, and Amber-Greece" ("The Argument of his Book," H1.1–2, 7–8). *Hesperides*—with its "piece by piece" attention to particulars, to the mundane, to the seemingly insignificant, and to the ephemeral—replicates in lyric form the devotional encounters of Hall's *Occasional Meditations*. Harold Fisch has described the structure and technique of Hall's *Occasional Meditations* as "the means of referring all his wayward thoughts and all seemingly insignificant worldly events to the higher life. It was to become the repository for all the miscellaneous gear which the ruminating but spiritually directed mind collected in its contacts with the

---

[31] Hall, *Occasional Meditations*, 89–91.
[32] Hall, *Arte of Diuine Meditation*, 7.
[33] Hall, *Occasional Meditations*, Meditations 29 (pp. 73–7), 49 (pp. 117–19), 69 (pp. 166–9), 101 (pp. 260–1), 62 (pp. 145–8), 63 (pp. 149–51), 88 (pp. 220–2), and 61 (pp. 143–5).
[34] Hall, *Occasional Meditations*, Meditations 7 (pp. 18–20), 4 (pp. 9–11), 96 (pp. 244–6), and 2 (pp. 4–6).
[35] Hall, *Occasional Meditations*, Meditations 105 (p. 269), 15 (pp. 34–7), 55 (pp. 128–30), and 86 (pp. 214–16).

HERRICK'S PLAYERS AND PRAYERS 95

world of books, men, and nature."[36] Strikingly, Fisch's description of Hall's book of meditations could have just as well been a description of Herrick's sprawling book of poems. Indeed, like Hall, Herrick found cause for devotional celebration in what others found unremarkable or vulgar, and his lyric prayers unfold within a devotional context that would have been recognized by contemporary proponents of extemporal meditation. But Herrick reimagines Hall's devotional technique in ways that might have stunned even Hall himself; in Herrick's love poems, the body itself provides the sensual scaffolding for a devotional practice that could replicate and even replace the official liturgies of the state church. The ceremonial love poems of the *Hesperides* unhinge Reformed worship from its ecclesiastical contexts, positing their private liturgies and rites of love as anti-ceremonial critiques of the narrowness of church worship. Far from being evidence of Herrick's lack of poetic seriousness, his lyric celebrations of the body and its desires in "piece by piece" fashion present his poems as acts of devotion. In *The Arte of Diuine Meditation*, Hall encouraged his reader to remain alert to the variety of the material world, which he saw as so many starting points for the cultivation of devotion: "God hath not straighted us for matter, having given us the scope of the whole world; so that there is no creature, event, action, speech which may not afford us new matter of meditation."[37] Herrick's poetry pushes Hall's assertion to its theological limits, demonstrating that every one of the body's fleshly desires offers an occasion for devotion.

***

Herrick's vision of himself as a participant in an array of private ceremonies and rites is not unique to his view of erotic desire; this view of life's fundamentally ceremonial impulse characterizes a number of other poems in *Hesperides*. Herrick wrote six poems about the Christmas and Candlemas celebrations: "Ceremonies for Christmasse" (H784), "Christmasse-Eve, another Ceremonie" (H785), "Ceremonies for Candlemasse Eve" (H892), "Ceremonies for Candlemasse Day" (H893), "Upon Candlemasse day" (H894), and "Ceremony Upon Candlemas Eve" (H980). Guibbory reads these poems on ceremony as Herrick's counterattack against Puritan encroachment on holiday rituals: "Where [William] Prynne finds it 'unlawfull' for Christians '*to decke up their Houses with Laurell, Yvie, and greene boughs*, (as we use to doe in the Christmas season),' Herrick encourages the tradition in poems like '*Ceremonies for Candlemasse Eve*' (H892)."[38] But contrary to Guibbory's view, what is surprising about these poems is that in spite of

---

[36] Harold Fisch, "Bishop Hall's Meditations," *The Review of English Studies* 25, no. 99 (1949): 210–1, see p. 211 for quotation. Similarly, Peter Damrau has noted that the bishop's devotional technique required that the worshipper maintain "an open mind for the things of the world." See Peter Damrau, *The Reception of English Puritan Literature in Germany* (London: Manley/Modern Humanities Research Association, 2006), 79.

[37] Hall, *Arte of Diuine Meditation*, 19–20.

[38] Guibbory, *Ceremony and Community*, 84.

96   DEVOTIONAL EXPERIENCE IN THE REFORMATION

their titles—of which all but one contain the word "ceremony"—none of them in fact describe anything like a formal religious ceremony or rite. Indeed, in the Candlemas poems, Herrick all but refuses to describe the ceremonies. Instead, in language that anticipates that of Prynne's iconoclastic attack on ceremony, the poems detail the dismantling of the holiday rites: "Down with the Rosemary and Bayes, / Down with the Misleto" (H892.1–2), and similarly, "Down with the Rosemary, and so / Down with the Baies, & mistletoe: / Down with the Holly, Ivie, all" (H980.1–3). His ambivalence about formal ceremonies is most apparent in his two-line Candlemas epigram: "End now the White-loafe, & the Pye, / And let all sports with Christmas dye" (H894). It could be that Herrick was satirizing the sentiments of Puritan opponents of formal worship, but nothing about the poems seems to suggest that these are not reflections of Herrick's own ambivalent views of religious ceremonies.

"Ceremonies for Christmasse," for instance, details less of a ceremony than a celebration—a simple home-cooked feast of mince pie, a loaf of bread, plum pastry, and "strong Beere" (H.784.12–18). Odder still, the second Christmas lyric, "Christmasse-Eve, another Ceremonie," details neither a ceremony nor a celebration, but captures the thoughts of a would-be celebrant on the night before Christmas, alone in the dark with his own ruminations and the freshly baked Christmas pie of the previous poem:

> Come guard this night the Christmas-Pie,
> That the Thiefe, though n'er so slie,
> With his Flesh-hooks, don't come nie
>   To catch it.
>
> From him, who all alone sits there,
> Having his eyes still in his eare,
> And a eale of nightly feare
>   To watch it.
>
> (H785.1–8)

Ceremony, in its traditional meaning, is all but absent in the poem. Indeed, the poem's only "ceremonies" are the watching and private musings of the person in the poem, vigilantly guarding the Christmas pie from the unnamed thief who threatens to seize it with his "Flesh-hooks"—an unexpectedly violent thought for the night before the Christmas feast, but one that apparently reflected the mood and ruminations of the man in the poem. Richard Brathwait, a contemporary of Herrick and a fellow student at Cambridge while he was at the university, described death as an "Earth-turn'd, mole-ei'd, flesh-hook that puls vs hence."[39]

---

[39] Richard Brathwait, "A Description of Death," in *Remains after Death* (Imprinted at London by Iohn Beale, 1618), sig. F. (*EEBO*, STC (2nd ed.) / 3568.5.) Bound with *The Good VVife: or, A rare one*

HERRICK'S PLAYERS AND PRAYERS   97

Whatever the flesh-hook might symbolize for the man in Herrick's Christmas Eve poem, his thoughts are far removed from the merriment of the holiday celebrations. The title of the poem makes sense only when we realize that the man's private thoughts *are* the ceremonial occasion. Rather than constituting misnomers, the titles of Herrick's Christmas ceremony poems seem to suggest that what was formerly relegated to the rarefied sphere of the church is in fact replicable in less formal, unofficial contexts. For Herrick, an individual's unuttered ruminations might count as a private ceremony and a devotional occasion. Indeed, Hall suggested as much in a devotional meditation occasioned by a table of food set for a feast: "I am not so austerely scrupulous as to deny the lawfulness of these abundant provisions, upon just occasions; I find my Savior himself more than once at a feast. ... Doubtless our bountiful God hath given us his creature, not for necessity only, but for pleasure."[40] While Herrick's poems celebrate ceremonies, it is clear that those ceremonial moments are less like those that would have been recognized by Laud and more like the private devotional moments described by Hall. Although Herrick seemed to regard the ceremonies with ambivalence, he persisted in his belief in the ceremonial power of the Christmas and Candlemas celebrations. As these poems suggest, Herrick understood that the devotional power of festive occasions wasn't limited to the traditional rites and ceremonies, but often inhered in the pleasure of sharing a home-baked pie and a pint of beer, or in a celebrant's own access to his affect and thoughts.

Herrick's puppet-priests

That Herrick remained ambivalent about formal ceremonies is apparent in "The Fairie Temple: or, Oberons Chappell" (H223), an imaginative account of a diminutive fairy community's worship rites. Herrick most likely wrote the poem in the 1620s, while he was at Cambridge, and circulated the poem among his university colleagues and London friends.[41] Given the early dating of the poem and the similarities between the fairies' religion and papal practice, it is unlikely that Herrick intended the poem as a commentary on the Laudian–Puritan controversies of the 1640s, but rather one about earlier anxieties about distinguishing Reformed religion from the older Catholic ceremonies and rites.[42] Herrick took care to draw links between the fairies' ceremonies and those of the Catholic church: "Theirs

---

amonst VVomen (At London: Printed [by John Beale] for Richard Redmer, and are to be sold at his shop at the west end of St Pauls Church, 1618).

[40] Hall, Meditation 81, in *Occasional Meditations*, 201–4.

[41] Cain, "Robert Herrick, Mildmay Fane, and Sir Simeon Steward," 312–17.

[42] Cain and Connolly note that "Though allusions in the first part could be either to Catholic or Laudian ritual, from l. 52 onward it becomes increasingly clear that the relatively genial satire is directed at Roman Catholicism." See commentary note in Cain and Connolly, *Complete Poetry of Robert Herrick*, eds. Cain and Connolly, 2:581. Additionally, Herrick's reference to Sir Thomas Parson, a generic

98   DEVOTIONAL EXPERIENCE IN THE REFORMATION

is a mixt Religion" (H223.29), Herrick states, "Part Pagan, part Papisticall" (31). "They much affect the *Papacie*" (116). The poem describes the sights and sounds that await a visitor to the fairies' "Temple of Idolatry" (12), built with "small bones, instead of walls" (16). Moving past the display of insectoid holy relics—the fairies pay homage to their "Idol-Cricket" (18), "Idol-Beetle-Fly" (20), and "Idol-Canker" (22)—the visitor next comes upon the temple divine: "A little-Puppet-Priest doth wait, / Who squeaks to all the comers there" (45–6). Herrick's critique of idolatrous ceremony also doubles as a critique of bad acting; the fairies' priest is guilty for propagating both.

In Chapter 2, I argued that Shakespeare's *Sonnets* co-opt and challenge Cranmer's arguments against the Catholic liturgy. Cranmer attacked the Catholic liturgy for enabling devotional insincerity in much the same way that antitheatrical campaigners attacked stage plays. As per their view of the papal rites, these campaigners alleged that playacting fostered hypocrisy by encouraging insincerity. As Jonas Barish has argued, criticism of the English theater and the state liturgy both stemmed from anxiety about how these performances encouraged an individual to obfuscate genuine affect, introducing what Barish has described as "a fatal discrepancy between the established gesture and the nuances of feeling."[43] Likewise, Brian Morris has noted that English antitheatricalists like Philip Stubbes attacked the theater by arguing for its similarity to public worship: "the attention which the plays commanded is not unlike the involvement of worship; the ritual participation of the actor and audience sets up a relationship between them and the experiencer represented by the play, which has close affinities with the spiritual communion at the heart of religion."[44] Early modern critics of both church ceremony and the public stage were eager to draw parallels between these two kinds of ritual performances in their attacks on both. John Field and Thomas Wilcox likened the Communion sacrament to "that old stagelike frisking & horrible Idol gadding." The performance of the ceremony was, they averred, "more mete for stage plays ... than for an holy action. ... [T]he true worship of God was by this means especially transformed into vain, and at the length mere stagelike songs."[45]

---

term for a pre-Reformation priest, seems to suggest that his poem is a critique on pre-Reformation Catholic ceremonies, not the High Church Anglicanism of the 1640s.

[43] Jonas Barish, *The Antitheatrical Prejudice* (Berkeley: University of California Press, 1981), 95.

[44] Brian Morris, "Elizabethan and Jacobean Drama," in *English Drama to 1710*, ed. Christopher Ricks (London: Sphere, 1971), 65–117, esp. 65–6. Other critics who have noted the resonance between the cultural purposes of public worship in the state church and secular stage performance include Barish, *Antitheatrical Prejudice*, 165; Margot Heinemann, *Puritanism and Theatre: Middleton and Opposition Drama under the Early Stuarts* (Cambridge: Cambridge University Press, 1980), 20, 30–1; Judith Maltby, *Prayer Book and People in Elizabethan and Early Stuart England* (Cambridge: Cambridge University Press, 1998), 3; Ramie Targoff, *Common Prayer: The Language of Public Devotion in Early Modern England* (Chicago: University of Chicago Press, 2001), 36–56; and Jeffrey Knapp, *Shakespeare's Tribe: Church, Nation, and Theater in Renaissance England* (Chicago: University of Chicago Press, 2002), 1–9.

[45] John Field and Thomas Wilcox, *An Admonition to the Parliament* (Hemel Hempstead: Printed by J. Stroud, 1572), unnumbered page. (*EEBO*, STC (2nd ed.) / 10848, document image 27.)

HERRICK'S PLAYERS AND PRAYERS 99

Writing exactly sixty years after Field and Wilcox published their criticism of church worship, William Prynne amplified their argument in his lambasting of the public stage in *Histrio-mastix*. Prynne saw Catholic priests as players in their acting out of the papal rites and ceremonies, and he saw aspects of these papal rituals in English state worship. These rites and rituals turn "their Priests into Players, their Temples, into Theaters," Prynne insisted.[46] Whereas Field and Wilcox argued that ceremonial worship merely participated in aspects of the public stage plays, Prynne took their argument a step further. For Prynne, playacting not only offered a metaphor to explain the dangers inherent in public worship and ceremony. In a much more literal sense, Prynne feared that the church services would be infiltrated directly by playacting. According to Prynne, the continental Catholic churches were led by "playerlike priests and friars" who, in enacting the Passion, willfully bring "profane ridiculous Stage-play[s]" into the church.[47] Prynne saw no difference between these Catholic "playerlike priests" on the continent and his fellow English people who continued to partake in holiday pastimes and ceremonies: "our riotous, ludicrous & voluptuous Christmasses, (together with Stage-plays, dancing, masques and such like Pagan sports) had their original from Pagan, their revival and continuance from Popish Rome, who long since transmitted them over to England."[48] For Prynne, participation in any religious and holiday ceremony was tantamount to contaminating public worship with playacting and papal influence. Prynne's ideal Christmas celebration, a reader of *Histrio-mastix* might infer, might look a lot like the occasion of Herrick's "Ceremonies for Christmasse" and "Christmasse-Eve, another Ceremonie," which, despite their titles, do not describe any actual ceremonies in the formal sense.

Much like Field, Wilcox, and Prynne, Herrick draws upon the cultural parallels between bad acting and false religion in "Upon Trap" (H1076). In the poem, Herrick turns to the fraught intersection between secular and stage performances in a meditation on the transformative power of theater: "Trap, of a Player turn'd a Priest now is; / Behold a suddaine *Metamorphosis*" (H1076.1–2). The poem takes a satirical view of Trap, a player turned priest, who oscillates between his two professions in order to serve his own machinations. But in his "metamorphosis" from one playacting role to another, Trap is not completely successful in pulling off his transformation. The boundaries between his old and new roles remain permeable, and Trap muddles his performances both as player and as priest. In his new role as priest, Trap continues to perform all the old country dances and entertainments—such as the "Tythe-pigs" jig—that he used to perform in his capacity as a professional player: "If Tythe-pigs faile, then will he shift

---

[46] William Prynne, *Histrio-mastix: The Players Scourge, or, Actors Tragaedie* (London: E[dward] A[llde, Augustine Mathewes, Thomas Cotes] and W[illiam] I[ones] for Michael Sparke, 1633), 118. (*EEBO*, STC (2nd ed.) / 20464a.) See also Prynne's similar arguments on pp. 114 and 148.

[47] Prynne, *Histrio-mastix*, 765.

[48] Prynne, *Histrio-mastix*, 766.

the scean, / And, from a Priest, turne Player once again" (3–4). Herrick presents a transformation that condenses the present and the past instantiations of Trap's various modes of playacting into an integrated theatrical role. The scene may shift, but Trap remains a consummate performer and dissembler in his singular role as player–priest.

Herrick's Trap embodies the "playerlike" priests that were the target of Prynne's invectives in *Histrio-mastix*. Like Prynne, Herrick's Trap moves seamlessly between the stage and the pulpit, his commitment to the former disqualifying him for the latter. In *Histrio-mastix*, Prynne writes anxiously of priests who were also professional stage actors. Whether or not this scenario was common, Herrick's poem seems to echo Prynne's fear about priests moonlighting as players. Not only was Prynne concerned about "playerlike" priests bringing playacting into the church, he also feared that they might bring the church to the secular stage: "Clergy men ... may not come forth upon the stage as actors, nor act comedies in their mother tongue: they shall make no spectacle of their body in any public or private place ... as they are unseemly to all ministers, and much derogatory from the clerical order."[49] Prynne, like Herrick's poem, articulates a wider cultural anxiety about the performative porousness of playacting and public religion.

Herrick's conflation of both secular and sacred dissembling in "Upon Trap" and "The Fairie Temple" anticipated antitheatricalist critiques of secular and sacred performance. Indeed, at the time of the poems' publication in the 1640s, Herrick's derision of the puppet-priest's ceremonies and the playacting of the player-turned-priest would have sounded very similar to the critique of performance advocated by critics of the theater and church rites. Trap, Herrick's player-priest, is in some sense the ultimate poetic representation of the antitheatricalists' most feared public menace: the player who insists on corrupting the public, not only in the playhouses but in the state church as well. Indeed, Prynne maintained that playing and praying held sufficient spiritual correspondence, and that they engaged the participant in such similar ways that simply gazing upon a playhouse performance held spiritually dangerous consequences for an individual's ability to pray: "The twelve effect of stage-plays is this: That they wholly indispose their actors and spectators to all religious duties: that they withdraw and keep them from God's service: that they bring the Word, the worship, yea all the ordinances of God into contempt; making them vain and ineffectual to their souls."[50] Prynne went so far as to state that a career in the public theaters—and even exposure to theatrical spectacle as a passive observer—roundly disqualified one from a life of clerical duty:

> Moreover those *sundry councils and authors, which debar all clergy men from the acting and beholding of stage-plays, either in public or private, lest their eyes, their*

---

[49] Prynne, *Histrio-mastix*, 612.
[50] Prynne, *Histrio-mastix*, 521.

HERRICK'S PLAYERS AND PRAYERS 101

ears and hearts, set apart, and consecrated to God's holy mysteries, should be defiled by them, and so indispose them to discharge their ministerial function; are a most pregnant evidence of this irrefragable truth; that stage-plays disable men from the right performance of all holy duties.[51]

As I argued in Chapter 2 on Shakespeare's *Sonnets*, for certain early modern reformers, secular stage plays shared in the idolatry associated with improper devotional performance. In his argument about religious idolatry, Prynne's critique of theatrical performance melds the logic of D'Ewes and earlier antitheatricalists such as Field and Wilcox.[52] As I have noted above, D'Ewes described ritual genuflection during the Communion sacrament as a form of idolatry, and before Prynne, Stubbes had described stage plays as worship of "false idols," a variety of "heathenish idolatry." In his argument, Prynne conflates these two forms of cultural anxiety about idolatrous performance. According to Prynne, secular playacting is itself a form of idolatry, and he saw "profane, and poisonous stage-plays" as nothing short of "the common idol, and prevailing evil of our dissolute, and degenerate age."[53] In Prynne's logic, the consequences of watching or acting in stage plays held direct bearing upon an individual's ability to access and participate in proper devotion. For him, secular stage performance was mutually exclusive with the "right performance" of religious duties; in effect, participation in spiritually dangerous performance made the performance of proper devotion all but impossible.

Although Prynne and his antitheatrical predecessors who inveighed against the theaters have often been presented as radical Puritans,[54] in fact, antitheatrical sentiment was not necessarily synonymous with puritanism nor was it necessarily associated with any particular confessional outlook or identity.[55] As Jeffrey Knapp has pointed out, "[t]hree of the five best known antitheatricalists in Elizabethan England—Stubbes, Anthony Munday, and Stephen Gosson—do not seem to have sided with puritans in any consistent way. By the same token, puritans are known to have attended plays, bought playbooks, and even patronized dramatists."[56] Indeed, Brian Morris has noted that by the time Prynne wrote his *Histrio-mastix*, at least forty others had published antitheatrical tracts in England, judging by Prynne's citations alone.[57] It seems that by the 1630s, criticism of the stage was no longer a fringe view but an increasingly mainstream one.[58] By the early Caroline period, the antitheatricalist sentiment of Prynne's *Histrio-mastix* would have been

---

[51] Prynne, *Histrio-mastix*, 528.

[52] See my treatment of Field and Wilcox in Chapter 2, 54–55.

[53] Prynne, *Histrio-mastix*, 2.

[54] For example, as in Barish's argument about English puritanism and antitheatricalism. See Barish, "Puritans and Proteans," chap. 4 in *Antitheatrical Prejudice*, 80–131.

[55] Heinemann, *Puritanism and Theatre*, 22, 26–30; Martin Butler, *Theatre and Crisis, 1632–1642* (Cambridge: Cambridge University Press, 1984), 91; and Knapp, *Shakespeare's Tribe*, 14.

[56] Knapp, *Shakespeare's Tribe*, 14.

[57] Morris, "Elizabethan and Jacobean Drama," 81.

[58] For a contrary view, see Butler, *Theatre and Crisis*, 95–6.

102   DEVOTIONAL EXPERIENCE IN THE REFORMATION

regarded not as a religious position but as a political one—specifically, as Margot Heinemann has argued, one that would have been associated with anti-royalist sentiment: "[A]s the court, the exclusive patron of theatrical companies, became increasingly remote in its standards and attitudes from the majority of citizens, the conflict of codes (expressed among other things in customary Sunday plays at court) hardened into the familiar clash of principle around Prynne's *Histriomastix*."[59] According to Heinemann, Prynne's criticism of public playacting was covert criticism of the court itself, as a patron of both the public theater houses and of Sunday court performances. The latter in particular drew Prynne's ire, as he believed that these Sunday plays drew audiences away from the state church services.[60] If Heinemann's argument is correct, and Prynne's antitheatrical tract encoded an indirect critique of the Caroline court and of Charles himself, then Herrick's own antitheatrical poems lend credence to my argument that Herrick should not be regarded as either a royalist or a conservative poet—contrary to how scholars such as Guibbory and Marcus have portrayed his literary output. As it turns out, his poems about public performance—both theatrical and ceremonial— offer more complicated, and perhaps even critical, political commentary upon the state church and court.

In light of Prynne's excoriation of players and their unwitting spectators, Herrick's poems read as not only antitheatricalist but also anti-establishment in their sentiments about performance and clerical duty. Rather than indicating any royalist sympathies, Herrick's poems seem to echo rather than disavow the political positions that modern critics have associated with those who regarded the church establishment with skepticism. It is not difficult to see how Herrick's conflation of secular and sacred modes of performance into a single act of dissembling might have pleased both the antitheatricalists as well as the iconoclasts who made it their mission to dismantle the "popish" rites and ceremonies of the English church. Herrick's satirical treatment of Trap—whose name announces the performative and spiritual snares he sets for his audience and congregants alike—affirms reformist critiques both of the theater and of church ceremony. Indeed, not only does Herrick assume what might be regarded as a decidedly anti-establishment

---

[59] Heinemann, *Puritanism and Theatre*, 35. See also 22. Butler reads Prynne as a royalist of sorts, in that he is careful in *Histrio-mastix* to avoid direct criticism of Charles while reserving his critique solely for Laud and the English ecclesiology. Yet, as I argue in my discussion of Milton, Charles and Laud had a close political relationship and Butler seems to overlook the fact that the two worked in tandem to implement church policy regarding state worship. See Butler, *Theatre and Crisis*, 89–90, and Chapter 6 in this book.

[60] Prynne, *Histrio-mastix*, 530–1, 312. Earlier antitheatricalists made the same argument: see Stephen Gosson, *The Schoole of Abuse Conteining a Pleasaunt Inuectiue against Poets, Pipers, Plaiers, Iesters, and such like Caterpillers of a Comonwelth* (London: for Thomas VVoodcocke, 1579), unnumbered pages. (*EEBO*, STC (2nd ed.) / 12097.5, document images 22–3 and 17); Anthony Munday, *A Second and Third Blast of Retrait from Plaies and Theaters* (London: By Henrie Denham, dwelling in Pater noster Row, 1580), 17. (*EEBO*, STC (2nd ed.) / 21677, document image 15); and Philip Stubbes, *The Anatomie of Abuses, Part 1* (London: By [John Kingston for] Richard Iones, 1583, unnumbered page. (*EEBO*, STC (2nd ed.) / 23376, document image 85).

HERRICK'S PLAYERS AND PRAYERS   103

stance toward church ceremonies in his poems; moreover, he goes so far as to link
religious performances with the dangers of secular theater.

Yet to read Herrick's antitheatricalism through the lens of the Anglican–Puritan
controversies of the 1640s is to overlook the earlier contexts for his skepticism of
the theater. As I have demonstrated in my Introduction and Chapter 1, Herrick's
belief that devotional performances were valuable, so long as they corroborated
prior affect, was a widely held conviction during the half-century after the Elizabethan settlement—a view that was shared by clerics as diverse as Richard Hooker
and William Perkins. When *Hesperides* was published in 1648, Herrick's skepticism of ceremonial practice would have assumed additional political and religious
valences for his readers in light of the Laudian religious reforms. But the religious
skepticism toward ceremonial and theatrical performance that had become newly
controversial in the 1640s would have been a widely held view in the 1620s and
earlier. When Herrick had written and circulated "The Fairie Temple" and possibly "Upon Trap" in the 1620s or earlier, the poems reflected an ambivalence about
performances and ceremonies—a sentiment that would not have been uncommon
in the Elizabethan and Jacobean eras, reflecting the same unease that Shakespeare
imagined both the young man of the *Sonnets* and his readers would have felt when
confronted with the poems' formal rites, rituals, and ceremonies of love.

Herrick registers this uneasy view of ceremonies and performances in "The
Wake," another lyric account of the Maytide celebrations.[61] Much like "Corinna's
going a-Maying," "The Wake" describes Herrick's desire to join in with the rituals
and rites while simultaneously undercutting those ceremonies. By way of wooing
Anthea to join him, Herrick details a catalogue of the kinds of performances that
they can expect to encounter at the wake:

> Come *Anthea* let us two
> Go to Feast, as others do.
> ...
> Morris-dancers thou shalt see,
> Marian too in Pagentrie:
> And a Mimick to devise
> Many grinning properties.
> Players there will be, and those
> Base in action as in clothes:
> Yet with strutting they will please
> The incurious Villages.
>
> (H761.1–2, 7–14)

What appears to be a celebration of the holiday ceremonies develops into a
criticism not just of the performances, the players, their costumes, and their

---

[61] Although the term "wake" in contemporary English is now associated with funerary proceedings,
the term was used up until the 1890s to refer to annual celebrations and rituals performed by rural
English parishes.

104   DEVOTIONAL EXPERIENCE IN THE REFORMATION

parts—the "grinning properties" that the mimes assume—but also of the "incurious" spectators, incapable of grasping the import of the performances. Paradoxically, Herrick woos Anthea with the promise of the wake's plays and festivities, even as he regards the players and their spectators with suspicion: "Happy
Rusticks, best content / With the cheapest Merriment: / And possesse no other
feare, / Then to want the Wake next year" (H761.21–4). Poems like "Corinna's
going a-Maying" and "The Wake" poetically recreate ceremonial performances for
Herrick's readers while also regarding those same performances with skepticism.
In his treatment of ceremony in *Hesperides*, Herrick's ambiguous stance on performance reflects the contradictory positions on performance that were in circulation
in early seventeenth-century England.

In 1644, three years before Herrick published *Hesperides*, the English Parliament issued an ordinance that banned maypoles—"a heathenish vanity, generally
abused to superstition and wickedness." The ordinance also issued fines—a hefty
five shillings per offense—for those found in attendance at wakes and other Sunday pastimes: "And be it further ordained, that no person or persons shall hereafter
upon the Lords-day, use exercise, keep, maintain, or be present at any wrestlings,
shooting, bowling, ringing of bells for pleasure or pastime, masque, wake, otherwise called feasts, church-ale, dancing, games, sport or pastime whatsoever."[62]
Although they were most likely written in the 1610s or 1620s, when Herrick published poems like "The Wake" and "Corinna's going a-Maying" in the late 1640s,
he did not bother emending or eliding the portions of the poem that criticized
the wake ceremonies. Amid the political climate of that decade, it is not difficult
to imagine that the poem might have pleased both Puritan and parliamentar-
ian opponents of the recently outlawed wakes, performances, and ceremonies.
The moderate skepticism about performances and ceremonies, widespread from
the 1590s to the 1620s, assumed new political and religious dimensions during
the decade when Herrick pursued publication. This is surely something that Herrick would have been alert to when gathering his poems for print. Yet if Herrick's
views on performance in "The Wake" resonate with Puritan critiques of public
and sacred performances, his actions in the poem do not. While Herrick deni-
grates the people who participate in the wake performances, his wariness of the
ceremonies do not prevent him from including himself and Anthea among those
spectators. The poem suggests a contradictory stance on playacting and ceremony that adopts arguments from a range of contemporary views of performance
without sympathizing with any one polemical position.

Despite his skepticism about rites, wakes, and rituals, Herrick was unable to
imagine his devotional commitments apart from the roles and playacting intrinsic
to theater. This is the case in Herrick's poetic rendition of Catullus's fifth ode. In

---

[62] *An Ordinance of the Lords and Commons Assembled in Parliament, for the better Observation of
the Lords-Day, April 6, 1644* (London: Printed for Edward Husbands, April 10, 1644). (*EEBO*, Wing /
E1943A.)

HERRICK'S PLAYERS AND PRAYERS   105

imploring Anthea to have sex with him, Herrick adapts the erotic argument from Catullus while nevertheless departing from the original poem's conclusion:

> Give me a kisse, and to that kisse a score;
> Then to that twenty, adde a hundred more:
> A thousand to that hundred: so kisse on,
> To make that thousand up a million.
> Treble that million, and when that is done,
> Let's kisse afresh, as when we first begun.
>
> ("To Anthea," H74.3–8)

As it turns out, in both Catullus's and Ben Jonson's versions of the poem, the ever-multiplying number of kisses stolen from Lesbia and Celia are collected with a third-party onlooker in mind. As Jonson writes: "the enuious, when they find / What their number is, be pin'd."[63] Jonson's poem marks a departure from Catullus's version, in which the dizzying number of kisses provokes the third-party onlooker not to envy but confusion: "then when we've notched up all these many thousands, / shuffle the figures, lose count of the total, / so no maleficent enemy can hex us / knowing the final sum of our kisses."[64] By contrast, the only onlookers in Herrick's rendition of the poem are Anthea and himself, the amorous pursuit culminating not in public recognition but a private act of sexual consummation. Herrick reimagines the kisses as a kind of theatrical foreplay, scenes leading up to the dramatic culmination: "But yet, though Love likes well such Scenes as these, / There is an Act that will more fully please: / Kissing and glancing, sooth, all make way / But to the acting of this private Play" (H74.9–12). Having banished the third-party onlooker in his version of the poem, Herrick posits himself and Anthea as both actors and spectators of their own private performance. For Herrick, erotic desire is fundamentally like playacting, and the roles that lovers assume in their wooing and retreat are not unlike the acting of parts.

Ceremonial theater in *His Noble Numbers*

The world is a stage; every man an actor; and plays his part here either in a comedy, or a tragedy; The good man is a comedian; which however he begins ends merrily: but the wicked man acts a tragedy, and therefore ever ends in horror.

—Joseph Hall, *Meditations and Vowes* (1605)[65]

---

[63] Ben Jonson, "VI. To the Same [To Celia], *The Forrest*," in *The works of Beniamin Ionson* (Imprinted at London: By Will Stansby, 1616), 826–7. (*EEBO*, STC (2nd ed.) / 14751.)

[64] 5.10–13. Catullus, *The Poems of Catullus: A Bilingual Edition*, trans. Peter Green (Berkeley: University of California Press, 2007), 49.

[65] Joseph Hall, *The Second Booke of Meditations and Vowes, Divine and Morall* (At London: Imprinted by *Humfrey Lownes*, for *Iohn Porter*, 1607 [1605]), in *Meditations and Vowes, Diuine and*

106 DEVOTIONAL EXPERIENCE IN THE REFORMATION

At the outset of this chapter, I argued that the dominant critical view of Herrick's approach to ceremonial performance is anachronistic, being based on the assumption that his ceremonial poems were responses to the Laudianism of the 1640s rather than to earlier religious debates about Reformed devotion in the Elizabethan and Jacobean churches. Additionally, there is a second reason for the inadequacy of extant critical interpretations of Herrick's ceremonial poems: not only anachronistic, these arguments rest partially on omission. Indeed, while there has been significant critical attention to Herrick's ceremonialism in the secular poems of *Hesperides*, the critical treatment of Herrick's engagement with the religious controversies about the role of performance all but overlooks *His Noble Numbers*. Moreover, where *His Noble Numbers* has elicited critical responses, readers have vigorously dismissed these poems as evidence of Herrick's literary and devotional failures. "Bone-dry, prosaic, stripped of metaphor," one critic avers, "Herrick's divine poems seem at times designed to alienate the reader from poetry itself."[66] "I find most of his religious verse either dull or unconvincing," writes another.[67] "Certainly," a third critic adds, "he is not thought of as a 'religious' poet, despite his *Noble Numbers*, a collection of rather dull poems on conventionally Christian devotional topics."[68] One critic claims that the poems were hastily written as "padding" for the tail end of the collection, "at the cost of rendering it monotonous and trivial."[69] And harshest still: the poems of *His Noble Numbers* "appear thin, flat, and barren of intellectual or psychological complexity."[70] These are but a sampling of the extant critical views of Herrick's devotional poems.[71]

Morall; Seruing for direction in Christian and Ciuill Practise. Diuided into two Bookes (At London: Printed by *Humfrey Lownes*, for *Iohn Porter*, 1607 [1605]), 153–4. (STC/12681.) Bound with *The Arte of Divine Meditation: Profitable for all Christians to know and practice, Exemplified with a large Meditation of eternall life* (At London: Printed by *H. L.* for *Samuel Macham*: and are to be sold at his shop in Paules Church-yard, at the signe of the Full-head. 1607 [1605]). Copy from the Houghton Library, Harvard University.

[66] Coiro, *Robert Herrick's "Hesperides,"* 27.

[67] Joseph H. Summers, *The Heirs of Donne and Jonson* (New York: Oxford University Press, 1970), 57.

[68] Achsah Guibbory, "Enlarging the Limits of the 'Religious Lyric': The Case of Herrick's *Hesperides*," in *New Perspectives on the Seventeenth-Century English Religious Lyric*, ed. John R. Roberts (Columbia, MO: University of Missouri Press, 1994), 28–45, esp. 28.

[69] Creaser, "'Times Trans-Shifting,'" 184.

[70] Leah S. Marcus, "Herrick's *Noble Numbers* and the Politics of Playfulness," *English Literary Renaissance* 7 (1977): 108–26, esp. 108. See also Leah S. Marcus, *Childhood and Cultural Despair* (Pittsburgh: University of Pittsburgh Press, 1978), 95.

[71] Earlier critics have espoused similarly dim views of Herrick's *Noble Numbers*. "Yet if any reader turns to *His Noble Numbers* with the hope of finding religious enlightenment he has come to the wrong place," Marchette Chute insists, "for Herrick was perhaps the least meditative Christian that the seventeenth century produced." See Marchette Chute, *Two Gentle Men: The Lives of George Herbert and Robert Herrick* (New York: E. P. Dutton, 1959), 251. Likewise in the late nineteenth century, Edward Everett Hale revealed his own distaste for the divine poems in his introductory note to his edition of Herrick's poems: "It must be confessed that it is on the whole a most inferior part, inferior in thought and inferior in handling. ... There are hardly a dozen of the *Noble Numbers* that come up even to the average excellence of *Hesperides*." See Edward Everett Hale, Introduction to *Selections from the Poetry of Robert Herrick*, ed. Edward Everett Hale (Boston: Ginn, 1895), xlvii.

HERRICK'S PLAYERS AND PRAYERS 107

Yet despite the longstanding critical dislike of *His Noble Numbers*, it is imperative to take into account Herrick's religious poems if we are to fully understand his religious outlook.

His Noble Numbers reflects Herrick's mature view of devotional intimacy; the poems claim a private and intimate familiarity with Christ's body, much as the earlier love poems of *Hesperides* laid claim to the bodies of Julia, Corinna, and Anthea. At moments in *His Noble Numbers*, Herrick seems to count Christ among one of his several amorous interests, describing his desire for Christ in much the same way that he often expresses his desire for his girlfriends.[72] In one poem addressed to God, Herrick resorts to coyness in his devotional negotiations: "lay thy stately terrours by, / To talke with me familiarly ... Speak thou of love and I'le reply / By way of *Epithalamie*" ("To God," N1362.7–8, 11–12). Like his poems in pursuit of women, Herrick's poems of praise imagine devotional intimacy with God in ceremonial and performative terms.

In *His Noble Numbers*, it is not just priests and players who are implicated in the evasions that come from acting a part. Herrick criticizes God himself for his playacting. More astonishing still, as an actor, God often falls short of performing his part—with disastrous consequences for his devotees and worshippers, who are unwittingly drawn into his theatrics. *His Noble Numbers* is replete with Herrick's many references to God's theatrical shortcomings. Herrick's relationship with God *is* theater, and most often, that stage play is badly performed. "He may seem to over-act His part," Herrick writes, describing God's maddening tendency to mete out unendurable punishment ("Affliction," N1140.2). Like Shakespeare's "unperfect actor" of Sonnet 23, whose stage fright causes him to fumble his part, Herrick's overzealous God tramples the boundaries of his roleplaying. But if, in his negotiations with his worshippers, God at times overperforms his part, at other times he underperforms: "GOD still rewards us more then our desert: / But when He strikes, he quarter-acts his part" ("God sparing in scourging," N1372.1–2). Herrick cannot rid himself of the sense that all of his encounters with God involve a measure of playacting; even at his most merciful, God reveals his clemency by

---

Graham Parry puts forth the sole contrarian view against criticism of *His Noble Numbers*, arguing in favor of their theological liberality: "Throughout the collection of *Noble Numbers* there runs a generosity of spirit that cheers one by its inclusiveness. ... This generosity of spirit extends across the ages and across creeds. ... The desire to worship God, to praise God, to expiate sin and ward off misfortune is universal, and the history of worship is the history of the human race, with variations on a central theme." See Parry, "His Noble Numbers," 276–99. See pp. 295 and 296 for the quotation.

[72] Compare the striking similarities between "*Upon* Julia's *Breasts*" ("Display thy breasts, my *Julia*, there let me / Behold that circummortall purity: / Between whose glories, there my lips Ile lay, / Ravisht, in that faire *Via Lactea*" [H230.1–4]) and "*To Christ*" ("My mouth I'le lay unto Thy wound / Bleeding, that no Blood touch the ground: / For, rather then one drop shall fall / To waste, my JESU, I'le take all" [N1259.5–8]). All quotations from *His Noble Numbers* are taken from Herrick, *Hesperides* (1648), with poem titles and their numbers in *Complete Poetry of Robert Herrick*, eds. Cain and Connolly (denoted "N"), followed by line numbers, given parenthetically in the text.

108   DEVOTIONAL EXPERIENCE IN THE REFORMATION

"quarter-acting" his part. In each of these encounters, Herrick yearns for unfettered access to God, but is instead met with a theatrical guise. In either of his diametrically opposed moods, God the actor misses his mark.

Nor is Herrick's God only culpable for playing his own roles badly. Herrick censures God for his duplicitous dissembling, and his oscillating—like Trap—between multiple parts. When "by stripes" God saves his penitents, Herrick claims that "then 'tis known, / He comes to play the part that is His own" ("God has a twofold part," N1152.3–4). But the obverse maintains as well: "GOD when for sin He makes His Children smart, / His own He acts not, but anothers part" (N1152.1–2). Herrick leaves his reader with only a murky sense of the distinction between God's two parts. God beats his children in the role of another, but he beats them when he is playing his own part, too.[73] In this account of divine punishment and wrath, negotiating with God without the use of scripted roles remains impossible for Herrick. Regardless of what role God chooses to adopt at any given moment, Herrick's poems suggest that each of God's theatrical parts is a cause for human suffering: "Where God is merry, there write down thy fears: / What He with laughter speaks, here thou with tears" ("Gods mirth, Mans mourning," N1193.1–2). What is clear is that, for Herrick, playacting is the sole vehicle by which one *must* negotiate with a fundamentally performative God. Even when he is at his best, God is still putting on an act—playing "the part that is His own."

In the divine encounters of *His Noble Numbers*, Herrick's God is either blundering his part or disregarding it entirely. In doing so, God emerges as anything but the amiable being described by critics of Herrick's religious poems, who maintain that such a God was the invention of a naive and childlike country clergyman: "[T]he truth is that [Herrick's] conception of religion in spite of his reading of the Fathers, was scarcely more mature than that of a child of eight," Frederic W. Moorman writes, describing the religious sentiment of *His Noble Numbers*. "His God ... is an amiable Being with whom the poet stands on very intimate terms."[74] Yet contrary to Moorman's assessment, Herrick's numerous epigrams and short poems present his God as a thoroughly unlikeable character, prone to capriciousness and a tendency to mete out suffering for his own amusement. In fact, Herrick's criticism of God is reminiscent of Prynne's excoriating attack on playactors, who,

---

[73] So pervasive are God's theatrics that his playacting seems to animate even the inanimate props that bolster his performances; the shepherd's staff that he uses to discipline his flock might, Herrick hopes, "come to play the friendly part" ("The Staffe and Rod," N1371.4). Of course, the implicit alternative obtains as well, and Herrick fears that his staff-brandishing God might adopt a more sinister role in one of his less jovial moods.

[74] Frederic W. Moorman, *Robert Herrick: A Biographical and Critical Study* (New York: Russell and Russell, 1910), 305–6, 309. Other critics have likewise argued for Herrick's childish and childlike religious temperament in their readings of *His Noble Numbers*, including Marcus, *Childhood and Cultural Despair*, 95; Chute, *Two Gentle Men*, 205; and Starkman, "*Noble Numbers*," 9, 17.

HERRICK'S PLAYERS AND PRAYERS   109

in always performing another's part, implicate themselves in "gross hypocrisy." Prynne writes, "They are always *acting others*, not themselves."[75]

It is God, not Herrick, who emerges in *His Noble Numbers* as temperamental and childish in his whims. Acknowledging this allows us to consider the implications of Herrick's extraordinary caricature of a theatrical God for a culture that harbored profound anxiety about what happens when devotion and performance are mixed. It is not the worshipper but God who becomes the target of Herrick's antitheatrical and iconoclastic ire. What does it mean that Herrick attacks not the idolatrous practice of performed devotion but instead attributes those practices to the very nature of God? In his reflections upon his own ongoing negotiations with God, Herrick reappropriates the current of hostility against the theatrical arts in giving dimension and scope to his ambivalence toward God. In appropriating arguments against allegedly idolatrous practices, Herrick paradoxically ends up placing himself in a profoundly uncomfortable, and arguably idolatrous, devotional position. *His Noble Numbers* echo the antitheatricalist critique of performance, while also mobilizing that argument to articulate anxieties about his own devotional access to God. In doing so, Herrick reappropriates the widespread cultural resistance to the institution of the theater in ways that would have surprised even his own contemporary readers. What concerns Herrick most is not the consequences of his own devotional dissembling; rather, his preoccupation with performance reveals rifts in his relationship with a God whose intentions he reads as both opaque and changeable. In doing so, Herrick furthers a devotional vision that would have rested uneasily with both defenders and critics of the secular theater as the poems weigh the nature of God's commitments to even his most dedicated devotees.

Desire is at once the impetus and the aftershock of Herrick's skeptical appraisal of God, who appears at his most monstrous and most marvelous at precisely the moments when he is under attack. Herrick presents a problematic reading of devotional access, one both complicated by and contingent upon theatrical performance. Herrick's devotional impasse lies in the seemingly insurmountable distance between the penitent, whose gestures of devotion lack performative force, and his God, who is equally enigmatic in his theatrical whims. Herrick's God encompasses oppositions, demanding that his worshippers negotiate with the whole gamut of his various personae. Indeed, Herrick describes the task of

---

[75] Prynne, *Histrio-mastix*, 156. Prynne's full invective against the playactors describes their dissembling and counterfeiting at great length: "All things are counterfeited, feined, dissembled; nothing really or sincerely acted. Players are always counterfeiting, representing the persons, habits, offices, calling parts, conditions, speeches, actions, lives; the passions, the affections, the anger, hatred, cruelty, love, regence, dissentions; yea, they very vices, sinnes, and lusts; the adulteries, incests, rapes, murthers, tyrannies, thefts, and such like crimes of other men, of other sexes, of other creature; yea, oft-times of the Devell himself, and Pagan Divell gods." See Prynne, *Histrio-mastix*, 156.

110 DEVOTIONAL EXPERIENCE IN THE REFORMATION

knowing God as a Herculean endeavor: "'Tis hard to finde God, but to comprehend / Him, as He is, is labour without end" ("God not to be comprehended," N1138.1–2). But negotiating with a theatrical God, for Herrick, requires further theatrics. Indeed, while theater is the vexed medium through which Herrick conveys his profound frustration about a fundamentally opaque God, it is also the medium by which Herrick renders this otherwise opaque God materially and spiritually accessible. Rather than abolishing divine performance, Herrick assumes the direction of it in the closing Crucifixion poems of *His Noble Numbers*.

***

In what is probably the most well-known devotional lyric of *His Noble Numbers*, Herrick casts the Crucifixion as a public stage play, with Christ as the lead actor. In "*Good Friday*: Rex Tragicus, *or Christ going to His Crosse*" (N1393), Herrick imagines speaking with Christ as he faces his executioners during the moments before his death. But in searching for causes for Christ's present plight, Herrick casts blame upon the unfeeling bystanders who gape and gawk at the sufferings of Christ: "Long before this, the base, the dull, the rude, / Th'inconstant, and unpurged Multitude / Yawne for Thy coming" (N1393.5–7). Here Herrick's antipathy for the "unpurged Multitude" is reminiscent of his disdain in "The Wake" for the "incurious Villages," who gape at the "strutting" players, "base in actions as in clothes." In "Good Friday," the audience regards the Passion performance as if it were a cheap stage play, alternately yawning and bickering among themselves in a running commentary upon the lead actor's part: "some e're this time crie, / How he Deferres, how loath He is to die" (N1393.7–8). Like spectators who interrupt the theatrical performance, the crowd—"this scumme," "the Skurfe," and the "Bran"—join voices with Christ's torturers, taunting him as he makes his way to the place of execution:

> Among this scumme, the Souldier, with his speare,
> And the sowre Fellow, with his *vineger*,
> His *spunge*, and *stick*, do ask why Thou dost stay?
> So do the *Skurfe* and *Bran* too: Go thy way,
> Thy way, Thou guiltlesse man, and satisfie
> By Thine approach, each their beholding eye.
>
> (N1393.9–14)

Unexpectedly, Herrick joins in on the crowd's challenge to Christ: "Go thy way, / Thy way, Thou guiltlesse man." Somewhere in the address to Christ, the crowd's derision becomes elided with Herrick's own private address to Christ. At its outset, the sentence is spoken by the multitude; by its end, it is spoken by Herrick, who has taken it upon himself to commandeer the Passion performance. As in his criticism of the wake performances in *Hesperides*, here Herrick takes issue not with all ceremonies but with badly performed ones. Under his direction, the Passion performance—which has until now provoked only jeers—promises to "satisfie /

HERRICK'S PLAYERS AND PRAYERS   111

By Thine approach, each their beholding eye." In making his artistic intervention, Herrick objects to Christ's bad acting of his part: "No, no, this Scene from Thee takes life and sense, / And soule and spirit, plot, and excellence" (N1393.26–7). According to Herrick's interjection, the present rendition of the stage play is not just a spiritual travesty against "soul and spirit" but also an aesthetic violation of "plot" and poetic "excellence." For the performance to have its intended effect upon its viewers, Christ must "keep / The Lawes of Action" (N1393.37)—that is, the dramatic unities required for *katharsis*.[76]

At this point in the poem, Herrick assumes responsibility for the direction of the stage play. In his set directions, he outlines the theatrical parameters of Christ's performance:

> The *Crosse* shall be Thy *Stage*; and Thou shalt there
> The spacious field have for Thy *Theater*.
> Thou art that *Roscius*, and that markt-out man,
> That must this day act the Tragedian,
> To wonder and affrightment.
> ...
> Why then begin, great King! ascend Thy Throne,
> And thence proceed, to act Thy Passion
> To such a height, to such a period raised.
>
> (N1393.17–21, 28–30)

Under Herrick's creative direction, a skillful performance might reverse the negative effects of the theater, turning the multitude's taunts to "wonder and affrightment." Herrick regards Christ's performance in "Good Friday" much as Cicero did in praising the professional Roscius, according to Prynne's retelling of the account: "Did not their Cicero when as he commended one Roscius a stage-player, say, that he was so skillful, that he only was worthy to come upon the stage: that he was so good a man, that he only was worthy not to come upon it?"[77] Like Cicero's Roscius, Herrick's Christ is such a superlative actor that his skill almost seems to undercut the performance itself. Indeed, Herrick contrasts Christ's art with that of the two criminals slated for executed alongside him—"those poor Theeves that act their parts with Thee: / Those act without regard" (N1393.23–4). At this point in the poem, the Passion play almost seems to undo its theatrical medium, as Christ's skillful performance shows the imperfections of the performance itself.

Herrick's re-enactment of the Crucifixion threatens to dismantle the very medium demarcating the boundaries between theatrical fiction and reality. The unpurged multitude, by their very disengagement and dumb participation in the divine performance, undergo spiritual transformation—not just within the parameters of theater but for all eternity: "those, who see Thee nail'd unto the Tree, /

---

[76] See Aristotle, *Poetics*, in *The Basics Works of Aristotle*, ed. Richard McKeon (New York: Modern Library/Random House, 2001), 1449b21–8.

[77] Prynne, *Histrio-mastix*, 525.

112 DEVOTIONAL EXPERIENCE IN THE REFORMATION

May (though they scorn Thee) praise and pitie Thee" (N1393.34–5). The scorn and yawns of the minor players morph into pity and praise. Not only does Herrick's Passion play undo its own theatrical parameters mid-performance; by the end of the play, his actors have dropped their initial roles. The haphazardness of the poem's theatrical conceit has puzzled Herrick's readers. Roger B. Rollin, for example, has doubted the effectiveness of the poetic conceit of "Good Friday," writing that the devotional success of the Passion poem is debatable: "it may be regarded as at best incongruous and at worst blasphemous."[78] But the incongruity of the theatrical conceit is what lends it its devotional power. "Good Friday" explores the implications of this claim about the power of theater, borrowing from antitheatricalist critiques of performance while simultaneously undermining their validity.

While readers of Herrick's Passion poems have noted the theatrical import of the pieces, none have pointed to the way in which the religious theatrics of these poems provide the foundation for Herrick's particular vision of devotional intimacy with God. In fact, among critics, there has been a tendency to do the opposite, to associate the theatrical valences of Herrick's Passion poems with frivolity—as if modern readers of the poems had internalized an antitheatrical wariness of performance. Marcus, in her reading of the closing poems of *His Noble Numbers*, asserts that "even these poems curiously reduce the emotionally-charged events they purport to commemorate: the Nativity becomes a glorified birthday party, and the Crucifixion a stage play performed to the astonishment of its spectators."[79] But despite his own wariness of performance, Herrick understood devotional intimacy in decidedly theatrical terms. In a companion poem to "Good Friday," an unnamed poem formatted in the shape of a cross (N1398), Herrick once more describes the Crucifixion in theatrical terms, casting himself as stage director of the performance. Imagining himself at the scene of the Crucifixion, Herrick hastens to make preparations for Christ's death as if his execution were a public stage play:

---

[78] Rollin, "Missing the Hock-Cart," 156.

[79] Marcus, "Herrick's *Noble Numbers*," 108–9, 121–2. Graham Parry and Alistair Fowler note the theatrical import of "Good Friday," and Starkman notes the poem's liturgical elements. See Graham Parry, *The Arts of the Anglican Counter-Reformation: Glory, Laud and Honour* (Woodbridge: Boydell, 2006), 148–9; Alistair Fowler, "Robert Herrick" (Warton Lecture on English Poetry, 23 October, 1980), in *Proceedings of the British Academy*, vol. 66 (1980), (London: Oxford University Press, 1982), 262; and Starkman, "*Noble Numbers*," 11. Corns reads the theatrics of the poem in terms of Herrick's poetics, reading the poem's performative dimension as an expression of Herrick's "anguished royalism in the miserable 1640s." See Corns, *Uncloistered Virtue*, 127. Deming comes to the opposite conclusion in his book-length study on the ceremonialism of Herrick's poems, in his assertion that *His Noble Numbers* as a whole is not overly ceremonious relative to the more ceremonial secular lyrics of *Hesperides*. See Deming, *Ceremony and Art*, 78.

This Croſſe-Tree here
Doth JESUS beare,
Who ſweet'ned firſt,
The Death accurs't.

HEre all things ready are,make haſt,make haſt away;
For,long this work wil be, & very ſhort this Day.
Why then, go on to act : Here's wonders to be done,
Before the laſt leaſt ſand of Thy ninth houre be run ;
Or e're dark Clouds do dull,or dead the Mid-dayes Sun.

Act when Thou wilt ,
Bloud will be ſpilt ;
Pure Balm, that ſhall
Bring Health to All.
Why then , Begin
To powre firſt in
Some Drops of Wine,
In ſtead of Brine ,
To ſearch the Wound,
So long unſound :
And,when that's done,
Let Oyle, next , run,
To cure the Sore
Sinne made before.
And O! Deare Chriſt,
E'en as Thou di'ſt,
Look down , and ſee
Us weepe for Thee.
And tho(Love knows)
Thy dreadfull Woes
Wee cannot eaſe ;
Yet doe Thou pleaſe,
Who Mercie art ,
T'accept each Heart,
That gladly would
Helpe , if it could.
Meane while, let mee,
Beneath this Tree ,
This Honour have ,
To make my grave.

To

Figure 3.2 An unnamed shape poem from *His Noble Numbers*, formatted in the image of the Cross. London: Printed for John Williams and Francis Eglesfield, 1648. Copy from the Henry E. Huntington Library.

114   DEVOTIONAL EXPERIENCE IN THE REFORMATION

> Why then, go on to act: Here's wonders to be done,
> Before the last least sand of Thy ninth houre be run;
> Or e're dark Clouds do dull, or dead the Mid-dayes Sun.
>
> (N1398.7–9)

Herrick's primary concern is one of aesthetics; here Christ's act is constrained by matters of weather and lighting—as would have been the case in early modern outdoor theaters such as The Globe, which began productions in the early afternoon and relied on the day's shifting light to set the scene.[80] The shape poem consists of a tightly blocked stage performance with Christ's every dying moment scripted and accounted for, and its description of Christ's execution is presented as a list of stage directions, written for Christ's part: "Act when Thou wilt" (10), "Why then Begin" (14), "And, when that's done, / Let Oyle, next, run" (20–1), and "Look down, and see / Us weep for Thee" (26–7). Herrick's Crucifixion poems make clear that despite his skepticism of ceremonial performance, he made exceptions if the performances were aesthetically well-constructed—if they had poetic gravitas and poise.

In matters of ceremony and ritual, Herrick gave special license to poets and their art, going so far as to insinuate himself into the performance as director, actor, and spectator. Despite his wariness of performances, Herrick could not stop himself from participating in them. Indeed, these performances were foundational to Herrick's peculiar vision of devotional access, both erotic and spiritual. In the unnamed cross poem, the poem's theatrics afford Herrick intimate access to Christ's body. In writing out the part of Christ's tormenter—imagined in "Good Friday" as "that sowre Fellow, with his *vineger*, / His *spunge*, and stick" (N1397.10–11)—Herrick replaces the vinegar with "Some Drops of Wine, / Instead of Brine, / To search the Wound, / So long unsound" (N1398.16–19). In what appears at first to be a minor rewriting of the Passion story, Herrick swaps out Christ's brine for wine—replacing the rancid drink that Christ's crucifiers mockingly offer to him when forcing him to drink from the vinegar-soaked sponge.[81] Christ emerges here as what Richard Rambuss, in his treatment of Crashaw's verse, has called, "the form of Jesus *in extremis*, as an iconic male body rendered visible and open to desire."[82] Just as the visual shape of Herrick's poem highlights the sensory aspects of Christ's bodily form, so too does his retelling of the Crucifixion render Christ's body open to observers, his interior made accessible—with probes, sounds, and sticks.

---

[80] For a discussion on the use of daylight in both outdoor and indoor early modern English commercial theaters, see Martin White, "'When Torchlight Made an Artificial Noon': Lightness and Darkness in the Indoor Jacobean Theatre," in *The Oxford Companion to Shakespeare*, eds. Andrew Gurr and Farah Karim-Cooper (Oxford: Oxford University Press, 2014), 115–136, esp. 116–18.

[81] See Matthew 27:46; Mark 15:36; Luke 23:36; and John 19:29–30. See also Psalms 69:21.

[82] Richard Rambuss, *Closet Devotions* (Durham, NC: Duke University Press, 1998), 34. See also Richard Rambuss, "Pleasure and Devotion: The Body of Jesus and Seventeenth-Century Lyric," in *Queering the Renaissance*, ed. Jonathan Goldberg (Durham, NC: Duke University Press, 1994), 253–79.

Although the lines begin as stage directions to Christ, their intended addressee seems to shift as the poem progresses. Ultimately, the lines read like Herrick's private instructions to himself. What begins as a public performance at the opening of the poem becomes, by the end of it, an intimate negotiation between Herrick and Christ.

Much like Herrick's ceremonial Christmas and Candlemas poems, the Crucifixion poems of *His Noble Numbers* constitute private ceremonies, ones that take place not as part of but in spite of the public spectacle. Christ isn't meant to drink the wine; instead, Herrick himself pours the wine into Christ's open wounds. In pouring the wine—with its dual medicinal and sacramental functions—into the open body of Christ, Herrick describes a curative effect on the wound, until now left untreated ("so long unsound"). But the line also suggests Herrick's desire to probe Christ's body itself, to penetrate and to sound the interior of his body. In Herrick's rewritten Passion performance, Herrick gains access to the innermost parts of Christ's being.

In both his erotic and religious poems, Herrick remained wary of public devotional performances. But what is clear is that Herrick—like John Donne, as I will demonstrate in Chapter 4—saw himself as the erotic and spiritual exception to the norm. As a spectator of performances and a director of them, Herrick believed that the dangers these spectacles posed to others had little bearing on himself. In this sense, Herrick's stance on performance hardly seems different from that of the antitheatricalists, who despite their vehement criticism of public spectacle both religious and secular often made exceptions for some performances, under the right circumstances. Indeed, Herrick's poems capture Gosson's view that the very best plays may have their value for a select few, provided that they were not used as mass entertainment: "These plays are good plays and sweet plays, and of all plays the best plays and most to be liked, worthy to be song of the Muses, or set out with the cunning of Roscius himself, yet are they not fit for every man's diet: neither ought they commonly to be shows. Plays are not to be made common."[83] And even for their ideal and select audience, Prynne thought plays were best read instead of performed, admitting that it could be "lawful to *read* plays or comedies now and then for recreation sake."[84] Likewise, in that they are poems, Herrick's erotic and devotional performances are meant to be read—not performed. Much like Shakespeare's *Sonnets*, Herrick's lyric medium at once captures the performative

---

[83] Gosson, *Schoole of Abuse*, unnumbered page. (*EEBO*, document image 23)
[84] Prynne, *Histrio-mastix*, 98, emphasis added.

116 DEVOTIONAL EXPERIENCE IN THE REFORMATION

aspects of drama while insisting upon the reader's participatory and individual engagement with the devotional aspects of the poems.

**

What the Holy Communion rites could do for the soul, Herrick posited that his poetry could do for his reader. His cross poem offers a lyric equivalent of the spiritual oneness afforded by the Communion rites, which Joseph Hall described as a process by which the souls of the communicants "receive the flesh, and blood of Christ" and are made "partakers of his most blessed body and blood."[85] In line with the majority of mainstream Reformed clerics, who adhered to a Calvinist-inspired view of sacramental worship, Hall did not ascribe any inherent devotional power to ceremonial performance. For him, like both Hooker and Perkins, the sacraments were valuable only as signs and remembrances.[86] For Hall, the Holy Communion rites were devotionally useful solely as indicators of a prior grace: "If therefore we shall look upon and take these sacred elements as the pledges of our Savior's love to us, and remembrances of his death for us, we shall not need, neither indeed can we require by the judgment of our Church to set any other value on them."[87] Because the sacramental performances were just one sign among many of an inward grace, Hall reasoned that their devotional potential could be replicated in any number of informal, everyday occasions. The communicant did not ingest the body of God only during the sacramental rites, for the reason that "every simple act of our faith feeds on Christ."[88] For Hall, ceremonial practice and extemporal devotion were two manifestations of the same spiritual practice.

Hall's insistence on the devotional potential that inhered in simple acts of faith, ordinary objects, and daily occasions, did not undercut his views on the value of formal ceremonies and rites. On the contrary, his insistence on informal devotional worship offered a justification for ceremonial performance, for the reason that the prior devotional affect cultivated by private devotion had the potential to spiritually animate set worship. As McCabe describes Hall's practical divinity, his extemporal devotion "quickens the spirit of formal rituals and ceremonies by rendering them spiritually meaningful."[89] Indeed, despite his adherence to Calvinist principles, Hall remained a strong defender of ecclesiastical polity. He saw the

---

[85] Joseph Hall, *A Plain and Familiar Explication of Christ's Presence in the Sacrament of His Body and Blood, out of the Doctrine of the Church of England for the Satisfying of a Scrupulous Friend* (1631), in *The Shaking of the Olive-Tree. The Remaining Works of that Incomparable Prelate Joseph Hall, D. D. Late Lord Bishop of Norwich. With Some Specialties of Divine Providence in His Life. Noted by His own Hand. Together with His Hard Measure: VVritten also by Himself* (London: Printed by J. Cadwel for J. Crooke, at the *Ship* in S. Pauls Church-Yard, 1660), 292. (*EEBO*, Wing (2nd ed.) / H416.) Reproduction from the British Library.

[86] See Chapter 1 for my discussion on Hooker and Perkins's shared views on Reformed sacramental practice.

[87] Hall, *Plain and Familiar Explication*, 291.

[88] Hall, *Plain and Familiar Explication*, 775.

[89] McCabe, *A Study in Satire*, 175.

HERRICK'S PLAYERS AND PRAYERS   117

value in prescribed prayer and the liturgy, and he vigorously opposed the Puritan practice of spontaneous preaching.[90] McCabe has argued that Hall's defense of prescribed forms of worship was crucial for his defense of his own method of extemporal meditation, which sought to arouse devotion through an artful construction of set mediations—much like the set liturgies and common prayers of the state church.[91] In short, Hall defended ceremonial worship in order to ensure that he could amplify its devotional effects to include all simple acts of faith and the things of the world around him.

In his poems, Herrick subscribes to a similar reformist view of ecclesiastical worship—open to formal ceremonies and rites, while denying them any inherent devotional power. Several early poems in *His Noble Numbers* celebrate the devotional potential of prescribed prayer ("A prayer, that is said alone, / Starves, having no companion" ["Prayer," N1288.1–2]), while also criticizing unpoised, spontaneous praise ("God He rejects all Prayers that are sleight, / And want their Poise: words ought to have their weight" ["Prayers must have Poise," N1146.1–2]). At the same time, elsewhere in *His Noble Numbers*, Herrick remains adamant that the externals of ceremonial worship—here embodied by the offering of the sacrificial calf—lack efficacy when performed without appropriate devotional affect:

> In the old Scripture I have often read,
> The calfe without meale n'ere was offered;
> To figure to us, nothing more then this,
> Without the heart, lip-labour nothing is.
>
> ("Lip-labour," N1164.1–4)

> In Prayer the Lips ne're act the winning part,
> Without the sweet concurrence of the Heart.
>
> ("The Heart," N1165.1–2)

These early, shorter poems of *His Noble Numbers* provide straightforward articulations of the reformist view of ceremonial performance that Herrick would return to later in the sequence in the paired Crucifixion poems. The Crucifixion poems describe Herrick's disruption of the Passion performances, even as he salvages scenes of the Passion into his own individual devotional ceremony with Christ. The poems' private devotional performances are valuable as outward confirmations of a prior devotional affect. In the untitled cross poem, Herrick asks Christ to look down at him from his position on the Cross, and to acknowledge the devotional affect that animates his outward performance of devotion: "accept each

---

[90] McCabe, *A Study in Satire*, 173.
[91] McCabe, *A Study in Satire*, 174. In much of his devotional writing, Hall intentionally modeled his prose style on the authoritative English of the King James Version of the bible and on the ceremonial language of the *Book of Common Prayer*. See McCabe, *A Study in Satire*, 202.

118   DEVOTIONAL EXPERIENCE IN THE REFORMATION

Heart, / That gladly would / Helpe, if it could" (N1398.33–5). For Herrick, the poem's Passion performance is but outward evidence of that which lies within, what Herrick calls "the sweet concurrence of the Heart."

Much like the majority of reform-minded clerics in the Church of England, Herrick regarded the devotional ceremonies of the state church with reservation, and his poems often contained echoes of the antitheatrical sentiments of religious radicals such as Prynne. But what is clear is that even as Herrick remained skeptical of ceremonial performance in many poems of *Hesperides* and *His Noble Numbers*, he so often ended up participating in those ceremonies—even as he sought to question or dismantle them. In *His Noble Numbers*, Herrick seems to intentionally make it difficult for his readers to distinguish the devotional performance from his critique of that performance. The poems reveal the near impossibility of participating in the debate about religious performance without inadvertently replicating the parameters and structures of performance.

Herrick's treatment of ceremonies in *Hesperides* and *His Noble Numbers* traffics in arguments from both sides of the early modern debate about devotional performance. His poems appropriate a range of contemporary arguments about performance in an effort to poetically imagine a materialist vision of devotional intimacy, both with women and with Christ. In doing so, Herrick presents a view of devotional access that astonishes precisely in its refusal to abide by the polemical positions of either the defenders or detractors of ceremonial and theatrical performance.[92] The result is a collection that, *in toto*, assumes a position on performance that remains decidedly ambiguous—one that undermines attempts to describe these poems in terms of a single political or religious ideological camp. As he put it in one of his autobiographical poems, "I am Sive-like, and can hold / Nothing hot, or nothing cold. .../ What comes in, runnes quickly out: ... / *Herrick* keeps, as holds nothing" ("Upon himselfe," H285.1–2, 6, 12). Although Herrick was neither a Laudian nor a straightforward ceremonialist, the devotional performances of *Hesperides* and *His Noble Numbers* show his openness to a particular kind of individual and imaginative ceremony, which borrowed from ecclesiastical polity as much as it did from techniques of private devotion. *Hesperides* and *His Noble Numbers* capture the range of confessional viewpoints that were available to English Protestants during the three decades spanning Herrick's poetic career, and remind us that ascertaining the religious allegiances of those who lived during the first decades of the seventeenth century is rarely a straightforward task.

---

[92] David Scott Kastan, for example, points out that the positions on ceremonial and theatrical performance were hardly clear cut. While Puritans were an uncontested majority in the antitheatricalist camp, that camp also included those like Laud, who himself worked to prevent the reopening of the theaters in 1637. See David Scott Kastan, "Performances and Playbooks: The Closing of the Theatres and the Politics of Drama," in *Reading, Society and Politics in Early Modern England*, eds. Kevin Sharpe and Steven N. Zwicker (Cambridge: Cambridge University Press, 2003), 167–84, esp. 168–9.

PART II
IMAGES, IDOLATRY, AND ICONOCLASM

4

Donne's Speaking, Weeping, Bleeding Images

Iconophobia and Iconophilia in the *Holy Sonnets* and the Sermons

The act of looking at God put Donne ill at ease, and he confessed as much before his congregation at St. Paul's Cathedral in a sermon on the dangers of images, which he delivered to an open-air audience on May 6, 1627. Before his congregants, Donne condemned those who sought "to make images of *God* who was never seen, and to make those images of God, *very gods*; to make their images do daily miracles; to transfer the honor due to God, to the image, and then to encumber themselves with such ridiculous riddles, and scornful distinctions, as they do, for justifying unjustifiable, unexcusable, uncolorable enormities."[1] According to Donne, perhaps the most insidious forms of idolatry were committed by people who sought to attribute lifelike powers and properties to inert images—even if those images were only intended to render the likeness of decidedly mortal beings. These idolaters, mired in the "pernicious errors" of the Roman Catholic Church, aspired to "make images of *men*, which never were." But above all, these idolaters desired to make their images—as if they possessed real presences and real bodies—do no less than "*speak*, and *move*, and *weep*, and *bleed*."[2] "*Vae idololatris*"—woe to the idolaters—"woe to such advancers of Images, as would throw down Christ rather than his Image."[3]

Despite his condemnation of idolaters, Donne remained conflicted on the issue of what role images should play in proper devotional practice. In the same sermon, he criticizes not just the idolaters but also the virulent iconoclasts: "But *Vae Iconoclastis* too, woe to such peremptory abhorrers of Pictures ... as had rather throw down a Church, then let a Picture stand."[4] Four years before delivering his sermon, during a bout of serious illness in 1623, Donne reflected privately upon the debate

---

[1] John Donne, Sermon 17, in *Sermons*, eds. Evelyn Mary Spearing Simpson and George Reuben Potter, 10 vols. (Berkeley: University of California Press, 1953–62), 7:432–3. Since Donne's sermons are preserved across ten manuscripts, I have chosen to work from Simpson and Potter's edition, which is the only complete edition of Donne's sermons at the time of writing. A new edition of Donne's sermons, under the auspices of the Oxford Centre for Early Modern Studies, is currently in its beginning stages.

[2] Donne, Sermon 17, in *Sermons*, 7:432.

[3] Donne, Sermon 17, in *Sermons*, 7:433.

[4] Donne, Sermon 17, in *Sermons*, 7:433.

Devotional experience and erotic knowledge in the literary culture of the English Reformation. Rhema Hokama, Oxford University Press. © Rhema Hokama (2023). DOI: 10.1093/oso/9780192886552.003.0005

122   DEVOTIONAL EXPERIENCE IN THE REFORMATION

over religious images in his *Devotions upon Emergent Occasions*. In Expostulation 16, he acknowledged that the best forms of worship did not rely on images at all. In his direct address to God, Donne asserted: "I know I cannot have any better image of thee than thy Son, nor any better of image of him than his Gospels." And yet Donne insisted that despite this knowledge, his affinity with God had often been strongest when gazing upon Christ's visual likeness: "yet must not I, with thanks confess to thee, that some historical pictures of his have sometimes put me upon better *Meditations* than otherwise I should have fallen upon?" These images, Donne maintained, remain valuable precisely because they "work upon the affections of natural men," visually stirring an individual to devotion.[5] During his tenure as a cleric in the Church of England, Donne wavered on his stance about religious images, acknowledging their devotional uses as well as their spiritual hazards. Indeed, Donne's sermon and his *Devotions* echo the theological uncertainty of his third satire: "To'adore, or scorne an Image, or protest, / May all be bad."[6]

By the time Donne entered the priesthood in 1615, he entered a state church that was committed to a forty-year-long position against image-based worship.[7] In 1571, Bishop John Jewel posed the hypothetical question in his *Homilie against perill of idolatrie*: "to whom then will ye then make God like?"[8] The question is, of course, a rhetorical one. According to Jewel, no icon, image, or bodily presence can approximate God's true nature. So thorough was the English church's crackdown against images that even those images that existed nowhere but in the mind were likewise causes for suspicion. Indeed, the church posited that interior idols were as dangerous, if not more so, than external ones. The third section of the *Homilie against idolatrie* launches an attack on what Jewel called idolatry that "standeth chiefly in the mind." Such idolaters, the *Homilie* maintains, "use the same outward rites and manner of honoring and worshipping their images, as the gentiles did

---

[5] John Donne, *Devotions upon Emergent Occasions*, ed. John Sparrow (Cambridge: Cambridge University Press, 1923), 95.

[6] John Donne, "Satyre 3" (original version), in *The Variorum Edition of the Poetry of John Donne*, ed. Gary A. Stringer, vol. 3, *The Satyres* (Bloomington: Indiana University Press, 2016), lines 76–7.

[7] That the Church of England had become solidly Genevan by the end of the sixteenth century and remained so well into the middle of the seventeenth is an argument whose primary contenders are Patrick Collinson and Nicholas Tyacke, who maintain that both the clergy and the educated laity within the Reformed church were united by a shared religious outlook that was primarily Calvinistic in its sympathies. See Patrick Collinson, *The Religion of Protestants: The Church in English Society 1559–1625* (Oxford: Clarendon Press, 1982); Nicholas Tyacke, "Puritanism, Armininism and Counter-Revolution," in *The Origins of the English Civil War*, ed. Conrad Russell (London: Palgrave Macmillan, 1978 [1973]); Nicholas Tyacke, *Anti-Calvinists: The Rise of English Arminianism, c. 1590–1640* (Oxford: Clarendon Press, 1990 [1987]); and Nicholas Tyacke, "Anglican Attitudes: Some Recent Writings on English Religious History, from the Reformation to the Civil War," *Journal of British Studies* 35, no. 2 (1996): 139–67.

[8] John Jewel, "An Homilie against *perill of idolatrie*, and *superfluous* decking of Churches," in *The second tome of homilees of such matters as were promised, and intituled in the former part of homilees* (Imprinted at London: In Poules Churchyarde, by Richarde Iugge, and Iohn Cawood, printers to the Queenes Maiestie, 1571), 35. (*EEBO*, STC (2nd ed.) / 13669, document image 18.) I cite subsequent references to the *Homilie* by page number.

DONNE'S SPEAKING IMAGES 123

use before their idols, and that therefore they commit idolatry, as well inwardly and outwardly, as did the wicked Gentiles idolaters."[9] Jewel echoes the Calvinist position that even one's thoughts could imperil one in spiritual dangers akin to those posed by material idols and visual images. In the *Institutio*, Calvin points to the dangers risked by those who seek God's likeness, albeit only in their mind:

> When ... we are in a manner forced to the contemplation of God ... we immediately fly off to carnal dreams and depraved fictions, and so by our vanity corrupt heavenly truth. ... [W]e substitute monstrous fictions for the one living and true God. ... Every individual mind being a kind of labyrinth of fictions, but that almost every man has had his own god.[10]

The potential to cultivate inner images meant that each individual was required to undertake a policy of inward iconoclasm. "Everyone was therefore under the obligation to deal with his own imagery, to act the iconoclast on the idol-processes of the mind," Margaret Aston writes in her sweeping study on English religious iconoclasm. "It was not enough to turn away from the objects made by cunning craftsmen set up in popish places. The destroying must burn within, in the 'house' of the imagination."[11]

---

[9] Jewel, "Homilie against *perill of idolatrie*," 98. Although he does not mention the English theological tradition in his transhistorical discussion of Western culture's wariness of images, W. J. T. Mitchell succinctly describes the iconoclastic impulse toward mental images in his study of verbal and visual representations: "In this scenario of intellectual history, the worship of graven images in the dark groves and caves of heathen superstition has given way to a superstitious belief in the power of graven mental images that reside in the dark cave of the skull." See W. J. T. Mitchell, *Iconology: Image, Text, Ideology* (Chicago: University of Chicago, 1986), 165.

[10] John Calvin, *Institutes of the Christian Religion: 1536 Edition*, trans. Ford Lewis Battles (Grand Rapids, MI: Eerdmans, 1986 [1975]), 1.5.11–12. I have chosen to work from a modern translation of Calvin's original Latin edition rather than from Thomas Norton's sixteenth-century English translation due to Norton's idiosyncratic use of terms that will no longer be familiar to modern-day readers. For example, Norton uses the term "godhead" instead of "image" or "idol" to refer to a number of false representations of the true God. Norton's descriptions of false worship practices, however strange to modern readers, suggest that English Protestants in the 1570s were still struggling to find a vocabulary to distinguish between the recusant and the orthodox.

The difficulty of fully eradicating idolatry, Calvin surmised in his treatise on church reform, stems from the fact that every idolater becomes enamored by the phantasms imparted by his or her own brain. These private idols are consequently more alluring and dangerous than those constructed *en masse* and for public consumption: "I am not unaware how difficult it is to persuade the world that God rejects and even abominates every thing related to this worship that is devised by human reason. The delusion on this head is owing to several causes—'Every one thinks highly of his own,' as the old proverb expresses it. Hence the offspring of our own brain delights us." See John Calvin, "The Necessity of Reforming the Church Presented to the Imperial Diet at Spires, A.D. 1544, in the name of all who wish Christ to reign," in *John Calvin: Tracts and Treatises*, trans. Henry Beveridge (Grand Rapids, MI: Eerdmans, 1959), 1:153.

[11] Margaret Aston, *England's Iconoclasts: Laws against Images* (Oxford: Clarendon Press, 1988), 460. James Simpson argues that the religious suppression of idols spread beyond the defacement and destruction of physical icons as it came to encompass any action or doctrine that was perceived to lack scriptural backing: "Repression of idolatry ... required internal, psychic regulation even more pressingly than external iconoclasm. The problem is much wider and deeper than physical iconoclasm can

124   DEVOTIONAL EXPERIENCE IN THE REFORMATION

In 1591, twenty years after the publication of the *Homilie against idolatrie* and around the time when Donne was writing his satires, the Reformed cleric William Perkins published a tract that reiterated Jewel's attack on image-based devotion. Part theological tract, part how-to devotional manual, *A Golden Chaine* single-handedly vaulted Perkins to pastoral stardom during the early decades of the seventeenth century. During the next sixty years, Perkins's works outsold Shakespeare's by a margin of two to one.[12] In the tract, Perkins argued that making and worshipping images depicting even the true God implicated one in idolatry: "If any man reply, that they worship not the image, but God in the image: let him know that the creature cannot comprehend the image of the creator, and if it could, yet God would not be worshipped in it, because it is a dead thing."[13] For Perkins, it did not matter whether an individual's devotional intentions were directed toward the true God; to use imagistic aids in those devotional entreaties was enough to make a worshipper guilty of idolatry.

Perkins's iconoclasm was thorough, sparing not even the images that only existed in the mind: "All relics, and monuments of idols: for these, after the idols themselves are once abolished, must be razed out of all memory."[14] But the peculiarity of Perkins's theology was that its iconophobia was bound up with an equally powerful iconophilia. While Perkins undeniably denigrated the senses and all material and mental depictions of God, paradoxically, he also promoted the possibility that those images might be preserved—if not in the material world then in the mind, enhanced and enabled by the outward senses: "The more obscure manifestation, is the vision of God's majesty in this life, by the eyes of the mind, through the help of things perceived by the outward senses."[15] Although Perkins insisted that images of even the true God were idols, and that all images of idols—even the memory of them—must be razed, he nevertheless remained committed to the belief that vision and the senses can and ought to play a role in fostering intimacy with God. Perkins was no lover of images, but he did acknowledge that the problem they posed affected not just idolaters but all sensing beings. The central barrier to proper devotion, Perkins maintained, was that human beings

address, since idolatry now encompasses all humanly-constructed figments and imaginations, including *false doctrine*." I am grateful to Simpson for generously sharing a written version of his "Evangelical Absolutism: Breaking the Mind's Images in the English Reformation" (Distinguished Fellow Lecture, Huntington Library, Pasadena, CA, March 17, 2014).

[12] In a discussion of the reading and print cultures of early seventeenth-century England, Kari Konkola argues that Perkins's widespread popularity reflected a reading population in England and the Continent that was keen to read theological works—even more so than literary ones. See Kari Konkola, "'People of the Book': The Production of Theological Texts in Early Modern England," *The Papers of the Bibliographical Society of America* 94 (2000): 5–34.

[13] William Perkins, *A Golden Chaine, or the description of theologie containing the order of the causes of saluation and damnation, according to Gods woord* (London: Printed by Edward Alde and are to be sold by Edward White at the little north doore of S Paules Church at the signe of the Gunne, 1591), unpaginated. (*EEBO*, STC (2nd ed.) / 19657, document image 46.)

[14] Perkins, *Golden Chaine*, unpaginated. (*EEBO*, document image 48.)

[15] Perkins, *Golden Chaine*, unpaginated. (*EEBO*, document image 7.)

DONNE'S SPEAKING IMAGES   125

could perceive an inherently imperceptible God through no other means than our external senses: "we in honor of the invisible God, are accustomed to adore visible images," he conceded.[16] In doing so, Perkins articulated the distinctly Reformed anxiety that the devotional hindrances posed by images were not so much remnants of Catholicism, but rather an epistemological condition common to all worshippers.

Substantial prior scholarly work has positioned Donne's literary output as evidence either of his crypto-Catholicism or of his proto-Laudian sentiment. In the former vein, scholars such as John Carey and R. V. Young have argued that Donne's poetry shows his attachment to his former Catholic religion, and that even after his conversion to the Church of England's variety of Protestantism, Donne never really gave up his Catholic outlook. The latter view of Donne's theological attachments, spearheaded by Achsah Guibbory, posits that Donne adopted what might be called an "Anglican" stance on episcopal polity; in this sense, his literature and sermons might be best understood through the ecclesiology of William Laud, Lancelot Andrewes, and Richard Montagu.[17] Donne's was an absorptive mind, and I have written elsewhere about the intellectual delight that he took in straddling theological boundaries and muddling confessional identity in his earlier elegies and satires.[18] For a mind as expansive as Donne's, there is no doubt that aspects of his poetry—even his later devotional writings such as the *Holy Sonnets* and his sermons—continued to pay homage to his Catholic roots and perhaps resonated with the theological movements that would eventually become High Church Anglicanism. However, to read Donne's poetry solely in these theological terms is to miss the major reformist thrust of his poems. I maintain that we need not read Donne as anything other than what he himself professed to be: a committed Reformed Protestant in the most orthodox sense—one whose views

[16] Perkins, *Golden Chaine*, unpaginated. (*EEBO*, document image 46.)

[17] Both John Carey and R. V. Young read into Donne's Calvinism the resurgent desires and impulses of his Catholic past. See John Carey, *John Donne: Life, Mind, and Art* (New York: Oxford University Press, 1980), 3; R. V. Young, *Doctrine and Devotion in Seventeenth-Century Poetry: Studies in Donne, Herbert, Crashaw, and Vaughan* (Woodbridge: Boydell and Brewer, 2000), 28–9. Achsah Guibbory has argued that Donne subscribed to religious sympathies aligned with the views of Laudians like Richard Montagu, in order to accommodate elements of the Catholic Church into Protestant worship. See Achsah Guibbory, "Donne's Religion: Montague, Arminianism and Donne's Sermons, 1624–1630," *English Literary Renaissance* 31, no. 3 (2001): 412–39.
For critics who have read Donne's theological stance as contrarian, unorthodox, or conflicted, see Jeanne Shami, "Political Advice in Donne's *Devotions*: No Man Is an Island," *Modern Language Quarterly* 50 (1989): 337–56; Annabel Patterson, *Censorship and Interpretation: The Conditions of Writing and Reading in Early Modern England* (Madison, WI: University of Wisconsin Press, 1984), 92–105; David Norbrook, "The Monarchy of Wit and the Republic of Letters: Donne's Politics," in *Soliciting Interpretation: Literary Theory and Seventeenth-Century English Poetry*, eds. Elizabeth D. Harvey and Katharine Eisaman Maus (Chicago: University of Chicago Press, 1990), 3–36; and Richard Strier, "Donne and the Politics of Devotion," in *Religion, Literature, and Politics in Post-Reformation England, 1540–1688*, eds. Donna B. Hamilton and Richard Strier (Cambridge: Cambridge University Press, 1996), 93–114.

[18] Rhema Hokama, "'Loves halowed temple': Erotic sacramentalism and reformed devotion in John Donne's 'To his Mistress going to bed,'" *Modern Philology* 119, no. 2 (2021): 248–75.

126   DEVOTIONAL EXPERIENCE IN THE REFORMATION

on the use of images in performed worship would have resonated with committed Calvinists like Perkins. Donne imagined his own Reformed Christianity as an orthodox Christianity, one that assented to the anti-Arminian sentiment of the Jacobean Church of England.[19] As Debora Kuller Shuger has rightfully argued, "Donne is not an eccentric convert but in many ways representative of the mainstream of English Reformation theology ... his theology is characteristic of the 'High Church Calvinism.'"[20]

Yet readers of Donne who acknowledge the Calvinist commitments of the *Holy Sonnets* have nevertheless interpreted the poems' devotional prevarications as evidence of Donne's inability to fully endorse Reformation doctrine. Most prominently, Richard Strier has suggested that "the pain and confusion in many of the 'Holy Sonnets' is not that of the convinced Calvinist but rather of a person who would like to be a convinced Calvinist but who is both unable to be so and unable to admit that he is unable to be so."[21] In part, Strier's assertion rests on the assumption that the body had a contested role in English Calvinist devotion. Throughout his argument, Strier associates the poems' attention to the body's role in devotional practice as evidence of theological subversion: "Donne could not yet enter fully enough into the psychological world of Reformation theology to conceive of grace" as anything other than "a physical model." Strier equates the "materialist" nature of the poems to "anti-Reformation" doctrine.[22] In a similar vein, Kimberly Johnson has equated the poems' materialism and attention to the body as evidence

---

[19] Several historians of Jacobean Anglicanism have pointed to pockets of theological resistance to the Church of England's largely Genevan brand of orthodoxy from within the English Protestant establishment. My stance is that Donne consciously opposed these alternatives to mainstream Reformed Protestantism, which he saw as opposed to James's official church policy. For a critical overview of Arminianism in the Church of England, see Peter White, "Revisionism Revised: Two Perspectives on Early Stuart Parliamentary History," *Past and Present* 92 (1981): 55–78; Peter White, "The Rise of Arminianism Reconsidered," *Past and Present* 110 (1983): 34–54; Peter White, *Predestination, Policy and Polemic* (Cambridge: Cambridge University Press, 1992); Peter Lake, "Calvinism and the English Church 1570–1635," *Past and Present* 114 (1987): 32–76; Peter Lake, "The Laudian Style: Order, Uniformity and the Pursuit of the Beauty of Holiness in the 1630s," in *The Early Stuart Church, 1603–1642*, ed. Kenneth Fincham (Palo Alto: Stanford University Press, 1993), 161–85; and Graham Parry, *The Arts of the Anglican Counter-Reformation: Glory, Laud and Honour* (Woodbridge: Boydell and Brewer, 2006).

[20] Debora Kuller Shuger, *Habits of Thought in the English Renaissance: Religion, Politics, and the Dominant Culture* (Toronto: University of Toronto Press, 1997 [1990]), 164. For others who have noted Reformed sympathies in Donne's poetry, see John Stachniewski, "John Donne: The Despair of the 'Holy Sonnets,'" *ELH* 48, no. 4 (1981): 677–705, reprinted in John Stachniewski, *The Persecutory Imagination: English Puritanism and the Literature of Religious Despair* (Oxford: Clarendon Press, 1991), 254–91; Paul M. Oliver, *Donne's Religious Writing: A Discourse of Feigned Devotion* (New York: Longman, 1997); Norbrook, "Monarchy of Wit," 3–36; Paul Sellin, *John Donne and Calvinist Views of Grace* (Amsterdam: VU Boekhandel, 1983); and Daniel W. Doerksen, "Polemicist or Pastor? Donne and Moderate Calvinist Conformity," in *John Donne and the Protestant Reformation*, ed. Mary Arshagouni Papazian (Detroit: Wayne State University Press, 2003), 12–34; and Strier, "Donne and the Politics of Devotion," 93–114.

[21] Richard Strier, "John Donne Awry and Squint: The 'Holy Sonnets,' 1608–1610," *Modern Philology* 86, no. 4 (1989): 357–84. See 361 for quotation.

[22] Strier, "John Donne Awry and Squint," 378, 374.

DONNE'S SPEAKING IMAGES   127

of theological confusion and obfuscation: "Donne locates spiritual significance not in the disembodied and abstract sphere but in the body itself."[23] Rather than treating sacramental topoi as Johnson assumes they would have been regarded, "as transparent symbols referring to abstract spiritual principles," Donne's attention to the sensible, visible, and particular confuse the devotional import of the poems. "For Donne, the particularizing of the sign renders it more opaque."[24]

Contrary to such claims that the materialism of the *Holy Sonnets* renders the poems un-Calvinist or somehow obfuscates their devotional outlook, I suggest in this chapter that the tenets of experiential Calvinism offer resolutions to the theological and interpretive problems raised by previous readers of the *Holy Sonnets*. I maintain that the devotional prevarications of the poems emerge from ruptures within the Reformed tradition itself—rather than in opposition to it.[25] Moreover, I assert that Donne's early modern readers would not have regarded the poems' attention to the material, the sensual, and the particular as un-Calvinist or as attempts at theological obfuscation. On the contrary, the materialism of Donne's theological outlook would have been regarded as part and parcel of a culturally sanctioned view of experience-based worship that understood the body as a vital medium through which one could ascertain devotional affect. The paradoxical, contentious devotion that emerges in the *Holy Sonnets* arises from the Church of England's own inconsistencies about the use of devotional images, and about the role of the body and the senses in the cultivation of spiritual intimacy with God. The tensions of the *Holy Sonnets* reflect an English Protestantism that affirmed a larger cultural iconophobia while simultaneously endorsing devotional practices that were inescapably linked to images. I maintain that these poetic tensions arise in the *Holy Sonnets* from Donne's dual commitments to the state church's official policy of iconoclasm and to the very idols he claims to disavow. Donne's iconoclastic intentions in the *Holy Sonnets* are subject to fissures, reversals, and contradictions as he negotiates his competing desires to destroy the idols of his past while preserving them as the foundation for devotional access to God.

---

[23] Kimberly Johnson, *Made Flesh: Sacramental Poetics in Post-Reformation England* (Philadelphia: University of Pennsylvania Press, 2014), 32.

[24] Johnson, *Made Flesh*, 31–2, 31. For Johnson's elaboration on this argument, see also 101.

[25] Both Louis L. Martz and Helen Gardner have proposed readings of the *Holy Sonnets* as expressions of veiled Ignatian meditation practices. Reactions against Martz and Gardner, such as the counter-reading posed by Barbara Kiefer Lewalski, have tended to swing to the polar opposite view, interpreting the *Holy Sonnets* as a straightforward model of English Protestant spiritual progression. See Helen Gardner, Introduction to *John Donne's Divine Poems*, ed. Helen Gardner (Oxford: Clarendon Press, 2000 [1952]), xv–lv; Louis Martz, *The Poetry of Meditation: A Study in English Religious Literature of the Seventeenth Century* (New Haven: Yale University Press, 1954); and Barbara Kiefer Lewalski, *Protestant Poetics and the Seventeenth-Century Religious Lyric* (Princeton: Princeton University Press, 1979).

128   DEVOTIONAL EXPERIENCE IN THE REFORMATION

Gazing at God

In Holy Sonnet 8, "At the round Earths Imagin'd corners," Donne contemplates the problematic position of being made to gaze upon an image of God. The poem presents us with an image of God presiding over a multitude of souls on the day of the Last Judgment. What is especially surprising about Donne's highly detailed description of the mental image, however, is that for all his gazing upon the scene, he is fundamentally excluded from what is arguably the most important act of looking in the sonnet's octet:

> At the round Earths Imagin'd corners blowe
> Your Trumpetts, Angells, and arise, arise
> From Death you numberles Infinities
> Of soules, and to your scattered bodies goe,
> All whome the floud did, and fire shall o're-throwe
> All whom Warre, death, age, agues, Tyrannies,
> Despair, Lawe, Chaunce, hath slayn, and you whose eyes
> Shall behold God, and neuer tast Deaths woe.[26]

Victims of war, tyrannical rule, flooding, and fire, those who died from fevers or the ailments of age, and even those who died (perhaps by their own hand) in the throes of despair—all of these souls return to their scattered bodies on Judgment Day, in preparation to meet God face to face. In particular, Donne regards with special awe those still alive on Judgment Day, "whose eyes / Shall behold God" without ever having to experience death. But among the "numberless Infinities / Of soules" who seek out God on the day of reckoning, one soul in particular is strikingly absent from the poem's litany of seekers. Out of the numberless infinities of sinners, Donne singles himself out as the most abject of all: "yf aboue all these my sinnes abound," Donne posits, "'Tis late to aske abundance of thy grace" (8.10–11). Despite his supreme confidence in the election of others—even of those who had died by suicide—Donne has no such confidence in his own salvation. Donne can look at others gazing upon God, but he himself cannot behold God himself. Holy Sonnet 8 reveals a poetic and visual paradox, presenting a devotional image that in fact highlights the problem of looking at God. Although Donne is barred from looking at God, he gazes upon the souls of the dead even when death has dimmed their senses: "But let them sleepe, Lord, and me mourne a space" (8.9). As it turns

---

[26] 8.1–8. John Donne, *The Variorum Edition of the Poetry of John Donne*, ed. Gary A. Stringer, vol. 7, pt. 1, *The Holy Sonnets*, ed. Gary A. Stringer (Bloomington: Indiana University Press, 2005). I have used this edition in conjunction with the 1633 print edition of Donne's *Poems*. All subsequent citations from the *Holy Sonnets* refer to the Variorum edition and are denoted parenthetically by sonnet and line number in the text.

DONNE'S SPEAKING IMAGES   129

out, Donne's status as supreme sinner also affords him a singular privilege: it is he—and not the resurrected or the never-dead—who apprehends the end of time while being fully in time. The stretch of mourning he must endure while his compatriots sleep unperturbed ensures his uninterrupted being at a moment when all other souls are rendered spiritually inert.

Donne vacillates between characterizing his exceptionalism as either a burden to be endured or as a spiritual prerogative afforded to him alone—one that exempts him from the cycle of repentance, death, judgment, and ultimate ascension that shapes the spiritual trajectory of all others. This tendency for prevarication informs even the grammatical shifts and ruptures in the poem's treatment of Donne's profound uncertainty about his own salvation. Donne's extreme penitential stance unravels as the sonnet moves toward its concluding volta:

> For yf aboue all these my sinnes abound,
> 'Tis late to aske abundance of thy grace,
> When we are there; here on this lowly ground
> Teach me howe to repent, for thats as good
> As yf th' hadst seal'd my pardon with thy blood.
>
> (8.10–14)

The enjambment of the final couplet has us believe until the poem's penultimate line that Donne is resigning himself to his status as the world's worst sinner: "Teach me howe to repent," he pleads, "for thats as good"—as good as if he were one of those "numberless infinities of souls" who rest easy knowing that they are elected to salvation. The enjambment succeeds in enabling Donne to maintain this posture until the poem's final line: "for that's as good / As if thou'dst sealed my pardon with thy bloud." Donne carries over the uncertainty of the octet's "if" ("For yf aboue all these my sinnes abound") into the final line of the poem, where the word serves to transform Donne's extreme spiritual self-castigation into an attempt to ascribe to his own repentance a redemptive power equal to that of the Passion.[27]

In the sonnet's final line, Donne proposes that he might enact a kind of redemption for himself, not in conjunction with Christ's Passion, but as an equally

---

[27] In her reading of the sonnet's final couplet, Ramie Targoff has argued that the lines reveal Donne's neediness for God's reassurance: "Donne represents himself in a state of unnecessary, extravagant dependence: he needs immediate contact with God to be reassured of his fundamental rights as his creature," she maintains. "This desire for immediate contact is also a desire for unmediated contact— even the gift of Christ's blood stands in the way of Donne's access to God." Targoff is certainly right in pointing to Donne's extraordinary anxiety about his salvation and his need for immediate reassurance. However, the syntax of the lines simultaneously suggests an opposite desire that is coterminous with Donne's extreme need of God. See Ramie Targoff, *John Donne: Body and Soul* (Chicago: University of Chicago Press, 2008), 120.

130   DEVOTIONAL EXPERIENCE IN THE REFORMATION

effective alternative to it. That is to say, Donne wants to imagine a relationship with God in which his salvation is no longer contingent upon God's whim. His repentance is *as good as if* Christ had died for his sins. The heretical overtones of the claim, moreover, are compounded by Donne's inclusion of the suppositional "if": "Teach me howe to repent, for that's as good / As *yf* th' hadst seal'd my pardon with thy bloud." Does Donne mean to imply here that Christ did *not* in fact die for his sins? Or is he suggesting that, somehow, Christ's sacrifice has failed to exert its intended redemptive effect, that Christ died for humankind at large but not for Donne? Once God teaches him how to repent, Donne claims that his own act of repentance will provide a redemptive function that will not only supplement, but supplant, Christ's sacrifice. The suppositional comment on the role of his own repentance, rather than functioning as a gloss on biblical history, actively seeks to rewrite that history.[28] The closing couplet from Holy Sonnet 8 captures a decisive reversal in Donne's devotional stance, effectively undoing his earlier insistence that his salvation lies with God (the "abundance of Thy grace") rather than with human penitential gestures. The sonnet makes claims to its own Eucharistic effectiveness; ultimately its final couplet has as much power as Christ's blood to ensure Donne's election.[29]

In Holy Sonnet 8, Donne's initial pose of penitential humbleness turns out to be a posture. What does it mean that here an apparently unambivalent expression of repentance looks startlingly like a rejection of the redemptive power of the Passion? Indeed, the structural similarities between proper worship and idolatrous longing are such that a number of critics of the *Holy Sonnets* have failed to notice the odd heresy of its final lines, reading them not as an attempt to undermine the self-effacing penitential attitude of the preceding lines, but seeing them merely as an extension of Donne's devotional logic.[30] Donne has a tendency to present

---

[28] Brian Cummings has made a similar observation in his reading of the culminating religious sonnets from Fulke Greville's *Caelica* sequence. Far from constituting a passive summation of existing orthodoxy, Cummings calls the poetry "an active participant in belief and doctrine," and claims that "Rather than theology happening elsewhere, before the poem is made, the poem shows theology in the making." See Brian Cummings, *The Literary Culture of the Reformation: Grammar and Grace* (Oxford: Oxford University Press, 2002), 301.

[29] In a reading of *La Corona*, David Chanoff has noted that Donne often ascribes to the sequence the sacramental force of liturgy, a claim that not even Catholic poets such as Robert Southwell made about their writing: "With Donne, however, the poem is not merely a pious imaginative exercise; it is to assume a role that is ordinarily performed by the sacramental rites of the Church." See David Chanoff, "Donne's Anglicanism," *Recusant History* 15, no. 3 (1980): 154–67, esp. 158. More recently, several critics have noted the sacramentalism of Donne's secular and devotional poems. See Regina M. Schwartz, *Sacramental Poetics at the Dawn of Secularism: When God Left the World* (Palo Alto: Stanford University Press, 2008), 7, 14, and esp. chap. 5, "Donne in Love: Communion of the Flesh," 87–116; and Robert Whalen, *The Poetry of Immanence: Sacrament in Donne and Herbert* (Toronto: University of Toronto Press, 2002), esp. 61–2.

[30] Critical readings that posit Donne as either wholly passive or open to cooperation in his relationship with God overlook his oblique claim to spiritual independence. Despite Donne's insistence upon the uniqueness of his position in his negotiations with Christ over his salvation, the antagonistic overtone of Holy Sonnet 8 has been downplayed—if not outright ignored—in critical readings of the sonnet's devotional stance. John Stachniewski, for example, claims that Donne's stance toward his own

DONNE'S SPEAKING IMAGES   131

theological orthodoxies that upon closer inspection look increasingly like theological unorthodoxies, with the result that sin and redemption look indistinguishable from one another in many of the sequence's poems.

The *Holy Sonnets* reveal an astonishing number of shifts, adjustments, and reversals, not only across the sequence, but even within single lines of poems. Donne manages to reverse an image of devotion—the scene of the Last Judgment—not only within the span of a single line, but within that sliver of the volta's counterfactual "as if." Perhaps that line reveals a grammatical playfulness on Donne's part, but we must take seriously his larger anxiety about the uneasy boundary separating proper devotion from idolatrous, heretical desire. In his reading of the poem, Strier has argued that the sonnet reveals Donne's failure to properly articulate and believe in the Calvinist doctrine of grace: "Personal repentance and Christ's atonement are again alternatives; again they are not coordinated but equated in value and efficacy. ... Donne seems to be able to imagine repentance but not grace."[31] But what Strier overlooks is that the poem's counterfactual is key to the success of the poem's prevaricating argument, as well as to a distinctly Calvinist understanding of the difficulty of discerning the state of grace from the state of damnation. In its grammatical turns, Holy Sonnet 8 experientially captures the spiritual veering of a Calvinist mind confronted with the task of interpretation, when indicators of grace often appear undiscernible from evidence of damnation.

Rather than indicating Donne's failure to take Calvinist doctrine to heart, Holy Sonnet 8 models the kind of spiritual interpretation that lay at the heart of Calvinist soteriology. "Now in the elect we set vocation to be the testimony of election,"

---

salvation was entirely passive in approach: "Nowhere in the sonnets does Donne think it lies in his power to 'make himself worthy' of redemption. ... Donne's extreme passivity is a strikingly consistent feature of the sonnets. Even as a suppliant he must wait for God to empower him to repent: 'here on this lowly ground, / Teach mee how to repent.'" See Stachniewski, *Persecutory Imagination*, 259, 281. More recently, P. M. Oliver has followed Stachniewski in arguing that Donne's passivity in his devotional poems plays a necessary role in securing his own redemption. In his reading of the fifth sonnet of Donne's *La Corona* sequence, Oliver makes a similar argument that Donne subscribes to the Calvinistic tenet on predestination in assuming a passive approach to salvation: "The request for Christ to '*Moist with one drop of blood my dry soul*' which closes the sonnet entitled 'Crucifying' implies a willingness to leave everything to him. Salvation viewed thus is an automatic process that lies in the gift of the Almighty and has nothing to do with faith or morals." See Oliver, *Donne's Religious Writing*, 101.

In a similar vein, Terry G. Sherwood suggests that Donne understood redemption as a collaborative process between himself and God: "Donne's request that God 'Teach mee how to repent' ... assumes a shared effort consistent with Donne's assertion elsewhere that God's contribution demonstrates his love." See Terry G. Sherwood, *Fulfilling the Circle: A Study in John Donne's Thought* (Toronto: University of Toronto Press, 1984), 149. Stachniewski, Oliver, and Sherwood's arguments for the penitential nature of Donne's sonnet are elaborations on readings first proposed by Helen Gardner and Barbara Lewalski. Gardner interprets the lines to mean that while Christ's death on the cross secures general pardon, Donne's repentance guarantees his individual salvation. See Gardner, ed., *John Donne's Divine Poems*, 68. Lewalski's supposition that the lines suggest "the growth of the speaker's faith and his recognition that nothing is impossible to God," likewise ignores the problems introduced by the lines' heretical implications. See Lewalski, *Protestant Poetics*, 269.

[31] Strier, "John Donne Awry and Squint," 372.

132   DEVOTIONAL EXPERIENCE IN THE REFORMATION

Calvin writes in his *Institutio*, "and then justification to be another sign of the manifest showing of it."[32] For Calvin, the individual's ability to look for signs of his election was the only mode of gaining intellectual and spiritual certainty of salvation, and one that placed an epistemological onus on the individual penitent. The paradox of the *Holy Sonnets* rests on the fact that, for Donne, the signs of damnation and the signs of salvation look astonishingly alike. Contrary to Strier's claim, Donne's interpretive problem in the poem does not stem from any tension between his desire to subscribe to Calvinism and a remnant crypto-Catholicism; rather, his interpretive dilemma emerges from fissures within the Calvinist tradition itself, which celebrated perceptible evidence of grace even as it acknowledged the difficult task of interpreting that evidence.

Profane devotion

The problem of being able to distinguish idolatrous desire from proper devotion is one that Donne considered in earnest in several lyric meditations on the tensions and overlaps between his longing for fleshly women and his love for God. In Holy Sonnet 15, an image of the brutalized face of Christ serves as a visual trigger for Donne's erotically charged account of his unusual obsession with this image:

> What yf this present were the worlds last night?
> Looke in my Hart, O Soule, where thou dost dwell
> The picture of Christ crucifyde and tell
> Whether that countenance can thee affright.
>
> (15.1–4)

At this point in the octet, the image of the crucified Christ confounds Donne's interpretive abilities, and he remains uncertain as to how to read the image he finds in his heart. He goes on to consider whether his beloved Christ, dwelling in his own being, can condemn him to eternal damnation. "And can that toung adiudge thee vnto hell," he wonders, "Which prayed forgiuenes for his foes ranck spite?" (15.7–8). Although Donne regards his spiritual suffering as deeply idiosyncratic at various other points in the *Holy Sonnets*, here his interpretive conundrum is a variation of the spiritual anguish that the Reformed preacher Thomas Goodwin likened to the act of looking upon a perspective painting—a perpetually oscillating image that revealed diabolical monstrosities from one angle, and beautiful and divine creatures from the other. Goodwin writes, "So some have looked over their hearts by signs at one time, and have to their thinking found nothing but hypocrisy, unbelief, hardness, self-seeking; but not long after examining their hearts again by

---

[32] Calvin, *Institutes*, 3.21.

the same signs, they have espied the image of God drawn fairly upon the tale of their hearts."[33]

In Holy Sonnet 15, Donne undertakes this arduous task of extracting stable meaning from the gory image in his heart. He goes about this process in an especially startling way, recycling the argument he once used to woo his many mistresses in his present devotional pursuit of Christ: "as in myne idolatree / I sayd to all my profane Mistressis / Bewty of pity, foulnes only is / A Signe of rigor; So I say to thee / To wicked Sprights are horrid shapes assignd, / This bewteous forme assures a piteous mind" (15.9–14). Christ's beauteous body and his material form, Donne asserts, should be sufficient to convince an onlooker of his benevolent and merciful feelings toward Donne. But contrary to Donne's description in line 14 of the image, Christ's form is hardly a "beauteous" sight to behold. His image might allure the sadomasochist, but is by standard definitions both repellant and troubling: "Teares in his eyes quench the amazing Light, / Blood fills his frowns which from his pierc'd head fell" (15.5–6). According to Strier, the fact that the image of Christ here is *not* conventionally beautiful renders the poem "weak and sophistical": "The force of the argument, taken as serious in the religious context, relies on the crucified Christ being immediately recognized as a 'beauteous forme.' But this is precisely what the octet has failed to establish. ... Christ's 'beauteous forme' is not present enough in the poem to bear the weight it must have."[34] Johnson makes a comparable claim in her reading of the poem, arguing that the poem's retreat into the materiality of Christ's body renders its devotional effect null: "the image [Donne] describes as a 'beauteous form' is difficult to conceive as beautiful. ... The picture is a gruesome one, to be sure, but again its ghastliness arises from its unsublimable particularity," she argues. Donne "offer[s] a Christ whose body is just too *bodily* to be sublimated into generally appropriable symbolism."[35]

I propose that the interpretive problem posed by Christ's paradoxically ugly yet "beauteous form" in Holy Sonnet 15 is in fact one that Donne himself addressed in a Trinity Sunday sermon, which he delivered in 1621. In the sermon, Donne insisted that Christ ought to be loved in all of his forms—not only when he was beautiful, but even when he was at his ugliest and most unlovable: "Thy love is not required only in the *Hosanna's* of Christ, when Christ is magnified, and his Gospel advanced, and men preferred for loving it: No, nor only in the *Transfiguration* of Christ, when Christ appears to thee in some particular beams, and manifestation of his glory; *but love him in his Crucifigatur, then when it is a scornful*

[33] Thomas Goodwin, *A childe of light vvalking in darknesse: or A treatise shewing the causes, by which God leaves his children to distresse of conscience* (London: By M[iles] F[lesher] for R. Dawlman and L. F[awne] at the Brazen Serpent in Pauls Church-yard, 1636), 32. (*EEBO*, STC (2nd ed.) / 12037, document image 115.) Quoted in John Stachniewski and Anita Pacheco, Introduction to *Grace Abounding: With Other Spiritual Autobiographies*, by John Bunyan, eds. Stachniewski and Pacheco (Oxford: Oxford University Press, 2008 [1998]), xiv.

[34] Strier, "John Donne Awry and Squint," 381.

[35] Johnson, *Made Flesh*, 96, 95.

134 DEVOTIONAL EXPERIENCE IN THE REFORMATION

thing to love him." Donne's Christ is as fickle as an earthly beloved, and his many transfigurations—not all of them winsome—challenge our ability to love him, continuously, at all times. And yet Donne insisted upon the necessity of loving Christ in all of his guises—"not only in spiritual transfigurations, when he visits thy soul with glorious consolations, but even in his inward eclipses, when he withholds his comforts, and withdraws his cheerfulness, even when he makes as though he loved not thee, love him."[36] Here Donne might as well be describing an off-and-on relationship with one of his many profane mistresses of Holy Sonnet 15; indeed, Christ's many transfigurations make him as vexing an object of desire as one of Donne's former girlfriends. In Holy Sonnet 15, the image of the crucified figure of Christ, imprinted into Donne's own being, presents Donne and Christ together at the spiritual nadir of their relationship. In the poem's vision of spiritual progression, Donne gives up his past trysts with women for an affair with Christ as various and uncertain as his earthly erotic pursuits. In effect, Donne's current pursuit of Christ does not so much replace as it *replicates* his old erotic idolatries.

The possibility that Donne's pursuit of Christ might be, like his pursuit of his profane mistresses, nothing other than idol worship is certainly amplified by the imagistic nature of Christ's form; Donne is seeking assurance, after all, by gazing upon a *picture* of Christ.[37] But the idolatrous import of the sonnet would have held additional resonances for an early modern reader attuned to broad conceptions of what idolatry entailed in the Elizabethan and Jacobean church. In his *Homilie against idolatrie*, Jewel drew specific attention to the intrinsic connection between idol worship and illicit sexual desire. In urging public magistrates to raze all idolatrous images from church spaces, Jewel described idolaters and image lovers as nothing short of "spiritual harlots." Idolatry, what Jewel called "spiritual fornication," threatened to hold the mind hostage, just as carnal fornication could

---

[36] Donne, Sermon 14, in *Sermons*, 3:305.

[37] Despite the idolatrous import of Holy Sonnet 15, readers of the poem have sought to ignore the uncomfortable overtones of Donne's admiration of Christ's image. For example, Richard Strier dismisses the poem's treatment of the image as "carefully non-iconophilic." See Strier, "John Donne Awry and Squint," 380. Others, like Ernest B. Gilman, insist that Donne's use of the image is essentially non-idolatrous only because that image will eventually be destroyed later in the sequence. Donne's behavior is undeniably idolatrous in *this* sonnet, Gilman argues, but he refuses to read the poem's articulation of idolatrous desire as something to be taken seriously: "the image of Christ formed by the poet must itself be regarded as a deformity, a scum of rust that must be burned off before the untarnished image of Christ can be restored—restored, paradoxically, by the artisan uniquely qualified for his craft by having submitted himself to be deformed on the cross, just as Donne had imagined him." See Ernest B. Gilman, "'To adore, or scorne an image': Donne and the Iconoclastic Controversy," *John Donne Journal* 5 (1986): 62–100, esp. 179–80. Gilman's article is an earlier form of his argument, republished in Ernest B. Gilman, "Donne's 'Pictures Made and Mard,'" chap. 5 in *Iconoclasm and Poetry in the English Reformation: Down Went Dagon* (Chicago: University of Chicago Press, 1986), 117–48. These readings of Holy Sonnet 15 fail to resolve the problem posed by idolatrous longing, either by ignoring the iconophilic import of the poem or by incorrectly regarding the image as a target of attack. Neither accurately captures the tender, albeit vexed, longing with which Donne regards the image of Christ.

DONNE'S SPEAKING IMAGES   135

ensnare the body itself.[38] The Reformed association between illicit sexual desire and idolatry is ultimately biblical; Ezekiel 16:17 describes image worship as a form of spiritual whoredom: "Thou hast also taken thy fair jewels of my gold and my silver, which I had given thee, and madest to thyself images of men, and didst whoredom with them."[39] Holy Sonnet 15 captures this cultural understanding of image worship as tantamount to deviant desire and sexual acts. Donne desires Christ as intensely—and as idolatrously—as he once desired his former mistresses. As he gazes longingly upon the picture of Christ, Donne's devotion assumes distinctly erotic overtones, and he woos Christ using the same logic that he once used to woo women. His idolatry is of the worst and most dangerous variety, inflected by and infected with the very kinds of desires that those like Jewel vehemently warned against. In appropriating this culturally specific understanding of image worship as deviant desire in his devotional pursuit of God, Donne succeeds in claiming powerful erotic control over Christ; the implication of the sonnet's logic is that Christ, like Donne's many fleshly lovers, might also be susceptible to flattery and erotic solicitation. In the devotional and sexual fantasy of Holy Sonnet 15, Donne renders Christ's body materially and spiritually accessible, subject to his petitions and pursuit.

Iconophobia and iconophilia are coextensive and mutually dependent in Holy Sonnet 15, which mobilizes a widespread understanding of idolatry only to reveal the way that the very fear of the sexualizing power of images can also foster an alluring, albeit unorthodox, devotional intimacy with God. But Donne's insistence on using idolatrous logic as the basis for the cultivation of devotional affect strikes us as surprising in light of his official position against the use of images in proper worship, a position that he outlined in his capacity as a preacher. In a 1626 sermon preached at St. Paul's, Donne disavows the devotional use of all idols. Idolatrous

---

[38] Jewel, "Homilie against *perill of idolatrie*," 133. This cultural linkage between image worship and sexual deviance appears in English religious tracts on idolatry as early as the mid-sixteenth century, when Nicholas Ridley anticipated the homily's description of the overlap between spiritual and carnal fornication in his posthumous *A Treatise on the Worship of Images* (1563). Ridley's treatise calls the invention of images, "the beginning of spiritual fornication," and describes the offending images themselves as "whores." See Nicholas Ridley, "A Treatise on the Worship of Images," in *The Works of Nicholas Ridley, D.D. sometime Lord Bishop of London, martyr, 1555*, ed. Rev. Henry Christmas (Cambridge: Cambridge University Press, 1841), 85, 87. Similarly, in his 1611 treatise *An Arrow against Idolatry*, Henry Ainsworth likened the effects of idolatry to a wanton woman's debilitating power over the fleshly body: "Ezekiel compareth the idolaters of Israel, to a vvoman inflamed with loue towards some goodly yong man, on whom she hath cast her eyes, and fixt her affections ... and bringeth him to her into the bed of love, so discovering her fornication and disclosing her shame. Teaching us by this similitude, that idolatry is as sweet to the corrupted conscience & mind of man, as lust and fornication, is to any wanton body." See Henry Ainsworth, *An arrow against idolatrie Taken out of the quiver of the Lord of hosts* (Amsterdam: Printed [by Giles Thorp], 1611), 43. (*EEBO*, STC (2nd ed.) / 221, document image 22.) For a useful discussion of the imaginative resonances between idolatry and sexual fornication in seventeenth-century English religious culture, see Alexandra Walsham, *The Reformation of the Landscape: Religion, Identity, and Memory in Early Modern Britain and Ireland* (Oxford: Oxford University Press, 2011), 84.

[39] Cited in Aston, *England's Iconoclasts*, 468. For a discussion on the cultural associations between idolatry and adultery—and illicit desire more broadly—see Aston, *England's Iconoclasts*, 468–79.

136 DEVOTIONAL EXPERIENCE IN THE REFORMATION

practices, he maintains, are only useful in so far as they serve as a present reminder of the Reformed church's sinful and papist past:

> But as the Christian in abolishing the idolatry of the gentiles, in some places, some times, left some of their idols standing, lest the gentiles should come to deny that ever they had worshipped such monsters. So it hath pleased the Holy Ghost to hover over the authors and writers in the Roman Church, so as that they have left some impressions of the iniquity.[40]

Donne makes his total rejection of devotional images absolutely clear in his public sermons against idolatry; even traces of idolatrous worship have no proper place in Reformed devotional practice. Yet in Holy Sonnet 15, Donne does not abjure all idolatry, and if anything, he succeeds in exchanging one kind of idolatry for another. Unable or unwilling to relinquish his past erotic intimacies, or his desire for his earthly lovers, Donne builds these past exchanges into his current negotiations with Christ. The poem chronicles an unorthodox spiritual progression whereby all previous lovers become subsumed, not rejected, within the parameters of Donne's present devotion to God. Donne's spiritual progression is not Diotimatian, which requires the rejection of individual lovers as one moves toward proper love of the Truth; nor does his spiritual progression follow the standard Protestant devotional trajectory outlined by Barbara Lewalski.[41] On the contrary, the spiritual movement of Holy Sonnet 15 is most reminiscent of the uncanny vision of desire outlined in Shakespeare's Sonnet 31, in which the poet locates images of his former lovers within the physical form of his current beloved: "Thou art the graue where buried loue doth liue," Shakespeare's poet declares. "Their images I lou'd, I view in thee."[42] In both Sonnet 31 and Holy Sonnet 15, desire for all former lovers is never eschewed, but rather assimilated into the poets' ongoing experiences of longing and desire.

Holy Sonnet 15 ends in an unexpected theological reversal, reclaiming and even celebrating the idolatries that the poem initially sets out to destroy. In his ongoing spiritual development, Donne's former idols become transformed into the very basis of devotional affect and intimacy, giving structure and dimension

---

[40] Donne, Sermon 6, in *Sermons*, 7:186.

[41] In their readings of Holy Sonnet 1, Barbara Lewalski and Paul Cefalu both point to Reformed models of devotion as the theological force driving the sonnet. Lewalski argues that the sonnet charts Donne's progression from anxiety about his own election toward a resolute acceptance of his spiritual calling, as evidenced by the sonnet's final line. See Lewalski, *Protestant Poetics*, 18. Although Donne never rids himself of fear in Cefalu's reading of the sonnet, by the end of the poem he does exchange his debilitating fear of the devil for a godly fear proper to penitents. See Paul Cefalu, "Godly Fear, Sanctification, and Calvinist Theology in the Sermons and 'Holy Sonnets' of John Donne," *Studies in Philology* 11, no. 1 (2003): 71–86, esp. 77. Yet both Lewalski and Cefalu ignore the uncomfortable comparison that Donne makes by positing Satan's allure as the prototype for his current attraction to God.

[42] Sonnet 31, lines 9, 13, in William Shakespeare, *Shake-speares sonnets Neuer before imprinted* (At London: By G. Eld for T[homas] T[horpe] and are to be solde by William Aspley, 1609). (*EEBO*, STC (2nd ed.) / 22353.)

DONNE'S SPEAKING IMAGES   137

to his present negotiations with God. But the uncomfortable tension between idolatry and devotion in the *Holy Sonnets* was not merely the reflection of a desire on Donne's part to adopt the role of religious miscreant. What constituted proper worship, and how one could secure the devotional satisfaction that Donne felt to be necessary to his spiritual life, were in fact questions that Donne regarded seriously in the *Holy Sonnets*. The tension between Donne's commitments to the flesh and to things divine assumes a central role in his efforts to chronicle the trauma of finding himself severed from the presence of his wife in the aftermath of her death—a rupture that threatens to sever Donne even from God himself.

Desire as sacrament

It is unclear whether Donne would have counted his wife, Anne More, among the profane mistresses of Holy Sonnet 15, who he both pits against and imagines as precursors for his love for God.[43] But what is undeniable is that in Holy Sonnet 17, "Since She whome I lovd, hath payd her last debt," Donne describes his longing for Anne as deeply incompatible with his present devotion to God. Donne probably wrote this sonnet in 1617, after both Anne and the child she was carrying—which would have been the couple's twelfth—died in childbirth. In coming to terms with Anne's untimely death—"her Soule early into heauen rauished" (17.3)—Donne imagines a scenario in which God has taken away his wife in a fit of jealousy, in order to establish himself as the sole object of Donne's devotional desires. This development is something, Donne imagines, that God thinks he ought to be grateful for: "But why should I begg more Love, when as thou / Dost woo my Soule, for hers offering all thine?"[44] The question is not rhetorical, but emerges out of Donne's sense that while he should be satisfied with God's sole attention, he nevertheless finds divine love alone acutely unfulfilling. What begins as a poetic meditation upon the underlying reasons for his ungratefulness reveals itself, by the end of the sonnet, as an oblique chastisement of God:

> And dost not only feare least I allow
> My Love to Saints and Angels, things diuine,

[43] I would like to think that Donne did not count his wife among his many idolatrous loves, but there is a critical tradition of reading Donne's relationship with Anne More as idolatrous, especially vis-à-vis his relationship with God. For example, Theresa M. DiPasquale and Frances M. Malpezzi both argue that Donne's love for Anne was akin to idol worship, and describe the various means that Donne undertakes to rid himself of his former idolatrous love for his wife as he progresses in his commitment to God. See Theresa M. DiPasquale, "Ambivalent Mourning in 'Since she whome I lovd,'" in *John Donne's "desire of more": The Subject of Anne More Donne in His Poetry*, ed. M. Thomas Hester (Newark: University of Delaware Press, 1996), 183–95; and Frances M. Malpezzi, "Love's Liquidity in "Since she whome I lovd,'" in Hester, *John Donne's "desire of more,"* 196–203.

[44] 17.9–10. In the Westmoreland Manuscript, the lines read, "But why should I beg more Love, when as thou / Dost *woe* my Soule, for hers offring all thine?" (emphasis added). The orthographical oscillation between wooing and woeing in the manuscript's original rendition of the line captures Donne's dismay over his wife's untimely death and his sense that he ought to be pleased by God's jealous preoccupation.

138   DEVOTIONAL EXPERIENCE IN THE REFORMATION

> But in thy tender iealosy dost doubt
> Lest the World, fleshe, yea Deuill putt thee out.

(17.11–14)

God has taken Anne away from him, Donne asserts, for no reason other than a jealous supposition that saints, angels, and earthly lovers might pose competition for Donne's devotion. God's apparent fear that "the World, fleshe, yea Deuill" might put him out casts God in a particularly uncharitable light—and especially so since Donne uses a nearly verbatim line to describe his own moments of spiritual weakness earlier in the sequence. The last line of Holy Sonnet 17 is an echo of the final lines of Holy Sonnet 6, "This is my Playes last scene," a poem in which Donne grapples with his own impending death. Holy Sonnet 6 ends with an imperative to God: "Impute me righteous, thus purg'd of evil, / For thus I leave the World, the flesh, and Devill" (6.13–14). The nearly verbatim echo of this phrase at the close of Holy Sonnet 17 serves to render God's jealousy as undeniably carnal; he fears that he will be overwhelmed by the very three encumbrances—"the World, fleshe, yea Devill"—that threaten to undermine Donne during his weakest spiritual moments in Holy Sonnet 6. Within the span of the final two lines of Holy Sonnet 17, God's dignity undergoes a considerable worsening of stature; what Donne terms "tender iealousy" in the sonnet's penultimate line quickly emerges as nothing other than a decidedly mortal insecurity in the closing line of the poem—a line jarring most of all because of its pronoun substitution. The world, the flesh, and the Devil threaten not to put *me* out, Donne insists, but *thee*. Here it is God, and not the mortal sinner of Holy Sonnet 6, who falls victim to carnal siege. The sonnet ends with the implicit suggestion that God is, at worst, no better than Donne at *his* spiritual worst; God fears the very triad that ought to threaten only the sinner incapable of repentance.

But the poem reverses more than just its pronouns; it also reverses the format of the state worship service's public call and response. For Donne's early modern audience, the holy sonnet's final line would have reverberated with the litany from the *Book of Common Prayer*. "Good Lorde deliver us," the congregation would have spoken in unison, to which the priest would have responded: "From fornication, and all other deadly sin, and from all the deceits of the world, the flesh, and the Devil."[45] In the poem, Donne transforms the litany's response into a private exchange between himself and God. What is more, Donne appears to reverse the role of parishioner and priest in adopting the priest's response as his own. In the poem, God no longer enjoys the role of ultimate arbiter; Donne has put him in the position of the common parishioner—uncertain about his own position vis-à-vis the world, the flesh, and the devil. In the ears of early modern churchgoers, the

---

[45] For the *Book of Common Prayer* litany in three early modern versions, see *The Book of Common Prayer: The Texts of 1549, 1559, and 1662*, ed. Brian Cummings (Oxford: Oxford University Press, 2011), 41–5, 117–23, and 259–64. I include the lines as they appear in the 1559 liturgy, on p. 117.

DONNE'S SPEAKING IMAGES   139

most concrete manifestation of the poem's triumvirate of threats would have been fornication—both spiritual and sexual. In a devotional poem that chronicles the deadly love triangle involving Anne, Donne, and God, the sonnet's final line had particular resonance for an early modern audience who themselves would have had participated in the public litany.

A particular problem emerges from this love triangle, in the aftermath of God's jealous abduction of Anne. If God has indeed stolen her away from Donne in a move designed to garner more devotion for himself, Donne reveals that God's calculated move has backfired. What God did not know before ravishing Anne to heaven is that earthly, sexual devotion between human lovers forms not just the model but the spiritual prerequisite for Donne's feelings of devotion toward God: "Here the admyring her my Mind did whett / To seeke thee God" (17.5–6). With Anne's bodily presence now absent from his daily life, Donne experiences a rupture in his devotional commune with God; his attachment to God was, he belatedly reveals, entirely contingent upon his wife's constant physical presence. In a 1626 sermon delivered on Easter day, Donne describes the role of sacramental practice in fostering devotional access to God: "Sacraments are mysteries, because though the grace therein be near me, yet there is *Velamen interpositum*, there is a visible figure, *a sensible sign, and seal*, between me, and that grace, which is exhibited to me in the Sacrament."[46] For Donne, adoration of Anne is an integral part of the sacramental devotion. Like the baptism and Communion rites, Anne functions as a visible and sensible sign of an otherwise invisible grace.

Anxieties about the idolizing of spouses preoccupied certain Reformed thinkers while Donne was writing the *Holy Sonnets*. In 1604, the Puritan John Reynolds argued that the Church of England's marriage ceremony encouraged sexual idolatry: "They make the new married man ... to an idol of his wife, saying: with this ring I thee wed, with my body I thee worship."[47] Along the lines of Reynolds's anxieties about matrimonial idolatry, Theresa DiPasquale has made the argument that Donne's devotion to Anne in Holy Sonnet 17 veers toward idol worship, rendering his desire for her theologically incompatible with his devotion to God.[48] But while radical Puritans like Reynolds would have certainly balked at Donne's descriptions of matrimonial longing, the sonnet offers a model of devotion that ultimately subscribes to mainstream Reformed devotional practices. Indeed, Holy Sonnet 17

---

[46] Donne, Sermon 3, in *Sermons*, 7:98, emphasis added.

[47] John Reynolds, "An Admonition to the Parliament," in *Puritan Manifestoes: A Study of the Origin of the Puritan Revolt*, eds. W. H. Frere and C. E. Douglas (New York: B. Franklin, 1972), 1–39, see p. 27 for quotation. Quoted in Aston, *England's Iconoclasts*, 467.

[48] See Theresa DiPasquale, "Ambivalent Mourning: Sacramentality, Idolatry, and Gender in 'Since she whome I lovd hath payd her last debt,'" *John Donne Journal* 10, nos. 1–2 (1991): 45–56; and a revised version, DiPasquale, "Ambivalent Mourning in 'Since she whome I lovd.'" For other views of Donne's sacramentalism in the sonnet, see also Malpezzi, "Love's Liquidity," 196–203; Achsah Guibory, "Fear of 'loving more': Death and the Loss of Sacramental Love," in Hester, *John Donne's "Desire of More,"* 204–27; and Maureen Sabine, "No Marriage in Heaven: John Donne, Anne Donne, and the Kingdom Come," in Hester, *John Donne's "Desire of More,"* 228–55.

140 DEVOTIONAL EXPERIENCE IN THE REFORMATION

mobilizes a standard Reformed understanding of the role of sensible signs of grace in the devotional process. Indeed, Donne's description of the devotional utility of the sacraments adheres to Calvin's own view of Reformed sacramental worship: "We have determined, therefore, that sacraments are truly named the testimonies of God's grace and are like seals of the good will that he feels toward us, which by attesting that good will to us, sustain, nourish, confirm, and increase our faith."[49] The devotional value of the sacraments, Calvin argues, rests on their participation in the visible and sensible world; they confirm grace not through rational apprehension, but through knowledge that comes from bodily engagement: "because we are of flesh, they are shown us under things of flesh. ... Augustine calls a sacrament 'a visible word' for the reason that it represents God's promises as painted in a picture and sets them before our sight, portrayed graphically and in the manner of images."[50] With the arrival of his theology in England, Calvin's understanding of the experiential and imagistic dimensions of sacramental practice influenced clerics like Perkins, for whom visible and outward signs of grace could be a source of spiritual comfort and assurance. For Perkins, like Donne, these sensible signs are testament of God's commitment to the elect: "we may behold in ourselves, some sure representations of all these imprinted, and even stamped in us by the word: and so by the beholding of these forms and impressions in ourselves, we shall easily be brought to the knowledge of those patterns (as it were) which are in the Lord himself." Perkins writes: "[A]s by certain marks imprinted in us, he doeth seal us to himself in Christ."[51]

The sonnet's argument about the importance of visible and sensible signs in Donne's devotional access to God could thus be described as sacramental, in the Reformed sense, in which outward rites do not contain spiritual efficacy but operate as signs and symbols of grace. But Holy Sonnet 17 offers, more broadly put, an argument about the kind of spiritual certainty that comes from sensory perception. In Donne's poetic logic, his desire for Anne is not idolatrous precisely because he counts his relationship with her as one of the many visible and sensible indications of God's grace. It is this certainty that God has swept away by ravishing Anne's soul to heaven. The poem's ostensible intention to describe the mutual exclusiveness of earthly and divine devotion unravels during Donne's meditation upon his intertwined love for both Anne and God. Holy Sonnet 17 underscores Donne's tendency to incorporate, rather than to eschew, the material, corporeal, and fleshly substratum undergirding his religious devotion. In the *Holy Sonnets*, desire for embodied lovers is the central prerequisite for devotional longing for

---

[49] Calvin, *Institutes*, 4.14.7.

[50] Calvin, *Institutes*, 4.14.6.

[51] William Perkins, *A case of conscience of the greatest that ever was, how a man may know, whether he be the son of God or no* (Imprinted at London: By Thomas Orwin, for Thomas Man and Iohn Porter, 1592), 55, 53. (*EEBO*, STC (2nd ed.) / 19665, document images 30, 29.) Copy from the Bodleian Library.

DONNE'S SPEAKING IMAGES   141

God. That longing for God is so porous and vast that it must be structured and made comprehensible by other forms of desire—whether matrimonial, erotic, or even idolatrous. Former erotic attachments, even illicit ones, give dimension and force to Donne's ongoing devotional commitments to God.

Idolatrous devotion

That former idolatry looks startlingly like devotion in the *Holy Sonnets* reveals more than just Donne's intellectual playfulness. On the contrary, he takes seriously the problem of being unable to discern proper from improper devotion. In Holy Sonnet 3, "O might those sighes and teares returne againe," he revisits the conundrum of finding himself incapable of distinguishing the state of sinfulness from the state of grace. This sonnet, like Holy Sonnets 15 and 17, initially appears to be a poem about repentance. In turning away from his past sins, Donne wishes that he could undo the aftereffects of his idolatrous desire:

> O might those sighes and teares returne againe
> Into my brest and eyes, which I have spent;
> That I might in this holy discontent
> Mourne with some fruite, as I haue mournd in vaine.
> In my Idolatry what showrs of raine
> Myne eyes did wast? what griefes my hart did rent?
> That sufferance was my Sin, now I repent.
>
> (3.1–7)

The opening line makes us think that Donne's request is initially a straightforward one in which he seeks to return to his former state of grief, but the enjambed clause transforms Donne's gestures of devotion into a request for a bodily and temporal impossibility: "Oh might those sighes and teares returne againe / Into my brest and eyes." Catherine Gimelli Martin has described Holy Sonnet 3 as a lyric account of spiritual "emptying," a process that would lead to the penitent's ultimate apprehension of Christ. The sonnet models "the 'emptying' process," she writes, "a pouring out of 'griefs' sadly insufficient to attest to the speaker's wished-for adoption."[52] But Donne is advocating for precisely the opposite process in his description of spiritual turmoil; what he really wants is to reabsorb his already expended sighs and tears. It is not sufficient for Donne to be able to sigh and cry again; he wants to emit the very same sighs and tears that he has already expended on his idolatrous loves, as if the number of sighs and tears an individual can expend are finite

---

[52] Catherine Gimelli Martin, "Experimental Predestination in Donne's *Holy Sonnets*: Self-Ministry and the Early Seventeenth-Century *Via Media*," *Studies in Philology* 110, no. 2 (2013): 350–81, esp. 373.

142 DEVOTIONAL EXPERIENCE IN THE REFORMATION

in number. Indeed, those tears would have been better spent, Donne insists, in the present state of spiritual upheaval. Despite eschewing his former idolatry, in some sense Donne's impossible request encodes a desire not to eschew the past, but to repeat it. He desires to reverse his tears, not because he wishes that he had never sighed and cried, but because he wants to grieve over again. Donne conserves the structures of his former idolatry in his present attention to God. In fact, Donne's expression of devotion looks alarmingly like his former idolatrous commitments: in his holy discontent, Donne wants to "Mourne with some fruite, *as I haue mournd in vaine*." Devotional mourning is a counterpart, a consequence, and an analogue to an idolatrous past.

The devotional significance of sighs and tears had shifting valences in Reformation religious culture; by no means was there a consensus about what those outward gestures of penitence might entail. As Alec Ryrie has noted, a subset of popular Reformed culture maintained that these bodily gestures of penitence had the devotional force of prayer itself: "A more comforting—and less common—variant held that people can sometimes pray without knowing it."[53] The Oxford-trained reformer Ezekiel Culverwell asserted that even penitents who "can do nothing but sigh and groan, not able to set aright their hearts to pray to God" nevertheless still inadvertently capture the devotional essence of prayer itself.[54] In a similar vein, the devotional writer Robert Linaker stated the case directly: "If you can sigh and groan, after this manner, be of good comfort. For ... you pray very effectually."[55] As Ryrie has pointed out, reformist arguments that a penitent's sighs and groans might themselves be a form of wordless prayer had scriptural support: "Likewise the Spirit also helpeth our infirmities: for we know not what we should pray for as we ought: but the Spirit itself maketh intercession for us with groanings which cannot be uttered" (Romans 8:26).[56]

In the twenty-third stanza from *A Litanie*, Donne appears to dabble in the view, articulated by Culverwell and Linaker, that sighs and groans might have the devotional force of prayer itself. In the poem, Donne reworks the refrain from the litany of the *Book of Common Prayer*—"We beseche thee to heare us good Lorde"—in the poem's appeal to God: "Heare us, O heare us, Lord" (23.1).[57] While the

---

[53] Alec Ryrie, *Being Protestant in Reformation Britain* (Oxford: Oxford University Press, 2013), 104. For another excellent overview of the Reformed devotional tradition that equated sighs and groans with forms of prayer, see also John Craig, "Bodies at Prayer in Early Modern England," in *Worship and the Parish Church in Early Modern Britain*, eds. Natalie Mears and Alec Ryrie (Farnham: Ashgate, 2013), 173–96, esp. 181–2.

[54] Ezekiel Culverwell, *A Treatise of Faith* (London: Printed by I. L. for William Sheffard, 1623), 331–2. Cited in Ryrie, *Being Protestant*, 104.

[55] Robert Linaker, *A comfortable treatise for the reliefe of such as are afflicted in conscience* (London: Valentine Simmes for R. Boyle, 1595), 47–8. (*EEBO*, STC (2nd ed.) / 15638.)

[56] *The Holy Bible, Conteyning the Old Testament and the New* (London: Imprinted by Robert Barker, 1611). (*EEBO*, STC (2nd ed.) / 2217.)

[57] Helen Gardner, ed., *John Donne: The Divine Poems* (Oxford: Oxford University Press, 2000 [1952]). For the refrain as it appears in the 1559 liturgy, see *Book of Common Prayer*, ed. Cummings, 118.

congregants in the state church services would have exhorted God to hear their petitions, Donne goes a step further in his refashioned litany in that he actually instructs God *how* to hear and interpret his private prayers in moments when "[w]e know not what to say" (23.6). Importantly, Donne's sighs and tears still demand interpretation, but it is up to God to act as interpreter of those outward signs of penitence: "Thine eare to'our sighes, teares, thoughts gives voice and word" (23.7). In adopting the set form of the litany of the state worship service, Donne nevertheless uses that form to advocate for a broadened definition of prayer—one that goes beyond the bounds of official set prayer, and even beyond language itself. In his reimagined litany, Donne pays homage to the communal litany even as he simultaneously obviates the need for those very forms of communal prayer; in Donne's litany, a penitent needs neither a congregation nor even words in order for God to know the import of his sighs and groans. Contrary to the import of the *Holy Sonnets*, in *A Litanie*, Donne avers that even the non-verbal gestures of penitence and devotion—one's sighs, tears, and even unarticulated thoughts—have the devotional force of prayer itself. Donne's private litany adopts the comforting view espoused by his Reformed contemporary John Winthrop, a founder of the Massachusetts Bay Colony, who argued that his own struggle to pray posed no barriers for God: "when I set myself seriously to prayer etc: though I be very unfit when I begin, yet God doth assist me and bows his ear to me."[58]

Donne's private litany is an elaboration upon Winthrop's view of devotional assistance. In the poem, Donne suggests that since it is ultimately God himself who imparts his devotional intentions to us, in the end, God's help makes it possible for him to hear his own devotional desires reflected back in the prayer: "Heare thy selfe now, for thou in us dost pray" (23.9). In the penultimate stanza of *A Litanie*, Donne seems to suggest that God's interpretive powers are so all-encompassing that they defy the usual empiricist categories upon which human knowledge rests: "Heare us, weake ecchoes, O, thou eare and eye" (27.9).[59] God's modes of knowing and interpretation are so expansive, Donne suggests, that they benefit from something akin to a divine synesthesia. God hears Donne's prayers not only with his ears, as we mortals do, but even with his eyes.

Donne's private litany shares in the devotional optimism articulated by Reformed thinkers such as Winthrop, Linaker, and Culverwell, and explores that optimistic view of prayer in startling poetic turns. But in his public facing sermons, as in his *Holy Sonnets*, Donne insisted that the interpretive onus of one's sighs and tears rested not on God and his synesthetic capacities for sense, but rather upon the one who prayed. In a sermon delivered at Sir William Cokayne's funeral in 1626, Donne described the monumental difficulty of effective prayer:

---

[58] John Winthrop, *Winthrop Papers*, vol. 1, 1498–1628 (Boston: Massachusetts Historical Society, 1929), 167. Cited in Ryrie, *Being Protestant*, 104.

[59] Although Gardner renders the line "eare, and cry," she notes that the line appears as "eare and cry" in manuscripts classified under Group III, the largest grouping of the divine poems.

144   DEVOTIONAL EXPERIENCE IN THE REFORMATION

But when we consider with a religious seriousness the manifold weaknesses of the strongest devotions in time of prayer, it is a sad consideration. I throw my self down in my chamber, and I call in, and invite God, and his angels thither, and when they are there, I neglect God and his angels, for the noise of a fly, for the rattling of a coach, for the whining of a door; I talk on, in the same posture of praying; Eyes lifted up; knees bowed down; as though I prayed to God; and, if God, or his angels should ask me, when I thought last of God in that prayer, I cannot tell; Sometimes I find that I had forgot what I was about, but when I began to forget it, I cannot tell. A memory of yesterday's pleasures, a fear of tomorrow's dangers, a straw under my knee, a noise in mine ear, a light in mine eye, an anything, a nothing, a fancy, a chimera in my brain, troubles me in my prayer. So certainly is there nothing, nothing in spiritual things, perfect in this world.[60]

Donne's anxiety about his inability to pray echoes his concern about his own devotional worthiness as a partaker in the Communion sacrament—just as the counterfactual "as if" of Holy Sonnet 8 reveals doubt about Donne's confidence in his own ability to secure grace for himself. In a Christmas sermon delivered in 1626, Donne articulated precisely this anxiety about his ability to secure grace as he reflected upon his participation in the Communion sacrament: "I am sure I receive him effectually, when I look upon his mercy; I am afraid I do not receive him worthily, when I look upon mine own unworthiness," he confessed. Donne admitted his own prevaricating position on his worthiness as a recipient of the sacrament: "Though I have a holy confidence of my salvation, yet the foundation of this confidence is a modest, and a tender, and a reverential fear, that I am not diligent enough in *the performance of those conditions* which are required to the establishing of it."[61]

In the Christmas sermon, Donne articulates the paradox of being at once certain of his salvation—that Christ did indeed die for him—and yet uncertain about his own ability to perform the conditions needed to secure it. Lurking in the subtext of the sermon's confession is Donne's fear—the same one that he revealed in Holy Sonnet 8—that he may not be able to undertake the necessary actions required to secure Christ's imputed righteousness for himself. In the sermon, Donne seems to be suggesting, as he does in Holy Sonnet 8, that Christ's Crucifixion alone might not be enough to secure grace for himself. Like the "unperfect actor" of Shakespeare's Sonnet 23, whose fear puts him beside his part, Donne fears that he is unable to perform the role of one worthy of grace.[62] The performance of those conditions of grace, Donne believes, is key to the devotional effectiveness of the Communion sacrament: "Thou art a prophet upon thyself, when you comest to the

---

[60] Donne, Sermon 10, in *Sermons*, 7:265–6.
[61] Donne, Sermon 11, in *Sermons*, 7:290, 289–90, emphasis added.
[62] For my discussion of Shakespeare's Sonnet 23, see Chapter 2, 52–7.

DONNE'S SPEAKING IMAGES   145

Communion; Thou art able to foretell, and to pronounce upon thyself, what thou shalt be forever; Upon thy disposition then, thou mayest conclude thine eternal state; then thou knowest which part of St. *Paul's* distribution falls upon thee."[63]

It is notable that Donne's devotional optimism regarding his sighs and groans in *A Litanie* is nowhere to be found in Holy Sonnet 3, in which Donne himself bears the burden of chief interpreter—a prophet—of his outward show of penitence. In the sonnet, Donne's sighs and tears do not evidence his repentance of his past idolatries; instead, he fears they mark a continuation of those former sins. Rather than marking a clean break with his past idolatries, Holy Sonnet 3 problematizes Donne's task of untethering proper devotion from the sins that prompted the repentance. Perkins warns against precisely this inability to repent, despite the penitent's sincere desire to do so, in his description of the reprobate:

> After [the reprobate] hath committed a sin, he *sorroweth and repenteth*: yet this repentance hath two wants in it. First he doth not detest his sin, and his former conversation when he repenteth: he doth bewail the loss of many things which he once enjoyed ... yet for his life, he is not able to leave his filthy sin: and if he might be delivered, he would sin as before.[64]

Like Perkins, Donne himself remained deeply wary of the resurgent power of old desires, sins, and idols. The problem of remnant idolatrous practices within the Reformed church fascinated and haunted Donne, who, in his capacity as a cleric, repeatedly preached against the dangers of unwittingly partaking in idol worship. In a sermon on Deuteronomy 12:30 delivered on Ascension Day, 1622, Donne points out the latent danger remnant idolatry poses for the church—and even for those deeply committed to Reformed Christianity:

> Thou art bred in a Reformed Church, where the truth of Christ is sincerely preached, bless God for it; but even there thou mayest contract a pride, an opinion of purity, and uncharitably despise those who labor yet under their ignorances or superstitions; or thou mayest grow weary of thy manna and smell after *Egyptian* Onions again. *It is not enough that the state and the church hath destroyed idolatry so far as we said before; still there are weeds, still there are seeds.*[65]

Donne remained deeply wary about the possibility that an individual might accidentally partake in idol worship, due to the fact that the state and church might have failed to eradicate the roots of idolatry. Despite official safeguards against

---

[63] Donne, Sermon 11, in *Sermons*, 7:290.

[64] William Perkins, *A treatise tending vnto a declaration whether a man be in the estate of damnation or in the estate of grace* (London: By R. Robinson, for T. Gubbin, and I. Porter, 1590), 7. (*EEBO*, STC (2nd ed.) / 19752, document image 11.)

[65] Donne, Sermon 4, in *Sermons*, 4:137, emphasis added.

146 DEVOTIONAL EXPERIENCE IN THE REFORMATION

image worship, he maintained, an individual could unwittingly fall victim to idol-atrous desire. In this regard, Donne takes the opposite view of the one articulated by Richard Hooker, who argued that Reformed worship practices that paid cultural homage to older image-based rituals were *adiaphora*—practices that were moral and spiritually indifferent—rather than indicative of shared idolatry:

> And when God did by his good Spirit put it into our hearts, first to reform ourselves (whence grew our separation) and then by all good means to seek also their reformation; had we not only cut off their corruptions but also estranged ourselves from them in things indifferent; who seeth not how greatly prejudicial this might have been to so good a cause.[66]

Contrary to Hooker's conviction that the Reformed church had sufficiently excised the sources of former idolatry, for Donne, the old forms of idol worship continued to hold powerful sway over Reformed worshippers. Remnant idolatry held particularly dangerous ramifications precisely because the worshipper could conceivably partake in that idol worship without ever intending to do so.

Donne's unwitting idolater is neither papist nor pagan, but the Reformed Christian—one's very self. In the unabashedly iconoclastic Ascension Day sermon, Donne departs from the paradigmatic position on the power of idols, disclosing his profound fear that idols might exert power even over those who overtly deny their spiritual potency. Iconoclasm is always motivated by a belief in the power of images, but these images, the iconoclasts claim, only have power over others. "[I]conoclasm typically proceeds by assuming that the power of the image is felt by someone *else*," W. J. T. Mitchell writes. "The idol, then, tends to be simply an image overvalued (in our opinion) by an *other*: pagans and primitives; by children or foolish women; by Papists and ideologues."[67] The dangerous power of images touches only those, the image breakers maintain, whom the iconoclasts deem spiritually weaker than themselves. "*They* are the ones who are susceptible to the effectiveness of pictures; not us," David Freedberg describes this iconoclastic rhetoric. "With us there is no danger of the adoration of pictures, or of fetishization, or of being misled by bad subjects. This seems to have been the party line for hundreds and hundreds of years."[68] The fact that Donne includes himself and his parishioners among those susceptible to images makes his iconophobia particularly unusual and his idols especially fearful: these idols compel even those who deny their power.

---

[66] Richard Hooker, *Of the Lavves of Ecclesiasticall Politie. Eyght Bookes* [books 1–4] (Printed at London by Iohn Windet, dwelling at the signe of the Crosse keyes neare Powles Wharffe, and are there to be solde, [1593]), 4.7.181. (*EEBO*, STC (2nd ed.) / 13712.) Hooker printed the first four books of the *Lawes* in 1594 [1593], and the fifth book in 1597. I refer to both printed editions in this chapter.

[67] Mitchell, *Iconology*, 111.

[68] David Freedberg, *The Power of Images: Studies in the History and Theory of Response* (Chicago: University of Chicago Press, 1989), 399.

DONNE'S SPEAKING IMAGES   147

The epistemological impossibility of discerning proper devotion from idolatrous worship, which Donne describes in the Ascension Day sermon, is the very situation that he explores poetically in Holy Sonnet 3. In the sonnet, the external marks of both sin and redemption look identical, and the psychological and spiritual states of Donne's past and present griefs become indistinguishable from each other: "Because I did suffer, I must suffer paine," he laments (3.8). "[T]o poore me is allowd / No ease; for long yet vehement griefe hath beene / The effect and cause; the punishment and Sinne" (3.12–14). At the close of the poem, we see no distinction between the outward markers of the sinner and the penitent. As a result, we cannot discern whether Donne's current grief is the consequence of a sinful past or a sign of redemption from that past. In the *Holy Sonnets*, scripture and prayer are rarely causes for celebration, but rather tend to provoke Donne to profound anxiety about his election. The opposite was true for George Herbert, for whom the scripture afforded a certainty about salvation and offered a foretaste of the raptures of heaven; he described the bible as "joyes handsels" and "a masse / Of strange delights."[69] Prayer, too, eased Herbert's vexed spirit, engendering only "Softnesse, and peace, and joy, and love, and bliss."[70] Joy is similarly the baseline feeling motivating Richard Crashaw's *Steps to the Temple* (1646), his devotional sequence modeled after Herbert's. For Crashaw, Christ's outpouring of blood provided assurance of salvation; it is, he called it, "A deluge of deliverance."[71] But while Herbert and Crashaw both celebrated the joys that come from discovering one's election, Donne's poetry of praise is strangely silent about what the experience of being saved entails. In the *Holy Sonnets*, Donne never depicts the joys of salvation because he can never quite convince himself that he has yet successfully repented—or that he really wants to do so.[72] In Holy Sonnet 3, the fine distinction—or perhaps even confusion—between idolatry and true worship of God poses an epistemological problem not just for Donne, but for his reader as well. Here I do not think that Donne is being merely witty in his conflation of the emotional states that distinguish idolatry from true worship. On the contrary, the

[69] George Herbert, "The H[oly] Scriptures I," in *The Temple: Sacred poems and private ejaculations* (Cambridge: Thom[as] Buck, and Roger Daniel, printers to the Universitie, 1633), p. 50, lines 13, 6–7. (*EEBO*, STC (2nd ed.) / 13183, document image 30.)

[70] Herbert, "Prayer (1)," in *The Temple*, p. 43, line 9. (*EEBO*, document image 26).

[71] Richard Crashaw, "Upon the Bleeding Crucifix A Song," in *Steps to the Temple: sacred poems, with other delights of the muses* (London: Printed by T.W. for Humphrey Moseley, and are to be sold at his shop at the Princes Armes in St. *Pauls* Church-yard, 1646), p. 24, line 39. (*EEBO*, Wing / C6836, document image 18).

[72] Barbara Lewalski has made the argument that the *Holy Sonnets* charts a typically Protestant spiritual progression across the sequence, embodying the Protestant paradigm of salvation. See Lewalski, *Protestant Poetics*, 264–75. Yet I am more inclined to agree with David Chanoff's suggestion that the sequence as a whole reveals spiritual paralysis rather than spiritual progression. The recognition of Christ's grace only highlights for Donne his paralysis in the face of that saving act. As Chanoff writes, "Rather than a prayer of offering, the 'Holy Sonnets' are desperate pleas for grace; they contemplate nothing beyond repentance." See Chanoff, "Donne's Anglicanism," 161. Indeed, contrary to Lewalski's reading of the sonnets, Donne cannot make spiritual progress so long as he remains frustrated about his inability to repent, and this is especially true of the conundrum of Holy Sonnet 3.

148   DEVOTIONAL EXPERIENCE IN THE REFORMATION

poem embodies a genuine fear that it might be impossible—even for a thinker as perceptive as Donne—to interpret definitively the marks of election.

The monumental task of interpretation is Donne's primary conundrum in Holy Sonnet 3. Are his external signs of grief indication of his successful repentance—and thus, of his salvation—or are they resurgent remnants of his former idolatry? But the problem of interpretation aside, Donne faced an additional problem. The very fact that he must gauge the status of his election by observing his own bodily behavior (his sighs and his tears) means that he is forced to rely on the very outward gestures of devotion that he so feared would trigger a relapse into the sins of his past. In the Ascension Day sermon, Donne argues that the most dangerous form of idolatry stems from the belief that one has already successfully repented of it. Of the many varieties of idolatry, one of the worst types grants the false sense of security that comes from ineffectual acts of repentance. The sermon warns that it is as easy, as a result of sacramental shows of devotion, to relapse into sin as it is to request forgiveness: "As many habitual sins as we have, so many idols have we set up. True repentance destroys this idolatry, 'tis true; but then, *Take heed of being snared,* post ea, *by coming after them,* by exposing thy self to dangers of relapses again, by consideration how easily thou madest thy peace last time with God."[73] Donne did not conceive of himself as a moderate along the theological lines of Hooker, who saw the ease of participating in official church worship as a devotional benefit—"the service of God in the solemn assembly of saints is a work though easy yet withal so weighty and of such respect"—one that enabled even children to sound God's praise.[74] Easy prayer, on the contrary, put Donne ill at ease. For Donne, prescribed prayer and external gestures of devotion serve as catalysts for relapse into idolatry, precisely because they tend to be interpreted as sufficient evidence of complete repentance. In most cases, the Ascension Day sermon suggests, such acts of repentance are ineffectual, despite appearing otherwise to the outside observer. The elusive task of reading spiritual states is complicated by the fact that often they are not only illegible to the outside observer; they are most often illegible even to the very one wishing to repent. The interpretive problems that arise from this spiritual illegibility are compounded when one mobilizes external gestures of devotion to bolster an act of repentance. Holy Sonnet 3 imagines the spiritual ramifications of erroneous interpretation and unwitting relapse into sin, the twin concerns that Donne outlined in such strident terms in the Ascension Day sermon.

---

[73] Donne, Sermon 4, in *Sermons,* 4:140.

[74] Richard Hooker, *Of the Lawes of Ecclesiasticall Politie. The fift Booke* (London: Printed by John Windet dvvelling at Povvles wharfe at the signe of the Crosse Keyes and are there to be solde, 1597), 5.31.66. (*EEBO,* STC (2nd ed.) / 13712.5.)

Iconoclasm and iconophilia

What causes the particular variety of spiritual paralysis Donne so brilliantly captures in Holy Sonnet 3? The answer, as I have suggested, has to do with the illegibility of the signs indicating election. In "O might those sighes and teares returne againe," Donne either does not want to or does not know how to put an end to his religious despair; he both dreads it as a mark of his idolatrous past and relishes it as an indication of redemption. Indeed, the poem reveals the impossible task of reading for signs of election—signs that ostensibly look, at least as they were imagined by Donne in the *Holy Sonnets*, remarkably indistinguishable from the marks of sinfulness. In his assessment of the predominant critical readings of the doctrine underlying the *Holy Sonnets* (i.e., that Donne was a renegade Anglican, a tortured victim of Calvinist despair, or a closet Jesuit), Brian Cummings argues that the many conflicting interpretations of the emotional states described in the sonnets all point to the fact that reading poetic emotion is hardly a straightforward task of interpretation: "These accounts, so different in their conclusions, are identical in their assumption of the legibility of emotion. Yet the difference in the conclusions itself belies such legibility," Cummings writes. "By the early seventeenth century religious identities in England are not constructed around fixed points of doctrine. Donne, like any intellectual interested in divinity, has to fashion his religion by means of a bewildering process of interpretation."[75] Similarly, in his reading of Holy Sonnet 15, Gary Kuchar attributes the poem's spiritual shortcomings to the fact that Donne remained indebted to both Ignatian meditative traditions and Reformed Christianity: "Like many of the *Holy Sonnets*, 'What if this present' fails devotionally because its speaker is caught within competing traditions."[76] What this chapter has sought to demonstrate, however, is that the devotional illegibility of the *Holy Sonnets* is not primarily the result of tensions between Reformed theology and competing traditions, so much as it is the product of tensions with the Reformed tradition itself. As Alexandra Walsham has noted, religious identity in the century after the Reformation was hardly a straightforward matter: "Even at the end of the Jacobean period, it seems clear, outward adherence to the Church of England's rites continued to camouflage a bewildering range of religious convictions and standpoints. Confessional identities were still in a state of transition and flux."[77] If Donne's readers have difficulty reading the emotional

---

[75] Cummings in particular refers to the insufficiencies of the interpretations put forth by John Carey, John Stachniewski, and Helen Gardner. See Cummings, *Literary Culture*, 369.

[76] Gary Kuchar, "Petrarchism and Repentance in John Donne's Holy Sonnets," *Modern Philology* 105, no. 3 (2008): 535–69, esp. 560. See also a revised version of this article with the same title in Gary Kuchar, *The Poetry of Religious Sorrow in Early Modern England* (Cambridge: Cambridge University Press, 2008), 151–83.

[77] Alexandra Walsham, "The Parochial Roots of Laudianism Revisited: Catholics, Anti-Calvinists and 'Parish Anglicans' in Early Stuart England," *Journal of Ecclesiastical History* 49, no. 4 (1998): 620–51, esp. 637.

150   DEVOTIONAL EXPERIENCE IN THE REFORMATION

import of the sonnets, this is due to the fact that Donne himself—much like his post-Reformation contemporaries—found his interpretive frameworks subject to the uncertainties brought about by this period of religious transformation.

Donne captures those uncertainties in Holy Sonnet 10, "Yf faithfull Soules be alike glorify'd," in which outward signs of repentance can only offer up inconclusive evidence upon a penitent's spiritual state. The central problem in the poem is an epistemological one: Donne discovers that he cannot make interpretive sense of the external signs that ought to assure him that he, too, is among the souls who have escaped Hell's eternal damnation:

> Yf faithfull Soules be alike glorify'd
> As angells, then my Fathers soule doth see
> And adds this ev'n to full felicity,
> That valiantly I Hells wide mouth ore-stride.
> But yf our mindes to these soules be descry'd
> By circumstances, and by signes that be
> Apparent in vs, not Immediately,
> Howe shall my mindes white truth to them be try'de?
>
> (10.1–8)

Here Donne depicts an account of spiritual judgment—but he makes it intentionally difficult to know who is judging whom, and what. The density and obliqueness of the syntax in lines 5–8 mirrors the epistemological confusion that he is attempting to describe. It appears that "these soules" of line 5 are the same "faithfull Soules" of line 1, but that they differ from those denoted by "our mindes" in the same line. There are two groups of souls here, and Donne positions the faithful as witness to the outward circumstances and signs that can reveal the true spiritual status of "our mindes"—a second category of souls who are far less certain than the faithful of their election. Uncertain as of yet as to what the faithful will judge of him, Donne frets about the fact that he cannot anticipate the conclusions that they may draw. Indeed, the real problem in the poem is that those circumstances and signs are illegible to himself; that those outward indicators are "[a]pparent in vs, not Immediately" is the central source of Donne's epistemological anxiety. At the same time, however, Donne does not appear to believe that those circumstances and signs are inherently illegible, only that they are so to him. In fact, he remains committed to the idea that those signs might hold interpretive possibilities for others. Rarely in the *Holy Sonnets* is Donne preoccupied about what other people may think about him, but in Holy Sonnet 10, before a jury of the faithful set to judge, he wonders, "Howe shall my mindes white truth by them be try'de?"

At this point in the poem, Donne introduces a third category of souls, the reprobates, who are also subject to the spiritual judgment of the faithful, the "They" of line 9:

DONNE'S SPEAKING IMAGES   151

> They see Idolatrous Lovers weepe and mourne,
> And vile blasphemous coniurers to call
> On Iesus name; and Pharisaicall
> Dissemblers faine devotion.

(10.9–12)

As Donne gazes at the faithful, who in turn look on at the reprobates as they weep and mourn, it is uncertain as to how any of the spectators of these scenes of penitence and devotion have access to the actual spiritual statuses of the so-called idolaters, blasphemers, and dissemblers. What makes these audiences certain that these worshippers are indeed reprobate? This is the question that Donne raises implicitly in the closing lines of the poem, in which he prioritizes God's judgment over that of those who regard themselves as elect: "then turne / (O pensiue soule) to God, for He knowes best / Thy greife, for he put it into my brest" (10.12–14). At this point in the sonnet Donne seems to contradict himself, suggesting that no one can truly know the mind of God while also raising the possibility of the spiritual comfort that comes from the certainty of experience. Even as Donne has just discredited the value of outward circumstances and signs as indicators of spiritual grace, paradoxically, he makes a final case for the devotional value of penitential grief.

Importantly, though, the unexpected resolution of Holy Sonnet 10 is not indicative of either a devotional or poetic failure on the part of the poem; on the contrary, the sonnet captures the tensions surrounding performed devotion within Reformed doctrine itself. Much like the argument of Donne's sonnet, Perkins likewise recognized that visible signs of devotion have the capacity to mislead, while nevertheless insisting on their devotional power. Despite Perkins's cautionary tales of the reprobate, who persists in sin despite outward signs of repentance, he also insisted that observable, sensible signs could serve as the foundation for knowledge of salvation. In *A graine of musterd-seede* (1611), which takes its title from Matthew 17:20,[78] Perkins ascribed to these outward marks of penitence the devotional potency of prayer itself:

> [W]hen a man in his weakness prays with sighs and groans, for the gift of lively faith, the want thereof he finds in himself, his very prayer on his manner made, is as truly in acceptation with God, as a prayer made in lively faith.[79]
>
> Understand that ... grief of the heart for the want of any grace necessary to salvation, is as much with God as the grace itself. *When being in distress, we cannot*

---

[78] "And Jesus said unto them, Because of your unbelief: for verily I say unto you, If ye have faith as a grain of mustard seed, ye shall say into this mountain; Remove hence to yonder place; and it shall remove; and nothing shall be impossible unto you." *The Holy Bible, Conteyning the Old Testament and the New* (London: Imprinted by Robert Barker, 1611). (*EEBO*, STC (2nd ed.) / 2217).

[79] William Perkins, *A graine of musterd-seede or, the least measure of grace that is or can be effectuall to saluation* (Printed at London: By Iohn Legate, Printer to the Vniuersitie of Cambridge. And to be sold in Pauls Church-yard at the signe of the Crowne by Simon Waterson, 1611), 24–5. (*EEBO*, STC (2nd ed.) / 19725, document image 15.)

152   DEVOTIONAL EXPERIENCE IN THE REFORMATION

*pray as we ought, God accepts the very groans, sobs, and sighs of the perplexed heart,
as the prayer itself.*[80]

[F]or if we can but grieve because we cannot pray, we now pray indeed.[81]

Even as Perkins suggests elsewhere that the most devout Protestants might nevertheless be unwittingly reprobate, he insists that these sighs and tears might serve as
fair indicators of grace, and provide the kernel—the proverbial "musterd-seede"—
of an eventual, stronger faith.

Perkins coupled his insistence on the devotional value of outward performances
of penitence with the assertion, in *A case of conscience* (1592), that there are numerous, diverse signs of grace; these signs of election are so various that no one judging
from without could possibly deny assurance of election to another. Assurance
through experiential encounters takes many forms: it comes "not one way, but
many ways."[82] Perkins chastises the "school-men" who attempt to discredit others'
attempts to ascertain their election; these academic theologians are much like the
faithful souls of Donne's Holy Sonnet 10 in their attempts to "descry" the elected
status of others: "The school-men demand, whether a man may be made sure of
his election. And they determine that a man cannot, except it be by divine revelation: because predestination is in God, and not in us. ... But they are deceived, for
God, not only by this one manner, which they spake of, doth reveal his will and
his counsels, but by many ... by inward and outward effects."[83]

According to Perkins, it is the school-men and not the reprobates who emerge
as the real hypocrites in the ongoing struggle to determine election. While these
theologians, who ostensibly subscribe to a form of radical puritanism, attempt to
narrowly circumscribe the indications of grace, Perkins argues for the opposite:
he makes a case for the devotional value of a wide range of sensible occurrences,
investing each of these with something akin to sacramental potential.

At the core of Donne's *Holy Sonnets* lies Perkins's paradoxical theology,
which insisted on the interpretive value of sensible, observable performances of
devotion—even as it denies the possibility of fully knowing the spiritual import
of such performances. But for Donne, that freewheeling process of interpretation

---

[80] Perkins, *Graine of musterd-seede*, 42–3, emphasis added. (*EEBO*, document image 24.)

[81] Perkins, *Graine of musterd-seede*, 23. (*EEBO*, document image 24.) Here Perkins cites Augustine in
support of his argument about the devotional power of outward signs of penitence; earlier in the treatise, he discusses Ignatius along with Lucifer and Beza to make similar points. Perkins's wide-ranging
source material is further testament to the fact that the Reformed theology of those like Perkins preserved continuities of Catholic thought. Donne's poetry, thus, could be both thoroughly Reformed and
still retain continuities with Catholic meditative practices. For a detailed treatment of Catholic resonances in English Protestant state worship, especially with regards to the 1559 *Book of Common Prayer*,
see Daniel R. Gibbons, *Conflicts of Devotion: Liturgical Poetics in Sixteenth- and Seventeenth-Century
England* (Notre Dame, IN: University of Notre Dame Press, 2017); and my treatment of Gibbons's
book in Rhema Hokama, Review of Daniel R. Gibbons, "Conflicts of Devotion," *Liturgical Poetics in
Sixteenth- and Seventeenth-Century England* (Notre Dame, IN: University of Notre Dame Press, 2017),
Parergon 34, no. 2 (2017): 207–8.

[82] Perkins, *Case of conscience*, 29. (*EEBO*, document image 15.)

[83] Perkins, *Case of conscience*, 31–2. (*EEBO*, document images 16–17.)

DONNE'S SPEAKING IMAGES   153

and the sense that he moved within a world replete with innumerable images—potentially idolatrous, potentially redemptive—made for a particularly expansive access to God. Despite his public sentiments as a preacher, as a poet, Donne's relationship with devotional images subverted the Church of England's official position on what constituted idolatry. In "The Crosse," Donne captures the paradox of a Reformed iconoclasm that was bound up with an undercurrent of iconophilia. Donne opens the poem with what would have been an especially inflammatory question for a Protestant in post-Reformation England: "Since Christ embrac'd the Crosse it selfe, dare I / His image, th'image of his Crosse deny?"[84] The answer to that question, for Perkins, would have been an assured reply in the affirmative. In *A Golden Chaine*, Perkins insisted that the image of the cross—being none other than an idol and a false image of the true God—must be banished from the church: "The image also of the cross and Christ crucified, ought to be abolished out of churches, as the brazen serpent was."[85] In his poem, Donne initially appears to take the opposite view, insisting that no pulpit preacher, reform-minded legislation, or scandalous shift in theological outlook could remove his image of the Cross: "From mee, no Pulpit, nor misgrounded law, / Nor scandall taken, shall this Crosse withdraw" ("The Crosse," 9–10). To do so would be tantamount to a tremendous devotional loss: "It shall not, for it cannot; for, the losse / Of this Crosse, were to me another Crosse" (11–12). Theologically, Donne imagines that devotional loss as a spiritual reenactment of the Crucifixion; syntactically, the lines serve to demonstrate the impossibility of ever losing the image of the Cross, which necessarily involves the creation of another Cross. But in his defense of images, Donne does not assume either a crypto-Catholic or a proto-Laudian position toward the use of church images. Instead, in the remainder of the poem, Donne uncouples the image of the Cross from the rarified world of the church space, linking it instead to a wide range of worldly sights and occurrences. As in Joseph Hall's *Occasions Meditations*, which sought to locate devotional possibilities in the ordinary and mundane,[86] Donne offers a litany of visual "crosses" made available by the variety and bounty of the natural world:

> Looke downe, thou spiest out Crosses in small things;
> Looke up, thou seest birds rais'd on crossed wings;
> All the Globes frame, and spheares, is nothing else
> But the Meridians crossing Parallels.

(21–5)

---

[84] John Donne, "The Crosse," in *Poems, by J.D. VVith elegies on the authors death* (London: Printed by M[iles] F[lesher] for Iohn Marriot, and are to be sold at his shop in St Dunstans Church-yard in Fleet-street, 1633), p. 64, lines 1–2. (*EEBO*, STC (2nd ed.) / 7045, document image 36.) I cite subsequent references to the poem parenthetically by line number.

[85] Perkins, *Golden Chaine*, unpaginated. (*EEBO*, document image 46.)

[86] For my discussion of Robert Herrick's poetry in the context of Joseph Hall's *Occasional Meditations*, see Chapter 3.

154   DEVOTIONAL EXPERIENCE IN THE REFORMATION

Like the *Holy Sonnets*, "The Crosse" presents a devotional process that reveals inescapable linkages to images. The poem describes a material world teeming with innumerable approximations, substitutes, and successors to the Cross, each of which, according to Donne, possesses the sacramental force of its prototype. Even access to one's own physical body is sufficient, Donne maintains, to replicate and ultimately replace the formal church images: "Who can deny mee power, and liberty / To stretch mine armes, and mine owne Crosse to be?" (17–18). In her reading of the poem, DiPasquale offers the striking suggestion that even the printed poem itself ought to be included among Donne's many material renderings of the cross: "[readers] will see the cross in the printed page. They will see it in the frequent repetition of the word 'cross,' and they will also see it in the individual cruciform letters x … and t … Donne ensures that the readers' eyes will gaze continually on crosses as they scan the lines of his poem."[87] In the visual rendering of the printed poem, the page itself offers yet another physical and visual prompt for occasional devotion. Although Donne did not advocate for the removal of the image of the Cross from church spaces, as Perkins did, in some sense the poem does just that—splintering the image into innumerable variations, semblances, and duplicates of the original. Eradicating the visual image of the Cross frees Donne to seek its likeness in every part of the natural world.

In a sermon delivered on Easter day, 1628, Donne argues that the entirety of the material world ought to be the basis for an experiential devotional practice. Like Hall, Donne refuses to limit devotional encounters to official church spaces or state worship practices; on the contrary, he argued that "[o]ur knowledge cannot be so dilated, nor God condensed, and contracted so, as that we can know him that way, comprehensively."[88] A multifaceted and inclusive God must be seen and understood in his entirety. To that end, Donne asserted that "for our sight of God here, our theatre, the place where we sit and see him, is the whole world, the whole house and frame of nature, and our *medium*, our *glass*, is the Book of Creatures, and our light, by which we see him, is the light of natural reason. … The world is the theatre that represents God, and everywhere every man may, nay must see him."[89] "The Crosse" captures the devotional sentiments described in Donne's Easter sermon. The poem describes the encounters that Donne believed could arise from any number of ordinary sights and sounds from the natural world, interpreted and rendered meaningful by means of our natural reason and understanding.

In "The Crosse," Donne delineates a number of occasional meditations—the devotional encounters, as described by Hall, inspired by the particularity of the physical world. As is the case with experiential Calvinism, the poem argues that the devotional benefits of formal worship need not be found solely within

---

[87] Theresa M. DiPasquale, *Literature and Sacrament: The Sacred and the Secular in John Donne* (Pittsburgh: Duquesne University Press, 1999), 39.
[88] Donne, Sermon 9, in *Sermons*, 8:236.
[89] Donne, Sermon 9, in *Sermons*, 8:221.

DONNE'S SPEAKING IMAGES   155

the state-sanctioned liturgy and sacraments. This position on formal ecclesiology and public worship—a position, I have shown, that was shared by Calvin, Cranmer, and Hooker—was hardly unorthodox by the time that Donne articulated it in his poems and sermons.[90] Similarly, that informal worship could afford devotional benefits previously limited to the formal sacraments was the central premise of popular devotional practices, such as those modeled by Hall and Perkins. Nonetheless, readers such as DiPasquale have been correct to note that there remained the possibility of unintentional idolatry in Donne's desire to replicate the image of the cross in a number of material instantiations. "There is little chance," DiPasquale has suggested, "that the poem will prove delightful for readers who object to the sign of the cross. ... What if [Donne's readers] are (as it seems more likely) comfortable conformists all too ready to mock 'Puritan' sensitivity to the peril of idolatry?"[91] Although DiPasquale is correct to note that the poem registers a potentially idolatrous import, she misattributes the nature of this idolatry. Donne's participation in the sacrament would not have angered so called Puritans, who would have celebrated his retreat from formal sacramentalism and his embrace of experiential Calvinism. On the contrary, Donne's idolatry is of the variety that Perkins most feared: an inward idolatry—one that had no bearing on the debate between conformists and Puritans, or on remnant Catholic worship.

As much as certain Reformed thinkers celebrated the material devotional prompts that afforded opportunity for occasional meditation, they also feared those same objects as potential idols. Even objects in the natural world were suspect, according to Jewel's *Homilie against idolatrie*, all too prone to being transformed into private idols of the mind: "And by and by he showeth how that the things which were the good creatures of God before (as trees or stones) when they be once altered and fashioned into images to be worshipped, become abomination, a temptation unto the souls of men, and a snare for the feet of the unwise."[92] Moreover, at least in his official clerical capacity, Donne echoed the sentiment of the *Homilie* in a Candlemas Day sermon on Matthew 5:8, which he delivered in either 1626 or 1627. In the sermon, he insisted that "when a man adores the sacrament, he must be sure, that he carry not his thoughts upon any thing that he sees, not only not upon bread and wine, (for, that they must not believe to be there, whatsoever they see or taste) ... he must carry all his thoughts upon the person of Christ, who is there, though he see him not; for otherwise, say they, if he

---

[90] See the Introduction and Chapter I in this book for my overview of Reformed sacramentalism and ecclesiology.

[91] DiPasquale, *Literature and Sacrament*, 44, 45.

[92] Jewel, "Homilie against *perill of idolatrie*," 33. The homily's fear that even objects in the natural world reveal idolatrous potentialities is echoed by Ainsworth, who claims that "every man is forbidden to make unto himself *any forme, shape,* or *resemblance,* of things in the heave[n]s, earth or waters, of *any similitude, shew,* or *likenes;* any *frame, figure, edifice* or *structure,* of man or beast, fowl or fish, or any creeping thing." See Ainsworth, *Arrow against idolatrie,* 9–10.

156   DEVOTIONAL EXPERIENCE IN THE REFORMATION

should adore that which he sees, he should commit idolatry."[93] As I have pointed out, Reformed theologians like Perkins included among idolatrous acts not only the worship of material relics and icons, but also the mental idols conjured by the mind. Because such mental images strive to approximate material objects, Perkins posited, they must necessarily fail to describe an immaterial God. But this immaterial conception of God poses a problem for Donne, for whom God was never immaterial. The devotional feeling that he cultivates in his religious poetry makes free use of objects in the material world that approximate, replicate, and even contain God when he threatens to make himself physically absent.[94] Even were the material Cross upon which Christ died to become inaccessible, this material loss would not be tantamount to a devotional loss for Donne.

Despite his sermon's rejection of the material basis of sacramental worship, in his devotional poetry Donne celebrates the role the material world plays in cultivating devotional affect. In fact, his celebration of Christ's Passion in "The Crosse" veers dangerously close to claiming the relative ease with which that divine event might be replicated—and even replaced. In addition to claiming the interchangeability of Christ's Cross and the many cross-like instantiations of the physical world, he also claims the redundancy of the Passion. More than simply serving as a token of remembrance, Donne suggests the possibility that these signs and images might function not as substitutes for the Cross but for Christ himself: "Then are you to your selfe, a Crucifixe. / ... Let Crosses, soe, take what hid Christ in thee, / And be his image, or not his, but hee" (32, 35–6). What begins as an iconoclastic rejection of material images of the Cross culminates in an attempt to usurp

---

[93] Donne, Sermon 13, 7:333.

[94] Despite their radically dissimilar conclusions about the *Holy Sonnets*, both William Kerrigan and Stanley Fish have pointed to the ways Donne's conception of God strives for approximation rather than direct representation. Donne's God, Kerrigan claims, is like the God of Milton's *Paradise Lost* in that he must be conceptually "accommodated" to fit the parameters of the human mind. See William Kerrigan, "The Fearful Accommodations of John Donne," *English Literary Renaissance* 4, no. 3 (1974): 340–63. Although Fish takes a disparaging view of the *Holy Sonnets* and their creator (claiming both are "sick"), he is correct to note that Donne conceptualizes his current devotion to God through the framework of his past erotic encounters. See Stanley Fish, "Masculine Persuasive Force: Donne and Verbal Power," in *Soliciting Interpretation: Literary Theory and Seventeenth-Century English Poetry*, eds. Elizabeth D. Harvey and Katharine Eisaman Maus (Chicago: University of Chicago Press, 1990), 223–52, esp. 241.

Similar observations have been made about materiality in the *Songs and Sonnets*. That parts of the material world absorb, subsume, and stand in for the absent beloved is a hallmark of Donne's erotic lyrics, as several readers of the poems have noticed. Elaine Scarry observes that the mimetic relationship between Donne's language and the material world enables his love lyric itself to function like a "place holder, occupying the person's space until he returns." See Elaine Scarry, "But yet the Body is his Book," in *Literature and the Body: Essays on Populations and Persons*, ed. Elaine Scarry (Baltimore: Johns Hopkins University Press, 1988), 70–105, esp. 80. John Carey maintains that the boundaries of the human body subsume various parts of its material surroundings in the *Songs and Sonnets*: "The human body is regularly assimilated to, or blended with, inanimate objects ('larders', 'cellars', 'vaults'), and the effect of this is not to deaden it but to intensify its bulk and actuality." See Carey, *John Donne*, 137. Finally, James B. Leishman traces the absorptive, mimetic quality of Donne's poetry to Petrarchan roots, noting that both the *Songs and Sonnets* and *Il Canzoniere* reveal a tendency to imagine objects and places as compensation for the absent lover. See James B. Leishman, *Themes and Variations in Shakespeare's Sonnets* (New York: Harper Torchbooks, 1966), 185–9.

Christ's singular position for those who gaze upon and delight in images. In Holy Sonnet 8, with which I began this chapter, Donne asserts that his repentance holds a redemptive force as powerful as Christ's Passion. In "The Cross," Donne goes a step further, inserting himself into the very role of the crucified Christ.

Donne's simultaneous rejection and celebration of the image of the Cross captures the logic of Reformed sacramentalism as it was described and understood by church clerics like Perkins. Perkins's endorsement of the sacraments might be understood as an extension of his larger experimental predestinarianism, one that posits the bodily signs and symbols of devotion—whether formal or not—as outward indicators of one's intentions, desires, and spiritual standing. Indeed, Perkins's stance on the church's ceremonial performances bears striking resemblance to his applied divinity; his assessment of the devotional value of official worship practices might be understood as an extension of his position on the many unofficial devotional performances that unfolded on a continual basis even outside the parameters of the state worship services. According to Perkins, the official rites and ceremonies of the church comprised only a few of the innumerable outward signs of inward grace; the worshipper did not need to rely on the official rites and ceremonies to determine one's inward state. There were numerous means, apart from the official ceremonies of the church, through which an individual might discern his spiritual standing vis-à-vis God. Any number of unofficial bodily performances, Perkins maintained, could serve as equally powerful signifiers of one's devotional access to God. The devout could find God's presence and likeness "in every natural action, belonging to each living creature, as to nourish, to engender, to moue, to perceive." Liberated from the need to rely wholly on formal worship for devotional proximity to God, it was now possible to find God's presence "in every humane action, that is, such as belong to all men."[95] Although it might be unlawful to create material images of God's likeness—and indeed, Perkins utterly forbade participation in "all such processions, plays, and such feasts, as are consecrated to the memorial and honor of idols"—he nevertheless insisted that the material, sensible world ought to play a vital role in the devotional process: "The more obscure manifestation, is the vision of God's majesty in *this life*, by the eyes of the mind, *through the help of things perceived by the outward senses*."[96] As the sacraments were devotionally valuable in their capacity to make God's grace "visible to the eye," similarly, human life and the natural world worked in concert to make God's presence perceptible by means of one's bodily senses.[97]

Like Perkins's sacramentalism, Donne's poetics is a poetics of both iconoclasm and iconophilia. His devotional poems swerve perilously close to the idolatrous

---

[95] Perkins, *Golden Chaine*, unpaginated. (*EEBO*, document image 20.)

[96] Perkins, *Golden Chaine*, unpaginated, emphasis added. (*EEBO*, document image 7.)

[97] William Perkins, *A commentarie or exposition, vpon the fiue first chapters of the Epistle to the Galatians* (Cambridge: Printed by Iohn Legat, printer to the Vniuersitie of Cambridge, 1604), 254. (*EEBO*, STC (2nd ed.) / 19680, document image 135.)

practices that he so vigorously condemns as a preacher. But what is undeniable is that the very images that provoke such unease also foster devotional affect. Donne sees within his interior landscape a host of mental pictures that not only bolster his devotional entreaties, but moreover serve to facilitate a fusional identification between himself and God.[98] Images—both visual and mental—have an absorptive quality for Donne, not only mimetically representing but even subsuming their likenesses within their physical parameters. This tendency, the hallmark of both his erotic and devotional lyrics, perpetually undermines Donne's iconoclastic intentions in the *Holy Sonnets*. The idols of the mind can never be destroyed so long as they comprise the essential medium through which Donne processes all thought and devotional feeling as he negotiates his relationship with God. These idols are vexations as much as they are spiritual salves for Donne. Incapable of abjuring his past idolatry, Donne ultimately consigns himself to the necessity of embracing the very idols that he sets out to dismantle. The *Holy Sonnets* move toward establishing this dilemma, rather than toward any spiritual resolution or progression, as the sequence navigates among the shifting spiritual states of the sonnets.

[98] For Donne, physical proximity to God was an integral aspect of his understanding of effective worship. In his study of Donne's *Devotions upon Emergent Occasions*, Richard Strier has made the argument that the physical world—and in particular, the place of worship—played a key role in Donne's attempt to foster devotional affect. Strier points to Donne's deep anxiety about what effect his inability to worship within the physical space of the church would have on his spiritual wellbeing: "Donne is obsessed with the physical distance that his disease forces him to keep from the church as a physical place." See Strier, "Donne and the Politics of Devotion," 103.

5

Greville's Iconoclastic Desire

Reformed and Literary Devotion in *Caelica* and *The Life of Sir Philip Sidney*

If poetry offered a way for early modern writers to imagine a distinctly Reformed understanding of the body in devotion, Fulke Greville's lyric sequence *Caelica* is a poetic wellspring for readers of English Reformation culture. While overlooked for much of the last century of critical scholarship on *Caelica*, Greville's erotic lyrics nonetheless offered important contributions to English Reformation theology. In the sequence's devotional entries to the poet's earthly lovers and to God as his ultimate beloved, *Caelica* reveals Greville's radically original view of devotion—one that both challenged and reimagined the Calvinist experientialism of English clerics such as William Perkins.

Despite Greville's theological and poetic originality, for much of the twentieth century, the critical scholarship on Greville has presented his biography and his literary output in terms of orthodox Calvinist thought.[1] Paradoxically, many of these readings have regarded the erotic lyrics of *Caelica* as incompatible with this variety of mainstream English Calvinism—an assumption that reflects a misunderstanding of Greville's poetics as much as it does a misunderstanding of English Reformed devotion. Consequently, these critical approaches have read the sequence's early erotic poems as evidence of religious immaturity, describing the poet's longing as inherently opposed to proper Reformed devotion to God. As Greville moves through the sequence, such readings maintain, he demonstrates the process whereby idolatrous attachments are relinquished in exchange for a mature Reformed religion.[2]

---

[1] See Elaine Y. L. Ho, "Fulke Greville's *Caelica* and the Calvinist Self," *Studies in English Literature* 32, no. 1 (1992): 35–57; James Biester, "'Nothing Seen': Fear, Imagination, and Conscience in Fulke Greville's *Caelica* 100," *Hellas: A Journal of Poetry and the Humanities* 7, no. 2 (1996): 123–5; Kenneth J. E. Graham, *The Performance of Conviction: Plainness and Rhetoric in the Early English Renaissance* (Ithaca, NY: Cornell University Press, 1994), *passim* but esp. 93–6.

[2] Two recent essays challenge this prevailing view, and make excellent cases for how Greville's erotic poems are revealing of his Calvinist outlook. Dan Breen offers a valuable account of the flaws in the longstanding tendency to view desire in the sequence as an obstacle to proper Calvinist spiritual development. In Breen's view, on the contrary, desire remains a constant throughout *Caelica*'s narrative progression, and plays a vital role in Greville's processes of repentance and conversion. In a similar vein, Freya Sierhuis has argued that the sequence's erotic poems serve as conceptual frameworks for understanding not only Greville's theology and philosophy, but also his view of creative output and

Devotional experience and erotic knowledge in the literary culture of the English Reformation. Rhema Hokama, Oxford University Press. © Rhema Hokama (2023). DOI: 10.1093/oso/9780192886552.003.0006

160   DEVOTIONAL EXPERIENCE IN THE REFORMATION

In spite of these narrow approaches to Greville's theology, critical attention to Greville's Calvinism is not unmerited. Indeed, as Russ Leo, Katrin Röder, and Freya Sierhuis have argued, according to Genevan standards, Greville was arguably "the most orthodox English poet of his generation."[3] Although Greville's Calvinism reflected the dominant variety of English Reformed religion, new attention to his theology can reveal how even "orthodox" Reformed culture proved capacious and even contradictory during a time when confessional identity in England was still in flux. As Leo, Röder, and Sierhuis rightfully point out, new critical attention to Greville's Calvinism has the potential to "remap the contours of English Reformation thought, much more so than it confirms existing assumptions about confession and identity."[4] During the sixteenth and seventeenth centuries, Greville contributed to the making of English Reformation thought as much as he did to the emergence of English literary culture.

I see this present chapter contributing to an exciting new revival of scholarly interest in Greville. In including *Caelica* in this study, my intention is to elevate Greville's stature as a poet as much as it is to demonstrate how his poetics actively contributed to an emerging English Calvinism.[5] As Brian Cummings has argued, rather than functioning as a passive conduit of static theological doctrine, Greville's poetry reveals "theology in the making"—a theology that reveals "subtle counter-balances of thought and feeling. It is a theology with a living syntax rather than a fixed order of ideas."[6] Importantly, whatever contradictions and tensions arise from Greville's poetry need not be understood as conflict between Greville and the Reformed religious establishment, as previous readers of Greville have assumed. Cummings offers an alternate way of approaching those fissures:

the value of fiction. See Dan Breen, "Redeeming the Sonnet Sequence: Desire and Repentance in *Caelica*," in "Fulke Greville and the Arts," eds. Freya Sierhuis and Brian Cummings, special issue, *Sidney Journal* 35, nos. 1–2 (2017): 141–63, esp. 141–9; and Freya Sierhuis, "Centaurs of the Mind: Imagination and Fiction-Making in the World of Fulke Greville," in *Fulke Greville and the Culture of the English Renaissance*, eds. Russ Leo, Katrin Röder, and Freya Sierhuis (Oxford: Oxford University Press, 2018), 99–118.

[3] Russ Leo, Katrin Röder, and Freya Sierhuis, "The Resources of Obscurity: Reappraising the Work of Fulke Greville," in Leo, Röder, and Sierhuis, *Fulke Greville and the Culture of the English Renaissance*, 1–26, esp. 19.

[4] Leo, Röder, and Sierhuis, "Resources of Obscurity," 18.

[5] This revival of interest in Greville studies includes Leo, Röder, and Sierhuis's 2018 essay collection *Fulke Greville and the Culture of the English Renaissance*. Oxford University Press has also commissioned a five-volume *Collected Works of Fulke Greville*, based on the Warwick manuscripts. In 2009, Bradin Cormack published an influential new afterword to Thom Gunn's edition of *Caelica*, which brought renewed attention to the eroticism of Greville's poems. Additionally, during the past two decades, the *Sidney Journal* has commissioned two special issues dedicated to essays on Greville— one in 2017 edited by Freya Sierhuis and Brian Cummings, and one in 2001 edited by Matthew C. Hansen and Matthew Woodcock. See Bradin Cormack, "In the Labyrinth: Gunn's Greville," Afterword to *The Selected Poems of Fulke Greville*, ed. Thom Gunn (Chicago: University of Chicago Press, 2009), 161–77; Freya Sierhuis and Brian Cummings, eds., "Fulke Greville and the Arts," special issue, *Sidney Journal* 35, nos. 1–2 (2017); and Matthew C. Hansen and Matthew Woodcock, eds., "Fulke Greville," special issue, *Sidney Journal* 19, nos. 1–2 (2001).

[6] Brian Cummings, *The Literary Culture of the Reformation: Grammar and Grace* (Oxford: Oxford University Press, 2002), 301.

GREVILLE'S ICONOCLASTIC DESIRE   161

"If Greville's religious affiliation sometimes seems ambiguous, this can be said of the national church as a whole."[7] *Caelica*'s poetic contradictions are telling of Greville's ongoing efforts, as he wrote and revised the sequence, to work through the various and sometimes contradictory valences of Reformed devotion.

Greville's sequence is unusual in that it spans both secular love poems and devotional ones. But for the majority of the twentieth century, scholarship on Greville has favored attention to the divine poems at the expense of the erotic ones.[8] This critical oversight stems in part from the misapprehension that Greville's divine poems are better expressions of his Calvinism than his erotic lyrics. This outcome is also the result, I surmise, of the critical establishment's discomfort with the homoerotic nature of many of Greville's erotic poems, which celebrate the poet's desire for the young man Cupid as much as they do his attraction to Caelica, Myra, and Cynthia. By drawing attention to Cupid as one of the central love obsessions of the earlier lyric poems, it is possible to situate Greville's *Caelica* alongside Shakespeare's *Sonnets*—the preeminent early modern English lyric sequence that describes homoerotic love. Additionally, widening our critical attention to encompass not only Greville's entreaties to his girlfriends but also to his male beloveds allows us to recognize that Greville never really relinquishes his attraction to beautiful men in the sequence. Ultimately, Greville shifts his attention away from Cupid to another equally complicated object of longing: God. What becomes clear is that the argument of Greville's early erotic poems is key to understanding the devotional import of the sequence's later poems. Greville does not relinquish his early attraction so much as he transfers that attention to God, his ultimate love object.

If critical attention to Greville has overlooked the erotic poems as a whole, it has especially overlooked Greville's homoerotic lyrics. In 2019, Gina Filo published one of the few full-length articles about the homoerotic import of *Caelica*, but despite her readings of the erotic poems, she regards Greville's homoeroticism as at times antithetical to his larger Calvinist outlook, rather than key to understanding that outlook. Filo maintains that the sequence's early homoerotic encounters are "fleeting within the larger context of the work," and sets up her readings of these moments as alternatives to the critical tendency to focus exclusively on what she calls "Greville's religio-ethical system."[9] What Filo overlooks, however, is that Greville's erotic lyrics—including his homoerotic ones—should not be regarded as anomalies within the larger sequence, but should be acknowledged as key to our

---

[7] Cummings, *Literary Culture*, 299.

[8] In a recent essay, Sierhuis provides an excellent overview of the critical tendency to overlook Greville's love poems as she makes a case for the philosophical value of *Caelica*'s erotic lyrics. See Sierhuis, "Centaurs of the Mind," esp. 99–102.

[9] Gina Filo, "Fulke Greville's 'Sweet Boy': Homoerotic Desire in *Caelica*," *Sidney Journal* 37, nos. 1–2 (2019): 133–49, see pp. 136 and 134 for quotations. For a brief but excellent discussion of Greville's homoeroticism, see Cormack, "In the Labyrinth: Gunn's Greville." For a biographical discussion of Greville's apparent lack of erotic interest in women, see also Ronald A. Rebholz, *The Life of Fulke Greville, First Lord Brook* (Oxford: Clarendon Press, 1971), 50–67.

162   DEVOTIONAL EXPERIENCE IN THE REFORMATION

understanding of the work's distinctive vision of Calvinist theology and poetics. If Greville is the most Genevan of early modern English poets, situating his poems within both Elizabethan and Jacobean religious contexts can help to broaden the surprising ways in which English Calvinism found expression during this pivotal moment in Reformation culture.

In this chapter, I argue that *Caelica's* early love poems articulate a reformist view of the body's role in cultivating devotion. The sequence's earlier erotic poems provide an essential intellectual and theological framework for understanding the religious poems in the latter part of the sequence. For Greville, the erotic poems were ways of thinking through Reformed doctrine and identity during a long and productive career as a poet and political administrator. Like Montaigne's lifelong revision of the Bordeaux *Essais*, Greville's *Caelica* is a palimpsest that bears the impressions of nearly four decades of his creative, political, and religious expression. Greville likely began writing *Caelica* in the 1580s, and continued to edit and expand the sequence as late as the 1620s—well into the final decade of his life.[10] Greville's active editing of the sequence effectively makes *Caelica* a work of both the Elizabethan and Jacobean courts. In this sense, the sequence is unique in that is a product of confessional developments spanning two English reigns.

Caelica was never a work that grew solely out of Sidney's late-sixteenth-century milieu, but one that Greville actively edited and rewrote throughout his productive career. Approaching the sequence with this in mind allows us to regard Greville as he ought to be regarded—as an outstanding poet in his own right, and not just a satellite figure in Sidney's biography. It is worth noting, too, that Greville's status as a minor poet is partly the result of his own self-fashioning as a politician and a writer. In his *Life of the Renowned Sr Philip Sidney*, Greville presents himself as a skeptic of the arts, and a poet whose output was second to that of his friend. But this is calculated self-presentation on Greville's part, and did not reflect his actual stature as a politician, administrator, or poet. Indeed, Sierhuis and Cummings have argued that we should be "wary of believing too literally Greville's self-abasement. ... While many scholars have again taken him at his word in this, and emphasized his gloominess and even grumpiness, it is necessary to challenge such a stereotype because it is as much a self-conscious

---

[10] Norman Farmer, Jr. dates the sequence's late lyrics to the 1610s, and more recently, Gavin Alexander has argued for an even later date for the writing and final arrangement of the sequences—a process that he maintains persisted well into the 1620s. Morris W. Croll, in his analysis of the sequence's metrical variation among lyrics, likewise claims that the second half of *Caelica* was written later than the earlier sections—probably after 1600. See Norman Farmer, Jr., "Fulke Greville and the Poetic of the Plain Style," *Texas Studies in Literature and Language* 11, no. 1 (1969): 657–70, esp. 669; Gavin Alexander, *Writing after Sidney: The Literary Response to Sir Philip Sidney, 1586–1640* (Oxford: Oxford University Press, 2006), 244; and Morris W. Croll, *The Works of Fulke Greville: A Thesis* (Philadelphia: J. B. Lippincott, 1903), 17.

creation as Sidney's own constructed ego of *sprezzatura*, ease, and fancy. Neither image may be taken as fact."[11] Greville's decades-long work on the sequence means that *Caelica* invites comparison to an astonishing range of literary outputs; Greville's poems reveal correspondences with late sixteenth- and early seventeenth-century lyric sequences such as Sidney's *Astrophil and Stella* and Shakespeare's *Sonnets*, while also suggesting affinity with lyric expressions by slightly later seventeenth-century poets such as Herrick and Donne. In including Greville in a book alongside four more celebrated English writers, my intention is to present Greville as he should be read: as an original literary innovator, and as an indispensable figure in literary studies of Reformation culture and thought.

In this chapter, I maintain that in *Caelica*'s attention to the sensing body, Paradise emerges as a conceptual pivot by which Greville explores his anxiety about intimate access against the backdrop of a Reformed emphasis on experiential devotional practice. Foreshadowing Milton's *Paradise Lost*, Greville returns again and again to that moment in time that forever severs human beings from direct access to God.[12] In his rewriting of the Fall, Greville makes claims about what it means to be denied access—not only to God, the supreme object of desire, but also to the experiential evidence that Greville so desperately requires to interpret his affinities and intimacies, both erotic and spiritual. The second part of this chapter focuses on the question of what we ought to make of Greville's powerful impulse to inhabit the experience of desire, which he explicates in his poetry on the loss of Paradise. I argue that Greville's obsession with the evidence of experience—and specifically, the experience of desire—inflects his core conception of what moral poetry entails and what its responsibilities are to those who read it. Looking, lusting, and sexual revulsion held profound implications for Greville's vision of creative expression, and his negotiations with desires that he felt to be both unnatural and perverse inflect his attempts to describe a moral poetics grounded foremost in bodily and sensual experience. His lyric accounts of the desiring body chronicle a deeply personal response to his lifelong friend, literary hero, and erotic icon: Philip Sidney. Both *Caelica* and Greville's biography of Sidney reveal oblique challenges to Sidney's philosophy of moral poetics. While Sidney's *Defence of Poesy* hails the poet's imaginative license as the most important prerequisite for the creation of effective moral poems, for Greville, the process of poetic moral fashioning begins with direct encounters with desire. In the process of reimagining

---

[11] Freya Sierhuis and Brian Cummings, Introduction to "Fulke Greville and the Arts," eds. Sierhuis and Cummings, special issue, *Sidney Journal* 35, nos. 1–2 (2017): i–iv, ii.

[12] For an illuminating discussion of Greville's postlapsarian Calvinism, see Daniel Cadman, "'To fashion grounds, from whence artes might be coyn'd': Commerce and the Postlapsarian State in Greville's Poetry," in "Fulke Greville and the Arts," eds. Sierhuis and Cummings, special issue, *Sidney Journal* 35, nos. 1–2 (2017): 119–39.

164   DEVOTIONAL EXPERIENCE IN THE REFORMATION

Sidney's legacy, Greville found himself drawn into a paradoxical, complicated process of wanting to both preserve and dismantle the literary and erotic inheritances left in the wake of his friend's death. Sidney—like Greville's vision of Paradise—embodied both a lost literary ideal and a starting point for Greville's veiled acts of poetic iconoclasm as he actively sought to subvert, erase, unwrite, and rewrite Sidney's moral poetics.

***

Much like Donne, Greville grappled with the question of how to look at the objects of his desire. Early on in *Caelica*, Greville struggles in his attempts to regard his erotic love objects, in much the same way that Donne struggled to behold Christ—both as God and as an embodied object of desire. Greville's attempts to look at naked women strike us as among the most baffling encounters chronicled in his lyric sequence. In poem 56, Greville relates his plot to sneak into the sleeping Cynthia's chambers with the intention of stealing a glimpse of her beautiful body—and perhaps do more—while she sleeps unawares. The excursion into the woman's bedchamber is rewarded indeed with marvelous sights and visions. "Sweet God *Cupid*," Greville marvels, "where am I?"[13] In the bedroom, Greville launches into a highly wrought conceit, in which he imagines gazing not up toward the heavens, but down toward the "Milken Way" of Cynthia's porcelain thighs—what he calls the "Way unto that dainty throne, / Where while all the gods would play, / Vulcan thinks to dwell alone."[14] But in what might have been the start of a blazon detailing the wonders of Cynthia's body, Greville seems to look away from the naked woman before him. In his expedition to the bedroom, Greville tells us instead about the gods at play, the night's shooting stars, and heaven's pale lights. "Wonders I saw, who can tell?" he asks (C56.11). Not Greville, it would seem. Despite his extensive *looking* during his unannounced visit to Cynthia's bedroom, poem 56 never does *tell* us what we hunger to know: what did Greville see of Cynthia herself, and what does she look like? The poem expends few words in describing Cynthia's bodily form. At the end of the evening, the sight of Cynthia's naked body—on her bed she "did naked lye" (C56.31)—culminates only in Greville's erotic paralysis: "There stand I, like *Articke* pole," he recounts (C56.37). "There stand I like Men that preach / From the Execution place" (C56.41–2).

---

[13] Fulke Greville, *Caelica*, 56.13, in *Certaine Learned and Elegant Workes of the Right Honorable Fvlke Lord Brooke, Written in his Youth, and familiar Exercise with Sir Philip Sidney* (London: Printed by E. P. for *Henry Seyle*, and are to be sold at his shop at the signe of the *Tygers* head in St. *Paules* Church-yard, 1633), 200. (*EEBO*, STC (2nd ed.) / 12361, document image 131.) I take all quotations from *Caelica* (denoted C) from this edition. For ease of reference, I also parenthetically cite the poem and line numbers as they are given in Thom Gunn's edition of the poems. See Fulke Greville, *The Selected Poems of Fulke Greville*, ed. Thom Gunn (Chicago: University of Chicago Press, 2009 [1968]).

[14] C56.21, 22–4. Greville draws closer to a detailed physical description of Cynthia in one manuscript version of the poem, in which he continues the conceit. In these lines, Greville describes the "Nets of sullen golden hair" that shadow Cynthia's pudendum, woven by Vulcan to ensnare Greville—much like the god's other rival, the unsuspecting Mars. See *Selected Poems of Fulke Greville*, ed. Gunn, 84 for a reprint of the lines from the manuscript.

For Greville, objects of longing are often best left unseen. *Caelica* couples the desire to behold erotic delights with the impulse to destroy the material basis of those very forms. Always careful to avoid idolatrous import in his poems, Greville was clearly more at ease when he was negotiating with the *idea* of his love object than when he was encountering that presence in the flesh. In several early lyrics in the sequence, he describes erotic longing as a wholly spiritual and mental *askesis*—as if that desire could be extracted from its material and bodily origins. In poem 16, he yearns for a love "plac'd aboue these *middle* regions, / Where euery passion warres it selfe with legions" (C16.13–14). Evacuated of the passions and lifted above its fleshly origins, Greville's desire assumes the characteristics of a mental construct rather than a bodily transaction between beings. Greville's fantasy that devotion—whether erotic or divine—could operate within a realm wholly stripped of the material dimension is one that he voices early on in the sequence in a description of ideal, ethereal love untainted by matter or the body. Such love, he writes, "Must, as *Ideas*, only be embraced / Since excellence in other forme enioyed, / Is by descending to her Saints destroyed" (C10.22–4). In Greville's idealized vision of intimate access, the act of consummating desire—or even figuring that devotion using performed or written expressions of praise—was tantamount to a contamination of that originary love.

Greville's description of love as an *idea*, abstracted and extracted from material context, has an obviously Platonic valence. But his argument about perfect love also bears more immediate resemblance to a particular variety of Reformed iconoclasm that sought to describe God—the supreme object of devotional yearning—first and foremost as an abstraction rather than as a real presence. Like his yearning for women, Greville yearned for a God who existed solely within the realm of ideas. In his desire to make God less like an embodied presence and more like an avatar for spiritual good, Greville was not alone among Reformed Protestants. William Perkins, the Cambridge theologian and Church of England cleric, proposed a means of securing devotional access to God while also avoiding the problem of having to look at him—and thus running the risk of inadvertently participating in image worship.[15] Perkins conceded that one could indeed locate God's image within the world, but he argued that this image functions like a cognitive construct or a figment of one's conscience rather than like a visual impression: "The

---

[15] Despite a modern historical tradition of identifying Perkins as a Puritan opponent of the Church of England's theology and doctrine, the fact remains that he held positions within the Church of England until his death in 1602. Seventy-six editions of Perkins's religious works were printed during his lifetime, and his three-volume collected works had reached eight printings by 1653. By contrast, the religious works of Richard Hooker—described by contemporary scholars as the most influential church theologian during the reigns of Elizabeth and James—did not in fact gain widespread popularity until after 1660. See Bryan D. Spinks, *Two Faces of Elizabethan Anglican Theology: Sacraments and Salvation in the Thought of William Perkins and Richard Hooker* (Lanham, MD: Scarecrow Press, 1999), 3.

166 DEVOTIONAL EXPERIENCE IN THE REFORMATION

remnant of God's image, is certain motions concerning good & evil."[16] For Perkins, God's remnant "image" has been completely interiorized within the mind, serving as a guiding force for one's beliefs, actions, and above all, one's desires: "The remnant image of God's image in the conscience, is an observing and watchful power, like the eye of a keeper, reserved in man, partly to reprove, and partly to repress the unbridled course of his affections."[17]

As I argued in Chapter 4 on Donne's devotional poems, the striking feature of Perkins's iconophobia is its contingency upon a powerful iconophilia, a desire to conserve God's image as a devotional and moral aid—and indeed, to transpose that image onto the physical body of every Protestant believer and to every part of the material world. God's image is most clearly "seen [in] the creation of the world, being considered in his works," Perkins insisted.[18] That remnant image of God is to be found "in every natural action, belonging to each living creature, as to nourish, to engender, to move, to perceive," as well as "in every humane action, that is, such as belong to all men."[19] For Perkins, the image of divine perfection might be found in every human being's impulses and desires; even the movements of lower creatures were not too insignificant to contain versions of a divine semblance. In condemning those who worship images of God, Perkins nevertheless retained a commitment to preserving material likenesses of God's divine image, finding variations and reflections of it in the forms and movements of human and animal life. In describing the whole of the natural world as a dizzying assemblage of God's material likenesses, Perkins paradoxically destroys God's image by means of its endless reproduction; he obliterates the possibility of idolatry through the desacralization of God's image, by locating that image within innumerable facets of the material world.

Much like Perkins's paradoxical devotional practices, Greville's lyric poems maneuver between the irreconcilable urges both to behold and obliterate material forms. For Greville, the body and sensual experience were simultaneously sources of sexual idolatry and means of visualizing and confirming one's intimacy with God. His paradoxical vision of the material world reflects a cultural doubleness of vision that emerged in response to the English church's assimilation of the Reformed position on the role of the body in devotional life. Vilified as the wellspring of sensual weakness, the body nevertheless played a distinct role in spiritual life by virtue of the growing doctrinal emphasis upon the importance of what John Stachniewski and Anita Pacheco call the "evidence of experience"—the surest means of cataloging the outward and bodily indicators of one's own election, in an

---

[16] William Perkins, *A Golden Chaine, or the description of theologie containing the order of the causes of saluation and damnation, according to Gods woord* (London: Printed by Edward Alde, and are to be sold by Edward White at the little north doore of S Paules Church at the signe of the Gunne, 1591), unpaginated. (*EEBO*, STC (2nd ed.) / 19657, document image 18.)

[17] Perkins, *Golden Chaine*, unpaginated. (*EEBO*, document image 19.)

[18] Perkins, *Golden Chaine*, unpaginated. (*EEBO*, document image 18.)

[19] Perkins, *Golden Chaine*, unpaginated. (*EEBO*, document image 20.)

GREVILLE'S ICONOCLASTIC DESIRE   167

effort to decipher one's own standing relative to God.[20] This larger religious and cultural anxiety about the body—what it reveals and conceals about inward devotional affect—informs Greville's poems about the difficulty of looking upon and securing one's intimate access both to God and to an array of earthly beloveds.

Despite his wariness of what he felt to be the perversity of his own erotic longings, the body and its desires continued to play central and lively roles in Greville's devotional and erotic performances. In poem 56, there *is* an object of desire who receives great attention in Cynthia's bedroom—but that person is not Cynthia. That individual is Greville himself, who fancies himself a god as he approaches the sleeping, naked woman:

> I gaue reynes to this conceipt,
> Hope went on the wheele of lust:
> Phansies scales are false of weight,
> Thoughts take thought that goe of trust.
> I stept forth to touch the skye,
> I a God by *Cupid* dreames.
>
> (C56.25–30)

But does Greville indeed fancy himself a god? Or is it Cupid who fancies Greville a god in the convoluted syntax of this strange conceit? It is impossible to say with absolute finality what role Cupid plays in the poem's erotic encounter. Perhaps Greville's "by Cupid" is a mere interjection in his bombastic conceit, or perhaps Greville imagines himself as a kind of mythic boy god—one akin to Cupid himself. More likely, I think, Greville imagines that Cupid is the one who is looking at the erotic performance of poem 56, both as audience and director of the scene. Greville is a god in Cupid's mind, and his subsequent erotic paralysis might be regarded as a kind of stage fright, an inability to fully inhabit the aesthetic, erotic, and divine requirements of the theatrical role. In a poem about the power of *looking*, Greville finds out that he is not ultimately the gazer, but the gazee—a player in Cupid's erotic imagination. In the end, Greville finds himself more excited by the

---

[20] See John Stachniewski and Anita Pacheco, Introduction to *Grace Abounding: With Other Spiritual Autobiographies*, by John Bunyan, eds. Stachniewski and Pacheco (Oxford: Oxford University Press, 2008 [1998]), xxii. Stachniewski and Pacheco maintain that the English religious establishment's acceptance of the doctrine of double predestination led to a conflicted paradigm about the role of the body and the senses in spiritual life: "The doubleness of predestination produced a doubleness of vision: the paradigm of reprobation (as explicit as that of election, and statistically much more probable) was always an influential possibility. ... In the end, only one of the paradigms could discover itself to be true for any one life. So there was a constant pressure to nag at the contradictory evidence, to keep experience under daily review; to try to argue anxiety away, certainly, but without evading the apparent grounds of anxiety" (xiv). For a thorough discussion of the cultural and psychological implications of the doctrine of double predestination in Perkins's devotional works, see Erin Sullivan, "Doctrinal Doubleness and the Meaning of Despair in William Perkins's 'Table' and Nathaniel Woodes's *The Conflict of Conscience*," *Studies in Philology* 110, no. 3 (2013): 533–61.

168 DEVOTIONAL EXPERIENCE IN THE REFORMATION

prospect of being looked at by Cupid than he does by the naked woman asleep in the bedroom.

A certain kind of performance anxiety coexists with the voyeurism of poem 56, and Greville remains deeply wary of finding himself unexpectedly onstage, in the spotlight, even as that prospect also holds for him a powerful erotic allure. And yet the Greville who emerges in *Caelica* is a consummate actor, and in key lyrics throughout the sequence, he inserts himself into moments from biblical history with surprising theatrical force. In fact, *Caelica* reads as an erotic re-enactment of one singular moment in divine history: the Fall.

Looking and lusting in Eden

A surplus of passion was what first severed Adam and Eve from God, according to Greville's retelling of the Fall. That desire was kindled by the act of looking—at the visions and dreams conjured by the devil: "The Serpent, Sinne, by shewing humane lust, / Visions and dreames inticed man to doe / Follies, in which exceed his God he must, / And know more than hee was created to" (C102.1–4). Lust, the world's first sin, precipitates human beings headlong into the imperfect world of matter, into what Greville describes as "the hell of flesh and blood" (C102.12). But this originary account of sin confounds those who probe the causes of the Fall, since it assumes the existence of lust even before the introduction of sin, a premise that would undermine not just Adam's perfection but God's as well. The task of poetically describing the kinds of desires that would have been available to Adam and Eve before their banishment from Eden provided a source of poetic fascination for Greville. In poem 102, Greville isolates what he describes as Adam's singular passion prior to the Fall: "in Paradise, / Eternity was obiect to his passion" (C102.31–2). Before the Fall, Adam's perfection existed on par with God's: "And hee in goodnesse like his Maker wise" (C102.33). With no competing desires or longings, his sight fixed firmly on the eternal, how is it possible to account for the ruptures in Paradise that would eventually sever Adam from God? "What greater power there was to master this, / Or how a lesse could worke?" Greville asks.[21]

In his attempts to justify the origins of the Fall, Greville conducts a thought experiment, positing a world devoid of eternity. In this hypothetical world,

---

[21] C102.35–6. Greville pursues a similar line of reasoning in his late verse treatise *A Treatise on Religion*, in which he questions how an otherwise omniscient God could have underestimated humanity's capacity for temptation: "Why God commanded more then Man could do, / Being all things that he will, and Wisdom too." See Fulke Greville, *A Treatise on Religion*, poem 76, lines 5–8, in *The remains of Sir Fulk Grevill Lord Brooke: Being Poems of Monarchy and Religion: Never before Printed* (London: Printed by *T. N.* for *Henry Herringman* at the sign of the *Blew Anchor* in the *Lower Walk* of the *New Exchange*, 1670), 196. (*EEBO*, Wing / B4900, document image 102.) For a discussion of Greville's frustrated stance toward God for having allowed the Fall, see G. A. Wilkes, ed., *The Complete Poems and Plays of Fulke Greville, Lorde Brooke (1554–1628)* (Lewiston, NY: Edwin Mellen, 2008), 2:322.

GREVILLE'S ICONOCLASTIC DESIRE   169

stripped of eternal concerns, Greville avers that sin would nevertheless have a
diminishing effect upon human life:

> But grant that there were no eternity,
> That life were all, and Pleasure life of it,
> In sinnes excesse there yet confusions be,
> Which spoyle his peace, and passionate his wit,
> Making his Nature lesse, his Reason thrall,
> To tyranny of vice vnnaturall.
>
> (C102.13–18)

In imagining a world without eternity, Greville reveals for a moment a fantasy
of a heavenless world in which sin's pleasure is paramount. This world, absent of
eternity and full of confusion and tyranny, is foremost a world suffused with pleasure: "That life were all, and Pleasure life of it." The eternal exists strictly, it would
seem, to keep human beings from veering into "unnatural" desires—the involun-
tary state of those left to their whims—at once abhorrent and thrilling to Greville.
In his description of these deviant longings, Greville attributes to them both the
hazards and pleasures of the occult: "And as Hell fires, not wanting heat, want
light; / So these strange witchcrafts, which like Pleasures be, / Not wanting faire
inticements, want delight" (C102.19–21). In poem 102, Greville wavers between
condemnation of what he feels to be the perversity of his own yearnings and a
compulsion to celebrate the advent of the "unnatural" in the aftermath of original
sin. This prevarication is only enhanced by the ambiguity of Greville's rhetorical
question about the origins of the Fall: "Is there ought more wonderfull than this?"
he exclaims, "That *Man*, euen in the state of perfection, / ... Should fall from God,
and breake his Makers will" (C102.25, 26, 29). Ostensibly, Greville suggests that
there is something astonishingly tragic about the events leading up to the Fall.
But the predominantly laudatory import of the word *wonderful*—meaning both
marvelous and excellent—was already the dominant meaning in late sixteenth-
and early seventeenth-century England, as it had been since its introduction to
Middle English in the twelfth century. *Terrible* would have worked equally well
for Greville's metrical scheme in that line, and would have certainly been far less
ambiguous.

The closing couplet of poem 102 grapples with the impossibility of fully relin-
quishing the pleasures of subversive longing: "Sin, then we knew thee not, and
could not hate, / And now we know thee, now it is too late" (C102.77–8). Presum-
ably, the final line means that it is now too late to restore the prelapsarian perfection
that Greville so longs for in his meditation about the loss of Paradise; it is too late
to un-know sin. But the line's elliptical syntax enables us to read a second meaning
in the line: now that we know its *wonderful* allure, it is too late to hate our sins and

170   DEVOTIONAL EXPERIENCE IN THE REFORMATION

"vice unnatural." For his sexual sins, Greville is not only unable but also unwilling to repent.

Greville emerges similarly unrepentant in poem 83, which recounts the Fall in terms of a deeply personal fall from erotic grace. In a meditation upon life after the loss of his beloved's favor, which he describes as a second Fall, Greville recounts the illicit act of first tasting the fruit of the forbidden tree: "In Paradise I once did liue; and taste the tree, / Which shadowed was from all the world, in ioy to shadow me" (C83.41–2). The protective shadows of Greville's erotic paradise quickly assume an ominous quality after his fall: "The tree hath lost his fruit, or I haue lost my seate, / My soule both blacke with shadow is, and ouer-burnt with heat" (C83.43–4). Surprisingly, the poem bemoans not the loss of perfection, but the tree's present barrenness: "The tree hath lost his fruit." That arboreal barrenness marks Greville's own erotic barrenness, and later in the poem he describes himself as "a tree that doth not bear" (C83.64). Having eaten of the forbidden tree, Greville's sole regret is that he will never again partake of the fruit's gustatory pleasures; in his fallen state, he is now barred from his former erotic joys.

Greville's retelling of the Fall in poems 102 and 83 is not, as expected, a story of repentance, nor does it chronicle a nostalgia for Paradise per se. There is the sense that Paradise has already been lost in the moments leading up to Greville's first forbidden tasting of the fruit, after he has committed to his intention to sin. In fact, Greville's account of the Fall contains echoes of Perkins's version of the story. For Perkins, spiritual blindness is the prerequisite for heightened sensory and sensual perception: "[B]eing thus blinded" by Satan's guile, Adam and Eve were "moved to behold the forbidden fruit," and "no sooner saw the beauty thereof, but they desire it."[22] In both Perkins's and Greville's accounts of the Fall, the pleasures and delights of the body are the sole domain of those who have already broken their ties to the eternal. It is this liminal state, after the Fall but before the loss of Paradise, that Greville yearns for as he laments the loss of his former erotic standing.

It is not surprising that Greville's poetry is inflected by the soteriological anxieties inspired by Calvin's variety of predestinarianism; indeed, the majority of the scholarship to date on Greville's literary output has presented his poems as expressions of his reformist commitments.[23] What is surprising, however, is Greville's

---

[22] Perkins, *Golden Chaine*. (*EEBO*, document image 17.)

[23] Greville's Calvinist and Puritan commitments have been widely discussed by readers of his poetry and plays, and while these approaches to Greville's theology are not inaccurate, these commitments could be equally described as representative of the dominant religious establishment. Considering the Church of England's relative openness to the Genevan position on election, a position that even theologians like Hooker would come to modify and support, Greville might be more accurately described as a writer of poetry that subscribes to a distinctly English Protestant sensibility. For an overview of those who have discussed the importance of Greville's Reformed Christianity for his literary output, see Cummings, *Literary Culture*, 304–8; Biester, "'Nothing Seen,'" esp. 123; Yvor Winters, *Forms of Discovery: Critical and Historical Essays on the Forms of the Short Poem in English* (Chicago: Alan Swallow, 1967), 45; William Frost, *Fulke Greville's "Caelica": An Evaluation* (Brattleboro, VT: Vermont Printing, 1942), 26; Thom Gunn, Introduction to *Selected Poems of Fulke Greville*, ed. Thom Gunn, 13–44,

GREVILLE'S ICONOCLASTIC DESIRE   171

self-reflexive awareness of his spiritual prevarication, and his refusal to emend his poetic account of desire in an effort to ease his own suspicion about his status as moral and sexual reprobate. Greville not only acknowledges his sexual sins, but, more alarming than even Perkins's reprobate, he is not even certain whether he really wants to repent of them. "The reprobate may have a feeling of his sins, and so acknowledge them," Perkins conceded.[24] Moreover, the reprobate may be desperate in his desire to repent, but remain unable to do so: "The reprobate for all this knowledge, in his heart may be an atheist."[25] Greville remains cognizant of his sins, but like Donne's persona in the *Holy Sonnets*, concedes that his sexual idolatries provide a source of unparalleled delight.

Yet unlike Donne, Greville acknowledges that his status as sexual reprobate is the result of his own inclination, and not God's eagerness to condemn. Indeed, he harbors no uncertainty about his ability to receive forgiveness, were he to ask for it. His spiritual and erotic misgivings emerge from his fundamental unwillingness to accept this saving grace:

> *If* from the depth of sinne, this hellish graue,
> And fatall absence from my Sauiours glory,
> I could implore his mercy, who can saue,
> *And for my sinnes, not paines of sinne, be sorry:*
>   Lord, from this horror of iniquity,
>   And hellish graue, thou *wouldst* deliuer me.
>
>   (C98.13–18, emphasis added)

The question that Greville poses to himself in poem 98 is not whether God would deliver him; on that point he is certain about God's boundless grace. His question is a more troubling one; he ponders whether he could truly, for his sins, be sorry—and not just fear their repercussions. For while all vice originates from

---

esp. 33; Jonathan Dollimore, *Radical Tragedy: Religion, Ideology and Power in the Drama of Shakespeare and His Contemporaries* (Durham, NC: Duke University Press, 2003 [1984]), 120, 130; Joan Rees, *Fulke Greville, Lord Brook, 1554–1628: A Critical Biography* (London: Routledge and Kegan Paul, 1971), 111–13; Jean Jacquot, "Religion et raison d'état dans l'oeuvre de Fulke Greville," *Etudes anglaises* 5 (1952): 211–2, esp. 212; Matthew Woodcock, "'The World is Made For Use': Theme and Form in Fulke Greville's Verse Treatises," in "Fulke Greville," eds. Hansen and Woodcock, special issue, *Sidney Journal* 19, nos. 1–2 (2001): 143–60, esp. 158–9; Fred Inglis, "Metaphysical Poetry and the Greatness of Fulke Greville," *The Critical Review* 8 (1965): 101–9, esp. 103; Graham, *Performance of Conviction*, 96; Catherine Bates, *Masculinity and the Hunt: Wyatt to Spenser* (Oxford: Oxford University Press, 2013), 189; Geoffrey Bullough, ed., *Poems and Dramas of Fulke Greville, First Lord Brooke* (New York: Oxford University Press, 1945), 1:23; Croll, *Works of Fulke Greville*, 18, 29; Wilkes, ed., *Complete Poems and Plays of Fulke Greville*, 2:319–20, 322; Richard Waswo, *The Fatal Mirror: Themes and Techniques in the Poetry of Fulke Greville* (Charlottesville: University Press of Virginia, 1972), 142; Rebholz, *Life of Fulke Greville*, 310; and June Dwyer, "Fulke Greville's Aesthetic: Another Perspective," *Studies in Philology* 78, no. 3 (1981): 255–74, esp. 269–71.

[24] William Perkins, *A treatise tending vnto a declaration whether a man be in the estate of damnation or in the estate of grace* (London: By R. Robinson, for T. Gubbin, and I. Porter, 1590), 4–5. (*EEBO*, STC (2nd ed.) / 19752, document image 10.)

[25] Perkins, *Treatise tending vnto a declaration*, 3. (*EEBO*, document image 9.)

172   DEVOTIONAL EXPERIENCE IN THE REFORMATION

these desires, desire also comprises the central medium through which Greville experientially processes all subsequent bodily suffering and delight. Even in his outright censuring of the flesh, he covets its sensual allure.[26]

Yet Greville makes it clear that his inability to repent has little to do with an intentional refusal to regulate his body and its passions, but rather is the unhappy result of an interpretive dilemma. His inability to repent is the consequence of his inability to accurately discern the meaning of his own devotional experience: "So neither can I leaue my hopes that doe deceiue," he observes, "Nor can I trust mine owne despaire" (C83.21–2). In this account of the Fall, forbidden pleasure does not give way to forbidden knowledge, and the mechanisms of Greville's present despair remain as murky to him as the original forces that compelled him to act upon his overwhelming desire. At best, his spiritual and erotic suffering can only extend cryptic clues about the causes and meaning of his erotic disgrace.

Poem 83, then, is a lamentation on lost access—to the beloved's favor, and to the presence of God. But more significantly, the poem is a meditation upon what it means to lose the ability to participate in, and experientially process, the state of desire. The ultimate tragedy, for Greville, lies less in the loss of either his beloved or his God than in his loss of the very external and internal markers of his self-hood: "Let no man aske my name, nor what else I should be; / For *Greiv-Ill*, paine, forlorne estate doe best decipher me" (C83.97–8). Reduced to a collection of signs of bodily suffering, Greville must be deciphered—not only by onlookers, but even by himself.

Stripped from its bodily basis, Greville's experience of desire can neither be demonstrated to a lover nor witnessed from without. Ignorant of the cause of his fall, unable to repent, unsatisfied in his desire, and equally unable to extricate himself from desire's powerful sway, Greville resorts to poetic annihilation in an attempt to rid himself of the effects of desire. His parenthetical "(I would I were not)" captures his wish for self-obliteration (C83.57). Barred from a Paradise rendered barren—and barred even from his own experience of desire—Greville's simultaneous lust for the state of desire and his yearning to be evacuated of it manifests itself in his wish for total dissolution. But Greville's fantasy of total material annihilation was only as powerful as his competing need to behold material forms. His devotional and erotic transactions *required* that he look upon the very bodily presences of his objects of desire.

---

[26] In his reading of *Caelica* 98, Dan Breen has described the "radical instability of desire" at work in Greville's attempts to repent. According to Breen, Greville "is able to draw out the implications of his observations on the nature of desire as a permanent fixture within the self. Even at the imagined moment of repentance, he remains conscious of himself as existing within 'this depth of sin.'" See Breen, "Redeeming the Sonnet Sequence," 156.

The refusal to adhere slavishly to reason, or to commit oneself to a life of sexual restraint, patience, humility, and otherworldliness was widely discussed and celebrated in Renaissance thought, according to Richard Strier, *The Unrepentant Renaissance: From Petrarch to Shakespeare to Milton* (Chicago: University of Chicago Press, 2011). While Strier does not directly discuss Greville's poetics—and indeed, it is difficult to reconcile Greville's conflicted inability to repent with Strier's characterization of brazen, early modern irreverence—nevertheless, the predicament of wanting to repent while lacking the resources to do so is the central dilemma animating Greville's sequence.

GREVILLE'S ICONOCLASTIC DESIRE   173

Beholding Caelica

Like Perkins's Adam and Eve, for whom the acts of lusting and looking precipitated the Fall, in poem 64, Greville links his erotic downfall to his overwhelming compulsion to behold Caelica's bodily form: "*Caelica*, when I did see you euery day, / I saw so many worths so well vnited" (C64.1–2). When confronted by their erotic union, "All others eyes both wondred and delighted" (C64.4). Looking at Caelica is Greville's sole prerogative; at most, other men can only regard her form indirectly, looking at Greville looking at Caelica. But even as Greville desires to behold his beloved, he wants to look away from her material form as well. Greville persists in the fantasy that Caelica's being is both ethereal and otherworldly, a being—like Greville's God—that is fundamentally inaccessible to the human senses. "[N]o earthly metall" could possibly substantiate Caelica's form (C64.7); she is made of nothing less than "some heauenly mould" (C64.5). Bodily matter, Greville asserts, is anathema to her insubstantial self: "Such enemies are flesh, and blood to measure" (C64.8).

In the aftermath of his fall from Caelica's favor, Greville discovers that his position of erotic privilege has suffered a reversal. It is now he who cannot gaze upon Caelica's face, while all others have the liberty to look. But even in his fallen state, Greville persists in his preoccupation with his beloved's fundamentally substanceless form:

> And since my fall, though I now onely see
> Your backe, while all the world beholds your face;
> This shadow still shews miracles to me.
>
> (C64.9–11)

Even Caelica's insubstantial shadow, he claims, has the power to make miracles incarnate. But what appears as resigned praise of his former beloved reveals further anxieties, both spiritual and erotic, in the poem's final couplet: "For what before was fil'd by me alone, / I now discerne hath roome for euery one" (C64.13–14). The couplet is both a veiled charge of Caelica's sexual promiscuity and an expression of anxiety about the worthlessness of salvation in light of an open policy of election. While ecclesiastical promiscuity bolsters Donne's ideal church—"Who is most true, and pleasing to thee, then / When she is embraced and open to most men"[27]— that same openness applied to unconditional election causes Greville to interpret Caelica's love as both inadequate and suspect. More importantly, though, the final lines encode a critique of the poem's fantasy about the immaterial; stripped of material dimension and form, Caelica's inherent formlessness assumes a terrifying instability. Divorced from the material, she reveals an erotic capaciousness that

---

[27] John Donne, Holy Sonnet 18, lines 13–14, in *The Variorum Edition of the Poetry of John Donne*, ed. Gary A. Stringer, vol. 7, pt. 1, *The Holy Sonnets*, ed. Gary A. Stringer (Bloomington: Indiana University Press, 2005).

174   DEVOTIONAL EXPERIENCE IN THE REFORMATION

still manages to exclude, and demonstrates a maddening and seemingly limitless capacity for protean shape shifting, oscillation, and dissembling.

Greville spares neither Caelica nor *Caelica*—the woman nor the text—the force of his iconoclastic ire when he disavows the truthfulness of all amatory verse: "No man can print a kisse, lines may deceiue" (C22.30). The material manifestations of poetic desire—Myra's cheek or lips upon which a kiss is printed, or the very paper upon which Greville impresses his verse—is testament, in Greville's view, to the inherent falsity of all utterances or gestures of desire. The poem's ostensible fantasy lies in the belief that true love exists independently of outward expressions of devotion—whether performed, spoken, or printed on the page.[28] In effect, Greville justifies his own ineffectual praise of Caelica and Myra—and his failure to win their reciprocal acknowledgment—by claiming that any love that proclaims itself in either gestures or words renders itself devotionally suspect from the outset. Greville's poetry reveals a paradoxical, oscillating treatment of the desiring body and its senses. At once a prerequisite for Greville's poetic conception of erotic desire, the senses also remain profoundly inadequate in the poet's quest for the perfect erotic union. Encoded within *Caelica*'s "major, materialist argument that the reality of the senses must be acknowledged," Bradin Cormack argues, "is the obverse thought that the senses must also be an obstacle to the real."[29] Even as Greville's poetry concedes to the material conditions that enable erotic access, he nevertheless persists in his belief that neither the body nor printed verse could provide an effective vehicle for the expression of erotic devotion.

Greville desires a desire that operates within a vacuum of bodies and words, even as he intuits that the material and corporeal are required mediums through which he has no other choice but to negotiate his sexual longings. Greville's distrust of the body and of outward performances of devotion is coextensive with his distrust of words themselves—whether written, prayed, uttered aloud, or even privately conceived. But that alone seems too distant a reason for his aborted attempts to both behold and write about women's physical forms; after all, he never found the female body particularly arresting to begin with. *Looking* at women troubled Greville, and according to his own admission in poem 102, they

---

[28] Several critics have demonstrated the strong correlation between falsity and language—and specifically, poetic language—in Greville's poetry and his biography of Sidney. But what each of these critics fails to acknowledge is how Greville's wariness of language is a subset of his wariness of relying on outward performances and material forms to articulate what he felt to be an otherwise ineffable longing. Douglas L. Peterson notes the close association between language and dissembling in his reading of Greville's *Treatise of Humane Learning*. See Douglas L. Peterson, *The English Lyric from Wyatt to Donne: A History of the Plain and Eloquent Styles* (Princeton: Princeton University Press, 1967), 252–3. June Dwyer links Greville's deep suspicion of poetry and language to what she describes as his orthodox Calvinism. See Dwyer, "Fulke Greville's Aesthetic," 256. Richard Waswo, G. A. Wilkes, and Joan Rees each support the view that Greville's "plain" style emerges directly out of his suspicion of poetic language. Greville's "plainness," they aver, is not indicative of Greville's aesthetic failure as a poet but of his moral stance on the corrupting power of poetry. See Waswo, *Fatal Mirror*, 39–40; Wilkes, ed., *Complete Poems and Plays of Fulke Greville*, 267; and Rees, *Fulke Greville*, 190, 206.

[29] See Cormack, "In the Labyrinth: Gunn's Greville," esp. 167.

GREVILLE'S ICONOCLASTIC DESIRE   175

tended to leave him frigid like the "*Articke* pole." Far more tantalizing for Greville were the implications of the act of looking at men—boys, warriors, gods, idealized beloveds—who Greville describes in worshipful terms in his lyric sequence. In poem 62, he laments the fickleness of his boy lovers—and their painfully short erotic attention spans: "VVho worships *Cupid*, doth adore a boy, / Boyes earnest are at first in their delight, / But for a new, soone leaue their dearest toy," he bemoans (C62.1–3). But the frenzies of homoerotic longing encode self-destructive potentialities. Greville describes his longing for men as a form of corporal torture: these boys are the creations of our own erotic imagination— "Fruit of our boughs, whence heauen maketh rods" to punish and curtail desire (C62.21). In the end, Greville concedes that the objects of his homoerotic longings are nothing other than false idols, erected by the flesh: "*Mercurie, Cupid, Mars*, they be no Gods, / But humane Idols, built vp by desire" (C62.19–20). At the close of the poem, Greville vows to stop looking at beautiful men, to put an end to his prying into the homoerotic desires that would have been impossible to consummate freely within the environs of the Elizabethan and Jacobean courts.[30] Instead, it would appear, he turns his gaze toward heavenly matters: "Who sees their glories, on the earth must prye; / Who seeks true glory must looke to the skye" (C62.23–4). The transition from earthly to divine at the end of the iconoclastic poem would fail to elicit surprise if it did not reference an internal lexicon that complicates an otherwise straightforward abnegation of homoerotic longing. "*Mars is* an idol," Greville insists, "and Man's lust, his skye" (C62.7). Desire—man's lust—provides the fundamental medium by which one can inhabit the experience of adoring and worshipping a boy; it constitutes the essential dwelling place for the idealized lover, who could not—due to cultural and legal limitations—exist in any real place for men like Greville. Is it to heaven that Greville turns his attention, or is it to this personal sky—the habitat of Mars and the enabler of longing—to which he retreats at the close of poem 62?

---

[30] That Greville was most likely attracted exclusively to men has been noted by several of his readers and biographers, and it is likely that his poetic descriptions of sexual access and limitation in *Caelica* were inflected by the intimacies that he cultivated with Sidney during his lifetime. Katherine Duncan-Jones has written that "there is little doubt that Sidney's close friend Fulke Greville did approximate to what would now be called homosexual, and that Greville was determined to suggest that his friendship with Sidney had priority over all other bonds." According to Duncan-Jones, Sidney most likely reciprocated Greville's affection to a certain degree: "Sidney's marked lack of enthusiasm for marriage, combined with the fact that his two closest friends, Dyer and Greville, were both among the 'tiny handful' of Elizabethan aristocrats who never married, provokes the suspicion that male friendship was in some ways more congenial to him than heterosexual union." See Katherine Duncan-Jones, *Sir Philip Sidney: Courtier Poet* (New Haven: Yale University Press, 1991), 240. In a similar vein, the late literary critic and gay activist Ronald Rebholz has suggested that Greville's sole attraction to men might explain his perplexing encounters with women in his lyric poems: "We can only speculate about the reasons why Greville found a mutual and constant love of a woman impossible," Rebholz writes. "Perhaps his feelings had a homosexual bias which he controlled or could not admit: certainly the friendship of men seems to have given him the only deep emotional satisfaction he experienced in his private life." See Rebholz, *Life of Fulke Greville*, 54.

176   DEVOTIONAL EXPERIENCE IN THE REFORMATION

Greville's erotic sky resonates with the aesthetic and creative impulses of Sidney's famed zodiac of wit, which, like Greville's homoerotic poetic expressions, sought out what might be termed the supranatural—the things that could never exist on material earth. "[O]nly the Poet," Sidney writes, "disdaining to be tied to any such subjection, lifted up with the vigor of his own invention, doth grow in effect, another nature, in making things either better than Nature bringeth forth, or quite anew forms such as never were in Nature."[31] Greville's lifelong work on the sequence—his countless acts of poetic rewriting, reimagining, and recasting— provided him with a zodiac of sexual possibilities; writing *Caelica* enabled Greville to poetically imagine forms of longing perhaps best described not so much as contrary to nature, but better than what the world as he knew it could provide. The poems describe erotic desires and potentialities that would have been all but impossible to confess or realize within the circumscribed political and religious spheres of Elizabethan and Jacobean England. For Greville, the desires that he felt to be outside of nature formed the cornerstone of his creative vision, serving as the driving impulse of a poetics that sought to commemorate Sidney's legacy even while seeking to undermine it.

Ocean of images

What is most striking about Greville's discussion of his own creative output in his biography of Sidney is his complete silence about his ongoing work on *Caelica*, despite the fact that he continued work on the sequence throughout his life up until the years immediately preceding his death.[32] In *The Life of the Renowned Sr Philip Sidney*, which he finalized between 1610 and 1612, Greville dismisses his own literary pursuits as nothing more than youthful poetic dabbling: "Which with humble sayles after I had once ventured upon this spreading *Ocean* of Images, my apprehensive youth, for lack of a well touched compasse, did easily wander beyond proportion."[33] Greville's chief criticism of his own poems was not a moral gripe but an aesthetic one. His literary failures, he insists, lie in the fact that his poetic images had failed to approximate the conditions of lived experience. Greville insisted that his ideal reader first acquire a certain measure of lived experience as a prerequisite for effective encounters with literature. In his veiled critique of Sidney's poetics,

---

[31] Philip Sidney, *An Apologie for Poetrie. Written by the right noble, virtuous, and learned, Sir Phillip Sidney, Knight* (London: Printed for *Henry Olney*, and are to be sold at his shop in Paules Church-yard, at the signe of the George, neere to Cheap-gate, 1595), sig. C2v. (*EEBO*, STC 22534, document image 9.)

[32] Greville's omission of his short poetic verses in the *Life* is especially odd, considering his decision to discuss his verse treatises and closet dramas at length.

[33] Fulke Greville, *The Life of the Renowned S Philip Sidney. [...] Written by Sir Fulke Grevil Knight, Lord Brook, a Servant to Queen Elizabeth, and his Companion & Friend* (London: Printed for *Henry Seile* over against St *Dunstans* Church in Fleet-street, 1651), 173. (*EEBO*, Wing (2nd ed.) / B4899.)

Greville writes that his own poems have been inspired by what he calls "the images of life"—and that he writes his poems specifically for those who seek to explicate their own experiences through these poetic images:

> For my own part, I found my creeping genius more fixed upon the images of life, than the images of wit, and therefore chose not to write to them on whose foot the black ox had not already trod, as the proverb is, but to those only, that are weather-beaten in the sea of this world, such as having lost the sight of their gardens, and groves, study to sail on a right course among rocks, and quick sands.[34]

Championing a creative process informed by experience, Greville juxtaposes his own worldly muse against Sidney's brilliant but unrefined wit. For Greville, moral poetry ought to confirm for the reader some prior lived encounter. Greville criticizes Sidney's images of wit not because of their imperfections, but because they are too perfect; these images, like their creator, have not been trodden down by life. On the contrary, in drawing upon the images of life in his moral poetics, Greville seeks to describe a fallen reality to those who inhabit that reality. Like Adam in his state of prelapsarian bliss, the unfallen will never be privy to the images of life that comprise the cornerstone of Greville's moral poetics. Indeed, those who aspire to grasp the full import of poetry's moral dimension must have already "lost the sight of their gardens, and groves." Greville's moral poetics required both the poet and the reader to possess a fund of experiential knowledge; this requirement was especially important for Greville's ideal reader, whose direct participation in the reading process was essential to the process of moral reading.

Greville's insistence that literary encounters required direct, aggressive, and ongoing participation on the part of the reader emerges most clearly in his description of his closet dramas *Mustapha* and *Alaham*—published respectively in 1609 and, posthumously, in 1633. Greville claims that he never intended either play for stage production; he saw no need for public performance, since, he maintains, the act of solitary reading effectively served to insert the reader as lead actor into his own private dramatic performance: "But he that will behold these acts upon their true stage, let him look on that stage wherein himself is an actor, even the state he lives in, and for every part he may perchance find a player, and for every line (it may be) an instance of life, beyond the author's intention."[35] What is remarkable about Greville's authorial intention for his closet dramas is his ostensible *lack* of anything that resembles authorial intention. Every reader, he maintains, should have the freedom to direct his own dramatic interpretation of the script independently of the author's original vision for the work. For Greville, even the

---

[34] Greville, *Life*, 245–6.
[35] Greville, *Life*, 246.

178 DEVOTIONAL EXPERIENCE IN THE REFORMATION

most private act of reading functions like public performance, with the reader–actor constantly on display before an audience that includes both himself and God. In Greville's moral *ars poetica*, the readerly experience, the devotional experience, and the experience of desire coalesce in a single theatrical performance. Greville saw Sidney's legacy as a starting point for his efforts to outline this trifold performative process.

The idea that effective poetry must speak to, and start from, what it experientially *feels* like to bodily and spiritually inhabit the state of suffering made the act of reading poems a distinctly private and individual commitment. Greville's insistence that poetic images must be derived first from the images of life reveals a decidedly Reformed aesthetic and moral approach to literary creation, which insisted upon the primacy of individual experience as the basis for all subsequent moral and spiritual development. While Sidney sought to use writing as the starting point for a transformative readerly encounter—"his end was not writing, even while he wrote ... but ... to make himself, and others, not in words or opinion, but in life, and action, good and great"[36]—Greville sought to reverse the causal relationship between writing and moral transformation. In Greville's creative vision, the reader's prior experience is the necessary prerequisite for effective moral poetry. Greville took issue with Sidney's argument that being a good reader was enough to equip an individual to navigate his own labyrinth of longings and desires. In emphasizing the centrality of a human being's prior lived experience, which Greville saw as essential for a reader's effective encounter with poetry, he not only made the act of reading a deeply personal endeavor, but a distinctly embodied process as well.

Despite the veiled challenges Greville posed to Sidney's moral poetics, the *Life* does not reference any of Sidney's lyrics, and Greville only obliquely comments upon his friend's literary output. His only direct critical treatment of Sidney's creative work in the *Life* is a brief discussion of poetic images in the *Arcadia*, a lengthy prose work interspersed with eclogues, ballads, and shorter lyric poems. Despite describing the *Arcadia* as an unparalleled masterpiece of creative expression, Greville nevertheless hopes that the epic will be the last work of its kind ever written: "So that howsoever I liked them too well (even in that unperfected shape they were) to condescend that such delicate (though inferior) pictures of himself, should be suppressed; yet I do wish that work may be the last in this kind, presuming no man that follows can ever reach, much less go beyond that excellent intended pattern of his."[37] In spite of the *Arcadia*'s imperfect shape and inferior pictures, Greville treats the work as a serious example of moral poetry, extending

[36] Greville, *Life*, 21.
[37] Greville, *Life*, 245. The posthumous 1651 edition of the *Life* prints this passage: "So that whosoever I liked them *not* too well." However, all modern editors of this passage have presented it without the addition of the "not," which is how the passage appears in the manuscript copy entitled "A Dedication." See, for example, Nowell Smith, ed., *Life of Sir Philip Sidney*, by Fulke Greville (Oxford: Clarendon

GREVILLE'S ICONOCLASTIC DESIRE   179

a fascinating reading of the romance in one of the first critical readings of the work by a contemporary of Sidney. In what appears as praise of Sidney's epic, Greville ignores its author's ostensible intentions for the work while reinterpreting its literary functions and moral purpose:

> And my noble friend had that dexterity, even with the dashes of his pen to make the *Arcadian* antiques beautify the margents of his works; yet the honor which (I bear him record) he never affected, I leave unto him, with this addition, that his end in them was not vanishing pleasure alone, but moral images, and examples, (as directing threads) to guide every man through the confused *labyrinth* of his own desires, and life.[38]

It is the reader's own desires and prior experience, Greville insists, that should direct the reading experience of works like the *Arcadia*. Rather than being understood in purely fictional terms—what Sidney described as "forms such as never were in Nature"—the *Arcadia* should be read, in Greville's estimation, as a reflection of human beings' most deeply felt desires. As much as Greville used the *Life* to both commemorate and undermine Sidney's view of moral fashioning and poetic creation, the biography also enabled Greville to use Sidney's poetics as a means of underscoring his own materialist conception of desire—one that would ultimately be shaped by the reader's own labyrinthine longings and experience.

Greville's attempts to apply his poetic images of life to his creative output emerge most fully in his decision to rewrite Sidney's lesser known lyric sequence of thirty-two poems, entitled *Certain Sonets*. Early in this short sequence, Sidney draws attention to the relatively unconflicted relationship between eros and the eternal in a refrain that recurs throughout the work: "O my heavens for taste by thie heavenly pleasure."[39] In Sidney's formulation, desire offers an anticipatory taste of eventual

---

Press, 1907), 223–4. In "A Dedication," Greville may well have been writing in earnest about his admiration for the poem, considering the fact that in 1590, two decades earlier, he had personally overseen the first official publication of *Arcadia*, four years after Sidney's death. But his praise nevertheless reads like a veiled concession given his subsequent insistence that the *Arcadia* must not spawn any more poetry like itself—that Sidney *not* serve as inspiration for fledgling poets. The 1651 edition's addition of "not" attempts to resolve Greville's ostensibly contradictory views on the *Arcadia* in what might be the first of many editorial and critical attempts to make Greville seem less paradoxical a writer than he truly was.

[38] Greville, *Life*, 224–5.

[39] Philip Sidney, *Certain Sonnets*, poem 5, lines 2, 6, in *The Poems of Sir Philip Sidney*, ed. William A. Ringler (Oxford: Clarendon Press, 1962). This poem was omitted from the 1598 folio edition of the *Arcadia*, which is the first sixteenth-century text to include the *Certain Sonets*. Unless otherwise specified, all citations of the *Certain Sonets* refer to the text of the 1598 folio edition. See Philip Sidney, *Certaine Sonets*, in *The Countesse of Pembrokes Arcadia* (London: Imprinted [by R. Field] for William Ponsonbie, 1598). (*EEBO*, STC (2nd ed.) / 22541.) Citations for sonnet 5 refer to Ringler's edition, based on the Clifford manuscript (Folger MS. H.b.I) and the Bodleian manuscript (Bodleian e Museo 37). I parenthetically cite references to *Certain Sonnets* (denoted as CS) using Ringler's numbering of the poems and lines, since the poems are unnumbered in both the 1598 folio and the early modern manuscripts.

180   DEVOTIONAL EXPERIENCE IN THE REFORMATION

heavenly pleasure, a sentiment all but absent in Greville's poetry. But there is an additional oddity about Sidney's line, which describes a desire contingent upon the realness of another's experience of erotic pleasure: Sidney anticipates the pleasures of heaven not through his own but by means of his beloved's pleasure, "by *thy* heavenly pleasure."[40] On the contrary, Greville makes no attempt to imagine the desires or pleasures of the women or the men who feature in his own love poetry, nor does he attempt to imagine his own desires in concert with the reciprocal desires of his beloveds. Greville's desire is fundamentally unlike Sidney's, unfolding as it does within a lyric space without beloveds who reciprocate—or at least respond to—that desire. And while this consequently makes Greville's erotic and spiritual yearnings read more like abstractions than exchanges between beings, it also lends his descriptions of desire an attentiveness to miniscule shifts within one's deeply personal experience of that desire. Greville's sequence modulates the raw states of being that elude language, that unfold subterranean to one's actions and interactions in this world.

In the *Certain Sonets*, the pursuit of desire and the pursuit of the eternal never seem to exist side by side as an interconnected process, as they do in *Caelica*. These pursuits, for Sidney, instead eclipse each other at alternative points within the sequence, and within individual poems within the sequence. The frustration for Sidney is that in trying to pursue both his beloved and God, he finds that he is effectively rendered incapable of securing access to either. Sidney's neglect of the eternal in favor of the pleasures of the body prompts his realization that he has neither the emotional nor spiritual reserves to afford the cost of both:

> Desire, desire I haue too dearely bought,
> With prise of mangled mind thy worthlesse ware;
> Too long, too long a sleep thou hast me brought,
> Who should my mind to higher things prepare.
>
> (CS31.5–8)

What begins as a triumphant rejection of the beloved confirms Sidney's ongoing yearning for her presence. In his quest to liberate himself from all longing, Sidney finds himself mired in the frenzy of desire, "Desiring naught but how to kill desire" (CS31.14). The act of killing off desire ultimately serves to reinforce the self-perpetuating nature of that desire. As Catherine Bates has noted about this poem, desire is the poetic persona's permanent state of being: "he desires to

---

[40] In a similar vein, Sidney dedicates the bulk of the lyric ballads in *Astrophil and Stella* to giving Stella a direct platform for articulating—and eventually consummating—her erotic desires, a formal decision especially astonishing in a lyric genre that typically relegated the female beloved to a silent object of desire, rather than a desiring agent in her own right. For my discussion of Sidney's attention to female desire in *Astrophil and Stella*, see Rhema Hokama, "'Wanton child': Fantasies of infanticide, abortion, and monstrous birth in Mary Wroth's *Pamphilia to Amphilanthus*," *SEL Studies in English Literature 1500–1900* 62.2 (forthcoming).

GREVILLE'S ICONOCLASTIC DESIRE   181

renounce desire but has not done so yet, and indeed cannot do so because the desire to renounce desire is only another fiendish form desire can take."[41] The paradox of Sidney's abnegation of desire in favor of eternal preoccupations is that the very rejection of desire encodes its own preservation.

Eros poses an ever-present barrier to Sidney's intended spiritual progression, but Sidney's preoccupation with moral uprightness also hinders his amorous pursuits. This anxiety about his desire's resurgent power is apparent in poem 32's verbatim echo of poem 31: "Leave me ô Loue which reachest but to dust, / And thou my mind aspire to higher things" (CS32.1–2). The pair of poems, when read together, reveal Sidney's obsession with his intention to aspire to "higher things" at all costs. By the close of both poems, however, his intentions remain only that: intentions. Despite his liturgical-like repetition of his rejection of love, Sidney ends the sequence before he achieves the state of eternal love to which he aspires.[42] There is little about Sidney's short sequence—part secular, part divine—that would convince his reader that he thought it possible to take seriously both God and sexual yearning within the framework of a unified literary work. If, as Greville maintains, Sidney's is a moral poetics crafted to guide one—like "directing threads"—through the thicket of life's desires, then the *Certain Sonets* registers not only a poetic but a moral failure.

Sidney's failure to kill desire—his failure to imagine poetic images that can contain that desire—serves as the starting point for Greville's iconoclastic poetics. Despite his insistence that the *Arcadia* must be the last instance of poetic experimentation—"I do wish that work may be the last in this kind"—Greville nevertheless refused to forego his own poetic output. In spite of his wariness of poetic images, Greville continued to write—and rewrite—erotic poems throughout his entire life. If Greville's poems refuse to provide satisfactory accounts of his fascination with the pleasures of the flesh, they nevertheless take those longings seriously as the starting point of his moral poetics—one that sought to give full attention to both secular and sacred expressions of devotion. In his rewriting of Sidney's short lyric sequence, Greville succeeded in writing poems directed toward the practical purpose he outlines in the *Life*; *Caelica* directs its readers through the maze-like expanse of unfathomable longings, offering a catalyst for the expression of desires that otherwise would fall outside the limits of description.

Even the most vehemently anti-love poems of *Caelica* encode endorsements of the flesh and its desires. In poem 86, the lyric about the loss of Paradise, Greville's despair is not a response to the pain that comes from desire; on the contrary, he reacts to the trauma of having been compelled to relinquish that desire, and to the anguished realization that he will never entirely extricate himself from the sway of

---

[41] Bates, *Masculinity and the Hunt*, 175.

[42] In fact, the final poem leaves us unsettled by Sidney's farewell to the world and his intention to eclipse erotic desire with eternal love: "Then farewell, world; thy uttermost I see; / Eternal love, maintain thy life in me" (CS32.13–14).

182 DEVOTIONAL EXPERIENCE IN THE REFORMATION

his fleshly longings: "Then Man, endure thy selfe, those clouds will vanish; / Life is a Top which whipping Sorrow driueth; / Wisdome must beare what our flesh cannot banish" (C86.9–11). He reiterates this sentiment again in poem 96: "Flesh but the *Top*, which onely *Whips* make goe" (C96.49), he concedes. "Peace is the seed of grace, in dead flesh sowne" (C96.48). Greville's sadomasochistic rendering of the flagellated body is the material basis for his eventual spiritual regeneration. In his final estimation, the flesh—the target of Greville's sexual rage—emerges as the battered, vexed convergence point at which his erotic and spiritual lives become inextricably linked.

Greville's fullest condemnations of desire are, paradoxically, also his fullest examinations of what it means to move through the world as a desiring, fleshly being.[43] As Thom Gunn notes, the power of *Caelica*'s final lyrics "lies in the clarity and strength of the poignancy he gives to the despair that can be cured only by the end of life. And in these poems, too, the body cries out in pain at the rejections it is being forced to make, and in the note of the cry we recognize the very humanity it is a cry against."[44] Until the moment that marks the end of life, Greville concedes to an existence in which the flesh and its desires will always play a role in directing one's spiritual progression: "Wisdome must beare what our flesh cannot banish" (C86.11). So long as one inhabits the realm of the flesh, there remain longings—Greville's indeterminate *what*—that even the most devout can never dispel.

In writing *Caelica*, a work that refuses to be contained by either wholly secular or wholly religious concerns, Greville succeeds in imagining a state of longing that defies the formal conventions of Sidney's lyric form. Freed from the need to create wholly from within Sidney's aesthetic parameters—a constellation of poetic images within a zodiac of wit—Greville writes of desires that emanate from and respond to the present world in which he finds himself, translating lived experience into poetic image.

As much as *Caelica* offers a sustained response to Sidney's moral poetics, the sequence also reads like a lyric precursor to Milton's *Paradise Lost*, the seventeenth century's most brilliant, iconoclastic rewriting of the biblical account of the Fall. More than a disjointed sequence by a minor Renaissance poet, or merely the

---

[43] Only after his renouncement of sensual pleasure in poem 84 can Greville capture the full depths of his erotic and spiritual despair, a fullness that affords us a poetic pleasure entirely unique to our encounters with the sequence's late poems. These expressions unexpectedly prove more compelling than any written about or to the particular women—Caelica, Myra, or Myrabella—who make shadowy appearances in Greville's sequence. We get the opposite sense about Donne's treatment of his beloveds in both his erotic and religious poems, which are vivified by virtue of our sense that they are written with a very specific woman in mind. The converse is true for Greville, whose best and most compelling articulations of erotic despair occur in poems that are written *not* to a woman but to God.

[44] Gunn, Introduction to *Selected Poems of Fulke Greville*, 41.

repository of a lifelong output of miscellaneous short writing,[45] *Caelica* offers a sustained meditation upon a Paradise known and lost, sexual idols worshipped, destroyed, and covertly restored, and the deep poetic compulsion to conjure poetic images that describe forbidden desire and seek to make that desire endurable. In *Caelica*, Greville presents both a practical theology and a practical *poesis*; at the heart of both lies Greville's uneasy attachment to the desiring, sensing body. Longstanding views of *Caelica* have treated desire as something to be annihilated and forgotten, an obstacle to be overcome as Greville moves from the early poems of love to the later devotional ones. On the contrary, across the sequence's progression, as the poems move from eros to devotional preoccupations, I have endeavored to show that desire remains a constant in Greville's twin visions of Reformed and literary devotion.

[45] Both Bullough and Croll have made claims to this end in their discussion of *Caelica*'s ordering and structure. See Bullough, ed., *Poems and Dramas of Fulke Greville*, 1:34; and Croll, *Works of Fulke Greville*, 11.

6

Adam and Eve in Bed and at Prayer

Recasting Milton's Iconoclasm in *Eikonoklastes* and *Paradise Lost*

When Fulke Greville wrote that he hoped Sidney's *Arcadia* would "be the last in this kind, presuming no man that follows can ever reach, much less go beyond that excellent intended pattern of his,"[1] his ostensible praise of the epic also encoded a fear about the moral effects that Sidney's literary images might have on the book's readers. Greville's latent anxiety about the moral uses and abuses of Sidney's fiction assumed fresh urgency and a new political application in the aftermath of the execution of Charles I in January 1649. Writing in October of that year, Milton published *Eikonoklastes*, a justification of Charles's execution and the longest of Milton's polemical works. Milton's tract was a response to the king's own *Eikon Basilike, The Pourtraicture of His Sacred Majestie in His Solitudes and Sufferings*, which circulated immediately following Charles's execution and generated widespread sympathy for the king's plight. Amid the diary-like entries of *Eikon Basilike*, Charles interspersed his prayers, which he modeled on the Psalms of David as well as poetic selections from Sidney's *Arcadia*. For these acts of devotional appropriation, Milton deemed Charles guilty not only of literary "plagiary" but also of a more serious breach in devotional propriety.[2] In using Sidney's "unhallow'd" and "unchrist'nd" prayers, "stol'n word for word from the mouth of a Heathen fiction praying to a heathen God," Charles made use of devotional models that were unfit for proper worship. Milton argued that the *Arcadia* was "no serious Book," and a "vain amatorious Poem."[3] Although Milton, like Greville, acknowledged the *Arcadia*'s literary merits as "a Book in that kind full of worth and witt," he had no qualms about listing its flaws: Sidney's book is "among religious thoughts, and duties not worthy to be named; nor to be read at any time without good caution; much less in time of trouble and affliction to be a

---

[1] Fulke Greville, *The Life of the Renowned Sʳ Philip Sidney.* [...] *Written by Sir Fulke Grevil Knight, Lord Brook, a Servant to Queen Elizabeth, and his Companion & Friend* (London: Printed for *Henry Seile* over against St *Dunstans* Church in Fleet-street, 1651), 245. (*EEBO*, Wing (2nd ed.) / B4899.) See my discussion in Chapter 5 of Greville's prevaricating treatment of Sidney's literary legacy.

[2] John Milton, *Eikonoklastes*, in *Complete Prose Works of John Milton*, 8 vols., ed. Don M. Wolfe et al. (New Haven: Yale University Press, 1953–82), 3:547. I have cited *Eikonoklastes* and Milton's antiprelatical tracts using the Yale edition of the *Complete Prose Works*, hereafter denoted YP.

[3] Milton, *Eikonoklastes*, YP 3:362.

Devotional experience and erotic knowledge in the literary culture of the English Reformation. Rhema Hokama, Oxford University Press. © Rhema Hokama (2023). DOI: 10.1093/oso/9780192886552.003.0007

ADAM AND EVE IN BED AND AT PRAYER   185

Christian's Prayer-Book."[4] In attacking Charles's plagiarized prayers—which, Milton maintained, were tantamount to heathenish idolatry—he also assailed what he felt to be Sidney's dangerous poetics, which could so easily be appropriated by readers for morally dubious purposes.

Considering Milton's criticism of Charles's appropriation of the Psalms and the prayers from Sidney's epic, it is surprising that he himself would make extensive use of set prayers in writing his own epic poem, *Paradise Lost*. In this chapter, I propose that Milton's inclusion of liturgical and sacramental devotion in his poetic account of Edenic worship constituted a literary application of his polemical arguments against set worship. In disavowing common worship, Milton nevertheless sought to extricate the liturgy and Psalmic prayers from the rarefied realm of state worship, recasting them as a part of daily experience and giving the sensing body a pivotal role in proper Reformed devotion.

Adam and Eve's prayers in *Paradise Lost* constitute Milton's literary contribution to the debate about set worship that vexed the Caroline church. During Charles's reign, Archbishop William Laud's ecclesiastical policy aimed at restoring the political power and economic wealth of the state church. Laud saw the unified church as a political body that could offer direct support to the monarch, without being overseen by Parliament. In Charles, Laud found a monarch sympathetic to his vision of church reform. The archbishop played a key role in Caroline church policy, cultivating a close political partnership with the king that lasted throughout Charles's personal rule. At the heart of Laud's ecclesiastical reforms lay his insistence upon the importance of uniformity in public worship and ceremony. According to Laud, the strength of the church required uniformity in observance of outward forms of devotion: "I laboured nothing more, than that the external public worship of God ... might be preserved, and that with as much decency and uniformity, as might be; being still of opinion, that unity cannot long continue in the Church, where uniformity is shut out at the church door." For Laud, outward forms of worship were hardly spiritual *adiaphora*. On the contrary, he regarded these externals as essential scaffolding for true inward devotion: "the public neglect of God's service in the outward face of it ... had almost cast a damp upon the true and inward worship of God; which while we live in the body, needs external helps, and all little enough to keep it in any vigour."[5]

Laud offered his apologia for his ecclesiastical polity from his prison chambers in the Tower of London, where he remained from 1640 until his execution in 1645. His political downfall came at the hands of his chief detractors, the nonconformist Puritans who dominated the Long Parliament, and who—like Milton—regarded set prayer as a hindrance to genuine devotional expression and as evidence of popery. Of the five poets that feature in this book, Milton is the only one who

---

[4] Milton, *Eikonoklastes*, YP 3:362–3.
[5] William Laud, *The History of the Troubles and Tryal of the Most Reverent Father in God, and Blessed Martyr, William Laud* (London: Printed for Ri[chard] Chiswell, at the Rose and Crown in St: Paul's Church-Yard, 1695), 224. (*EEBO*, Wing / L596, document image 123.)

186   DEVOTIONAL EXPERIENCE IN THE REFORMATION

articulated an overtly anti-liturgical stance. Milton's position would have been a marginal one in the late sixteenth and early seventeenth centuries, but his anti-liturgical stance reflected a wider shift in how a number of English nonconformists understood the use of set forms in both public and private worship in the Caroline period. As I have argued throughout this book, the majority of Protestants in Elizabethan and Jacobean England would not have regarded the use of external and outward worship as incompatible with Reformed Calvinism. Indeed, as Alexandra Walsham maintains, those who celebrated church ritual and ceremony would not have been regarded as Catholic recusants but "committed Prayer Book Protestants."[6] Alec Ryrie echoes this view, noting that "[i]n England, before 1640, flat opposition to the use of any set forms of prayer was a fringe view, the province of a few separatists."[7] But the liturgical practices that were regarded as mainstream prior to the early Stuart church assumed new political valences with the solidification of Laud's efforts to tighten ecclesiastical uniformity from the 1630s onward. "By then," Ryrie writes, "the two most clearly staked-out positions were those of the royalist establishment and the puritan radicals. The former held that public prayer must always, and private prayer should usually, follow set forms which provided full, authorized texts—in particular, the Book of Common Prayer. The latter rejected the use of any set forms at all, arguing that all prayers should be conceived by the person speaking them."[8] It was this latter position that Milton subscribed to, and detailed with vehement force in his polemical condemnations of Charles and the king's use of prescribed prayer. And yet, what is striking about Milton's view of set prayer is that while his polemical writing articulates an indisputably nonconformist view of the liturgy, his poetry nonetheless reverberates with the language of the *Book of Common Prayer*. In this chapter, I maintain that Milton's reappropriation of the prayer book was an intentional poetic act of iconoclasm, one that allowed him to reimagine the role of state liturgy and worship within entirely new devotional contexts.

***

During his wide-ranging career as both polemicist and poet, Milton proved himself adept at recasting his opponents' ideologies by framing familiar practices in startling new light. Milton undertakes precisely this act of recasting in *Eikonoklastes*, which offers a sustained and devastating response to Charles's *Eikon Basilike*. Published as the official parliamentary response to the king's tract, *Eikonoklastes* demolishes *Eikon Basilike*'s image of Charles as a martyred ruler—an image that emerges not only through the simple prayers and prose of Charles's tract, but even more strikingly in its frontispiece portrait of the monarch kneeling at prayer (see Figure 6.1). In the portrait, Charles gazes toward the

---

[6] Alexandra Walsham, "The Parochial Roots of Laudianism Revisited: Catholics, Anti-Calvinists and 'Parish Anglicans' in Early Stuart England," *Journal of Ecclesiastical History* 49, no. 4 (1998): 620–51, 636.

[7] Alec Ryrie, *Being Protestant in Reformation Britain* (Oxford: Oxford University Press, 2013), 215.

[8] Ryrie, *Being Protestant*, 214.

Figure 6.1 Frontispiece image of King Charles I at prayer from *Eikon basilike the pourtracture of His Sacred Majestie in his solitudes and sufferings*. London: Reprinted in R. M., Anno Dom. 1648 [1649]. Copy from the Houghton Library, Harvard University. The tract was published ten days after the king's beheading on January 30, 1649.

heavens as he raises a crown of thorns—reminiscent of the one worn by Christ at Gethsemane. According to Milton, the sole purpose of this frontispiece image, with its implicit parallel between Charles and Christ, was "to catch fools and silly gazers."[9] In undertaking the project of tearing down the *Eikon Basilike*'s literal and ideological icons, Milton establishes a precedent for his own polemics by positioning them within an extensive tradition of early Christian iconoclasm: "For which reason this answer also is entitled *Iconoclastes*, the famous surname of many Greek

[9] Milton, *Eikonoklastes*, YP 3:342.

188   DEVOTIONAL EXPERIENCE IN THE REFORMATION

emperors, who, in their zeal to the command of God, after a long tradition of idolatry in the church, took courage, and broke all superstitious images to pieces."[10]
In response to what he saw as Charles's fictions and pretensions, Milton countered with an act of role-playing of his own. In the figurative act of appending
"Iconoclastes" to his own name, Milton sets himself up as the last in a long line of
image-breaking emperors, and creates a genealogical tradition for his own visual,
political, and textual iconoclasms.

But if Milton crafts a genealogy for himself as the most recent of the Christian
iconoclasts, he is equally invested in crafting a genealogy for the executed king as
well. Milton Iconoclastes wanted to demolish not only the singular and historically
specific icon of Charles I, but also the larger tradition of monarchical tyranny that
the executed king represented. Pointing to the violence of the English Civil War,
Milton contextualized what he viewed as Charles's acts of tyranny by juxtaposing them against the historical persecution of the early Christians. In his criticism
of Charles's military leadership, Milton writes, "there hath been more Christian
blood shed by the commission, approbation, and connivance of King Charles,
and his father James in the latter end of their reign, than in the ten Roman per-
secutions." With respect to "those many whippings, pillories, and other corporal
inflictions" that marked Charles's reign in both war and peace, Milton argued that
the monarch was comparable to that early persecutor of Christians the "tyrant
Nero," who allegedly had a penchant for lighting the imperial premises by setting Christians ablaze.[11] If Charles's tyranny rivaled that of the Romans, Milton
also made sure to emphasize that the monarch's ineffectualness as a ruler had
ancient precedents as well. David Loewenstein points to the abundance of historical analogies comparing Charles to ancient, biblical, and Near Eastern despots in
Eikonoklastes, all of which support what Loewenstein sees as a vision of historical
recurrence: "Charles is, in a sense, just one more figure in a long and crowded
history of oppression and tyranny."[12] Indeed, in his Preface to *Eikonoklastes*,

---

[10]   Milton, *Eikonoklastes*, YP 3:343.

[11]   Milton, *Eikonoklastes*, YP 3:439. See also Tacitus, *Annals*, 15.44, in *Annals and Histories*, trans.
William Jackson Brodribb (New York: Alfred A. Knopf, 2009), 332–70.

[12]   David Loewenstein, *Milton and the Drama of History: Historical Vision, Iconoclasm, and the
Literary Imagination* (Cambridge: Cambridge University Press, 1990), 70. Loewenstein's suggestion
that the parallels Milton draws between Charles and various historical despots constitute a vision of historical recurrence is elaborated upon in James Simpson, "Statues of Liberty: Iconoclasm and Idolatry
in the English Revolution," chap. 3 in *Under the Hammer: Iconoclasm in the Anglo-American Tradition* (Oxford: Oxford University Press, 2011), 85–115. Simpson points to idolatry's "resurgent past"
and its tendency to express itself in repeated waves of idol worship. Milton identifies the idolatrous
implications of *Eikon Basilike* when he points out that the work's idolatry was not limited to the religious kind; indeed, the idolization of kings was tantamount "to a civil kinde of Idolatry." See Milton,
Eikonoklastes, YP 3:343. According to Milton, Charles's circumventing of parliamentary rule established him as an early modern Caligula, whose notions about his own self-sufficiency made him "think
himself a God." See Milton, *Eikonoklastes*, YP 3:467. Simpson's work follows an established tradition
of reading Milton's iconoclasm as a creative endeavor. See Lana Cable, *Carnal Rhetoric: Milton's Iconoclasm and the Politics of Desire* (Durham, NC: Duke University Press, 1995); Lana Cable, "Milton's
Iconoclastic Truth," in *Politics, Poetics, and Hermeneutics in Milton's Prose*, eds. David Loewenstein

ADAM AND EVE IN BED AND AT PRAYER 189

Milton compares the deceptions of *Eikon Basilike* to the posthumous recitation of Caesar's will before the people, an act that detailed "what bounteous legacies he had bequeathed them, wrought more in that vulgar audience to the avenging of his death, then all the art he could ever use, to win their favor in his lifetime."[13] As the text's reconstructed genealogy of tyranny makes clear, demolition is not Milton's preferred mode of iconoclasm; rather than entirely razing the image of the king, Milton elects instead the monumental task of recasting Charles's image.

"Defacement leaves behind a face," writes Joseph Koerner in his study on Reformation iconoclasm.[14] This is certainly true in the case of Milton's polemics. His defacing of the king in *Eikonoklastes* does not leave behind a featureless personage, but sears into the public imagination an image of Charles as the very face of devotional insincerity and political corruption. The figure of the English monarch then becomes the most recent instantiation in Milton's constructed history of tyrannical rule. In *Eikonoklastes*, Milton sets out to shatter the image of the executed king. But in fact, he does something else entirely. After successfully breaking the fictions linking the image of the executed king to Christ, Milton Iconoclastes recasts the royalist figurehead as an icon for his own construct—the genealogy of political tyranny.[15]

Breaking idols

Nearly twenty years after constructing historical genealogies that recontextualized royalist ideology in *Eikonoklastes*, Milton showed himself no less invested in the project of establishing historical precedents for the political issues of his own cultural moment. Indeed, Milton's response to the icon of Charles resonates with his treatment of the problem of idolatry in *Paradise Lost*. While Milton's genealogy of tyranny stretches backward toward antiquity, *Paradise Lost* opens and closes with genealogical catalogues of idolatrous acts that extend into the future. At the outset of the poem, the fallen demons dispersed throughout the world pass on their

---

and James Grantham Turner (Cambridge: Cambridge University Press, 1990), 135–51; Laura Lunger Knoppers, *Historicizing Milton: Spectacle, Power, and Poetry in Restoration England* (Athens, GA: University of Georgia Press, 1994); Achsah Guibbory, "Charles's Prayers, Idolatrous Images, and True Creation in Milton's *Eikonoklastes*," in *Of Poetry and Politics: New Essays on Milton and His World*, ed. P. G. Stanwood (Binghamton, NY: Medieval and Renaissance Texts and Studies, 1995), 283–94; and Achsah Guibbory, *Ceremony and Community from Herbert to Milton: Literature, Religion, and Cultural Conflict in Seventeenth-Century England* (Cambridge: Cambridge University Press, 1998), 147–227.

[13] Milton, *Eikonoklastes*, YP 3:342.

[14] Joseph Leo Koerner, *The Reformation of the Image* (Chicago: University of Chicago Press, 2008 [2004]), 106.

[15] Kristen Poole has noted Milton's use of similar historical and political genealogies in his antiprelatical tracts in his efforts to discount the ecclesiastical authority of the bishops. See Kristen Poole, "The Descent of Dissent: Monstrous Genealogies and Milton's Antiprelatical Tracts," in *Radical Religion from Shakespeare to Milton: Figures of Nonconformity in Early Modern England* (Cambridge: Cambridge University Press, 2000), 124–46.

190 DEVOTIONAL EXPERIENCE IN THE REFORMATION

names and personae to an astonishing array of false gods and deities, "known to men by various Names / And various Idols through the Heathen World."[16] Likewise, at the close of the epic, Michael's outline of human history provides a parallel genealogy of human folly and idol worship. As the archangel foretells the various sins and transgressions of humans yet unborn, Adam learns to his dismay that within a single generation of the deluge, Noah's descendants will have resumed their idolatrous worship:

> O that men
> (Canst thou believe?) should be so stupid grown,
> While yet the Patriark liv'd who scap'd the Flood,
> As to forsake the living God, and fall
> To worship thir own work in Wood and Stone
> For Gods!

(12.115–20)

The postdiluvian idol worshippers, of course, provide a direct historical precedent for the acts of idolatry—both religious and secular—that Milton witnessed in his own time. The angel concludes the vision of human history by announcing the unfortunate fact that few will discover true faith: "the rest, farr greater part," Michael reveals, "Well deem in outward Rites and specious formes / Religion satisfi'd."[17]

For a polemicist who two decades earlier had argued against the use of prescribed prayer and had denounced Charles for his use of set forms of worship, the catalogue's inclusion of the vast majority of those who worship only in "outward Rites and specious formes" extends the epic's concluding genealogy of human depravity all the way up to Milton's present moment. Indeed, Milton held strong opinions about how his fellow Christians ought *not* to conduct themselves during their prayers. He dedicated an entire chapter of *Eikonoklastes* to arguing against the practice of using set forms of prayer, in which he criticized the *Book of Common Prayer* and what he perceived as its underlying royalist ideology. For Milton, the prescribed prayers of the state church were nothing other than thinly

---

[16] John Milton, *Paradise Lost, a poem in twelve books* (London: Printed by S. Simmons, 1674), Book 1, lines 374–5. (*EEBO*, Wing / M2144.) I cite throughout from the 1674 edition of *Paradise Lost*, which divides the epic into twelve books and contains additions and emendations. (The 1667 text organizes the poem into ten books.) However, although I cite the text of the 1674 edition, for ease of reference I use Gordon Teskey's line numbers from his modern spelling edition of *Paradise Lost*. See John Milton, *Paradise Lost*, ed. Gordon Teskey (New York: W. W. Norton, 2005). Further references are given by book and line number parenthetically in the text.

[17] 12.533–5. The 1667 edition of the poem prints the line as "*Will* deem in outward rites and specious forms," which captures the import Michael's prediction holds for future generations of idolaters. See John Milton, *Paradise Lost a poem written in ten books* (London: Printed, and are to be sold by *Peter Parker* under *Creed* Church near *Aldgate; And by Robert Boulter* at the *Turks Head* in *Bishopsgate-street; And Matthias Walker*, under St. *Dunstons* Church in *Fleet-street*, 1667). (*EEBO*, Wing / M2137, document image 170.)

ADAM AND EVE IN BED AND AT PRAYER   191

veiled acts of popery; he argued that the *Book of Common Prayer* "was no other than the old Mass book done into English," and insisted that use of the prayer book should be banned on the grounds that it was "superstitious, offensive, and indeed, though English, yet still the Mass book."[18] Moreover, common forms of prayer—including those prescribed by the Church of England—constrain both an individual's prayerful sentiment and the Holy Spirit's ability to inspire prayer, "imprison[ing] and confin[ing] by force, into a pinfold set of words, those two most unimprisonable things, our prayers, [and] that divine spirit of utterance that moves them."[19] Those who subscribe to set forms of prayer "put on a servile yoke of liturgy," while a true Christian offers up prayer "without our premeditation."[20] Milton insisted that "Neither can any true Christian find a reason why liturgy should be at all admitted."[21]

Milton had made similar arguments against the liturgy nearly a decade earlier in his antiprelatical tracts, which he wrote and circulated during 1641 and 1642. In *Animadversions*, he condemned the liturgy as "an extract of the Mass book translated,"[22] and characterized prescribed prayer as "arbitrary," "unlawful," and nothing more than an Englishized liturgy, "prank[ed]" "in the weeds of a popish mass," an inheritance from "the corruptest times."[23] Likewise, in his *Apology for Smectymnuus*, published in 1642 and the last of his antiprelatical tracts, Milton vigorously criticized what he saw as the English church's reappropriation of "scandalous ceremonies and mass borrowed liturgies."[24] In warning against the dangers of set forms of prayer, Milton argued that prescribed worship "hinders piety rather than sets it forward, being more apt to weaken the spiritual faculties, if the people be not weaned from it in due time."[25] Rather than bolstering a worshipper's nascent devotional affect—as establishment clerics like Richard Hooker and even Calvinist-inspired theologians such as William Perkins and Samuel Hieron were inclined to believe—Milton saw corporate forms of worship as posing a hazard to genuine devotional expression: "Whereas they who will ever adhere to liturgy, bring themselves in the end to such a pass by overmuch leaning as to loose even the legs of their devotion. These inconveniences and dangers follow the compelling of set forms."[26] The spiritual implications of the inconveniences and dangers posed by set prayer moved Milton to depict a striking vision of a soul deformed by the constraints posed by the liturgy and religious ceremonies. Overburdened by

[18] Milton, *Eikonoklastes*, YP 3:504, 508.
[19] Milton, *Eikonoklastes*, YP 3:505.
[20] Milton, *Eikonoklastes*, YP 3:505, 506.
[21] Milton, *Eikonoklastes*, YP 3:504.
[22] Milton, *Reason of Church-Government*, YP 1:787.
[23] Milton, *Animadversions*, YP 1:690, 687, 688.
[24] Milton, *An Apology against a pamphlet call'd a modest confutation of the Animadversions upon the Remonstrant against Smectymnuus*, YP 1:912.
[25] Milton, *An Apology*, YP 1:937.
[26] Milton, *An Apology*, YP 1:938.

192   DEVOTIONAL EXPERIENCE IN THE REFORMATION

the performance of religious duties, the soul "forgot her heavenly flight, and left the dull and droyling carcass to plod on in the old road, and drudging trade of outward conformity."[27]

Eikonoklastes largely expounds upon Milton's earlier vituperation against the English liturgy. In his attack on the king, Milton condemns Charles for reappropriating David's Psalms in his own prayers throughout *Eikon Basilike*, an act that Milton sees as indicative of the king's spiritual disingenuousness. Although Charles engages with the Psalmic formalities, Milton claims that his external gestures of devotion belie his insincerity. What Milton found so alarming about Charles's appropriation of scriptural hymns for his own political purposes was the fact that although the king preoccupied himself with an outward show of praise, he did so, Milton believed, without genuine spiritual affect. Responding to a chapter of *Eikon Basilike* that cautioned against the dangers of overzealous reformist iconoclasm, Milton positions Charles's use of the Psalms as an act of literary and spiritual thievery: "He borrows *David's* Psalmes, as he charges the *assembly of divines* in his twentieth discourse, *to have set forth old catechisms, and confessions of faith new dressed.* Had he borrowed *David's* heart, it had been much the holier theft. For such kind of borrowing as this, if it be not bettered by the borrower, among good authors is accounted *plagiary*."[28] Milton argued that Charles was so incapable of mustering even a kernel of original sentiment that, throughout the *Eikon Basilike*, the king sings "to his soul vain psalms of exultation, as if the Parliament had assailed his reason with the force of arms."[29]

Yet despite Milton's vituperation against Charles for his use of the Psalms in his attempts to pray, he nonetheless engages in a similar act of appropriation in his efforts to poetically imagine Edenic prayer. Acts of repeated and rehearsed prayer abound in *Paradise Lost* and Milton unabashedly incorporates elements of both the Psalms and the *Book of Common Prayer* into his own vision of Adam and Eve's worship rites. In an essay on Milton's religious paradoxes, Daniel Shore makes the daring argument that Milton was not an iconoclast at all. According to Shore, Milton had no interest in enacting violence against religious images, but rather sought to leave us profoundly disenchanted with these icons, now hollowed out and utterly "void of spirit, value, and power."[30] Although Shore is right to note that Milton was not an iconoclast in any straightforward sense of that term, he overlooks the fact that Milton was deeply preoccupied with the task of preserving much more than the empty form of the icons. If Milton hollowed out inherited forms, his recasting of prescribed prayer in *Paradise Lost* indicates his refusal to

---

[27] Milton, *Of Reformation in England*, YP 1:522.

[28] Milton, *Eikonoklastes*, YP 3:547.

[29] Milton, *Eikonoklastes*, YP 3:435.

[30] Daniel Shore, "Why Milton Is Not an Iconoclast," *PMLA* 127, no. 1 (2012): 22–37, quote on 24. In a similar vein, David Gay, "Prayer and the Sacred Image: Milton, Jeremy Taylor, and the *Eikon Basilike*," *Milton Quarterly* 46, no. 1 (2012): 1–14, observes that Milton's method of iconoclasm did not strictly entail violence; the paradox of iconoclasm for Milton was that it involved simultaneous destruction and creation (3).

ADAM AND EVE IN BED AND AT PRAYER   193

leave them devoid of spiritual potential. In spite of his vigorous denouncement of Charles's prescribed prayers, Milton gives implicit assent to the power of formal worship in choosing to include elements of liturgical praise in *Paradise Lost*. Milton reimagined Eden as a historical and conceptual space in which he could dismantle the forms of worship that he found so spiritually repugnant, while also animating their devotional power.[31] What, precisely, is Milton doing when he imagines Adam and Eve participating in the very forms of worship and praise that made his contemporaries not only liable to receive substantial prison terms, but more important—as in the case of Charles—guilty of spiritual thievery?[32]

Prayer before the Fall

The vehement anti-liturgical sentiments of his prose tracts did not deter Milton from incorporating liturgical overtones into his poetic portrayal of Edenic prayer in *Paradise Lost*. Ever since Thomas Newton noted the liturgical and Psalmic import of Adam and Eve's morning hymn in Book 5, scholars have observed the various formal genres to which the epic's moments of spontaneous prayer allude. The hymn, Newton rightly observes, "is an imitation, or rather a sort of paraphrase of the 148th Psalm, and (of what is a paraphrase upon that) the Canticle placed after *Te Deum* in the Liturgy, 'O all ye works of the Lord, bless ye the Lord.'"[33] Both Psalm 148 and the canticle from the *Book of Common Prayer* serve as calls

---

[31] In this regard, Milton's conflicted portrayal of the power of common forms of prayer embodies the paradox of David Freedberg's observation that acts of violence against an image suggest the iconoclast's belief in the power of that image. See David Freedberg, *The Power of Images: Studies in the History and Theory of Response* (Chicago: University of Chicago Press, 1989), 378–428. Koerner has a provoking discussion of Freeberg's argument in his treatment of the sixteenth-century Münster Anabaptists' destruction of pre-Reformation church icons and monuments: "By [Freedberg's] account, the Anabaptists' hammerblows become a version of volt sorcery, where one attempts magically to harm one's enemies via images of them." See Koerner, *Reformation of the Image*, 109.

[32] During its tenure as a parliamentary advisory committee between 1643 and 1649, the Westminster Assembly issued several documents suggesting a restructuring of the Church of England, one of which, *The Directory of the Publick Worship of God*, was approved by Parliament in 1645 as a replacement for the church's standard *Book of Common Prayer*. Milton supported the assembly's rejection of the prayer book in favor of the *Directory* as well as the proposed year-long prison term for third-time offenders who practiced a form of worship not prescribed by the *Directory*. Despite its proscription during the interregnum, a number of churches continued to use the *Book of Common Prayer* during services. Although the criminal statutes against using the prayer book were rarely enforced, one imagines that these statutes nevertheless profoundly affected those who chose to pray using the proscribed liturgical forms. For a historical overview of the Westminster Assembly's proceedings, see Barbara Kiefer Lewalski, *The Life of John Milton: A Critical Biography* (Malden, MA: Blackwell, 2002), 161–2; and Regina M. Schwartz, *Remembering and Repeating: On Milton's Theology and Poetics* (Chicago: University of Chicago Press, 1993 [1988]), 75.

[33] Thomas Newton, ed., *Paradise Lost: A Poem, in Twelve Books*, by John Milton, 2 vols. (London: J. and R. Tonson and S. Draper, 1754), 1: 359. Modern editors and critics of the epic who have noted the morning hymn's resonance with the liturgy and the Psalms include Joseph H. Summers, *The Muse's Method: An Introduction to "Paradise Lost"* (London: Chatto and Windus, 1962), 78; Kathleen M. Swaim, "The Morning Hymn of Praise in Book 5 of *Paradise Lost*," *Milton Quarterly* 22 (1988): 7–16; John Carey and Alastair Fowler, eds., Introduction to *The Poems of John Milton* (London: Longmans,

194   DEVOTIONAL EXPERIENCE IN THE REFORMATION

to worship, exhorting first the heavenly and angelic hosts to offer up praises to God before moving down the chain of creation, appealing in turn to the sun, moon, and stars, and finally to the small creatures that populate the earth itself. The voices of the many parts of creation—animate and inanimate, imposing and diminutive—coalesce in a chorus of praise, a universal chorus that is itself structurally united by the refrain calling each part of the creation to contemplation and worship.

The refrain runs throughout the King James Version of the psalm—"Praise ye the Lord from the heavens: praise him in the heights. / Praise ye him all his angels: praise ye him all his hosts. / Praise ye him sun and moon: praise him all ye stars of light"[34]—as it does in the prayer book canticle: "O ye Angels of the Lord, bless ye the Lord: praise him, and magnifie him forever. / O ye heavens, bless ye the Lord: praise him, and magnifie him for ever ... / O ye Sun and Moon, blesse ye the Lord: praise him, and magnifie him forever."[35] In his own refashioning of the psalm and the canticle in Adam and Eve's morning prayer, Milton evokes echoes of the refrain as well as the prayer book's cosmic vision of the various parts of creation joining together in this chorus of praise. The hymn begins by exhorting those in Heaven— "ye Sons of light, / Angels" (5.160–1)—and the celestial bodies to join their voices in the hymn of praise, and moves down the cosmic chain as Adam and Eve proceed to address even the smallest of living creatures: "Joyn voices all ye living Soules, ye Birds / That singing up to Heaven Gate ascend" (5.197–8). The first morning prayer, as Milton imagines it, also retains something of a refrain that serves to structure the hymn's blank verse, prompting all of creation to "sound his praise" (5.172), "resound / His praise" (5.178–9), "Varie ... still new praise" (5.184), "still advance his praise' (5.191), "tune his praise" (5.196), "Bear ... his praise" (5.199), and be "taught his praise" (5.204). Despite Milton's insistence that Adam and Eve perform their morning rites "Unmeditated" (5.149), their orisons—"each Morning duly paid" (5.145)—nevertheless resonate profoundly with the display of outward show and liturgy to which Milton vehemently objected in his polemical tracts. In moments of what ought to be a deeply spontaneous outburst of praise, Milton presents us with an act of worship that startles us with its oddly rehearsed and reiterative nature.

1968); and Thomas B. Stroup, *Religious Rite and Ceremony in Milton's Poetry* (Lexington, KY: University of Kentucky Press, 2015 [1968]), esp. 15–47. Barbara Lewalski, "Paradise Lost" and the Rhetoric of Literary Forms (Princeton: Princeton University Press, 1985), esp. 202–5, has written the most detailed study to date on the liturgical and scriptural forms that inform *Paradise Lost*, and specifically the morning hymn. Additionally, Mary Ann Radzinowicz, *Milton's Epics and the Book of Psalms* (Princeton: Princeton University Press, 1989), esp. 135–99, argues that the structures of both *Paradise Lost* and *Paradise Regained* are indebted to Milton's own reading of and appreciation for the Psalms.

[34] Psalm 148:1–3, in *The Holy Bible, Conteyning the Old Testament and the New* (London: Imprinted by Robert Barker, 1611). (EEBO, STC (2nd ed.) / 2217.)

[35] Thomas Cranmer, "An Order for Morning Prayer daily throughout the Year," in *The book of common-prayer and administration of the sacraments and other rites & ceremonies of the church, according to the use of the Church of England* (London: Printed by His Ma[jes]ties Printers, 1662), unpaginated. (*EEBO*, Wing / B3622, document image 35.)

ADAM AND EVE IN BED AND AT PRAYER 195

Of course, Milton had appropriated elements of the state liturgy in his literary writings prior to *Paradise Lost*. Milton had previously described a similar scene of universal worship in his Nativity ode, which he wrote in 1629 at the age of twenty-one. In stanza 13, the younger Milton imagines the heavenly spheres, enthralled by the birth of the Messiah, offering up joyful praise in celebration of the Nativity occasion:

> Ring out ye Crystall sphears,
> Once bless our human ears
>   (If ye have power to touch our senses so)
> And let your silver chime
> Move in melodious time;
>   And let the Bass of Heav'ns deep Organ blow,
> And with your ninefold harmony
> Make up full consort to th' Angelike symphony.[36]

In Milton's ode, the sun, moon, stars, and planets join their voices with the heavenly angels "in loud and solemn quire" (115). The Nativity is perhaps the only postlapsarian occasion that Milton thought warranted the chorus of heavenly praise—both angelical and astronomical—that he would eventually describe more fully in Adam and Eve's Edenic prayers. Indeed, the liturgical resonances of the universal praise in Milton's ode anticipates the morning prayer from *Paradise Lost*, with its echoes of the *Te Deum* canticle from the *Book of Common Prayer*. While the Nativity ode's liturgical and ceremonial resonances certainly would have been apparent to Milton's contemporary readers, it is nonetheless telling that the poem never resorts to verbatim recitation or reiteration of the words of the liturgy itself. Thomas Stroup has aptly described the poem's praise as "the remembered, though unrecited, portion of liturgy"—Milton recreates the liturgical occasion without having to reiterate the words of the official liturgy itself. The twenty-one-year-old Milton appears to have already been committed to the belief—one he would eventually expound upon in his polemical writings—that true worship required one to add his own words of prayer and praise to the standard liturgical models. As Stroup describes the liturgical aspects of the Nativity ode, "underneath lies the form and the cue to [the liturgy's] presence, but the new words refresh its meaning."[37]

When Milton imagined Adam and Eve's prayers before the Fall in *Paradise Lost*, he could have done what he had already done in the Nativity ode, which adopted

---

[36] John Milton, "On the Morning of Christs Nativity," in *Poems of Mr. John Milton both English and Latin* (London: Printed by Ruth Raworth for Humphrey Moseley, and are to be sold at the signe of the Princes Arms in S. Pauls Church-yard, 1645), p. 7, lines 125–32. (*EEBO*, Wing / M2160, document image 7.) While I use the orthography from the first print edition of the poem, I have used line numbers from John Milton, *The Complete Shorter Poems*, ed. John Carey (Harlow: Pearson Education, 2007 [1968]).

[37] Stroup, *Religious Rite and Ceremony*, 7.

196   DEVOTIONAL EXPERIENCE IN THE REFORMATION

liturgical models without imitating the actual words of the liturgy itself. But Milton incorporates the liturgy much more directly in his crafting of Edenic prayer and praise, appropriating nearly verbatim phrases from the *Te Deum* canticle. In the epic, Milton conserves the words of the liturgy, incorporating them into Adam and Eve's prayers, while situating those prayers within fundamentally non-liturgical contexts.

In a similar vein, Milton's peculiar treatment of the liturgy in *Paradise Lost* becomes apparent when we consider the liturgical references of his early masque. Readers have long noted the association between Milton's *A Maske* and the scriptural lessons from the *Book of Common Prayer* that would have been read during Michaelmas, the day on which the masque was performed at Ludlow Castle in 1634. William B. Hunter has noted the thematic overlaps between *A Maske*'s focus on childhood innocence and virtue and Christ's celebration of children and child-like faith in Matthew 18, which features in the prayer book's Michaelmas Communion service.[38] Likewise, Hunter also suggests that the masque's depiction of the struggle between the Lady and Comus contains echoes of the battle between good and evil outlined in Psalms 140 and 141 and the apocryphal Ecclesiasticus 39—the scriptural topics of the Michaelmas morning lessons. In addition to its scriptural associations with the Michaelmas service lessons, James Taaffe, Anthony Mortimer, R. Chris Hassel, John Creaser, and Leah Marcus have noted the parallels between the masque and various aspects of the popular, festive, administrative, and calendrical associations of Michaelmas.[39] Without a doubt, Milton wrote *A Maske* with a mind to the fact that the people of Ludlow Castle would have been

---

[38] William B. Hunter, Jr., "The Liturgical Context of *Comus*," *English Language Notes* 10 (1972): 11–15, esp. 12–13.

[39] James Taaffe notes overlaps between the masque's attention to proper governance and the administrative functions of Michaelmas, which was a traditional date for the election of magistrates and a common due date for semiannual rents. In a similar vein, John Creaser notes the masque's thematic attention to the liturgical and administrative associations with Michaelmas, in both its attention to childhood and to self-governance. Michael Wilding has noted that the power struggles within the masque reference the borderland power struggles between England and Wales—a fitting topic since Ludlow Castle was the administrative seat of the Council of Wales and the marches, and the masque was presented on the occasion of John Egerton, 1st Earl of Bridgewater's installation as Lord President of Wales. Finally, R. Chris Hassel, Jr., Anthony Mortimer, and Leah Marcus have noted the festival, holiday, and ritual associations between *A Maske* and Michaelmas. See James Taaffe, "Michaelmas, the 'Lawless Hour,' and the Occasion of Milton's *Comus*," *English Language Notes* 6, no. 4 (1969): 257–62, esp. 260–2; John Creaser, "'The present aid of this occasion': The Setting of *Comus*," in *The Court Masque*, ed. David Lindley (Manchester: Manchester University Press, 1984), 111–34, esp. 114 and 127; Michael Wilding, "Milton's 'A Masque Presented at Ludlow Castle, 1634': Theatre and Politics on the Border," *Milton Quarterly* 21, no. 4 (1987): 35–51, esp. 46, 50; R. Chris Hassel, Jr., "Michaelmas, Hallowmas, and Saint Bartholomew's," in *Renaissance Drama and the English Church Year* (Lincoln, NE: University of Nebraska Press, 1979), 157–160; Anthony Mortimer, "*Comus* and Michaelmas," *English Studies* 65, no. 2 (1984): 111–19, esp. 111–13; Leah S. Marcus, "Milton's Anti-Laudian Masque," in *The Politics of Mirth: Jonson, Herrick, Milton, Marvell, and the Defense of Old Holiday Pastimes* (Chicago: University of Chicago Press, 1986), 169–212; and Leah S. Marcus, "The Earl of Bridgewater's Legal Life: Notes toward a Political Reading of Comus," *Milton Quarterly* 21, no. 4 (1987): 13–23.

alert to the morning's scriptural lessons from the *Book of Common Prayer*, and to the day's wider cultural valences.

Importantly though, as is the case with his Nativity ode, Milton succeeded in highlighting the masque's connection to the Michaelmas occasion without any verbatim repetition of the prayer book's liturgies. *A Maske* successfully references the *Book of Common Prayer* without resorting to direct imitation or use of repeated utterances. What Milton does with the liturgy as a younger writer in *A Maske* offers an example of how he *could* have treated the liturgical aspects of Adam and Eve's prayers in *Paradise Lost*. But rather than referencing scriptural themes or cultural occasions in *Paradise Lost*, Milton seems uninterested in contextualizing Adam and Eve's Edenic prayers in terms of the prayer book's attention to thematic and festival associations. On the contrary, he imagines Adam and Eve's prayers as verbatim recitation straight from the liturgy itself.

What is clear is that Milton imagines his engagement with the liturgy in *Paradise Lost* as doing something fundamentally different both from his earlier thematic and cultural references to the Michaelmas festivities in *A Maske* and from his earlier rewriting of liturgical elements in the Nativity ode. And yet, despite the indisputable liturgical and Psalmic echoes of Adam and Eve's prayers, no critic has considered the problems these forms of prayer pose when read alongside Milton's iconoclastic and anti-liturgical remarks. On the contrary, standard responses to the liturgical overtones of these Edenic prayers have avoided the paradox by pointing to the problems imposed by postlapsarian perception, arguing that our tendency to read set forms of prayer into these hymns indicates a failure of our own fallen perception. Our postlapsarian minds, such arguments contend, can neither situate these hymns within their original and unfallen contexts, nor fully appreciate the perfect poetry of these spontaneous outbursts of praise. For example, Joseph Summers explains the hymn's allusions to the various genres of worship as a means of approximating, for the benefit of postlapsarian readers, the perfection of unfallen human praise: "*Various*, here as always in the poem, has only the best connotations. No one ritual can suffice for the praise and thanksgiving due to God for the dazzling multiplicity of His perceived creation. More variety in sound is demanded than fallen man can conceive. Once again we are reminded that here we are dealing with yet perfect man, and once again the perfection of praise is described."[40] Summers justifies the problematic presence of liturgical overtones in the hymn by pointing to the limitations of postlapsarian perception; Adam and Eve's morning hymn is so supremely nuanced and variegated that fallen senses can never perfectly track the individual strains that come together in this most perfect moment of praise. This attempt at resolution is one to which Barbara Lewalski also subscribes when she describes the hymn's liturgical registers as an accommodation to the epic's postlapsarian reader: "This complexity and comprehensiveness

[40] Summers, *Muse's Method*, 75.

198   DEVOTIONAL EXPERIENCE IN THE REFORMATION

is at once a means of accommodation to us, suggesting the perfection of unfallen hymnody through a fusion of the most exalted hymnic forms we know, and also a testimony to the sublime artfulness of Adam and Eve's poetic accomplishment."[41] Nevertheless, the explanations provided by Summers and Lewalski do not directly resolve the question as to why Milton assumed the risks—both theological and political—of incorporating into Adam and Eve's prayers the very liturgical practices he argued were spiritually suspect and criminally punishable. We might be able to shed light upon the paradox of Milton's views on worship using common forms of prayer when we consider the limitations not only of our own decidedly postlapsarian senses, as Summers and Lewalski do, but also of those who inhabit Milton's Paradise.

***

On one of the first evenings of their newly created life together, Adam and Eve offer up their orisons and prayers to God: "under the open sky [they] adored / The God who made both sky, air, earth and heav'n / Which they beheld, the moon's resplendent globe / And starry pole" (4.721–4). Adam and Eve's nighttime prayers are variations of their morning hymns, which in turn jangle with the phrases and refrains from Psalm 148 and the prayer book canticle. In Book 4, Adam and Eve engage in a series of nocturnal rites that culminate in what is arguably the most sensational rite in *Paradise Lost*: sexual consummation. Under the open night sky, Adam and Eve pray, remembering and reflecting upon the various parts of creation—both vast and minuscule—and thanking God for each of these devotional occasions. With their prayers now completed, Adam and Eve hasten to their bower for the night:

> This said unanimous, and other Rites
> Observing none, but adoration pure
> Which God likes best, into their inmost bowre
> Handed they went; and eas'd the putting off
> These troublesom disguises which wee wear,
> Strait side by side were laid, nor turnd I weene
> *Adam* from his fair Spouse, nor *Eve* the Rites
> Mysterious of connubial Love refus'd.
>
> (4.736–43)

Adam and Eve's worshipful adoration of God spawns another register of "adoration pure" between devoted soulmates. The final rite that marks the evening's close, that of the mysteries of connubial love, becomes an extension of Adam and Eve's prayers and praise.

---

[41] Lewalski, "*Paradise Lost*," 203.

ADAM AND EVE IN BED AND AT PRAYER   199

According to Milton, prayer and sex are both facets of proper worship in Eden. Milton seems to be suggesting that the pleasures of sexual consummation between married partners might produce the devotional benefits of traditional forms of worship itself.[42] In making this claim about the devotional value of desire and sex, Milton's bower scene echoes other early modern reformist arguments that maintained that companionate love functioned as a spiritual aid for married couples.[43] The 1636 edition of Samuel Hieron's *A Helpe vnto Devotion*, a devotional manual of set prayers, includes two prayers for use by couples—the first for partners about to wed, and the second for married spouses.[44] The prayers describe married love as an extension of worship, allowing spouses to find "that sweetness which we find in Heavenly things" in each other. In Hieron's set prayers, marriage occasions moments of devotion, as per the formal prayers outlined in the handbook, but it also serves as a continuous and ongoing reminder of each spouse's relationship to God, allowing spouses to go—like Adam and Eve on their way to the bower—"hand in hand towards Heaven."[45] The view of married love described by both Milton and Hieron registers the view of Protestant love espoused by the Swiss reformer Heinrich Bullinger, who argued that the loving and daily actions of happily married spouses "please God no less than they do when they go to church to hear the word of God and to worship the Lord."[46] In Bullinger's view, companionate love is as devotionally powerful as the formal prayers and praise of ecclesiastical worship.

[42] For discussions of sex in Milton's Eden as an extension of sacred worship, see Achsah Guibbory, "Donne, Milton, and Holy Sex," *Milton Studies* 32 (1995): 3–21, reprinted in Achsah Guibbory, *Returning to John Donne* (Burlington, VT: Ashgate, 2015), 107–24; Guibbory, *Ceremony and Community*, 206–9; and Jennifer Waldron, *Reformations of the Body: Idolatry, Sacrifice, and Early Modern Theater* (New York: Palgrave Macmillan, 2013), 206.

[43] For my discussion of Protestant manuals on companionate marriage, in the context of Milton's polemics and Donne's elegies, see Rhema Hokama, "'Loves halowed temple': Erotic Sacramentalism and Reformed Devotion in John Donne's 'To his Mistress going to bed,'" *Modern Philology* 119, no. 2 (2021): 248–75, esp. 267–9.

[44] See Samuel Hieron, "The person intending Marriage, may be thus directed" and "The Married persons, their joynt request unto God," in *A Helpe vnto Devotion: containing certaine moulds, of formes of prayer, fitted to several occasions and penned for the furtherance of those, who haue more desire than skill to power out their soles by petition unto God* (London: Printed by John Beale, 1636), 337–46. (*EEBO*, STC (2nd ed.) / 13216.)

[45] Hieron, *Helpe vnto Devotion*, 345.

[46] Heinrich Bullinger, "The Second Decade, The Tenth Sermon," in *Fiftie godlie and learned sermons diuided into fiue decades, conteyning the chiefe and principall points of Christian religion, written in three several tomes or sections, by Henrie Bullinger minister of the churches of Tigure in Swicerlande. Whereunto is adioyned a triple or three-fold table verie fruitefull and necessarie. Translated out of Latine into English by H. I. student in diuinitie* (Imprinted at London: by [Henry Middleton for] Ralphe Newberrie, dwelling in Fleet-streate a little aboue the Conduite, 1577), 229. (*EEBO*. STC (2nd ed.) / 4056.) Cited in Roland Mushat Frye, "The Teachings of Classical Puritanism on Conjugal Love," *Studies in the Renaissance* 2 (1995): 148–59. For treatments of early modern Reformed views of married love, see also William Haller and Malleville Haller, "The Puritan Art of Love," *Huntington Library Quarterly* 5, no. 2 (1942): 235–72; Laurence Lerner, *Love and Marriage: Literature and Its Social Context* (London: Edward Arnold, 1979); and James Grantham Turner, *One Flesh: Paradisal Marriage and Sexual Relations in the Age of Milton* (Oxford: Clarendon Press, 1987).

200 DEVOTIONAL EXPERIENCE IN THE REFORMATION

Bullinger's vision of Reformed marriage sought to impart sacramental potential to ordinary experience. During the first decades of the seventeenth century, ideas like his inspired not only those like Hieron, but also Reformed-minded English theologians such as William Perkins, Thomas Gataker, William Whately, and William Gouge to author devotional handbooks on companionate Protestant marriage.[47] Those like Gouge saw sex within Protestant marriage as an antidote to Stoic or Catholic arguments in favor of celibacy, and nearly all of these handbook writers made the case that affection, desire, and sex—within the bonds of Protestant matrimony—might serve a devotional purpose. Gouge maintained that sex between married partners—what he calls a "due benevolence"—"is one of the most proper and essential acts of marriage," serving not only to satisfy bodily passion but also allowing the couple to partake in eternal, spiritual goodness: "Let us labor to cherish this natural affection in us, and to turn it to the best things, even to such as are not only apparently, but indeed good: and among good things to such as are most excellent, and the most necessary: such as concern our souls, and eternal life. ... Thus shall our natural affection be turned into a spiritual affection."[48] In his polemical writings, Milton himself attempted a handbook of sorts on companionate Protestant marriage. In his divorce tracts, Milton summed up the devotional and spiritual benefits of companionate love most succinctly, maintaining that "in matrimony there must be first a mutuall help to piety, next to civill fellowship of love and amity." The devotional benefits afforded by a well-matched marriage remained vital for Milton—so much so that he argued that a marriage ill-matched either intellectually or bodily ought to be grounds for divorce: the badly matched couple "can neither serve God together, nor one be at peace with the other, or be good in the family one to other, but live as they were dead, or live as they were deadly enemies in a cage together."[49]

For the writers of these handbooks on happy Protestant marriage, companionate love served as an ongoing form of worship, one that could be aided by the set forms of prayer of Hieron's handbook, but was, at the same time, not limited to

---

[47] A partial list of English sixteenth- and seventeenth-century tracts and handbooks on Protestant marriage includes Henry Smith's *A Preparatiue to Mariage* (1591); Robert Cleaver's *A Godlie forme of Householde Gouernment* (1598); William Perkins's *Christian Oeconomie, or, A Short Survey of the Right Manner of erecting and ordering a Familie according to the Scriptures* (1609); Samuel Hieron's *The Marriage-Blessing* (1611) and *The Bridegroome* (1613); Alexander Niccholes's *A Discourse, of Marriage and VViving* (1615); William Whately's *A Bride-Bush, or a VVedding Sermon* (1617) and *The Care-Cloth: or a Treatise on the Cumbers and Troubles of Marriage* (1624); John Wing's *The Crovvne Coniugall or, The Spouse Royall* (1620); Thomas Gataker's *Marriage Duties Briefely Couched together out of Colossians 3.18, 19* (1620), *A Good VVife Gods Gift and A VVife Indeed: Tvvo Marriage Sermons* (1623), and *A Marriage Praier* (1624); William Gouge's *Of Domesticall Duties* (1622); D[aniel] R[oger]'s *Matrimoniall Honour* (1642); and John Milton's four remarkable divorce tracts, which he wrote between 1643 and 1645.
[48] William Gouge, Treatise 2, pt. 2, in *Of Domesticall Dvties. Eight Treatises* (London: Printed by Iohn Haviland for William Bladen, and are to be sold at the signe of the Bible neere the great north doore of Pauls, 1622), 222; and William Gouge, Treatise 1, in *Of Domesticall Dvties. Eight Treatises* (London: Printed by Iohn Haviland, 1622), 83–4. (*EEBO*, STC (2nd ed.) / 12119.)
[49] Milton, *Tetrachordon*, YP 2:599.

any outward or prescribed model of praise. Although Milton would have likely disagreed with Hieron's use of set prayers, he would have no doubt supported the argument of those prayers—namely, the Reformed view that sex could be a form of prayer unto itself, one that had a devotional efficacy that rivaled the official worship of the state church. Milton's poetry describes an embodied desire that seems to transcend the formal registers of the poem's liturgical prayers while still retaining its literary debt to the language of liturgical praise.

The poem's sex scene quickly veers into one of Milton's polemical tirades against those who denounce sexual pleasure: "Whatever Hypocrites austerely talk / Of puritie and place and innocence, / Defaming as impure what God declares / Pure, and commands to som, leaves free to all."[50] In touching upon contemporary debates about Reformed love, Milton also makes an argument for how a companionate Protestant marriage might, in fact, serve as its own form of anti-ceremonial critique. Milton takes the set forms of common prayer, and, like Hieron, repurposes them in his efforts to describe private forms of devotion and desire. In Milton's Paradise, sex supplants formal liturgical worship, and the consummation of desire is its own act of performed devotion to God.

One of the features of sex before the Fall is its inextricable link to spoken language. Adam and Eve go to bed not only praying to God but conversing with one another: "Thus talking hand in hand alone they pass'd / On to thir blissful Bower" (4.689–90). The topic at hand is the proper way to worship God. As Adam explains to Eve, their prayers and praise join a whole chorus of voices:

> Millions of spiritual Creatures walk the Earth
> Unseen, both when we wake, and when we sleep:
> All these with ceaseless praise his works behold
> Both day and night.
>
> (4.677–80)

Milton situates Adam and Eve's nighttime rites of love in the vividly textured material and spiritual world of the Garden; the environs of the bower abound with an array of life forms. The bower is studded "with rich inlay" (4.701) and gem-like flowers—roses, jessamines, violets, crocuses, hyacinths, and "*Iris* all hues" (4.698). Milton describes the peripheries of the bower as teeming with small creatures, who retreat from the threshold in awe of the rites taking place therein: "Other Creature here / Beast, Bird, Insect, or Worm durst enter none; / Such was thir awe of Man" (4.703–5). These flowers and small beings, Milton seems to suggest, are some of the "Millions of spiritual creatures" whose voices offer up perpetual prayers and praise. In Adam's words, these spiritual creatures "With Heav'nly touch of instrumental sounds / In full harmonic number joind, thir songs / Divide the night,

---

[50] 4.744–7. For an illuminating discussion of the theological and historical context of this interjection, and of Milton's use of narrative interjections more broadly in the poem, see Peter Lindenbaum, "Lovemaking in *Paradise Lost,*" *Milton Studies* 6 (1974): 277–306, esp. 285–6.

202   DEVOTIONAL EXPERIENCE IN THE REFORMATION

and lift our thoughts to Heaven" (4.686–8). Much like Robert Herrick's poems of devotional and erotic praise, in Milton's Paradise the smallest details of the natural world—flowers, bees, and birds—offer occasions for worship and celebration.[51] In this regard, Adam and Eve's Edenic prayers and worship appear to make use of the Reformed devotional technique popularized by Joseph Hall, which used the objects, sights, and sounds of the natural world as prompts or occasions for private prayer and worship. Although Milton launched vigorous polemical attacks against Hall's conciliatory soteriological and ecclesiastical positions in his support of Smectymnuus—the *nom de plume* of five Reformed divines who published two pamphlets critiquing Hall's views of church worship—the devotional practices that Milton depicts in his Paradise undoubtedly adopt many of Hall's less controversial devotional techniques.[52] Indeed, after the Fall, upon learning of his imminent expulsion from Eden, Adam laments his impending loss of the features of the natural world that served as occasions for continuous prayer and praise:

> here I could frequent,
> With worship, place by place where he voutsaf'd
> Presence Divine, and to my Sons relate;
> On this Mount he appeerd, under this Tree
> Stood visible, among these Pines his voice
> I heard, here with him at this Fountain talk'd:
> So many grateful Altars I would reare
> Of grassie Terfe, and pile up every Stone
> Of lustre from the brook, in memorie,
> Or monument to Ages, and thereon
> Offer sweet smelling Gumms and Fruits and Flours:
> In yonder nether World where shall I seek
> His bright appearances, or foot-step trace?
>
> (11.317–29)

For all the losses incurred as a result of the Fall, the poem makes clear that Adam and Eve retain their access to these devotional aids—the "grateful Altars" that he devised from the turfs, stones, and brooks. As Michael reassures Adam, "surmise not then / His presence to these narrows bounds confin'd / Of Paradise or *Eden*. ... Yet doubt not but in Vallie and in plaine / God is here, and will be found

---

[51] G. Stanley Koehler has argued that Milton's Eden is modeled on the features of the English countryside. See G. Stanley Koehler, "Milton and the Art of Landscape," *Milton Studies* 8 (1975): 3–40. On the similarities between Herrick's lyric and Milton's *Paradise Lost*, Guibbory has likewise noted the uncanny parallels between poems like Herrick's "Corinna's gone a-Maying" and Adam and Eve's morning prayer in Book 5, although she sees this as evidence of Milton's ceremonialism rather than a Reformed attempt to find private devotional equivalents for ecclesiastical models of worship. See Guibbory, *Ceremony and Community*, 206.

[52] See Chapter 4 on Robert Herrick for my discussion of how Hall's devotional techniques shaped early modern English poetry in the mid-seventeenth century. For my discussion of William Perkins's development of experiential devotional practices, see Chapter 1.

ADAM AND EVE IN BED AND AT PRAYER   203

alike / Present" (11.340–2, 349–51). Michael's response cements the devotional continuity between pre- and postlapsarian worship. God does not strip away the devotional occasions offered by the natural features of Paradise; on the contrary, he widens the scope for worship by giving Adam and Eve the entirety of the material world as an aid for devotion. Just as he created a genealogy for his iconoclastic attacks against Charles, here Milton creates a literary genealogy for the kinds of devotional practices that were advocated by English adherents of Calvinist theology and experiential devotional practice. In doing so, he justifies Reformed devotional practice by attributing it to Edenic origins. By anchoring devotional practice to the sensible, material world, and stripping it of its ecclesiastical limitations, Milton suggests that Reformed worship methods hew most closely to the forms of prayer and praise that our original parents practiced in Paradise.

Similarly, Milton refuses to deny the fallen Adam and Eve the pleasures of sex. Just as *Paradise Lost* asserts the devotional continuity between pre- and postlapsarian prayer and praise, the poem also imagines a postlapsarian afterlife for the preeminent rite of Edenic worship: the rite of love. After their act of disobedience, a devastated Eve suggests to her husband that they might prevent future suffering by opting not to bear children into a wretched world, recommending that they "abstain / From Loves due Rites, Nuptial imbraces sweet" (10.993–4). Adam rejects Eve's solution in favor of prayer and supplication—what he calls "Some safer resolution" (10.1029). Adam rightfully warns that to give up sex and love "will provoke the highest / To make death in us live" (10.1027–8). To reject love's due rites, Adam maintains, would give assent to a kind of spiritual death; on the contrary, to make themselves available to the rites of love might avert spiritual dissolution. After the Fall, Milton establishes both prayer and sex as paired devotional aids, each of which fosters renewed access to God during the performance of the rites of worship.

Admittedly, Milton distinguishes fallen sex from Edenic sex by stripping it of its rich cognitive and intellectual contexts. Indeed, the poem's postlapsarian sex scene is devoid of both conversation and prayer, which had bound Adam and Eve to God and to each other as they performed love's rites in the bower of Book 4. As in Book 4, here Adam and Eve lead each other hand in hand to the bank on which they commence their "amorous play." But unlike the scene from Book 4, after the Fall they walk silently, relying on their glances and looks to bodily communicate their desires and intentions:

> So said he, and forbode not glance or toy
> Of amorous intent, well understood
> Of *Eve*, whose Eye darted contagious Fire.
> Her hand he seis'd, and to a shadie bank,
> Thick overhead with verdant roof imbowr'd
> He led her nothing loath;

204 DEVOTIONAL EXPERIENCE IN THE REFORMATION

> Flours were the Couch,
> Pansies, and Violets,
> And Asphodel, And Hyacinth, Earths freshest softest lap.
> There they thir fill of Love and Loves disport
> Took largely, of thir mutual guilt the Seale,
> The solace of thir sin, till dewie sleep
> Oppress'd them, wearied with thir amorous play.
>
> (9.1034–45)

For all its intellectual and spiritual shortcomings, Milton still finds devotional value even in fallen sexual yearnings. As James Grantham Turner puts it, "Forbidden sexuality is not suppressed in Milton's epic, but vividly registered as a potentiality."[53] Milton decks his description of fallen sex with the same litany of flowers that populated the bower of Book 4. Although removed from their marriage bed, and no longer attuned to the innumerable "spiritual creatures" that bolster their prayers to God, Adam and Eve's postlapsarian rites of love nevertheless retain the poetic features of paradisal sex. It is thus incorrect to suggest, as some readers have, that Adam and Eve's postlapsarian sex is not only inferior to its prelapsarian counterpart, but an outright perversion of it: as Achsah Guibbory puts it, the poem depicts fallen sex as "adulterous, a fit image for idolatry," and according to John Halkett, it is "a debasement of sexual love."[54] On the contrary, Milton refuses to imagine sex after the Fall as a perversion of married devotion. Postlapsarian lovemaking remains deeply pleasurable; if it binds Adam and Eve together in their "mutual guilt," it also links them together in mutual passion.

In imagining ideal companionate love between Adam and Eve, Milton could have imagined other modes of spiritual and sexual commune, modes that diminish the role of the physical body. Indeed, their sex is not the only kind that Milton describes in *Paradise Lost*; he also details sex among the angels. When angels have sex, their beings comingle entirely, "Easier then Air with Air" (8.626). Wholly unencumbered by any physical limits of the body, they "obstacle find none / Of membrane, joynt, or limb, exclusive barrs" (8.624–5). According to Gordon Teskey, what makes angelic sex so good in *Paradise Lost* is its ability to transcend material and bodily limitation; angelic sex is "not confined by the limitations of the body," he writes, "either by its barriers to total penetration or by specialized sexual organs." Milton's angels, as Teskey describes them, are "polymorphously erotic."[55] But while perfect angelic sex might be defined by its polymorphous eroticism, Milton makes clear that perfect human sex is necessarily an embodied act—and better for it. Like postlapsarian prayer, rooted in the robustness of the material world,

---

[53] Turner, *One Flesh*, 172.

[54] Guibbory, *Ceremony and Community*, 214; John Halkett, *Milton and the Idea of Matrimony: A Study of the Divorce Tracts and Paradise Lost* (New Haven: Yale University Press, 1970), 128.

[55] Gordon Teskey, *The Poetry of John Milton* (Cambridge, MA: Harvard University Press, 2015), 365.

ADAM AND EVE IN BED AND AT PRAYER   205

Milton does not deny Adam and Eve remnants of their former paradisal passion and desire; instead, he reimagines sex as an aid to devotion that might, as Adam surmises, stave off spiritual death.

***

Sex is not the only act of worship that is contingent upon bodily participation in Milton's Paradise. Eating, almost as inflammatory an act for Milton's contemporaries, likewise seems reminiscent (or perhaps anticipatory) of familiar postlapsarian forms of ritualized worship. Indeed, Milton manages to make Edenic consumption a theologically and politically charged event. During Raphael's visit to Eden in Book 5, Eve prepares a dinner feast for their guest. All present—both human and angel—partake of the Edenic fruits and vegetables; the ultimate purpose of paradisal digestion is "to transubstantiate" these delicacies into spiritual nourishment (5.438). To imagine the daily ritual of eating as a mode of transubstantiation was, of course, a comparison rife with theological and political connotations for Milton's seventeenth-century audience. But here, Milton's decision to reimagine eating not only as an act of praise, but specifically as an act of transubstantiation, removes the act from the rarified realm of the Eucharist and recontextualizes it as an everyday occurrence in the natural world.

Other reform-minded theologians, such as Milton's polemical antagonist Joseph Hall, had put forth similar arguments about the dual physical and spiritual valences of the Protestant Communion rites. In a sermon on the nature of Christ's presence in the Communion sacrament, Hall insisted that while the bodies of the Communion participants receive no more than ordinary bread and wine, their souls nevertheless continue to partake of Christ's body and blood: "so doth our mouth and stomach receive the bread and wine, as that in the meantime our souls receive the flesh and the blood of Christ. ... [W]hat come we to receive outwardly? The creatures of bread and wine. To what use? In remembrance of Christ's death and passion. What do we the whiles receive inwardly? We are thereby made partakers of his most blessed body and blood."[56] In making a case for the coexistence of the sacrament's material and spiritual valences, Hall—much like Calvin and Perkins before him—managed to defend the church's continued use of the sacrament while maintaining that the material scaffolding of the ceremony itself held no particular spiritual power. In *Paradise Lost*, Milton adopts the reformist logic of Hall's view of the dual nature of the Communion rites, but draws it out toward unexpected conclusions. If ordinary bread and wine, as Hall suggests, could serve

---

[56] Joseph Hall, *A Plain and Familiar Explication of Christ's Presence in the Sacrament of His Body and Blood, out of the Doctrine of the Church of England for the Satisfying of a Scrupulous Friend* (1631), in *The Shaking of the Olive-Tree. The Remaining Works of that Incomparable Prelate Joseph Hall, D. D. Late Lord Bishop of Norwich. With Some Specialties of Divine Providence in His Life. Noted by His own Hand. Together with His Hard Measure: VVritten also by Himself* (London: Printed by J. Cadwel for J. Crooke, at the *Ship* in S. *Pauls* Church-Yard, 1660), 292. (*EEBO*, Wing (2nd ed.) / H416.)

206   DEVOTIONAL EXPERIENCE IN THE REFORMATION

as spiritual reminders of Christ's Passion for the communicants, then by extension, the daily act of eating and drinking outside of the official church services
could surely do the same for the Reformed believer. By suggesting that the acts of
eating and drinking constitute a form of sacramental praise, Milton extricates the
devotional benefits of the Holy Communion from the rarified domain of the state
worship service. If the poem's description of paradisal food and drink undercuts
the sacramental practices of the state church, it does so by taking the reasoning
behind Calvinist Reformed ecclesiology to its logical conclusions.

As is the case with his treatment of paradisal sex, Milton's description of the
dinner scene in Book 5 is an argument for the absolutely vital role of the body and
the senses in proper devotional practice. Both angelic and human bodies alike
require food to fuel their reason, which itself contains within it "every lower facul-
tie / Of sense, whereby they hear, see, smell, touch, taste, / Tasting concoct, digest,
assimilate, / And corporeal to incorporeal turn" (5.410–13). Even the path toward
achieving incorporeality, as described by Raphael, involves profoundly sensual
and embodied processes. Indeed, although the ultimate end of Edenic feasting is
spiritual transubstantiation, that act of praise makes bodily pleasure a devotional
prerequisite. Adam and his angelic guest relish their food and partake of the meal
"with keen dispatch / Of real hunger" (5.436–7). Eating, as a spiritual practice and
as an act of devotion, constitutes one of the arenas in which Milton blurs the distinction between the sacred and the profane. Widening his definition of prayer
to include repeated acts of eating and sexual intercourse in Eden, Milton recasts
repeated acts of praise within the realm of the everyday.

As it turns out, the rituals of praise and worship not only provide means for
humans and angels to make each other sensorially and bodily present to one
another; prayer in *Paradise Lost* also serves to bring God himself within the limited perceptual ranges of human and angelic minds. The prefatory observations
that begin Adam and Eve's morning prayer register a disconnect between the
descriptors they use in their address to God and the occasion itself, a moment
of spontaneous worship that ought to draw Adam and Eve closer to God. They
begin, as they did the night before, by litanizing the parts of God's creation, before
attempting a description of God himself:

> thy self how wondrous then!
> Unspeakable, who first above these Heavens
> To us invisible or dimly seen
> In these thy lowest works.[57]

Repeated acts of praise serve to make what would otherwise prove an "unspeakable" and "invisible" God sensorially present to the Edenic worshippers as they

---

[57] 5.155–8. The 1667 edition of the poem prints the line, "Unspeakable, who *sitst* above these
Heavens." See Milton, *Paradise Lost* (1667). (*EEBO*, document image 63.)

move through the various parts of creation in which God's presence might nevertheless be "dimly seen." These addresses to God in the vocative, despite the fact that the God to whom they are directed is removed from sensory access, nevertheless have the effect of opening up Adam and Eve's senses, making it possible to overcome the distance posed by God's unspeakable and invisible qualities. For Milton, the act of drawing God's presence into the perceptive ken of the one who prays remained the objective not only of human prayers, but also of those sung by angels. Indeed, the prefatory address to God that commences what might be conceived of as the world's first act of praise is initiated by a chorus of angels who commemorate the newly created world:

> Eternal King; thee Author of all being,
> Fountain of Light, thy self invisible
> Amidst the glorious brightness where thou sit'st
> Thron'd inaccessible.

> (3.374–7)

The oddity of this description of God's glory lies in the devotional force of these angelic prayers, which paradoxically bring his presence into relief only by drawing a cloud about his radiance: "Dark with excessive bright thy skirts appeer" (3.380). If neither angels nor human beings can perceive God directly, as they can each other through the daily rites of eating and sex, they can nevertheless do so obliquely, through his creation or even by means of the fringes of his cloak.

For both heavenly and Edenic inhabitants, Milton imagines that certain forms of prayer would have the effect of making God's presence perceptible anew, with each instance of prayerful meditation.[58] Adam and Eve undoubtedly performed repeated acts of praise in Eden, and indeed, as Lewalski observes, Milton surely expects us to understand the pair's prayers and praise as repeated features of life in Paradise.[59] But Milton so radically redefines the boundaries of what it means to engage with these rites of worship that, by the end of Book 5, set forms of prayer as they are practiced in Eden seem to have little to do with the idolatrous

---

[58] The commemorative effect of prayer in *Paradise Lost* is detailed most thoroughly by Regina M. Schwartz, who argues that Adam and Eve's morning hymn serves "as a final cleansing of the poisoned atmosphere" created by Eve's foreboding dream the evening before. The hymn then returns Eden to a state of equilibrium, dispelling the malicious intent Satan has insinuated into Eve's ear and returning the couple to the remembrance of their obligations to God. Schwartz's argument about the morning hymn's function echoes Summers's earlier observation that the hymn's placement immediately after Eve's insidious dream charts the oscillation in Eden between temptation and reconciliation, as if Adam and Eve's prayers, even as they are still blameless, somehow serve to foreshadow good Christian practice after the Fall. While neither Summers nor Schwartz attempts to suggest the perceptual potentialities of repeated prayer as I have tried to do here, the idea that prayer serves as a continual safeguard against the twin threats of forgetfulness and sinfulness certainly resonates with my argument that perceptual awareness and proximity to God require repeated, and not isolated, acts of prayer and meditation. See Schwartz, *Remembering and Repeating*, 72; and Summers, *Muse's Method*, 73–4.

[59] Lewalski, *"Paradise Lost,"* 205.

208 DEVOTIONAL EXPERIENCE IN THE REFORMATION

and popish forms of worship that Milton denounces in the catalogues of human depravity that bookend the epic. Milton unhinges the very notion of prayer from its seventeenth-century contexts and recasts the practice as one that orders the fundamental structure of Edenic experience. Much as Milton recasts the image of Charles I in *Eikonoklastes*, we might similarly read *Paradise Lost* as Milton's twin effort at tearing down and reconceptualizing the practice of prescribed worship. Adam and Eve partake in a proto-liturgical form of public prayer, but they do so *without* the formalities of English liturgical worship. Milton gives us glimpses of familiar forms of praise, and yet he presents these moments within radically unfamiliar contexts. In redefining the boundaries of Edenic prayer, quotidian acts assume the solemnity of the liturgy while formal worship achieves the uninhibited qualities of spontaneous prayer. This tendency toward inversion—making prayer before the Fall look like postlapsarian worship—will likewise shape Milton's depiction of Adam and Eve's prayers after their expulsion from Eden.

The first common prayer

Despite the continuities in prayer, praise, and passion after the Fall, Milton nevertheless insinuates doubt as to whether truly perfect expressions of devotion could exist outside of Paradise. In the conversation between the couple immediately after Eve reveals that she has tasted the forbidden fruit, but before her husband has done so himself, Adam considers the merits of participating in Eve's disobedience— and incurring the ensuing punishment. His ultimate decision to eat the fruit is precipitated by his realization that his loss of Eve would far outweigh whatever punishments he might face for his act of disobedience. In a carefully reasoned inner monologue, Adam outlines his rationale for choosing Eve over a life alone in Paradise:

(A)	with thee
(A)	Certain my resolution is to Die;
(A)	How can I live without thee, how forgo
	Thy sweet Converse and Love so dearly joyn'd,
	To live again in these wilde Woods forlorn?
	Should God create another *Eve*, and I
	Another Rib afford, yet loss of thee
	Would never from my heart; no no, I feel
(B)	Nature draw me: Flesh of Flesh,
(B)	Bone of my Bone thou art, and from thy State
(B)	Mine never shall be parted, bliss or woe.

(9.906–16)

Milton makes clear that Adam's decision is not unreasoned, in part due to the fact that Adam first rehearses his reasoning inwardly to himself before outwardly outlining a similar reasoning in address to Eve. In his subsequent address to Eve, Adam's outward, reiterated speech hews almost exactly to the language and logic of his inward monologue:

(A)	I with thee have fixt my Lot,
(A)	Certain to undergoe like doom, if Death
(A)	Consort with thee, Death is to mee as Life;
(B)	So forcible within my heart I feel
(B)	The Bond of Nature draw me to my owne,
(B)	My own in thee, for what thou art is mine;
(B)	Our State cannot be severd, we are one,
(B)	One Flesh; to loose thee were to loose my self.

(9.952–9)

This speech is the first exchange between Adam and Eve that is decidedly rehearsed; until this point in the poem, their conversations have been extemporaneous and unscripted. Even prior to Adam's own fall, Eve's first act of disobedience introduces an intellectual and spiritual chasm between the spouses; like their prayers to God after the Fall, their expressions of devotion before each other are no longer artless and instinctive, but require prior deliberation. Additionally, while Adam's outward reiteration of his love for Eve is a reflection of his genuine affect, the speech's obvious omissions seem to suggest that it somehow misses the mark. As I have annotated the lines of both speeches above, Adam's inward and outward speeches articulate both (A) his commitment to die together with Eve, and (B) his rationale for his decision—that is, his sense of an inviolable unity with Eve, from which he cannot and does not want to extricate himself. But what is missing from his outward speech is his rejection of the possibility of marrying a second spouse—"should God create another Eve"—which has no counterpart in the second version of the speech. Milton's omission of Adam's profound expression of love for his wife is particularly striking, considering the nature of Eve's previous uncertainty about the depth of Adam's commitment to her. In her study of the development of scientific thought in early modern Protestant culture, Joanna Picciotto has astutely noted that Caroline and Interregnum depictions of Eve often exclude her from the possibility of pursuing intellectual inquiry and rational disputation, "removing Eve from what could have been a collective labor of understanding."[60] Picciotto's assertion that Eve was in effect excluded "from the laboratory" of reason and justification certainly resonates with Milton's depiction of the exchange in Book 9

[60] Joanna Picciotto, *Labors of Innocence in Early Modern England* (Cambridge, MA: Harvard University Press, 2010), 226.

210   DEVOTIONAL EXPERIENCE IN THE REFORMATION

between husband and wife.[61] Just as Eve was absent in Adam's conversation with Raphael in Book 5, called away from the conversation to attend to the food preparations for her guest, in Book 9 she is similarly excluded from knowing Adam's moving justification for why he picks devotion to Eve over obedience to God. In deciding whether to share the forbidden fruit with her husband or to keep its advantages for herself, Eve ultimately decides to allow Adam to share in her act of disobedience for fear that he may otherwise end up in Paradise without her, "wedded to another *Eve*" (9.838). In the end, Eve is never privy to her husband's expression of unassailable love for her. As a result, she persists in her belief that she might eventually be replaced by "another *Eve*"—the very misapprehension that impels her to encourage Adam to eat the fruit and fall with her in the first place. In the first failure of communication between the pair, it is as if Milton has deemed Eve undeserving of the reassurance that he has omitted from Adam's second speech.

In the strange exchange between husband and wife, Milton seems to suggest that rehearsed speech threatens to become disingenuous when extricated from its Edenic contexts and supports, as evidenced by Adam's puzzling elision in his expression of devotion to his wife. Although still in Eden, Eve's disobedience has already introduced a spiritual and intellectual rift between the spouses. But although Adam's reiterated expression of devotion reveals fissures in his spiritual access to his wife, Milton nevertheless saw redemptive value in postlapsarian acts of repeated prayer and praise. Indeed, Adam's reiteration stems from his commitment to reason; expressions that came spontaneously before disobedience must now be mentally mapped out both intellectually and emotionally prior to their outward expression. Although repetition and reiteration are markers of fallen speech, those features of postlapsarian speech might be repurposed as aids to devotion. To this end, the central verbal feature of post-Edenic prayer in *Paradise Lost* is its tendency toward repetition, and throughout the poem, Milton makes the case for the devotional value of repeated acts of prayer and praise.

Well before Adam and Eve's act of disobedience, Milton outlines the value of rehearsed supplication and prayer for the postlapsarian world. Early on in Book 3, God watches Satan descending upon his newly created world. Addressing the Son, God the Father foretells the fall of humankind, but not without outlining a means by which the fallen might be able to regain their lost status before their creator. To the select few, God promises to impart the proper mode of prayer and repentance:

> (C)   I will cleer their senses dark,
>   What may suffice, and soft'n stonie hearts
> (D)   To pray, repent, and bring obedience due.

---

[61] Picciotto, *Labors of Innocence*, 227.

ADAM AND EVE IN BED AND AT PRAYER   211

(D)   To Prayer, repentance, and obedience due,
         Though but endevord with sincere intent,
(C)   Mine ear shall not be slow, mine eyes not shut.

(3.188–93)

The chiastic structure of God's description of proper repentance juxtaposes two acts of sensual awareness (which I have designated C in the text above): first, God's promise to "cleer" humankind's "senses dark," and second, the subsequent opening up of God's ears and eyes to human prayer—provided that such prayers are properly performed. But even if we might bypass the description's first pairing of these two kinds of sensory awakening, its second juxtaposition (D) immediately strikes us even upon a cursory perusal of the lines. God reveals that proper contrition should lead the penitent "To pray, repent, and bring obedience due," and it is "To Prayer, repentance, and obedience due," offered by the sincere penitent, that God will willingly turn his attention. The nearly verbatim repetition of the two lines and their positioning one after another imbue God's description of proper prayer with a strangely rehearsed and repeated quality, even as the content of the speech underscores the penitent's "sincere intent." Only those penitents who come to God exactly as prescribed—here grammatically and, by extension, theologically—will prompt God to forgiveness. In this vision of proper contrition, contra that of *Eikonoklastes*, it seems that the sincerity of the penitent need not preclude the practice of particular set forms of prayer.[62] In the chiastic logic of God's outline of the Fall, sensual awareness becomes intimately bound up with certain modes of prayer, suggesting that these kinds of prayer lend themselves not only toward a kind of devotional effectiveness but toward a perceptual effectiveness as well.

Prior to the Fall, Adam and Eve's prayers shared many of the features of rehearsed forms of worship that Milton, in his polemical works, associated with disingenuous praise. But the reiterative nature of prayer in *Paradise Lost* is perhaps most fully realized *after* the Fall. Newly cognizant of their fallen state, Eve

---

[62] Ramie Targoff argues that certain early modern clerics in the Church of England did not make distinctions between inward sincerity and outward show of devotion. Targoff posits that this melding of inward and outward explains why the English church did not view private devotion as incompatible with the public liturgy: "the religious establishment could simultaneously seem uninterested in private belief and yet demonstrate repeatedly its desire to subsume private devotion within the public liturgy of the church." On the contrary, Targoff maintains that mainstream English theology postulated that outward display of devotion was conducive to cultivating genuine sincerity on the part of the one who prayed. See Ramie Targoff, *Common Prayer: The Language of Public Devotion in Early Modern England* (Chicago: University of Chicago Press, 2001), 4. Milton, of course, was hardly typical in his Protestantism, and he makes his disdain for common forms of prayer manifestly clear in his polemical tracts—for the very reason that he believed that there *was* a distinction between inward and outward, as per my opening discussion of Milton's response to Charles I's reappropriation of the Psalms. There nevertheless remains something to be said for Milton's willingness—whether conscious or not—to incorporate elements of prescribed prayer into his vision of Edenic (and thus ostensibly devotionally sincere) worship.

212 DEVOTIONAL EXPERIENCE IN THE REFORMATION

suggests to Adam the possibility of suicide as a means of terminating the cycle of sin and death that Adam has just predicted for generations of their descendants:

> Then both our selves and Seed at once to free
> From what we fear for both, let us make short,
> Let us seek Death, or he not found, supply
> With our own hands his Office on our selves.
>
> (10.999–1002)

Although it seems that Eve only corroborates the sentiments Adam has just artic- ulated prior to this moment—"Why comes not Death, / Said hee, with one thrice acceptable stroke / To end me?" (10.854–6)—Milton's narrative intervention nev- ertheless attributes Adam's levelheadedness amid his wife's despair to his sturdier spiritual and rational faculties: "But *Adam* with such counsel nothing sway'd / To better hopes his more attentive minde / Labouring had rais'd" (10.1010–12). Seek- ing some "safer resolution" (10.1029), Adam proposes that they instead move God to pity through penitence and prayer. He proceeds to outline the observable quali- ties of contrition that he deems will prove most effective in eliciting God's pity and forgiveness:

> What better can we do, then to the place
> Repairing where he judg'd us, prostrate fall
> Before him reverent, and there confess
> Humbly our faults, and pardon beg, with tears
> Watering the ground, and with our sighs the Air
> Frequenting, sent from hearts contrite, in sign
> Of sorrow unfeign'd, and humiliation meek.
>
> (10.1086–92)

Adam's description of the features proper to effective prayer inspires in the couple an overwhelming impulse to pray. Adam and Eve at once fall prostrate, commenc- ing their supplications in exactly the manner that he has just described:

> they forthwith to the place
> Repairing where he judg'd them prostrate fell
> Before him reverent, and both confess'd
> Humbly thir faults, and pardon beg'd, with tears
> Watering the ground, and with thir sighs the Air
> Frequenting, sent from hearts contrite, in sign
> Or sorrow unfeign'd, and humiliation meek.
>
> (10.1098–104)

ADAM AND EVE IN BED AND AT PRAYER 213

In extending their appeal for pity, Adam and Eve unwittingly perform the fallen world's first common prayer. Their highly rehearsed and measured prayer seems to hearken back to God's prescient observation, early on in Book 3 of the epic, that fallen worshippers will be able to regain their former favor with God through forms of prayer that are both premeditated and conscientiously performed.

By turning our attention to the interplay between repetition and memory in *Paradise Lost* we might be able to shed light on what exactly Milton is doing by imagining Adam and Eve's first postlapsarian prayer as a deeply rehearsed act of supplication. As he did with the genealogies of tyrants and idol worshippers, Milton also adeptly constructs a genealogy of memory for Eden's original inhabitants. At the close of Book 6, Raphael concludes his account of Satan's fall from Heaven by commanding Adam to remember, as if Adam too now has access to the memory of events that transpired before his creation: "firm they might have stood / Yet fell; remember, and fear to transgress." (6.911–12). In Book 7, the archangel continues his account of those events that occurred before human memory, which he outlines for Adam's benefit:

> how this World
> Of Heav'n and Earth conspicuous first began,
> When, and whereof created, for what cause,
> What within *Eden* or without was done
> Before his memorie.
>
> (7.62–66)

Memory, for the earth's first inhabitants, is constructed rather than naturally acquired over the course of a lifetime. But apart from the express purpose of constructing a genealogy of human memory that stretches backward in time to those events that happened even before Adam and Eve's creation, Raphael's retelling of the Creation story has another less obvious purpose as well. After relating those events before memory, Raphael continues with his account, reiterating even the circumstances surrounding Adam's own creation, the subsequent creation of Eve, and God's first conversations with the couple. The archangel's verbatim reiteration of God's commandment to refrain from eating the forbidden fruit—"In the day thou eat'st, thou di'st; / Death is the penaltie impos'd, beware" (7.544–5)—in effect functions as a present reminder of the continued validity of the prohibition.

Raphael's account of Creation is, of course, not the first Milton has presented to his readers. Before we receive Raphael's full account, we have already gleaned the central events of the Creation story in Book 4: first, through the perspective of the fallen Lucifer upon beholding the splendor of the world for the first time, and second, through the conversation between the couple overheard by Satan, in which Eve recounts the memory of her own creation and initial encounter with Adam. Raphael's account of the Creation story, then, serves as both extension and

214 DEVOTIONAL EXPERIENCE IN THE REFORMATION

reiteration, filling in gaps in our knowledge and reminding us of the details of Creation we have already culled from earlier moments in the epic. But Milton's own vision of the Creation story does not end with Raphael's. Immediately after Raphael's detailed retelling of Creation, Adam reiterates the events surrounding his own creation, despite the fact that the angel has just outlined these in great detail. After detailing his newly discovered sensory awareness and embodiedness, Adam then reiterates God's admonition in a much fuller account than the one just supplied by Raphael:

> This Paradise I give thee, count it thine
> To Till and keep, and of the Fruit to eate:
> Of every Tree that in the Garden growes
> Eate freely with glad heart; fear here no dearth:
> But of the Tree whose operation brings
> Knowledge of good and ill, which I have set
> The Pledge of thy Obedience and thy Faith
> Amid the Garden by the Tree of Life,
> Remember what I warne thee, shun to taste,
> And shun the bitter consequence.
>
> (8.319–28)

Adam's repeated account of God's prohibition clearly serves a function other than the dissemination of information, for Milton's readers have only just received a full account of Creation from Raphael in Book 7. On the contrary, Adam's compulsion to retell the angel's account is an act that functions not unlike the epic's vision of reiterated prayer. God's command to commit his admonition to memory—"Remember what I warne thee"—is literally carried out in Adam's verbatim reiteration of the prohibition itself; the simple act of retelling in Eden has in effect become an act of obedience to and praise of God.

But why would Milton have been invested in imagining a particular kind of recollection or reiteration that doubles as a form of worship? If we return our attention to God's justification for Creation, we perhaps also discern a theological precedent for this particular kind of remembrance that expresses itself precisely through repeated telling. After Satan's fall, God expresses his intent to create "another World" that will supplement the damage left in the wake of Lucifer's fall:

> But least his heart exalt him in the harme
> Already done, to have dispeopl'd Heav'n
> My damage fondly deem'd, I can repaire
> That detriment, if such it be to lose
> Self-lost, and in a moment will create
> Another World.
>
> (7.150–5)

ADAM AND EVE IN BED AND AT PRAYER 215

Here God's act of Creation—re-creation, in fact—is a response to Satan's fallenness; indeed, it seems that the heavenly counterreaction to sin is to crowd it out through repeated acts of divine power. In this newly made world God promises to create worshippers "out of one man a Race / Of men innumerable, there to dwell" (7.155–6). God's creative acts of repetition as well as Adam and Eve's (future) procreative acts of repetition serve as testament to the fact that divine power ultimately cannot be lessened even by Satan's attempts to "dispeople" Heaven when he drags a portion of the heavenly host with him on his descent to Hell. The logic of God's decision to create anew suggests that each part of the created universe serves as testament to his undiminished glory. God presents the creation of the new world as an extension of the rites of praise performed by all of Heaven:

> Heav'n yet populous retaines
> Number sufficient to possess her Realmes,
> Though wide, and this high temple to frequent
> With Ministeries due and solemn Rites.
>
> (7.146–9)

While the number of remaining angels in Heaven remains sufficient for the performance of worship rites, God argues that this, of course, is no reason why there should not also be additional voices that might join in upon the rites of praise from their dwelling places in this other world.

God's justification for creation—and re-creation—explains Milton's inclusion of Adam's seemingly redundant act of recollection. But like eating and sex, Milton insisted that prayer and worship in *Paradise Lost* need not be restricted to the rarified sphere of formal worship. Prayer and praise in *Paradise Lost* might be as simple as an act of remembering or retelling. Perhaps this explains why the epic includes so many separate retellings of the Creation story, even when the information conveyed by each retelling has been recently recounted. When Adam repeats God's prohibition verbatim, he is engaging in the very form of worship that God imagines inheres within the act of creation—and re-creation. The inherited story of humankind's creation is recast and refashioned, and in doing so, it is relived.

Recasting Paradise

According to the definitions of prayer and praise implicitly put forth by Milton's epic, the whole of *Paradise Lost*—which includes not just one but several retellings of the Creation account—might itself be read, as Samuel Johnson chose to read it, as akin to a kind of prayer, spurring its readers toward proper devotion.[63] The

---

[63] In his *Lives of the English Poets*, Samuel Johnson criticizes the genres of both devotional and sacred poetry for their aesthetic shortcomings and their potential sacrilegious import. Nevertheless, he

216 DEVOTIONAL EXPERIENCE IN THE REFORMATION

epic's portrayal of prayer, precisely because of its liturgical undertones, would have undoubtedly piqued those contemporaries of Milton who sympathized with his iconoclastic efforts. How would radical reformists have responded to a work, written by a man who argued against extra-scriptural aids to devotion, whose central premise was to "justify the ways of God to men" (1.26)? And how did Milton himself respond to the theological and poetic anxieties that he might have felt in writing an epic whose reformulation of Scripture might seem to veer dangerously close to sacrilege? The answers to these questions lie in the patterns of iconoclasm that shape both *Paradise Lost* and Milton's career as a polemicist.

At the moment when God establishes his prohibition against consuming the forbidden fruit, he offsets the heavy requirement by handing over to Adam and Eve Paradise itself and its plethora of edible fruits: "This Paradise I give thee, count it thine / To Till and keep, and of the Fruit to eate" (8.319–20). Adam and Eve's act of disobedience will eventually overwrite both God's prohibition and his paradisal gift to humankind. Like the covenant between God and human beings, ultimately destroyed by Adam and Eve's violation of God's prohibition, so too will Paradise itself meet destruction because of human shortcoming. It seems, then, that the epic's own narrative arc is self-destructing, so that by the close of *Paradise Lost* Milton's own act of poetic construction—the image of Paradise itself—undergoes a dissolution of sorts. Adam and Eve's expulsion from Eden at the close of *Paradise Lost* is thus perhaps the epic's final act of iconoclasm, undertaken by a poet who spent the whole of his political career demolishing an array of icons, both secular and religious.

In Book 11 of the epic, immediately after Adam and Eve conclude their first postlapsarian prayer, Adam beholds an approaching angel and imagines that the heavenly visitor bears tidings about the new laws God has issued for them as inhabitants of Eden. Adam attempts to placate Eve by suggesting, wrongly, that God might allow the two of them to continue living in Eden, only under slightly altered circumstances: "*Eve*, now expect great tidings, which perhaps / Of us will soon determin, or impose / New Laws to be observ'd" (11.226–8). And thus the pair meets bitter disappointment when Michael informs them of their imminent expulsion from the Garden: "O! unexpected stroke worse than of death!" Adam laments. "Must I thus leave thee Paradise?" (11.268–9). His question is only partly rhetorical, of course, and Milton Iconoclastes, always adept at pairing demolition with a parallel act of reformulation, is not prepared to relinquish the image of Paradise altogether. For although Milton builds into the very structure of his monumental

---

imagines that Milton manages to conserve the devotional purposes of these inferior forms of religious poetry within *Paradise Lost* without slavishly binding the epic to their formal requirements: "Whoever considers the few radical positions which the Scriptures afforded him will wonder by what energetic operations he expanded them to such extent and ramified them to so much variety, restrained as he was by religious reverence from licentiousness of fiction." See Samuel Johnson, *Lives of the English Poets*, 3 vols., ed. G. B. Hill (Oxford: Clarendon Press, 1905), 1:182–3. For a discussion of Milton's parallel acts of prayer and *poesis* in *Paradise Lost*, see Stephen Fix, "Johnson and the 'Duty' of Reading *Paradise Lost*," *ELH* 52, no. 3 (1985): 649–71, esp. 656–9.

vision of Paradise its own self-directed demolition, he manages to salvage the *idea* of Paradise. No longer tethered to a geographic locale, Paradise becomes a metaphorized description of one's inward terrain.

Michael finally supplies the answer to Adam's question at the close of Book 12: "then wilt thou not be loath / To leave this Paradise, but shalt possess / A paradise within thee, happier farr" (12.585–7). All his life Milton was profoundly preoccupied with the possibility of cultivating genuine devotion, so much so that he condemned those—monarchs, clergy, and laypeople alike—who seemed to him merely dissemblers in their religion and politics. Thus, it is unsurprising that Milton finds a way of reimagining the tragedy of human fallenness as an opportunity for furthering inwardness. For those who live after the Fall, Milton imagines the possibility of internalizing the various forms of Edenic prayer as part of a concerted attempt to reclaim our primordial losses and to approximate paradisal wholeness and joy. If Paradise and Edenic prayer are dismantled at the close of *Paradise Lost*, they are equally recast anew in Milton's suggestion of the life that awaits Adam and Eve as they leave the garden for the wide world before them.

***

Although Milton vigorously criticized the performative aspects of English devotional practices in his polemical tracts, *Paradise Lost* imagines forms of Edenic worship that would have struck early modern English churchgoers as intimately familiar—the poem's liturgical language and rites reverberate with phrases and refrains from the official services of the state church. But in imagining Adam at Eve in bed and at prayer, Milton so radically redefines the boundaries of what it means to engage with the rites of worship that set forms of devotion as they are practiced in Eden seem to have little to do with the idolatrous and popish ceremonies that Milton denounced in his polemical works. Milton unhinges the very notion of common prayer from its seventeenth-century contexts and recasts the practice as one that orders the fundamental structure of Edenic experience. Adam and Eve partake in a proto-liturgical form of public prayer, but they do so without the formalities of English liturgical worship. Milton gives us glimpses of familiar forms of praise, and yet he presents these moments within radically unfamiliar contexts. In recasting the forms of Edenic prayer, daily tasks and activities assume the devotional power of the liturgy, while formal worship assumes the qualities not just of spontaneous prayer, but of the act of sex itself.

One hundred years after the publication of the *Book of Common Prayer*, Milton's attack on the liturgy and the sacraments was in some sense a version of the iconoclastic logic that both Hooker and Perkins used to defend ceremonial worship—that is, the idea that sacraments and liturgies are devotionally inoffensive in that they have been devotionally neutered, stripped of any inherent power. Much like the common prayers and devotional displays sanctioned by the English state church, Milton strips Adam and Eve's rites of any inherent sacramental force.

But in doing so, he does not leave these rites evacuated of devotional power; on the contrary, he counts them among the many bodily rituals and rites that heighten Adam and Eve's devotion—not only to God, but to each other. In undercutting the original sacramental intent of the liturgy and ceremonies, Milton succeeds in placing the sensing body at the center of proper Reformed devotion.

Bibliography

Primary Sources

Ainsworth, Henry. *An arrow against idolatrie Taken out of the quiver of the Lord of hosts.* Amsterdam, Printed [by Giles Thorp], 1611. *EEBO.* STC (2nd ed.) / 221.

Aristotle. Poetics. In *The Basics Works of Aristotle.* Edited by Richard McKeon. New York: Modern Library/Random House, 2001.

Book of Common Prayer, The: The Texts of 1549, 1559, and 1662. Edited by Brian Cummings. Oxford: Oxford University Press, 2011.

Brathwait, Richard. "A Description of Death." In *Remains after Death.* Imprinted at London: By Iohn Beale, 1618. Bound with *The Good VVife: or, A rare one amonst VVomen.* At London: Printed [by John Beale] for Richard Redmer, and are to be sold at his shop at the west end of St Pauls Church, 1618. *EEBO.* STC (2nd ed.) / 3568.5.

Bullinger, Heinrich. "The Second Decade, The Tenth Sermon." In *Fiftie godlie and learned sermons diuided into fiue decades, conteyning the chiefe and principall points of Christian religion, written in three several tomes or sections.* Imprinted at London: by [Henry Middleton for] Ralphe Newberrie, dwelling in Fleet-streate a little aboue the Conduite, 1577. *EEBO.* STC (2nd ed.) / 4056.

Calvin, John. "The Necessity of Reforming the Church Presented to the Imperial Diet at Spires, A.D. 1544, in the name of all who wish Christ to reign." In *John Calvin: Tracts and Treatises,* vol. 1. Translated by Henry Beveridge. Grand Rapids, MI: Eerdmans, 1959.

Calvin, John. *Institutes of the Christian Religion: 1536 Edition.* Translated by Ford Lewis Battles. Grand Rapids, MI: Eerdmans, 1986 [1975].

Catullus. *The Poems of Catullus: A Bilingual Edition.* Translated by Peter Green. Berkeley: University of California Press, 2007.

Charles I. *Eikon basilike the pourtracture of His Sacred Majestie in his solitudes and sufferings.* [London?]: Reprinted in R.M., Anno Dom. 1648 [i.e. 1649]. EEBO. Wing / E276.

Covell, William. *A iust and temperate defence of the fiue books of ecclesiastical policie: written by M. Richard Hooker.* London: Printed by P. Short for Clement Knight, dwelling at the signe of the holy Lambe in Paules church-yard, 1603. *EEBO.* STC (2nd ed.) / 5881.

Cranmer, Thomas. *A defence of the true and catholike doctrine of the sacrament of the body and bloud of our sauiour Christ.* London: In Poules churcheyarde, at the signe of the Brasen serpent, by Reginald Wolfe. Cum priuilegio ad imprimendum solum, 1550. *EEBO.* STC (2nd ed.) / 6000.

Cranmer, Thomas. "The Supper of the Lorde, and the holy Communion, commonly called the Mass (1549)." In *The Book of Common Prayer: The Texts of 1549, 1559, and 1662.* Edited by Brian Cummings. Oxford: Oxford University Press, 2011.

Cranmer, Thomas and John Jewel. *The booke of common praier, and administration of the Sacramentes, and other rites and ceremonies in the Churche of Englande.* London: In officina Richardi Iugge, & Iohannis Cawode, 1559. *EEBO.* STC (2nd ed.) / 16292.

220 BIBLIOGRAPHY

Cranmer, Thomas and John Jewel. *The book of common-prayer and administration of the sacraments and other rites & ceremonies of the church, according to the use of the Church of England.* London: Printed by His Ma[jes]ties Printers, 1662. *EEBO.* Wing / B3622.

Crashaw, Richard. *Steps to the Temple: sacred poems, with other delights of the muses.* London: Printed by T. W. for Humphrey Moseley, and are to be sold at his shop at the Princes Armes in St. *Pauls* Church-yard, 1646. *EEBO.* Wing / C6836.

Culverwell, Ezekiel. *A Treatise of Faith.* London: Printed by I. L. for William Sheffard, 1623.

D'Ewes, Simonds. *The Autobiography and Correspondence of Sir Simonds D'Ewes, Bart., During the Reigns of James I and Charles I.* Edited by J. O. Halliwell. London: Richard Bentley, 1845.

Donne, John. *Poems, by J. D. VVith elegies on the authors death.* London: Printed by M[iles] F[lesher] for Iohn Marriot, and are to be sold at his shop in St Dunstans Church-yard in Fleet-street, 1633. *EEBO.* STC (2nd ed.) / 7045.

Donne, John. *Devotions upon Emergent Occasions.* Edited by John Sparrow. Cambridge: Cambridge University Press, 1923.

Donne, John. *Sermons.* Edited by Evelyn Mary Spearing Simpson and George Reuben Potter. 10 vols. Berkeley: University of California Press, 1953–62.

Donne, John. *The Variorum Edition of the Poetry of John Donne.* Edited by Gary Stringer. Vol. 7, part 1, *The Holy Sonnets.* Bloomington: Indiana University Press, 2005.

Donne, John. *The Variorum Edition of the Poetry of John Donne.* Edited by Gary A. Stringer. Vol. 3, *The Satyres.* Bloomington: Indiana University Press, 2016.

Erasmus, Desiderius. Preface to "The paraphrase of Erasmus vpon the gospell of sainct Iohn." In *The first tome or volume of the Paraphrase of Erasmus vpon the Newe Testamente.* Translated by Nicholas Udall. London: Enprinted at London in Fletestrete at the signe of the Sunne by Edwarde Whitchurche, the last daie of Ianuarie, 1546. *EEBO.* STC (2nd ed.) / 2854.5.

Field, John and Thomas Wilcox. *An Admonition to the Parliament.* Hemel Hempstead: Printed by J. Stroud, 1572. *EEBO.* STC (2nd ed.) / 10848.

Goodwin, Thomas. *A childe of light vvalking in darknesse: or A treatise shewing the causes, by which God leaves his children to distresse of conscience.* London: By M[iles] F[lesher] for R. Dawlman and L. F[awne] at the Brazen Serpent in Pauls Church-yard, 1636. *EEBO.* STC (2nd ed.) / 12037.

Gosson, Stephen. *The Schoole of Abuse Conteining a Plesaunt Inuectiue against Poets, Pipers, Plaiers, Iesters, and such like Caterpillers of a Comonwelth.* London: for Thomas VVoodcocke, 1579. *EEBO.* STC (2nd ed.) / 12097.5

Gouge, William. *Of Domesticall Dvties. Eight Treatises.* London: Printed by Iohn Haviland for William Bladen, and are to be sold at the signe of the Bible neere the great north doore of Pauls, 1622. *EEBO.* STC (2nd ed.) / 12119.

Greville, Fulke. *Certaine Learned and Elegant Workes of the Right Honorable Fvlke Lord Brooke, Written in his Youth, and familiar Exercise with Sir Philip Sidney.* London: Printed by E. P. for *Henry Seyle*, and are to be sold at his shop at the signe of the *Tygers* head in St. *Paules* Church-yard, 1633. *EEBO.* STC (2nd ed.) / 12361.

Greville, Fulke. *The Life of the Renowned Sr Philip Sidney.* [...] *Written by Sir Fulke Grevil Knight, Lord Brook, a Servant to Queen Elizabeth, and his Companion & Friend.* London: Printed for *Henry Seile* over against St *Dunstans* Church in Fleet-street, 1651. *EEBO.* Wing (2nd ed.) / B4899.

Greville, Fulke. *A Treatise on Religion.* In *The remains of Sir Fulk Grevill Lord Brooke: Being Poems of Monarchy and Religion: Never before Printed.* London: Printed by T. N. for *Henry Herringman* at the sign of the *Blew Anchor* in the *Lower Walk* of the *New Exchange*, 1670. *EEBO.* Wing / B4900.

BIBLIOGRAPHY 221

Greville, Fulke. *The Selected Poems of Fulke Greville*. Edited by Thom Gunn. Chicago: University of Chicago Press, 2009 [1968].

Hall, Joseph. *The Arte of Diuine Meditation profitable for all Christians to knowe and practise; exemplified with a large meditation of eternall life*. Imprinted at London by *Humfrey Lowes*, for *Samuel Macham*, and *Mathew Cooke*: and are to bee sold in Pauls Church-yard at the signe of the Tigers head, 1605. STC 12642.

Hall, Joseph. *Meditations and Vowes, Diuine and Morall; Seruing for direction in Christian and Ciuill Practise. Diuided into two Bookes*. At London: Printed by *Humfrey Lownes*, for *Iohn Porter*, 1607 [1605]. STC 12681. Bound with *The Arte of Divine Meditation: Profitable for all Christians to know and practice, Exemplified with a large Meditation of eternall life*. At London: Printed by *H. L.* for *Samuel Macham*: and are to be sold at his shop in Paules Church-yard, at the signe of the Full-head. 1607 [1605].

Hall, Joseph. *Occasional Meditations by Ios. Exon. Set forth by R. H. The third Edition: with the Addition of 49 Meditations not heretofore published*. London: Printed by M. F. for *Nathaniel Butter*, 1633 [1630]. STC 12689.

Hall, Joseph. *A Plain and Familiar Explication of Christ's Presence in the Sacrament of His Body and Blood, out of the Doctrine of the Church of England for the Satisfying of a Scrupulous Friend*. In *The Shaking of the Olive-Tree. The Remaining Works of that Incomparable Prelate Joseph Hall, D. D. Late Lord Bishop of Norwich. With Some Specialties of Divine Providence in His Life. Noted by His own Hand. Together with His Hard Measure: VVritten also by Himself*. London: Printed by J. Cadwel for J. Crooke, at the Ship in S. Pauls Church-Yard, 1660. *EEBO*. Wing (2nd ed.) / H416.

Hall, Joseph. "Epistle 7 (To Mr. William Bedell)." In *The Works of the Right Reverend Joseph Hall*. Edited by Philip Wynter. Vol. 6. Oxford: Oxford University Press, 1863.

Harris, Robert. *Peters enlargement upon the praryers of the Church*. London: Printed by H[umphrey] L[owns] for John Bartlet, at the golden Cup, in the Gold-Smiths Row in Cheape-side, 1627. *EEBO*. STC (2nd ed.) / 12842.

Harvey, Christopher. *The Synagogve, or, The Shadow of the Temple. Sacred Poems, and Private Ejacvlations. In Imitation of Mr. George Herbert*. London: Printed by J. L. for Philemon Stephens, 1647. *EEBO*. Wing / H1045.

Herbert, George. *The Temple: Sacred poems and private ejaculations*. Cambridge: Thom[as] Buck, and Roger Daniel, printers to the Universitie, 1633. *EEBO*. STC (2nd ed.) / 13183.

Herrick, Robert. *His noble numbers, or, His pious pieces vvherein (amongst other things) he sings the birth of his Christ: and sighes for his Saviours suffering on the crosse*. London: Printed for John Williams, and Francis Eglesfield, 1647. *EEBO*. Wing (2nd ed.) / H1596 and H1597.

Herrick, Robert. *Hesperides, or, The works both humane & divine*. London: Printed for John Williams and Francis Eglesfield, and are to be sold by Tho[mas] Hunt, 1648. *EEBO*. Wing / H1595.

Herrick, Robert. *The Complete Poetry of Robert Herrick*. Edited by Tom Cain and Ruth Connolly. 2 vols. Oxford: Oxford University Press, 2013.

Hieron, Samuel. *A defense of the ministers reasons for the refusal of subscription to the Book of Common Prayer, and of Conformitie against the seuerall ansvvers*. [S.I. and Amsterdam?]: Imprinted [by W. Jones's secret press, and J. Hondius?], 1607. *EEBO*. STC (2nd ed.) / 13395.

Hieron, Samuel. *A helpe vnto deuotion containing certain moulds or forms of prayer, fitted to seuerall occasions*. London: by H[umphrey] L[ownes] for Samuel Macham, and are to be solde at his shop in Pauls Church-yard at the signe of the Bull-head, 1608. *EEBO*. STC (2nd ed.) / 13406.3.

222 BIBLIOGRAPHY

Hieron, Samuel. *A Helpe vnto Devotion: containing certaine moulds, of formes of prayer, fitted to several occasions and penned for the furtherance of those, who haue more desire than skill to power out their soles by petition unto God.* London: Printed by John Beale, 1636. *EEBO.* STC (2nd ed.) / 13216.

The Holy Bible, Conteyning the Old Testament and the New. London: Imprinted by Robert Barker, 1611. *EEBO.* STC (2nd ed.) / 2217.

Hooker, Richard. *Of the Lavves of Ecclesiasticall Politie. Eyght Bookes* [books 1–4]. Printed at London: By Iohn Windet, dwelling at the signe of the Crosse keyes neare Powles Wharffe, and are thereto be solde, [1593]. *EEBO.* STC (2nd ed.) / 13712.

Hooker, Richard. *Of the Lawes of Ecclesiasticall Politie. The Fift Booke.* London: Printed by John Windet dvvelling at Povvles wharfe at the signe of the Crosse Keyes and are there to be solde, 1597. *EEBO.* STC (2nd ed.) / 13712.5.

Hooker, Richard. *The Fift Book of Ecclesiasticall Pollity.* 1597 [1594]. Bodleian MS Add. C.165.

Hooker, Richard. *On the Laws of Ecclesiastical Polity.* Edited by Arthur Stephen McGrade. Oxford: Oxford University Press, 2013.

Hooker, Richard. *A learned and comfortable sermon of the certaintie and perpetuitie of faith in the elect especially of the prophet Habakkuks faith.* At Oxford: Printed by Ioseph Barnes, and are to be sold by John Barnes dwelling neere Holborne Conduit, 1612. *EEBO.* STC (2nd ed.) / 13707.

Jewel, John. "An Homilie against *perill of idolatrie*, and *superfluous* decking of Churches." In *The second tome of homilees of such matters as were promised, and intituled in the former part of homilees.* Imprinted at London: In Poules Churchyarde, by Richarde Iugge, and Iohn Cawood, printers to the Queenes Maiestie, 1571. *EEBO.* STC (2nd ed.) / 13669.

Jewel, John. *The Apology for the Church of England and a Treatise of the Holy Scriptures.* Edited by William R. Wittingham. New York: Henry M. Onderdonk, 1846.

Jewel, John. *An Apology of the Church of England (1564).* Edited by John E. Booty. Ithaca, NY: Cornell University Press, 1963.

Jonson, Ben. "VI. To the Same [To Celia], *The Forrest.*" In *The works of Beniamin Ionson.* [Imprinted at London: By Will Stansby, 1616]. *EEBO.* STC (2nd ed.) / 14751.

Laud, William, *The History of the Troubles and Tryal of the Most Reverent Father in God, and Blessed Martyr, William Laud.* London: Printed for Ri[chard] Chiswell, at the Rose and Crown in St: Paul's Church-Yard, 1695. *EEBO.* Wing / L596.

Linaker, Robert. *A comfortable treatise for the reliefe of such as are afflicted in conscience.* London: Valentine Simmes for R. Boyle, 1595. *EEBO.* STC (2nd ed.) / 15638.

Luther, Martin. *A commentarie vpon the fiftene Psalmes, called Psalmi graduum, that is, Psalmes of degrees.* Imprinted at London: By Thomas Vautroullier, 1577. *EEBO.* STC (2nd ed.) / 16975.5.

Milton, John. *Poems of Mr. John Milton both English and Latin.* London: Printed by Ruth Raworth for Humphrey Moseley, and are to be sold at the signe of the Princes Arms in S. Pauls Church-yard, 1645. *EEBO.* Wing / M2160.

Milton, John. *Paradise Lost a poem written in ten books.* London: Printed, and are to be sold by *Peter Parker* under *Creed* Church near *Aldgate;* And by *Robert Boulter* at the *Turks Head* in *Bishopsgate-street;* And *Matthias Walker,* under St. *Dunstons* Church in *Fleet-street,* 1667. *EEBO.* Wing / M2137.

Milton, John. *Paradise Lost, a poem in twelve books.* London: Printed by S. Simmons, 1674. *EEBO.* Wing / M2144.

Milton, John. *Complete Prose Works of John Milton.* Edited by Don M. Wolfe. 8 vols. New Haven: Yale University Press, 1953–82.

BIBLIOGRAPHY   223

Milton, John. *Paradise Lost.* Edited by Gordon Teskey. New York: W. W. Norton, 2005.

Milton, John. *Milton: The Complete Shorter Poems.* Edited by John Carey. Harlow: Pearson Education, 2007 [1968].

Munday, Anthony. *A Second and Third Blast of Retrait from Plaies and Theaters.* London: By Henrie Denham, dwelling in Pater noster Row, 1580. *EEBO.* STC (2nd ed.) / 21677.

The Newe Testament of Ovr Lorde Iesvs Christ. Edited by Laurence Tomson. London: Christopher Barker, 1586 [1560]. *EEBO.* STC / 2887.

An Ordinance of the Lords and Commons Assembled in Parliament, for the better Observation of the Lords-Day. London: Printed for Edward Husbands, April 10, 1644. *EEBO.* Wing / E1943A.

Perkins, William. *A treatise tending vnto a declaration whether a man be in the estate of damnation or in the estate of grace.* London: By R. Robinson, for T. Gubbin, and I. Porter, 1590. *EEBO.* STC (2nd ed.) / 19752.

Perkins, William. *A Golden Chaine, or the description of theologie containing the order of the causes of saluation and damnation, according to Gods woord.* London: Printed by Edward Alde and are to be sold by Edward White at the little north doore of S Paules Church at the signe of the Gunne, 1591. *EEBO.* STC (2nd ed.) / 19657.

Perkins, William. *A case of conscience of the greatest that ever was, how a man may know, whether he be the son of God or no.* Imprinted at London: By Thomas Orwin, for Thomas Man and Iohn Porter, 1592. *EEBO.* STC (2nd ed.) / 19665.

Perkins, William. *A reformed Catholike: or, A declaration shewing how neere we may come to the present Church of Rome in sundrie points of religion.* Cambridge: Printed by Iohn Legat, printer to the Vniuersitie of Cambridge, 1598. *EEBO.* STC (2nd ed.) / 19736.

Perkins, William. *A Golden Chaine: or The description of theologie containing the order of the causes of saluation and damnation.* Cambridge: Printed by Iohn Legat, printer to the Vniuersitie of Cambridge, 1600. *EEBO.* STC (2nd ed.) / 19646.

Perkins, William. *A warning against the idolatry of the last times.* Cambridge: Printed by Iohn Legat, Printer to the Vniuersitie of Cambridge, 1601. *EEBO.* STC (2nd ed.) / 19763.5.

Perkins, William. *A commentarie or exposition, vpon the fiue first chapters of the Epistle to the Galatians.* Cambridge: Printed by Iohn Legat, printer to the Vniuersitie of Cambridge, 1604. *EEBO.* STC (2nd ed.) / 19680.

Perkins, William. *A cloud of faithful witnesses, leading to the heauenly Canaan, or, A commentary vpon the 11 chapter to the Hebewes.* London: Printed by Humfrey Lownes, for Leo. Greene, 1607. *EEBO.* STC (2nd ed.) / 19677.5.

Perkins, William. *A godly and learned exposition of Christs Sermon in the Mount.* Cambridge: Printed by Thomas Brooke and Cantrell Legge, printers to the Vniversitie of Cambridge, 1608. *EEBO.* STC (2nd ed.) / 19722.

Perkins, William. *Christian Oeconomie, or a Short Survey of the Right Manner of erecting and ordering a Familie, according to the Scriptures.* London: Imprinted by Felix Kyngston, and are to be sold by Edmund Weauer, 1609. *EEBO.* STC (2nd ed.) / 19677.

Perkins, William. *A graine of musterd-seede or, the least measure of grace that is or can be effectuall to saluation.* Printed at London: By Iohn Legate, Printer to the Vniuersitie of Cambridge. And to be sold in Pauls Church-yard at the signe of the Crowne by Simon Waterson, 1611. *EEBO.* STC (2nd ed.) / 19725.

Prynne, William. *Histrio-mastix: The Players Scourge, or, Actors Tragaedie.* London: E[dward] A[llde, Augustine Mathewes, Thomas Cotes] and W[illiam] I[ones] for Michael Sparke, 1633. *EEBO.* STC (2nd ed.) / 20464a.

224 BIBLIOGRAPHY

Reynolds, John. "An Admonition to the Parliament." In *Puritan Manifestoes: A Study of the Origin of the Puritan Revolt*, 1–39. Edited by W. H. Frere and C. E. Douglas. New York: B. Franklin, 1972.

Ridley, Nicholas. *A Treatise on the Worship of Images*. In *The Works of Nicholas Ridley, D.D. sometime Lord Bishop of London, martyr, 1555*. Edited by Rev. Henry Christmas. Cambridge: University of Cambridge Press, 1841.

Shakespeare, William. *Shake-speares sonnets Neuer before imprinted*. At London: By G. Eld for T[homas] T[horpe] and are to be solde by William Aspley, 1609. *EEBO*. STC (2nd ed.) / 22353.

Shakespeare, William. *Shake-speares Sonnets. Neuer before Imprinted*. At London: By G. Eld for T. T. and are to be solde by Iohn Wright, dwelling at Christ Church gate, 1609. STC (2nd ed.) / 22353a.

Shakespeare, William. *King Lear*. In *The Norton Shakespeare*. Edited by Stephen Greenblatt, Walter Cohen, Jean E. Howard, Katharine Eisaman Maus, Gordon McMullan, and Suzanne Gossett. New York: W. W. Norton, 2016.

Shakespeare, William. *The Winter's Tale*. In *The Norton Shakespeare*. Edited by Stephen Greenblatt, Walter Cohen, Jean E. Howard, Katharine Eisaman Maus, Gordon McMullan, and Suzanne Gossett. New York: W. W. Norton, 2015.

Sibbes, Richard. *The bruised reede, and smoaking flax*. London: Printed [by M. Flesher] for R. Dawlman, dwelling at the signe of the Brazen Serpent in Pauls Church-yard, 1630. *EEBO*. STC (2nd ed.) / 22479.

Sidney, Philip. *An Apologie for Poetrie. Written by the right noble, virtuous, and learned, Sir Phillip Sidney, Knight*. London: Printed for *Henry Olney*, and are to be sold at his shop in Paules Church-yard, at the signe of the George, neere to Cheap-gate, 1595. *EEBO*. STC (2nd ed.) / 22534.

Sidney, Philip. *Certaine Sonets*. In *The Countesse of Pembrokes Arcadia*. London: Imprinted [by R. Field] for William Ponsonbie, 1598. *EEBO*. STC (2nd ed.) / 22541.

Sidney, Philip. *Certain Sonnets*. In *The Poems of Sir Philip Sidney*, 133–62. Edited by William A. Ringler. Oxford: Clarendon Press, 1962.

Smectymnuus [pseud.]. *An answer to a booke entitvled An hvmble remonstrance in which the originall of liturgy, episcopacy is discussed*. London: Printed for I. Rothwell and to be sold by T. N., 1641. *EEBO*. Wing / M748.

Stubbes, Philip. *The Anatomie of Abuses, Part 1*. London: By [John Kingston for] Richard Iones, 1583. *EEBO*. STC (2nd ed.) / 23376.

Tacitus. *Annals and Histories*. Translated by William Jackson Brodribb. New York: Alfred A. Knopf, 2009.

Tyndale, William. *An exposycyon vpon the v.vi.vii. chapters of Mathewe*. London: 1536 [1533]. *EEBO*. STC / 24441.3.

Tyndale, William. *The Obedience of a Christian Man*. Edited by David Daniell. London: Penguin Books, 2000.

Winthrop, John. *Winthrop Papers*. Vol. 1, 1498–1628. Boston: Massachussetts Historical Society, 1929.

Secondary Sources

Alexander, Gavin. *Writing After Sidney: The Literary Response to Sir Philip Sidney, 1586–1640*. Oxford: Oxford University Press, 2006.

Aston, Margaret. *England's Iconoclasts: Laws against Images*. Oxford: Clarendon Press, 1988.

BIBLIOGRAPHY 225

Balke, Willem. "The Word of God and Experientia According to Calvin." In *Calvin Ecclesiae Doctor: International Congress on Calvin Research*, edited by Wilhelm H. Neuser, 19–31. Kampen, Neth.: Kok, 1978.

Barish, Jonas. "The Antitheatrical Prejudice," *Critical Quarterly* 8.4 (1966): 329–48.

Barish, Jonas. *The Antitheatrical Prejudice*. Berkeley: University of California Press, 1981.

Barkan, Leonard. "'Living Sculptures': Ovid, Michelangelo, and *The Winter's Tale*." *ELH* 48, no. 4 (1981): 639–67.

Bates, Catherine. *Masculinity and the Hunt: Wyatt to Spenser*. Oxford: Oxford University Press, 2013.

Beckwith, Sarah. "Shakespeare's Resurrections: *The Winter's Tale*." In *Shakespeare and the Grammar of Forgiveness*, 127–46. Ithaca, NY: Cornell University Press, 2011.

Beeke, Joel R. *Assurance of Faith: Calvin, English Protestantism, and the Dutch Second Reformation*. New York: Peter Lang, 1991.

Benedict, Philip. *Christ's Churches Purely Reformed: A Social History of Calvinism*. New Haven: Yale University Press, 2002.

Bevington, David. *Tudor Drama and Politics: A Critical Approach to Topical Meaning*. Cambridge, MA: Harvard University Press, 1968.

Biester, James. "'Nothing Seen': Fear, Imagination, and Conscience in Fulke Greville's *Caelica* 100." *Hellas: A Journal of Poetry and the Humanities* 7, no. 2 (1996): 123–35.

Bishop, T. G. "*The Winter's Tale*; or, Filling Up the Graves." In *Shakespeare and the Theater of Wonder*, 125–75. New York: Cambridge University Press, 1996.

Booth, Stephen, ed. *Shakespeare's Sonnets*. By William Shakespeare. New Haven: Yale University Press, 2000 [1977].

Breen, Dan. "Redeeming the Sonnet Sequence: Desire and Repentance in *Caelica*." In Sierhuis and Cummings, "Fulke Greville and the Arts," 141–63.

Breward, Ian, "The Significance of William Perkins," *The Journal of Religious History* 4, no. 2 (1966): 113–28.

Breward, Ian. Introduction to *The Work of William Perkins*, 3–131. Edited by Ian Breward. Abingdon: Sutton Courtenay Press, 1970.

Brydon, Michael. "The Establishment of Anglican Triumphalism." In *The Evolving Reputation of Richard Hooker: An Examination of Responses, 1600–1714*, 81–122. Oxford: Oxford University Press, 2006.

Bullough, Geoffrey, ed. *Poems and Dramas of Fulke Greville, First Lord Brooke*. 2 vols. New York: Oxford University Press, 1945.

Burrow, Colin, ed. *The Complete Sonnets and Poems*. The Oxford Shakespeare. Oxford: Oxford University Press, 2008.

Butler, Martin. *Theatre and Crisis, 1632–1642*. Cambridge: Cambridge University Press, 1984.

Cable, Lana. "Milton's Iconoclastic Truth." In *Politics, Poetics, and Hermeneutics in Milton's Prose*, edited by David Loewenstein and James Grantham Turner, 135–51. Cambridge: Cambridge University Press, 1990.

Cable, Lana. *Carnal Rhetoric: Milton's Iconoclasm and the Politics of Desire*. Durham, NC: Duke University Press, 1995.

Cadman, Daniel. "'To fashion grounds, from whence artes might be coyn'd': Commerce and the Postlapsarian State in Greville's Poetry." In Sierhuis and Cummings, "Fulke Greville and the Arts," 119–39.

Cain, Tom G. S. "Robert Herrick, Mildmay Fane, and Sir Simeon Steward." *English Literary Renaissance* 15, no. 2 (1985): 312–17.

Cain, Tom, and Ruth Connolly, eds. *"Lords of Wine and Oile": Community and Conviviality in the Poetry of Robert Herrick*. Oxford: Oxford University Press, 2011.

226 BIBLIOGRAPHY

Cain, Tom, and Ruth Connolly. Introduction to *The Complete Poetry of Robert Herrick*, xv–lxxv. Edited by Tom Cain and Ruth Connolly. Vol 1. Oxford: Oxford University Press, 2013.

Carey, John. *John Donne: Life, Mind, and Art*. New York: Oxford University Press, 1980.

Carey, John, and Alastair Fowler. Introduction to *The Poems of John Milton*. Edited by John Carey and Alastair Fowler. London: Longmans, 1968.

Cavell, Stanley. "The Avoidance of Love: A Reading of *King Lear*." In *Must We Mean What We Say?*, 267–353. Cambridge: Cambridge University Press, 2003 [1967].

Cefalu, Paul. "Godly Fear, Sanctification, and Calvinist Theology in the Sermons and 'Holy Sonnets' of John Donne." *Studies in Philology* 11, no. 1 (2003): 71–86.

Chanoff, David. "Donne's Anglicanism." *Recusant History* 15, no. 3 (1980): 154–67.

Chute, Marchette. *Two Gentle Men: The Lives of George Herbert and Robert Herrick*. New York: E. P. Dutton, 1959.

Coiro, Ann Baynes. *Robert Herrick's "Hesperides" and the Epigram Book Tradition*. Baltimore: Johns Hopkins University Press, 1988.

Coiro, Ann Baynes, ed. Special issue on Robert Herrick, *George Herbert Journal* 14, nos. 1–2 (1990–91).

Collinson, Patrick. *The Religion of Protestants: The Church in English Society, 1559–1625*. Oxford: Clarendon Press, 1982.

Collinson, Patrick. *The Elizabethan Puritan Movement*. Oxford: Clarendon Press, 1990 [1967].

Cormack, Bradin. "In the Labyrinth: Gunn's Greville." Afterword to *The Selected Poems of Fulke Greville*, 161–77. Edited by Thom Gunn. Chicago: University of Chicago Press, 2009.

Corns, Thomas N. *Uncloistered Virtue: English Political Literature, 1640–1660*. Oxford: Clarendon Press, 1992.

Craig, John. "Bodies at Prayer in Early Modern England." In *Worship and the Parish Church in Early Modern Britain*, edited by Natalie Mears and Alec Ryrie, 173–96. Farnham: Ashgate, 2013.

Creaser, John. "'The present aid of this occasion': The Setting of *Comus*." In *The Court Masque*, edited by David Lindley, 111–34. Manchester: Manchester University Press, 1984.

Creaser, John. "Herrick at Play." *Essays in Criticism* 56, no. 4 (2006): 324–50.

Creaser, John. "'Times trans-shifting': Chronology and the Misshaping of Herrick." *English Literary Renaissance* 39, no. 1 (2009): 163–96.

Creaser, John. "'Jocond his Muse was': Celebration and Virtuosity in Herrick." In Cain and Connolly, "*Lords of Wine and Oile*," 39–62.

Crockett, Bryan. *The Play of Paradox: Stage and Sermon in Renaissance England*. Philadelphia: University of Pennsylvania Press, 1995.

Croll, Morris W. *The Works of Fulke Greville: A Thesis*. Philadelphia: J. B. Lippincott, 1903.

Culler, Jonathan. *Theory of the Lyric*. Cambridge, MA: Harvard University Press, 2015.

Cummings, Brian. *The Literary Culture of the Reformation: Grammar and Grace*. Oxford: Oxford University Press, 2002.

Cummings, Brian. "Prayer, Bodily Ritual and Performative Utterance: Bucer, Calvin and the *Book of Common Prayer*." In *Prayer and Performance in Early Modern English Literature*, edited by Joseph William Sterrett, 16–36. Cambridge: Cambridge University Press, 2018.

Dailey, Alice. "Easter Scenes from an Unholy Tomb: Christian Parody in *The Widow's Tears*." In *Marian Moments in Early Modern British Drama*, edited by Regina Buccola and Lisa Hopkins, 127–40. Aldershot: Ashgate, 2007.

BIBLIOGRAPHY 227

Damrau, Peter. *The Reception of English Puritan Literature in Germany*. London: Maney/Modern Humanities Research Association, 2006.

Deming, Robert H. "Robert Herrick's Classical Ceremony." *ELH* 34, no. 3 (1967): 327–48.

Deming, Robert H. *Ceremony and Art: Robert Herrick's Poetry*. The Hague: Mouton, 1974.

DeNeef, A. Leigh. *"This Poetic Liturgie": Robert Herrick's Ceremonial Mode*. Durham, NC: Duke University Press, 1974.

Diehl, Huston. *Staging Reform, Reforming the Stage*. Ithaca, NY: Cornell University Press, 1997.

Diehl, Huston. "'Strike All that Look Upon With Marvel': Theatrical and Theological Wonder in *The Winter's Tale*." In *Rematerializing Shakespeare: Authority and Representation on the Early Modern English Stage*, edited by Bryan Reynolds and William N. West, 19–34. New York: Palgrave Macmillan, 2005.

Diehl, Huston. "'Does not the stone rebuke me?': The Pauline Rebuke and Paulina's Lawful Magic in *The Winter's Tale*." In *Shakespeare and the Cultures of Performance*, edited by Paul Yachnin and Patricia Badir, 69–82. Burlington, VT: Ashgate, 2008.

DiPasquale, Theresa M. "Ambivalent Mourning: Sacramentality, Idolatry, and Gender in 'Since she whome I lovd hath payd her last debt.'" *John Donne Journal* 10, nos. 1–2 (1991): 45–56.

DiPasquale, Theresa M. "Ambivalent Mourning in 'Since she whome I lovd.'" In Hester, *John Donne's "desire of more,"* 183–95, 1996.

DiPasquale, Theresa M. *Literature and Sacrament: The Sacred and the Secular in John Donne*. Pittsburgh: Duquesne University Press, 1999.

Dixon, Lief. *Practical Predestinarians in England, c. 1590–1640*. Farnham: Ashgate, 2014.

Doerksen, Daniel W. "Polemicist or Pastor? Donne and Moderate Calvinist Conformity." In *John Donne and the Protestant Reformation*, edited by Mary Arshagouni Papazian, 12–34. Detroit: Wayne State University Press, 2003.

Dollimore, Jonathan. *Radical Tragedy: Religion, Ideology and Power in the Drama of Shakespeare and His Contemporaries*. Durham, NC: Duke University Press, 2003 [1984].

Dubrow, Heather. *A Happier Eden: The Politics of Marriage in the Stuart Epithalamium*. Ithaca, NY: Cornell University Press, 1990.

Duffy, Eamon. *The Stripping of the Altars: Traditional Religion in England c. 1400–c. 1580*. New Haven: Yale University Press, 1992.

Duncan-Jones, Katherine. *Sir Philip Sidney: Courtier Poet*. New Haven: Yale University Press, 1991.

Dwyer, June. "Fulke Greville's Aesthetic: Another Perspective." *Studies in Philology* 78, no. 3 (1981): 255–74.

Eppley, Daniel. "Richard Hooker on the Un-Conditionality of Predestination." In Kirby, *Richard Hooker and the English Reformation*, 63–77.

Eppley, Daniel. *Reading the Bible with Richard Hooker*. Minneapolis, MN: Augsburg Fortress, 2016.

Farmer, Norman, Jr. "Fulke Greville and the Poetic of the Plain Style." *Texas Studies in Literature and Language* 11, no. 1 (1969): 657–70.

Ferry, Anne. *The "Inward" Language: Sonnets of Wyatt, Sidney, Shakespeare, and Donne*. Chicago: University of Chicago Press, 1983.

Filo, Gina. "Fulke Greville's 'Sweet Boy': Homoerotic Desire in *Caelica*." *Sidney Journal* 37, nos. 1–2 (2019): 133–49.

Fincham, Kenneth, and Nicholas Tyacke. *Altars Restored: The Changing Face of English Religious Worship, c. 1547–1700*. Oxford: Oxford University Press, 2007.

228   BIBLIOGRAPHY

Fineman, Joel. *Shakespeare's Perjured Eye: The Invention of Poetic Subjectivity in the Sonnets*. Berkeley: University of California Press, 1986.

Fisch, Harold. "Bishop Hall's Meditations." *The Review of English Studies* 25, no. 99 (1949): 210–21.

Fish, Stanley. "Masculine Persuasive Force: Donne and Verbal Power." In Harvey and Maus, *Soliciting Interpretation*, 223–52.

Fix, Stephen. "Johnson and the 'Duty' of Reading *Paradise Lost*." *ELH* 52, no. 3 (1985): 649–71.

Fowler, Alistair. "Robert Herrick." Warton Lecture on English Poetry, 23 October, 1980. In *Proceedings of the British Academy*. Vol. 66, 1980, 243–64. London: Oxford University Press, 1982.

Freedberg, David. *The Power of Images: Studies in the History and Theory of Response*. Chicago: University of Chicago Press, 1989.

Frost, William. *Fulke Greville's "Caelica": An Evaluation*. Brattleboro, VT: Vermont Printing, 1942.

Frye, Roland Mushat. *Shakespeare and Christian Doctrine*. Princeton: Princeton University Press, 1963.

Frye, Roland Mushat. "The Teachings of Classical Puritanism on Conjugal Love." *Studies in the Renaissance* 2 (1995): 148–59.

Gardner, Helen, ed. *John Donne: The Divine Poems*. Oxford: Oxford University Press, 2000 [1952].

Gash, Anthony. "Shakespeare, Carnival, and the Sacred: *The Winter's Tale* and *Measure for Measure*." In *Shakespeare and the Carnival: After Bakhtin*, edited by Ronald Knowles, 177–210. Basingstoke: Macmillan Press, 1998.

Gay, David. "Prayer and the Sacred Image: Milton, Jeremy Taylor, and the *Eikon Basilike*." *Milton Quarterly* 46, no. 1 (2012): 1–14.

Gibbons, Daniel R. *Conflicts of Devotion: Liturgical Poetics in Sixteenth- and Seventeenth-Century England*. Notre Dame, IN: University of Notre Dame Press, 2017.

Gilman, Ernest B. "Donne's 'Pictures Made and Mard.'" In *Iconoclasm and Poetry in the English Reformation: Down Went Dagon*, 117–48. Chicago: University of Chicago Press, 1986.

Gilman, Ernest B. "'To adore, or scorne an image': Donne and the Iconoclastic Controversy." *John Donne Journal* 5 (1986): 62–100.

Gosse, Edmund. "Robert Herrick." *The Cornhill Magazine* 32 (1875): 176–91.

Graham, Kenneth J. E. *The Performance of Conviction: Plainness and Rhetoric in the Early English Renaissance*. Ithaca, NY: Cornell University Press, 1994.

Grant, Patrick. "Augustinian Spirituality and the *Holy Sonnets* of John Donne." *ELH* 38, no. 4 (1971): 542–61.

Grantley, Darryll. "*The Winter's Tale* and Early Religious Drama." *Comparative Drama* 20, no. 1 (1986): 17–37.

Greenblatt, Stephen. *Shakespearean Negotiations*. Berkeley: University of California Press, 1988.

Greenblatt, Stephen. "Remnants of the Sacred in Early Modern England." In *Subject and Object in Renaissance Culture*, edited by Margreta de Grazia, Maureen Quilligan, and Peter Stallybrass, 337–45. Cambridge: Cambridge University Press, 1996.

Greenblatt, Stephen. *Hamlet in Purgatory*. Princeton: Princeton University Press, 2002.

Greenblatt, Stephen. *Renaissance Self-Fashioning: From More to Shakespeare*. Chicago: University of Chicago Press, 2005 [1980].

Green, Ian M. *Print and Protestantism*. Oxford: Oxford University Press, 2000.

BIBLIOGRAPHY 229

Greene, Thomas M. "'Pitiful Thrivers': Failed Husbandry in the Sonnets." In *Shakespeare and the Question of Theory*, edited by Patricia Parker and Geoffrey Hartman, 230–44. New York: Methuen, 1985.

Grislis, Egil. "Reflections on Richard Hooker's Understanding of the Eucharist." In Kirby, *Richard Hooker and the English Reformation*, 207–23.

Grosart, Alexander B. "Memorial-Introduction: Critical." In *The Complete Poems of Robert Herrick*, cxi–cclxxvi. Vol. 1. Edited by Alexander B. Grosart. London: Chatto and Windus, 1876.

Guibbory, Achsah. "Enlarging the Limits of the 'Religious Lyric': The Case of Herrick's *Hesperides*." In *New Perspectives on the Seventeenth-Century English Religious Lyric*, edited by John R. Roberts, 28–45. Columbia, MO: University of Missouri Press, 1994.

Guibbory, Achsah. "Charles's Prayers, Idolatrous Images, and True Creation in Milton's *Eikonoklastes*." In *Of Poetry and Politics: New Essays on Milton and His World*, edited by P. G. Stanwood, 283–94. Binghamton, NY: Medieval and Renaissance Texts and Studies, 1995.

Guibbory, Achsah. "Donne, Milton, and Holy Sex." *Milton Studies* 32 (1995): 3–21.

Guibbory, Achsah. "Fear of 'loving more': Death and the Loss of Sacramental Love." In Hester, *John Donne's "desire of more*," 204–27.

Guibbory, Achsah. *Ceremony and Community from Herbert to Milton: Literature, Religion, and Cultural Conflict in Seventeenth-Century England*. Cambridge: Cambridge University Press, 1998.

Guibbory, Achsah. "Donne's Religion: Montague, Arminianism and Donne's Sermons, 1624–1630." *English Literary Renaissance* 31, no. 3 (2001): 412–39.

Guibbory, Achsah. "Donne, Milton, and Holy Sex." In *Returning to John Donne*, 107–24. Burlington, VT: Ashgate, 2015.

Gunn, Thom. Introduction to *The Selected Poems of Fulke Greville*, 13–44. Edited by Thom Gunn. Chicago: University of Chicago Press, 2009 [1968].

Haigh, Christopher. *Reformation and Resistance in Tudor Lancashire*. Cambridge: Cambridge University Press, 1975.

Haigh, Christopher. *English Reformations: Religion, Politics, and Society under the Tudors*. Oxford: Clarendon Press, 1993.

Hale, Edward Everett. Introduction to *Selections from the Poetry of Robert Herrick*, xi–lxx. Edited by Edward Everett Hale. Boston: Ginn, 1895.

Halkett, John. *Milton and the Idea of Matrimony: A Study of the Divorce Tracts and Paradise Lost*. New Haven: Yale University Press, 1970.

Haller, William, and Malleville Haller. "The Puritan Art of Love." *Huntington Library Quarterly* 5, no. 2 (1942): 235–72.

Hammond, Gerard. *Fleeting Things: English Poets and Poems, 1616–1660*. Cambridge, MA: Harvard University Press, 1990.

Hansen, Matthew C., and Matthew Woodcock, eds. "Fulke Greville." Special issue, *Sidney Journal* 19, nos. 1–2 (2001).

Harvey, Elizabeth D., and Katharine Eisaman Maus, eds. *Soliciting Interpretation: Literary Theory and Seventeenth-Century English Poetry*. Chicago: University of Chicago Press, 1990.

Hassel, R. Chris, Jr. "Michaelmas, Hallowmas, and Saint Bartholomew's." In *Renaissance Drama and the English Church Year*, 157–60. Lincoln, NE: University of Nebraska Press, 1979.

230 BIBLIOGRAPHY

Heinemann, Margot. *Puritanism and Theatre: Middleton and Opposition Drama under the Early Stuarts*. Cambridge: Cambridge University Press, 1980.

Hester, M. Thomas, ed. *John Donne's "desire of more,": The Subject of Anne More Donne in His Poetry*. Newark, DE: University of Delaware Press, 1996.

Hill, Christopher. *Milton and the English Revolution*. New York: Viking, 1978 [1977].

Hill, W. Speed. "The Evolution of Hooker's Laws of Ecclesiastical Polity." In *Studies in Richard Hooker: Essays Preliminary to an Edition of His Works*, edited by W. Speed Hill, 117–58. Cleveland, OH: Press of Case Western Reserve University, 1972.

Ho, Elaine Y. L. "Fulke Greville's *Caelica* and the Calvinist Self." *SEL Studies in English Literature* 32, no. 1 (1992): 35–57.

Hokama, Rhema. "Love's Rites: Performing Prayer in Shakespeare's Sonnets." *Shakespeare Quarterly* 63, no. 2 (2012): 199–223.

Hokama, Rhema. "Praying in Paradise: Recasting Milton's Iconoclasm in *Paradise Lost*." *Milton Studies* 54 (2013): 161–80.

Hokama, Rhema. Review of Daniel R. Gibbons, *Conflicts of Devotion: Liturgical Poetics in Sixteenth- and Seventeenth-Century England* (Notre Dame, IN: University of Notre Dame Press, 2017). *Parergon* 34, no. 2 (2017): 207–8.

Hokama, Rhema. "'Loves halowed temple': Erotic Sacramentalism and Reformed Devotion in John Donne's 'To his Mistress going to bed.'" *Modern Philology* 119, no. 2 (2021): 248–75.

Hokama, Rhema. "'Wanton child': Fantasies of infanticide, abortion, and monstrous birth in Mary Wroth's *Pamphilia to Amphilanthus*." *SEL Studies in English Literature 1500–1900* 62.2 (forthcoming).

Hunt, Maurice. *Shakespeare's Religious Allusiveness: Its Play and Tolerance*. Aldershot: Ashgate, 2004.

Hunter, William B., Jr. "The Liturgical Context of *Comus*." *English Language Notes* 10 (1972): 11–15.

Ingalls, Ranall. "Hooker on Sin and Grace." In Kirby, *Companion to Richard Hooker*, 151–84.

Inglis, Fred. "Metaphysical Poetry and the Greatness of Fulke Greville." *The Critical Review* 8 (1965): 101–09.

Irish, Charles W. "'Participation of God Himselfe': Law, the Mediation of Christ, and Sacramental Participation in the Thought of Richard Hooker." In Kirby, *Richard Hooker and the English Reformation*, 165–84.

Jacobsen, Ken. "'The Law of a Commonweal': The Social Vision of Hooker's *Of the Laws of Ecclesiastical Polity* and Shakespeare's *The Taming of the Shrew*." *Animus* 12 (2008): 15–38.

Jacquot, Jean. "Religion et raison d'état dans l'oeuvre de Fulke Greville." *Etudes anglaises* 5 (1952): 211–22.

Jensen, Phebe. "Singing Psalms to Horn-Pipes: Festivity, Iconoclasm, and Catholicism in *The Winter's Tale*." *Shakespeare Quarterly* 55, no. 3 (2004): 279–306.

Jensen, Phebe. "Singing Psalms to Hornpipes: Festivity, Iconoclasm, and Catholicism in *The Winter's Tale*." In *Religion and Revelry in Shakespeare's World*, 194–233. Cambridge: Cambridge University Press, 2008.

Johnson, Kimberly. *Made Flesh: Sacramental Poetics in Post-Reformation England*. Philadelphia: University of Pennsylvania Press, 2014.

Johnson, Samuel. *Lives of the English Poets*. Edited by G. B. Hill. 3 vols. Oxford: Clarendon Press, 1905.

BIBLIOGRAPHY 231

Johnson, William C. "*In Vino—et in Amore—Veritas*: Transformational Animation in Herrick's 'Sack' Poems." *Papers on Language and Literature* 41, no. 1 (2005): 89–108.

Jones, Frederick J. *The Structure of Petrarch's "Canzoniere": A Chronological, Psychological, and Statistical Analysis.* Cambridge: D. S. Brewer, 1995.

Kambaskovic-Sawers, Danijela. "Carved in Living Laurel: The Sonnet Sequence and Transformations of Idolatry." *Renaissance Studies* 21 (2007): 377–94.

Kastan, David Scott. "Performances and Playbooks: The Closing of the Theatres and the Politics of Drama." In *Reading, Society and Politics in Early Modern England*, edited by Kevin Sharpe and Steven N. Zwicker, 167–84. Cambridge: Cambridge University Press, 2003.

Kaufman, Peter Iver. *Prayer, Despair, and Drama: Elizabethan Introspection.* Urbana, IL: University of Illinois Press, 1996.

Kendall, R. T. *Calvin and English Calvinism to 1649.* Oxford: Oxford University Press, 1979.

Kerrigan, William. "The Fearful Accommodations of John Donne." *English Literary Renaissance* 4, no. 3 (1974): 340–63.

Kerrigan, John, ed. *The Sonnets and "A Lover's Complaint."* By William Shakespeare. London: Penguin, 1986.

Kirby, W. J. Torrance, ed. *Richard Hooker and the English Reformation.* Dordrecht: Kluwer Academic Publishers, 2003.

Kirby, W. J. Torrance, ed. *A Companion to Richard Hooker.* Leiden: Brill, 2008.

Knapp, Jeffrey. *Shakespeare's Tribe: Church, Nation, and Theater in Renaissance England.* Chicago: University of Chicago Press, 2002.

Knoppers, Laura Lunger. *Historicizing Milton: Spectacle, Power, and Poetry in Restoration England.* Athens, GA: University of Georgia Press, 1994.

Koehler, G. Stanley. "Milton and the Art of Landscape." *Milton Studies* 8 (1975): 3–40.

Koerner, Joseph Leo. *The Reformation of the Image.* Chicago: University of Chicago Press, 2008 [2004].

Konkola, Kari. "'People of the Book': The Production of Theological Texts in Early Modern England." *The Papers of the Bibliographical Society of America* 94 (2000): 5–34.

Kuchar, Gary. "Petrarchism and Repentance in John Donne's Holy Sonnets." *Modern Philology* 105, no. 3 (2008): 535–69.

Kuchar, Gary. "Petrarchism and Repentance in John Donne's Holy Sonnets." In *The Poetry of Religious Sorrow in Early Modern England*, 151–83. Cambridge: Cambridge University Press, 2008.

Lake, Peter. *Moderate Puritans and the Elizabethan Church.* Cambridge: Cambridge University Press, 1982.

Lake, Peter. "Calvinism and the English Church 1570–1635." *Past and Present* 114 (1987): 32–76.

Lake, Peter. *Anglicans and Puritans? Presbyterianism and English Conformist Thought from Whitgift to Hooker.* London: Unwin Hyman, 1988.

Lake, Peter. "The Laudian Style: Order, Uniformity and the Pursuit of the Beauty of Holiness in the 1630s." In *The Early Stuart Church, 1603–1642*, edited by Kenneth Fincham, 161–85. Palo Alto: Stanford University Press, 1993.

Lake, Peter. "Business as Usual? The Immediate Reception of Hooker's Ecclesiastical Polity." *The Journal of Ecclesiastical History* 3 (2001): 456–86.

Lake, Peter, with Michael Questier. *The Antichrist's Lewd Hat: Protestants, Papists, and Players in Post-Reformation England.* New Haven: Yale University Press, 2002.

Leishman, James B. *Themes and Variations in Shakespeare's Sonnets.* New York: Harper Torchbooks, 1966.

232 BIBLIOGRAPHY

Leo, Russ, Katrin Röder, and Freya Sierhuis, eds. *Fulke Greville and the Culture of the English Renaissance*. Oxford: Oxford University Press, 2018.

Leo, Russ, Katrin Röder, and Freya Sierhuis. "The Resources of Obscurity: Reappraising the Work of Fulke Greville." In Leo, Röder, and Sierhuis, *Fulke Greville and the Culture of the English Renaissance*, 1–26.

Lerner, Laurence. *Love and Marriage: Literature and Its Social Context*. London: Edward Arnold, 1979.

Lewalski, Barbara Kiefer. *Donne's "Anniversaries" and the Poetry of Praise: The Creation of a Symbolic Mode*. Princeton: Princeton University Press, 1973.

Lewalski, Barbara Kiefer. *Protestant Poetics and the Seventeenth-Century Religious Lyric*. Princeton: Princeton University Press, 1979.

Lewalski, Barbara Kiefer. *"Paradise Lost" and the Rhetoric of Literary Forms*. Princeton: Princeton University Press, 1985.

Lewalski, Barbara Kiefer. *The Life of John Milton: A Critical Biography*. Malden, MA: Blackwell, 2002.

Lewis, C. S. *English Literature in the Sixteenth Century, Excluding Drama*. Oxford: Clarendon Press, 1965 [1954].

Lim, Walter S. H. "Knowledge and Belief in *The Winter's Tale*." *SEL Studies in English Literature, 1500–1900* 41, no. 2 (2001): 317–34.

Lindenbaum, Peter. "Lovemaking in *Paradise Lost*." *Milton Studies* 6 (1974): 277–306.

Loewenstein, David. *Milton and the Drama of History: Historical Vision, Iconoclasm, and the Literary Imagination*. Cambridge: Cambridge University Press, 1990.

Lupton, Julia Reinhard. "*The Winter's Tale* and the Gods: Iconographies of Idolatry." In *Afterlives of the Saints: Hagiography, Typology, and Renaissance Literature*, 175–218. Stanford: Stanford University Press, 1996.

McCabe, Richard A. *Joseph Hall: A Study in Satire and Meditation*. Oxford: Oxford University Press, 1982.

McCabe, Richard A. "Joseph Hall." In *Oxford Dictionary of National Biography*. Oxford University Press, 2004; online ed., 2008.

McCoy, Richard C. "Love's Martyrs: Shakespeare's 'Phoenix and Turtle' and the Sacrificial Sonnets." In McEachern and Shuger, *Religion and Culture in Renaissance England*, 188–209.

MacCulloch, Diarmaid. "Cranmer, Thomas (1489–1556), Archbishop of Canterbury." In *Oxford Dictionary of National Biography*. Oxford: Oxford University Press, 2004; online ed., 2015.

McEachern, Claire, and Debora Shuger, eds. *Religion and Culture in Renaissance England*. Cambridge: Cambridge University Press, 1997.

Malpezzi, Frances M. "Love's Liquidity in 'Since she whome I lovd.'" In Hester, *John Donne's "desire of more,"* 196–203.

Maltby, Judith. *Prayer Book and People in Elizabethan and Early Stuart England*. Cambridge: Cambridge University Press, 1998.

Marcus, Leah S. "Herrick's *Noble Numbers* and the Politics of Playfulness." *English Literary Renaissance* 7 (1977): 108–26.

Marcus, Leah S. *Childhood and Cultural Despair*. Pittsburgh: University of Pittsburgh Press, 1978.

Marcus, Leah S. "Herrick's 'Hesperides' and the 'Proclamation made for May.'" *Studies in Philology* 76, no. 1 (1979): 489–74.

Marcus, Leah S. *The Politics of Mirth: Jonson, Herrick, Milton, Marvell, and the Defense of Old Holiday Pastimes*. Chicago: University of Chicago Press, 1986.

BIBLIOGRAPHY   233

Marcus, Leah S. "The Earl of Bridgewater's Legal Life: Notes toward a Political Reading of Comus." *Milton Quarterly* 21, no. 4 (1987): 13–23.

Marcus, Leah S. "Afterword: Herrick and Historicism." In Coiro, Special issue on Robert Herrick, *George Herbert Journal*, 172–77.

Marno, David. *Death Be Not Proud: The Art of Holy Attention*. Chicago: University of Chicago Press, 2016.

Martin, Catherine Gimelli. "Experimental Predestination in Donne's *Holy Sonnets*: Self-Ministry and the Early Seventeenth-Century *Via Media*." *Studies in Philology* 110, no. 2 (2013): 350–81.

Martz, Louis. *The Poetry of Meditation: A Study in English Religious Literature of the Seventeenth Century*. New Haven: Yale University Press, 1954.

Mauer, Margaret. "The Circular Argument of Donne's *La Corona*." *SEL Studies in English Literature, 1500–1900* 22, no. 1 (1982): 51–68.

Milner, Matthew. *The Senses and the English Reformation*. New York: Routledge, 2011.

Mitchell, W. J. T. *Iconology: Image, Text, Ideology*. Chicago: University of Chicago Press, 1986.

Montrose, Louis. "The Purpose of Playing: Reflections on a Shakespearean Anthropology." *Helios* 7, no. 2 (1980): 51–74.

Montrose, Louis. *The Purpose of Playing*. Chicago: University of Chicago Press, 1996.

Montrose, Louis. "Shakespeare, the Stage, and the State." *SubStance* 25, no. 2 (1996): 46–67.

Moorman, Frederic W. *Robert Herrick: A Biographical and Critical Study*. New York: Russell and Russell, 1910.

Morris, Brian. "Elizabethan and Jacobean Drama." In *English Drama to 1710*, edited by Christopher Ricks, 65–117. London: Sphere, 1971.

Mortimer, Anthony. "*Comus* and Michaelmas." *English Studies* 65, no. 2 (1984): 111–19.

Moshenska, Joe. "'A Sensible Touching, Feeling and Groping': Metaphor and Sensory Experience in the English Reformation." In *Passions and Subjectivity in Early Modern Culture*, edited by Brian Cummings and Freya Sierhuis, 184–99. Farnham: Ashgate, 2013.

Moshenska, Joe. *Feeling Pleasures: The Sense of Touch in Renaissance England*. Oxford: Oxford University Press, 2014.

Neelands, W. David. "Richard Hooker and the Debates about Predestination, 1580–1600." In Kirby, *Richard Hooker and the English Reformation*, 43–61.

Neelands, W. David. "Christology and the Sacraments." In Kirby, *Companion to Richard Hooker*, 369–402.

Neelands, W. David. "Hooker and Predestination." In Kirby, *Companion to Richard Hooker*, 185–219.

Neelands, W. David. "Richard Hooker and the Debates about Predestination, 1580–1600." In Kirby, *Richard Hooker and the English Reformation*, 43–61.

Netzley, Ryan. *Reading, Desire, and the Eucharist in Early Modern Religious Poetry*. Toronto: University of Toronto Press, 2011.

Newton, Thomas, ed. *Paradise Lost: A Poem, in Twelve Books*. By John Milton. 2 vols. London: J. and R. Tonson and S. Draper, 1754.

Norbrook, David. "The Monarchy of Wit and the Republic of Letters: Donne's Politics." In Harvey and Maus, *Soliciting Interpretation*, 3–36.

O'Connell, Michael. *The Idolatrous Eye: Iconoclasm and Theater in Early-Modern England*. Oxford: Oxford University Press, 2000.

Oliver, Paul M. *Donne's Religious Writing: A Discourse of Feigned Devotion*. New York: Longman, 1997.

234   BIBLIOGRAPHY

Parker, Thomas H. L. *Calvin's Doctrine of the Knowledge of God*. Grand Rapids, MI: Eerdmans, 1959 [1952].

Parry, Graham. *The Arts of the Anglican Counter-Reformation: Glory, Laud and Honour*. Woodbridge, Suffolk: Boydell, 2006.

Parry, Graham. "His Noble Numbers." In Cain and Connolly, *"Lords of Wine and Oile,"* 276–99.

Patterson, Annabel. *Censorship and Interpretation: The Conditions of Writing and Reading in Early Modern England*. Madison, WI: University of Wisconsin Press, 1984.

Patterson, W. B. *William Perkins and the Making of a Protestant England*. Oxford: Oxford University Press, 2014.

Peguigney, Joseph. *Such Is My Love: A Study of Shakespeare's Sonnets*. Chicago: University of Chicago Press, 1985.

Peterson, Douglas L. *The English Lyric from Wyatt to Donne: A History of the Plain and Eloquent Styles*. Princeton: Princeton University Press, 1967.

Picciotto, Joanna. *Labors of Innocence in Early Modern England*. Cambridge, MA: Harvard University Press, 2010.

Platt, Peter G. *Shakespeare and the Culture of Paradox*. Farnham: Ashgate, 2009.

Poole, Kristen. *Radical Religion from Shakespeare to Milton: Figures of Nonconformity in Early Modern England*. Cambridge: Cambridge University Press, 2000.

Poole, Kristen. *Supernatural Environments in Shakespeare's England: Spaces of Demonism, Divinity, and Drama*. Cambridge: Cambridge University Press, 2011.

Pugh, Syrithe. *Herrick, Fanshawe and the Politics of Intertextuality: Classical Literature and Seventeenth-Century Royalism*. Farnham: Ashgate, 2010.

Questier, Michael C. *Conversion, Politics and Religion in England, 1580–1625*. Cambridge: Cambridge University Press, 1996.

Radzinowicz, Mary Ann. *Milton's Epics and the Book of Psalms*. Princeton: Princeton University Press, 1989.

Rambuss, Richard. *Closet Devotions*. Durham, NC: Duke University Press, 1998.

Rambuss, Richard. "Pleasure and Devotion: The Body of Jesus and Seventeenth-Century Lyric." In *Queering the Renaissance*, edited by Jonathan Goldberg, 253–79. Durham, NC: Duke University Press, 1994.

Rebholz, Ronald A. *The Life of Fulke Greville, First Lord Brooke*. Oxford: Clarendon Press, 1971.

Rees, Joan. *Fulke Greville, Lord Brook, 1554–1628: A Critical Biography*. London: Routledge and Kegan Paul, 1971.

Rollin, Roger. "Missing the Hock-Cart." *Seventeenth Century News* 24, no. 3 (1966): 39–40.

Rollins, Hyder Edward, ed. *A New Variorum Edition of Shakespeare*. 2 vols. Philadelphia: Lippencott, 1971.

Rosendale, Timothy. *Liturgy and Literature in the Making of Protestant England*. Cambridge: Cambridge University Press, 2007.

Rust, Jennifer R. *The Body in Mystery: The Political Theology of the* Corpus Mysticum *in the Literature of Reformation England*. Evanston, IL: Northwestern University Press, 2014.

Ryrie, Alec. *Being Protestant in Reformation Britain*. Oxford: Oxford University Press, 2013.

Sabine, Maureen. "No Marriage in Heaven: John Donne, Anne Donne, and the Kingdom Come." In Hester, *John Donne's "desire of more,"* 228–55.

Sanchez, Michelle Chaplin. *Calvin and the Resignification of the World*. Cambridge: Cambridge University Press, 2019.

BIBLIOGRAPHY 235

Scarry, Elaine. "But yet the Body is His Book." In *Literature and the Body: Essays on Populations and Persons*, edited by Elaine Scarry, 70–105. Baltimore: Johns Hopkins University Press, 1988.

Schalkwyk, David. *Speech and Performance in Shakespeare's Sonnets and Plays*. Cambridge: Cambridge University Press, 2002.

Schoenfeldt, Michael. *Prayer and Power: George Herbert and Renaissance Courtship*. Chicago: University of Chicago Press, 1991.

Schreiner, Susan E. "'The Spiritual Man Judges All Things': Calvin and the Exegetical Debates about Certainty in the Reformation." In *Biblical Interpretation in the Era of the Reformation: Essays Presented to David C. Steinmetz in Honor of His Sixtieth Birthday*, edited by Richard A. Muller and John L. Thompson, 189–215. Grand Rapids, MI: Eerdmans, 1996.

Schreiner, Susan E. *Are You Alone Wise? The Search for Certainty in the Early Modern Era*. Oxford: Oxford University Press, 2010.

Schwanda, Tom. *Soul Recreation: The Contemplative-Mystical Piety of Puritanism*. Eugene, OR: Pickwick Publications, 2012.

Schwartz, Regina M. *Remembering and Repeating: On Milton's Theology and Poetics*. Chicago: University of Chicago Press, 1993 [1988].

Schwartz, Regina M. *Sacramental Poetics at the Dawn of Secularism: When God Left the World*. Palo Alto: Stanford University Press, 2008.

Selleck, Nancy. *The Interpersonal Idiom in Shakespeare, Donne, and Early Modern Culture*. Basingstoke: Palgrave Macmillan, 2008.

Sellin, Paul. *John Donne and Calvinist Views of Grace*. Amsterdam: VU Boekhandel, 1983.

Shami, Jeanne. "Political Advice in Donne's *Devotions*: No Man Is an Island." *Modern Language Quarterly* 50 (1989), 337–56.

Sherwood, Terry G. *Fulfilling the Circle: A Study in John Donne's Thought*. Toronto: University of Toronto Press, 1984.

Shore, Daniel. "Why Milton Is Not an Iconoclast." *PMLA* 127, no. 1 (2012): 22–37.

Shuger, Debora Kuller. *Habits of Thought in the English Renaissance: Religion, Politics, and the Dominant Culture*. Toronto: University of Toronto Press, 1997 [1990].

Shuger, Debora Kuller. "'Society Supernatural': The Imagined Community of Hooker's *Laws*." In McEachern and Shuger, *Religion and Culture in Renaissance England*, 116–41.

Shuger, Debora Kuller. "Faith and Assurance." In Kirby, *Companion to Richard Hooker*, 221–50.

Siemon, James R. *Shakespearean Iconoclasm*. Berkeley: University of California Press, 1985.

Sierhuis, Freya, and Brian Cummings, eds. "Fulke Greville and the Arts." Special issue, *Sidney Journal* 35, nos. 1–2 (2017).

Sierhuis, Freya. "Centaurs of the Mind: Imagination and Fiction-Making in the World of Fulke Greville." In Leo, Röder, and Sierhuis, *Fulke Greville and the Culture of the English Renaissance*, 99–118.

Simpson, James. *Burning to Read: English Fundamentalism and Its Reformation Opponents*. Cambridge, MA: Harvard University Press, 2007.

Simpson, James. *Under the Hammer: Iconoclasm in the Anglo-American Tradition*. Oxford: Oxford University Press, 2011.

Simpson, James. "Evangelical Absolutism: Breaking the Mind's Images in the English Reformation." Distinguished Fellow Lecture, Huntington Library, Pasadena, CA, March 17, 2014.

Smith, Nigel. *Literature and Revolution in England, 1640–1660*. New Haven: Yale University Press, 1994.

236 BIBLIOGRAPHY

Smith, Nowell, ed. *Life of Sir Philip Sidney*. By Fulke Greville. Oxford: Clarendon Press, 1907.

Spinks, Bryan D. *Two Faces of Elizabethan Anglican Theology: Sacraments and Salvation in the Thought of William Perkins and Richard Hooker*. Lanham, MD: Scarecrow Press, 1999.

Spufford, Margaret. *Contrasting Communities: English Villagers in the Sixteenth and Seventeenth Centuries*. Cambridge: Cambridge University Press, 1974.

Stachniewski, John. "John Donne: The Despair of the 'Holy Sonnets.'" *ELH* 48, no. 4 (1981): 677–705.

Stachniewski, John. *The Persecutory Imagination: English Puritanism and the Literature of Religious Despair*. Oxford: Clarendon Press, 1991.

Stachniewski, John and Anita Pacheco. Introduction to *Grace Abounding with Other Spiritual Autobiographies*, by John Bunyan, ix–xliii. Edited by John Stachniewski and Anita Pacheco. Oxford: Oxford University Press, 2008 [1998].

Stallybrass, Peter. "'Wee feaste in our Defense:' Patrician Carnival in Early Modern England and Robert Herrick's 'Hesperides.'" *English Literary Renaissance* 16, no. 1 (1986): 234–52.

Starkman, Miriam K. "*Noble Numbers* and the Poetry of Devotion." In *Reason and the Imagination: Studies in the History of Ideas 1600–1800*, edited by J. A. Mazzeo, 1–27. New York: Routledge and Kegan Paul, 1962.

Stewart, Susan. *Poetry and the Fate of the Senses*. Chicago: University of Chicago Press, 2002.

Strier, Richard. *Love Known: Theology and Experience in George Herbert's Poetry*. Chicago: University of Chicago Press, 1986.

Strier, Richard. "John Donne Awry and Squint: The 'Holy Sonnets,' 1608–10." *Modern Philology* 86, no. 4 (1989): 357–84.

Strier, Richard. "Donne and the Politics of Devotion." In *Religion, Literature, and Politics in Post-Reformation England, 1540–1688*, edited by Donna B. Hamilton and Richard Strier, 93–114. Cambridge: Cambridge University Press, 1996.

Strier, Richard. *The Unrepentant Renaissance: From Petrarch to Shakespeare to Milton*. Chicago: University of Chicago Press, 2011.

Strier, Richard. "Mind, Nature, Heterodoxy, and Iconoclasm in *The Winter's Tale*." *Religion and Literature* 47, no. 1 (2015): 31–60.

Stroup, Thomas B. *Religious Rite and Ceremony in Milton's Poetry*. Lexington, KY: University of Kentucky Press, 2015 [1968].

Stuermann, Walter E. *A Critical Study of Calvin's Concept of Faith*. Ann Arbor: Edwards Brothers, 1952.

Sullivan, Erin. "Doctrinal Doubleness and the Meaning of Despair in William Perkins's 'Table' and Nathaniel Woodes's *The Conflict of Conscience*." *Studies in Philology* 110, no. 3 (2013): 533–61.

Summers, Claude J. "Herrick's Political Poetry: The Strategies of His Art." In *"Trust to Good Verses": Herrick Tercentenary Essays*, edited by Roger B. Rollin and J. Max Patrick, 171–83. Pittsburgh: University of Pittsburgh Press, 1978.

Summers, Claude J. "Tears for Herrick's Church." In Coiro, Special issue on Robert Herrick, *George Herbert Journal*, 51–71.

Summers, Joseph H. *The Muse's Method: An Introduction to "Paradise Lost."* London: Chatto and Windus, 1962.

Summers, Joseph H. *The Heirs of Donne and Jonson*. New York: Oxford University Press, 1970.

BIBLIOGRAPHY 237

Swaim, Kathleen M. "The Morning Hymn of Praise in Book 5 of *Paradise Lost*." *Milton Quarterly* 22 (1988): 7–16.

Taaffe, James. "Michaelmas, the 'Lawless Hour,' and the Occasion of Milton's *Comus*." *English Language Notes* 6, no. 4 (1969): 257–62.

Targoff, Ramie. "The Performance of Prayer: Sincerity and Theatricality in Early Modern England." *Representations* 60 (1997): 49–69.

Targoff, Ramie. *Common Prayer: The Language of Public Devotion in Early Modern England*. Chicago: University of Chicago Press, 2001.

Targoff, Ramie. *John Donne: Body and Soul*. Chicago: University of Chicago Press, 2008.

Teskey, Gordon. *The Poetry of John Milton*. Cambridge, MA: Harvard University Press, 2015.

Turner, James Grantham. *One Flesh: Paradisal Marriage and Sexual Relations in the Age of Milton*. Oxford: Clarendon Press, 1987.

Turrell, James F. "Richard Hooker on Uniformity and Common Prayer." In Kirby, *Companion to Richard Hooker*, 337–66.

Tyacke, Nicholas. "Puritanism, Arminianism and Counter-Revolution." In *The Origins of the Civil War*, edited by Conrad Russell, 119–43. London: Palgrave Macmillan, 1978 [1973].

Tyacke, Nicholas. *Anti-Calvinists: The Rise of English Arminianism, c. 1590–1640*. Oxford: Oxford University Press, 1990 [1987].

Tyacke, Nicholas. "Anglican Attitudes: Some Recent Writings on English Religious History, from the Reformation to the Civil War." *Journal of British Studies* 35, no. 2 (1996): 139–67.

Vendler, Helen. *The Art of Shakespeare's Sonnets*. Cambridge, MA: Harvard University Press, 1997.

Voak, Nigel. *Richard Hooker and Reformed Theology: A Study of Reason, Will, and Grace*. Oxford: Oxford University Press, 2003.

Waldron, Jennifer. "Of Stones and Stony Hearts: Desdemona, Hermione, and Post-Reformation Theater." In *The Indistinct Human in Renaissance Literature*, edited by Jean E. Feerick and Vin Nardizzi, 205–27. New York: Palgrave Macmillan, 2012.

Waldron, Jennifer. *Reformations of the Body: Idolatry, Sacrifice, and Early Modern Theater*. New York: Palgrave Macmillan, 2013.

Walsham, Alexandra. "The Parochial Roots of Laudianism Revisited: Catholics, Anti-Calvinists and 'Parish Anglicans' in Early Stuart England." *Journal of Ecclesiastical History* 49, no. 4 (1998): 620–51.

Walsham, Alexandra. *Charitable Hatred: Tolerance and Intolerance in England, 1500–1700*. Manchester: Manchester University Press, 2006.

Walsham, Alexandra. *The Reformation of the Landscape: Religion, Identity, and Memory in Early Modern Britain and Ireland*. Oxford: Oxford University Press, 2011.

Waswo, Richard. *The Fatal Mirror: Themes and Techniques in the Poetry of Fulke Greville*. Charlottesville: University Press of Virginia, 1972.

Whalen, Robert. *The Poetry of Immanence: Sacrament in Donne and Herbert*. Toronto: University of Toronto Press, 2002.

Whitaker, Virgil. *Shakespeare's Use of Learning: An Inquiry into the Growth of His Mind and Art*. San Marino, CA: Huntington Library, 1953.

White, Helen C. *Tudor Books of Private Devotion*. Madison, WI: University of Wisconsin Press, 1951.

238 BIBLIOGRAPHY

White, Martin. "'When Torchlight Made an Artificial Noon': Lightness and Darkness in the Indoor Jacobean Theatre." In *The Oxford Companion to Shakespeare*, edited by Andrew Gurr and Farah Karim-Cooper, 115–36. Oxford: Oxford University Press, 2014.

White, Peter. "Revisionism Revised: Two Perspectives on Early Stuart Parliamentary History." *Past and Present* 92 (1981): 55–78.

White, Peter. "The Rise of Arminianism Reconsidered." *Past and Present* 110 (1983): 34–54.

White, Peter. *Predestination, Policy and Polemic*. Cambridge: Cambridge University Press, 1992.

Wilding, Michael. "Milton's 'A Masque Presented at Ludlow Castle, 1634': Theatre and Politics on the Border." *Milton Quarterly* 21, no. 4 (1987): 35–51.

Wilkes, G. A., ed. *The Complete Poems and Plays of Fulke Greville, Lorde Brooke (1554–1628)*. 2 vols. Lewiston, NY: Edwin Mellen, 2008.

Williamson, Elizabeth. "'Things Newly Performed': Tomb Properties and the Survival of the Dramatic Tradition." In *The Materiality of Religion in Early Modern English Drama*, 37–69. Farnham: Ashgate, 2009.

Winters, Yvor. *Forms of Discovery: Critical and Historical Essays on the Forms of the Short Poem in English*. Chicago: Alan Swallow, 1967.

Woodcock, Matthew. "'The World is Made for Use': Theme and Form in Fulke Greville's Verse Treatises." *Sidney Journal* 19, nos. 1–2 (2001): 143–60.

Woodward, Daniel H. "Herrick's Oberon Poems." *Journal of English and Germanic Philology* 64, no. 2 (1965): 279–84.

Young, R. V. *Doctrine and Devotion in Seventeenth-Century Poetry: Studies in Donne, Herbert, Crashaw, and Vaughan*. Woodbridge: Boydell and Brewer, 2000.

Zysk, Jay. *Shadows and Substance: Eucharistic Controversy and English Drama across the Reformation Divide*. Notre Dame, IN: University of Notre Dame Press, 2017.

Index

actors
  in Donne 144
  in Greville 167–8, 177
  in Herrick 98–100, 103, 105, 107–9, 110–16
  in Shakespeare's *Sonnets* 52, 53, 107, 144
Adam and Eve
  and Edenic prayer 13
  in Greville's *Caelica* 168, 170, 173, 177
  in Milton's *Paradise Lost* 13, 193, 195, 197–8,
    201–3, 206, 208–12, 216
  prayers of 193, 195, 197–8, 201–3, 206, 211
adiaphora 39, 59, 90, 146, 185
altars 202
amens
  in Herrick 93
  in Perkins 39–40
  in Shakespeare's *Sonnets* 59, 61, 62, 74, 78, 93
Andrewes, Lancelot 125
angels
  in Donne 128, 137–8, 144
  in Milton 190, 194, 195, 202, 204, 205–6, 207,
    213–14, 215, 216
Anglicanism. *See also* Laudianism
  definitions of 23–6
  and Donne 125
  and Herrick 81, 87, 103
  and Hooker 20, 21, 23
  and puritanism 23–4, 25–6
  and Shakespeare's *Sonnets* 48
Aquinas, Thomas 15, 16
Aristotle 15–16, 17
Arminianism 87
Ascension Day 145–8
assurance. *See* certitude
Aston, Margaret 123
atheism 171
audiences
  in Greville 167, 178
  in Herrick 98, 110
  in Shakespeare's *Sonnets* 63, 68, 69, 71, 72
Augustine 15, 140
Augustinianism. *See* Augustine

baptism. *See* sacrament(s)
Barish, Jonas 54, 98
Bates, Catherine 180–1

Baynes, Paul 25
beads (of the rosary) 81, 92, 93
Benedict, Philip 28
bible, the
  and biblical history 168, 188
  and Donne 135, 145, 151, 155
  and Greville 168
  King James Version of 88, 194
  and Milton 188, 192, 193–4, 196–8, 215
  ownership of 48
  rewriting of 215
  sales of 48
  and Shakespeare 2, 48, 78
  in Tyndale 78
  Old Testament
    Deuteronomy 12:30 145
    Psalms 185, 192, 193–4, 196, 197
    Psalm 140 196
    Psalm 141 196
    Psalm 148 198
    Ezekiel 16:17 135
    Habakkuk 2:11 2
  Apocrypha
    Ecclesiasticus 39 196
  New Testament
    Matthew 5:8 155
    Matthew 6:6–7 48, 78
    Matthew 7:8–9 78
    Matthew 17:20 151
    Matthew 18 196
    Luke 19:40 2
    Romans 8:26 142
birds
  in Donne 153
  in Hall 93–4
  in Herrick 92–4
  in Milton 194, 201
blasphemy 62, 64–5, 151
blazon 63
blood 116, 129–30, 133, 168, 173, 205. *See also*
    Christ, blood of
bodily gestures. *See* gestures
body, the
  in Calvin 140
  of Christ 33–6, 133
  in the Communion 33

240 INDEX

body, the (*Continued*)
  in Donne 30, 126–7, 128, 133
  in Greville 159, 162, 163, 164–5, 166, 167,
    172, 173, 174, 182, 183
  in Hall 89–90
  in Milton 204, 205, 206, 218
  in Perkins 35
  in prayer 26, 31
  as proof 32
  and readers 76–7
  in Reformation culture 18
  and the senses 18
  in Sidney 180
  in worship 19, 32
Book of Common Prayer
  on ceremony 12
  on the Communion 3, 5–6
  and Donne 134, 138, 142, 155
  on gazers and lookers-on 3, 69
  and Hall 90
  and Herrick 81, 92–3
  and Jewel 134, 155
  and Milton 186, 189–90, 192, 193–5, 196–7
  on sacraments 3
  and Shakespeare's *Sonnets* 12, 48, 54, 60,
    61–2, 64, 67, 68–70, 73–4
books vi, 53, 55, 57
Booth, Stephen 48, 58, 64, 75, 78
bowing. *See* genuflection
Brathwait, Richard 96
Bucer, Martin 32
Bullinger, Heinrich 199–200

Caesar, Julius 189
Cain, Tom 83–4
Calvin, John
  on Augustine 140
  on bodily gestures 31
  on the body 140
  and cartography 20
  on Christ 35–6
  cosmology of 20
  and Donne 123, 131–2, 155
  on experience 9
  and experimental predestinarianism 9
  on grace 140
  and iconoclasm 123
  on knowledge 20–1
  on mental images 123
  and Milton 205
  and performed worship 31
  on proof 32, 41
  on the sacraments 140
  on salvation 35

  and science 20
  on signs 32, 104
  work:
    Institutio 7–8, 9, 20, 26, 35–6, 123, 131–2
Calvinism
  and anxiety 17, 22, 170
  and certitude 4, 41
  and confusion 17
  and Donne 126–7, 131–2, 154–5
  and the English tradition 9, 17, 25, 36
  as epistemology 4, 8, 11, 26, 32–3, 41
  and experientialism. *See* Calvinist
    experientialism
  and Greville 159–61, 163, 170, 172
  and Milton 206
  and popular divinity 10, 13, 24, 25
  and predestination 9–10
  and the senses 17
Calvinist experientialism
  in the Church of England 10, 13, 25, 30
  in Cranmer 30
  in Donne 31, 154–5
  in Greville 159, 163, 172
  in Herrick 88
  in Hooker 30
  in Jewel 30
  as knowledge 21, 41
  and Milton 203
  in Perkins 4, 9–10, 11, 20, 23, 25, 30
  in popular divinity 10, 13, 24, 25
  as the Real Presence 5, 14
  in Shakespeare's *The Winter's Tale* 13–14, 15
Cambridge University 85, 88, 96, 97
Candlemas 95–7, 115, 155–6
Caroline church 21, 31, 48, 68, 81–6, 101–2, 185
cartography 20
Catholicism
  and Catholic recusancy 24, 125, 132
  and Catholic residualism 7, 15–19, 31, 38–9,
    125, 155
  and ceremony 97
  and Donne 121–2, 125, 132, 153, 155
  and Herrick 81, 91, 97
  and the liturgy 15–19, 30, 65, 81
  and the Real Presence 5, 6, 14
  and the sacraments 15–19
  and Shakespeare 65
Catullus 104–5
ceremony
  in Catholicism 97
  in the Church of England 23
  in Cranmer 11–12
  in Donne 31
  in Hall 116–17

INDEX 241

in Herrick 91, 95, 97, 115, 117–18
and idolatry 39
in Jewel 11–12
in Perkins 41
private ceremony 91, 95, 97, 115
and puritanism 81–2
in Shakespeare's *Sonnets* 11–12
as signs 41
certitude
and Calvinism 4, 41
and Donne 151–2
and experience 5
and Perkins 152
and Shakespeare's *The Winter's Tale* 8, 42
Charles I
and Christ 187, 189
and Herrick 82, 102
image of 186–7, 189, 208
and Laud 185
and Milton 13, 184–91, 192, 203, 208
prayers of 184–5, 186, 192
work:
Eikon Basilike 184–5, 186–7, 192
Chatterton, Laurence 88
Christ
blood of 116, 129–30, 133
body of 33–6, 133
in Calvin 35–6
in the Communion 33–6
copulation with 34–5
in Donne 12, 132–5
in Herrick 86, 107, 110–16
in Hooker 36
images of 132–5, 153
incarnation of 35
Passion of. *See* Passion, the
Real Presence of 33–4
and relationship with believers 7
and sermon on Mount of Olives 2
in Shakespeare's *Sonnets* 48, 64–5, 70, 72, 74, 78
Christmas 95–7, 99, 115, 144, 195, 197
Church of England
ceremony in 23
ecclesiology of 24, 25
and experientialism 10, 13, 25, 30
images in 127
liturgy in 24
official worship in 4–5, 13, 15, 16–17
ritual in 19
sacraments in 24
and Shakespeare's *The Winter's Tale* 11
Cicero 111
Civil War. *See* English Civil War

Cokayne, William 143
Collinson, Patrick 49
Communion (sacrament). *See also* sacrament(s)
and the body 33
in the *Book of Common Prayer* 3, 5–6
in the Catholic tradition 16
and Christ 33–6
in Cranmer 6, 10, 14, 33–4
in Donne 120, 144–5
and eating 34
and gazers and lookers-on 3, 4, 5–6
in Hall 116
in Herrick 84, 87, 98, 116
in Hooker 33
in Jewel 3, 5–6, 10, 14
in Milton 196, 205–6
in Perkins 35, 42
and the Real Presence 33–4
in Shakespeare's *Sonnets* 67–8, 69, 70, 73–4, 84
confessional identity. *See* religious identity
confusion
in Calvinism 17
in devotion 12, 126, 150
in Donne 12, 126–7, 150
and the senses 1, 15
in Shakespeare's *The Winter's Tale* 1, 15
Connecticut Colony 25
Connolly, Ruth 83–4
copulation 34–5. *See also* sex
Cormack, Bradin 174
corpus mysticum 16
cosmology 20
Cotton, John 25
court, the (Elizabethan and Jacobean) 162, 175
Cranmer, Thomas
on the Communion 6, 10, 14, 33–4
and Donne 155
ecclesiology of 18
and experientialism 30
on the Real Presence 33–4
on the senses 14
and Shakespeare's *Sonnets* 11, 48, 60, 73–4, 75, 80, 98
and Shakespeare's *The Winter's Tale* 14
Crashaw, Richard 114, 147
Creaser, John 83–4, 196
Creation, the 213–15
Cross, the 111–15, 153–4, 156–7. *See also* Passion, the
Crucifixion, the. *See* Passion, the
crypto-Catholicism. *See* Catholicism, and Catholic recusancy
Culler, Jonathan 50

242 INDEX

Culverwell, Ezekiel 142, 143
Cummings, Brian 26, 32, 149, 160, 162–3
Cupid 13, 161, 164–5, 167–8, 175

damnation 9–10, 132, 150
Daniel, Samuel 63
David (biblical king) 192
death
  in Donne 128–9, 137
  in Milton 203, 208–9, 212, 216
demons 189–90
despair
  in Donne 128, 149
  in Greville 172, 181–2
devil, the. See Satan
devotion
  and confusion 12, 126, 150
  and eating 5, 13, 205–6
  and impropriety 2
  in medieval culture 18
  as plagiarism 13, 184, 192–3
  and sex 13, 203, 205
devotional access
  to God 41–2, 43, 65 n.56, 109–10, 127, 157,
    163, 165, 167, 172, 202–3, 206–7
  in Greville 65 n.56, 163, 165, 167, 172
  in Herrick 109–10
  in Milton 202–3, 206–7
  in Perkins 157
  in Shakespeare's Sonnets 51, 71
devotional aids
  in Donne 31
  eating as 13
  in Milton 202, 203, 205, 210
  sex as 13, 203, 205
devotional manuals
  of Bullinger 199–201
  of Gouge 10, 200
  of Hall vi, 10, 93–5, 153, 202
  of Hieron 10, 199–201
  and Milton 199–200
  of Perkins 10, 28, 30, 200
D'Ewes, Simon 87, 88, 101
digestion. See eating
Diotima 136. See also Plato
DiPasquale, Theresa 25, 139, 154, 155
disobedience 203, 208–9, 210, 216
Donne, Anne. See More, Anne
Donne, John
  actors in 144
  angels in 128, 137–8, 144
  and Anglicanism 125
  and Ascension Day 145–8
  and the baptism 139

and the bible 135, 145, 151, 155
birds in 153
blasphemy in 151
blood in 129–30, 133
and the body 30, 126–7, 128, 133
and the *Book of Common Prayer* 134, 138,
  142, 155
and Calvin 123, 131–2, 155
and Calvinism 126–7, 131–2, 154–5
on Candlemas 155–6
and Catholicism 121–2, 125, 153
and Catholic recusancy 125, 132
and Catholic residualism 125, 155
on ceremony 31
on certitude 151–2
on Christ 12, 132–5, 133–4
on Christmas 144
and Cokayne 143–4
on the Communion 120, 144–5
and Cranmer 155
and Crashaw 147
on the Cross 153–4, 156–7. See also Donne,
  John, on the Passion
Crucifixion, the. See also Donne, John, on the
  Passion
on damnation 132, 150
on death 128–9, 137
on despair 128, 149
on the devil 138
on devotional aids 31
and devotional confusion 12, 126–7, 150
and Easter 139, 154
on election 130–2, 149, 152, 173
and epistemology 132, 147, 150
and experientialism 31, 154–5
on externals in worship 31
eyes in 128, 141, 143, 144, 154
on the flesh 137–8
on genuflection 141
on gesture 144
on God 121–2, 127, 128, 137, 138, 153
on grace 126, 128–9, 131–2, 139–40, 151
and Greville 164, 171, 173
grief in 141–2, 147, 151
and Hall 153–4
Hell in 150
and Herbert 147
and Herrick 115
and Hooker 146, 148, 155
and iconoclasm 123–4, 127, 146, 157–8
idolatry in 121–2, 133–7, 141–2, 145–9, 151,
  153, 155–7
and idols 123, 127, 135–6, 145–6
on images 12, 121–4, 127, 128, 131–5, 153–4

INDEX 243

and inwardness 152
and Jewel 122–3, 134, 155
on Judgment Day. *See* Donne, John, on the
  Resurrection
and Laud 125
and Laudianism 125, 153
marriage of 137–41
on memory 144
on mistresses 12, 133, 134, 137
and Anne More 12, 137–9, 140
and occasional meditation 154. *See also*
  Donne, John, and Hall
on the Passion 129–30, 132, 133–4, 144,
  153–4, 156–7
and Perkins 12, 124, 126, 145, 151–4,
  156–7
on pictures. *See* Donne, John, on images
on plays. *See* Donne, John, and the theater
on prayer 144
on proof 132
and puritanism 139, 155
on reading 149, 154
and religious identity 125, 149–50
repentance in 129–30, 141, 148
on the Resurrection 128, 131
on ritual 31
on the sacraments 139–40
on salvation 128–30, 144, 151
on the senses 30, 127
on the serpent 153
sighs in 141–3, 145, 148, 149, 151–2
and sign-hunting 132
on signs 128–9, 132, 133, 139–40, 149,
  150–1
sin in 141, 145, 147–8
on the soul 128–9, 137, 150–1
and St. Paul's Cross (cathedral) 30, 121, 135
suicide in 128
tears in 141, 143, 145, 148, 149
and the theater 138
works:
"The Crosse" 153–4, 156–7
Devotions upon Emergent Occasions 122, 158
  n.98
Holy Sonnets
  Holy Sonnet 3 ("O might those sighes and
    teares") 141, 145, 147–9
  Holy Sonnet 6 ("This is my Playes last
    scene") 138
  Holy Sonnet 8 ("At the round Earths
    Imagin'd corners") 128–30, 145
  Holy Sonnet 10 ("Yf faithfull Soules be alike
    glorify'd") 150–1, 152
  Holy Sonnet 15 ("What yf this
    present") 132–7, 141, 149

Holy Sonnet 17 ("Since She whome I
  lovd") 137–41
Holy Sonnet 18 ("Show me deare
  Christ") 173
A Litanie 142–3, 145
sermons 30–1, 121, 125, 133–4, 143–4
Duffy, Eamon 38, 68

early church, the 188
Easter 139, 154
eating
  in the Communion 34
  as devotional aid 13
  in Milton's *Paradise Lost* 13, 205–6, 215
  in Shakespeare's *The Winter's Tale* 5
Eden. *See* Paradise
election
  in Donne 130–2, 149, 152, 173
  in Greville 166, 173
  in Perkins 152
Elizabethan church 85, 86, 106, 134
English Calvinism. *See* Calvinism, and the
  English tradition
English Civil War 16, 28, 83, 188
epistemology. *See also* knowledge; proof
  and bodily experience 5
  and Calvinism 4, 8, 11, 26, 32–3, 41
  in Donne 132, 147, 150
  in Perkins 23
  prayer as 40
  and sexual desire 5, 8
  and signs 43
Eppley, Daniel 24
Erasmus, Desiderius 35
Eucharist. *See* Communion (sacrament)
evidence. *See* proof
experience
  and the body 5, 18
  in Calvin 9–10
  and certitude 5
  and cognition 34
  in Greville 163, 166, 176–8, 179, 182
  and individual experience in prayer 37
  and sexual longing 5
experientia 9. *See also* experience
experientialism. *See* Calvinist experientialism
experimentum 9. *See also* experience
experiri 9. *See also* experience
externals in worship
  in Donne 31
  in Hooker 37
  interpretive value of 31, 56
  in Laud 185
  in Milton 190, 192
  in Shakespeare's *Sonnets* 56–7

244 INDEX

eyes
   in Donne 128, 141, 143, 144, 154
   in Greville 173
   and Herrick 96, 111
   in Milton 203, 211
   in Shakespeare's *Sonnets* 53–4, 57, 76, 77, 79

fairies 97–8
Fall, the
   in Greville's *Caelica* 163, 168–70, 172, 182
   in Milton's *Paradise Lost* 13, 201–2, 203–4,
      208–9, 217
Field, John 54–5, 98–9, 101
Filo, Gina 161
Fisch, Harold 94
flesh, the
   in Donne 137–8
   in Greville 165, 168, 172–3, 175, 181–2
   in Milton 208–9
flesh-hooks 96–7
Flood, the 190
Freedberg, David 146

Galenic humoral theory 15–16
gazers and lookers-on
   in the *Book of Common Prayer* 3
   in the Communion 3, 4
   in Jewel 3
   in Shakespeare's *Sonnets* 66–8, 69
   in Shakespeare's *The Winter's Tale* 2, 3–4, 6,
      14, 31
genealogies 188, 189, 213
genuflection
   in Donne 141
   in Hall 89–90
   in Herrick 87, 89–90, 101
   in Milton 186
gestures
   in Calvin 31
   in Donne 144
   in Greville 174
   in Hall 89–90
   in Herrick 84, 89–90, 98
   in Milton 192
   in prayer 26, 42, 142
   in Shakespeare's *Sonnets* 47, 55, 63, 64, 66, 72
girlfriends. *See* mistresses
glossolalia 59, 60–1
God. *See also* Christ
   access to 41–2, 43, 65 n.56, 109–10, 127, 153,
      157, 163, 165, 167, 172, 202–3, 206–7
   appearance of 202–3
   as audience 178
   chastisement of 137

   in Donne 121–2, 127, 128, 137, 138, 153
   in Greville 65 n.56, 161, 163, 165–8, 172, 178
   in Herrick 107–10
   idea of 165
   images of 121–2, 128, 132–5, 153, 165–6
   jealousy of 138
   looking at 121, 164, 165, 167
   as love object 161
   in Milton 202–3, 206–7, 210–11, 214–15
   perfection of 168
   in Sidney 180
Good Friday 110–12
Goodwin, Thomas 132
Gosson, Stephen 101, 115
Gouge, William 10, 200
grace. *See also* salvation
   in Calvin 140
   and damnation 9–10
   in Donne 128–9, 131–2, 139–40, 151
   in Greville 170, 171, 182
   in Hall 116
   in Hooker 37–9
   in Perkins 157
   in Shakespeare's *Sonnets* 71
Greeks, the 187–8
Greenblatt, Stephen 18, 33, 74
Greene, Thomas M. 67, 68
Greville, Fulke
   and actors 167–8, 177
   Adam and Eve in 168, 170, 173, 177
   and audiences 167, 178
   and the bible 168
   blood in 168, 173
   on the body 159, 162, 163, 164–5, 166, 167,
      172, 173, 174, 182, 183
   Caelica in. *See* Greville, Fulke, girlfriends in
   and Calvinism 159–61
      and anxiety 170
      and experientialism 159, 163, 172
      and predestinarianism 170
   and the court (Elizabethan and
      Jacobean) 162, 175
   Cupid in 13, 161, 164–5, 167–8, 175
   Cynthia in. *See* Greville, Fulke, girlfriends in
   on despair 172, 181–2
   and Donne 164, 171, 173
   Eden in. *See* Greville, Fulke, Paradise in
   on election 166, 173
   and erotic paralysis 164
   on evidence. *See* Greville, Fulke, on proof
   on experience 163, 166, 176–8, 179, 182
   eyes in 173
   on the Fall 163, 168–70, 172, 182
   on the flesh 165, 168, 172–3, 175, 181–2

gestures in 174
girlfriends in 161, 164, 167, 173–4
and God
  access to 65 n.56, 163, 165, 167, 172
  as audience 178
  idea of 165
  image of 165–6
  looking at 164, 165, 167
  as love object 161, 165
  perfection of 168
on grace 170, 171, 182
Hell in 169
and homoeroticism 161, 175–6
iconoclasm of 13, 174, 175, 181
ideas (abstractions) in 165
on idolatry 165, 166, 171
idols in 175, 183
on images 176–7, 181, 182
immaterialism in 173–4
on imputation 138
on knowledge 172, 177
looking in 164, 165, 167, 168, 172–3, 174
lust in 168
materialism in 174, 179
on mental images 13. See also Greville, Fulke
  on images
and Milton 163, 182, 184
and Montaigne 162
Myra in. See Greville, Fulke, girlfriends in
Nature in 169, 175, 179
pages (of book) in 174
Paradise in 13, 163–4, 168–70, 172, 181, 183
and Perkins 159, 165–6, 170–1, 173
and Plato's Symposium 165.
pleasure in 169, 172, 179–80
on poetry 176–9, 182
on proof 163, 166, 172
on reading 177–8
on repentance 171–2
Satan in 168, 170
senses in 174
on the serpent 168. See also Greville, Fulke,
  Satan in
and Shakespeare's Sonnets 63, 161, 163
and Sidney 13, 162–4, 176–83, 184
  and Arcadia 178–9, 181, 184
  and Astrophil and Stella 163
  and Certain Sonets 179–80
  and Denfense of Poesy 163, 175
sin in 168–9, 170, 171
and the soul 170
and stage fright 167
and theater 167, 177
tree (of knowledge) in 170

"unnatural" vice in 169–70
and women 174–5
works:
Alaham 177
Caelica 12, 63
  dating of 162
  divine poems of 161
  erotic poems of 159, 161–2
  poems in:
  poem 10 165
  poem 16 165
  poem 22 174
  poem 56 164, 167
  poem 62 175
  poem 63 175
  poem 64 173
  poem 83 170, 172
  poem 86 181–2
  poem 98 171
  poem 102 168–9, 170, 174–5
The Life of the Renowned Sᵣ Philip Sidney 162,
  176–8, 181
Mustapha 177
grief 141–2, 147, 151
Guibbory, Achsah 82, 95, 102, 204
Gunn, Thom 182

Haigh, Christopher 38
Halkett, John 204
Hall, Joseph
  and adiaphora 90
  birds in 93–4
  and the body 89–90
  and the Book of Common Prayer 90
  and books vi
  on ceremony 116–17
  on the Communion 116
  devotional manuals of vi, 10, 93–5, 153, 202
  and Donne 153–4
  and genuflection 89–90
  and gestures 89–90
  on grace 116
  and Herrick 12, 85–6, 88–9, 92, 93–5, 97, 105,
    116–17
  and inwardness 205
  and Milton 202, 205–6
  popular divinity of 12, 17, 116
  on prayer 90–1
  and puritanism 117
  works:
  The Arte of Diuine Meditation 89, 95
  Meditations and Vowes 105
  Occasional Meditations vi, 93–5, 153

246 INDEX

Harris, Robert 55–6, 57
Harvey, Christopher 62
Hassel, R. Chris 196
Heaven 194, 195, 202, 213, 214–15
Heinemann, Margot 102
Hell 150, 169, 215
Herbert, George 62, 147
Herrick, Joan 87
Herrick, Robert
  and actors 98–100, 103, 105, 107–9, 110–16
  and amen 93
  and anachronisms 12, 83, 87, 106
  and Anglicanism 81, 87, 103
  and antitheatricalism 98–103, 109
  and Arminianism 87, 126
  and audiences 98, 110
  and beads 81, 92, 93
  birds in 92–4
  and the *Book of Common Prayer* 81, 92–3
  and bowing. *See* Herrick, Robert, and
    genuflection
  and Richard Brathwait 96
  and Calvinist experientialism 88
  and Cambridge University 85, 88, 96, 97
  Candlemas in 95–7, 115
  and Caroline church 81–6, 101–2
  and Catholicism 81, 91, 97
  and Catullus 104–5
  and Charles I 82, 102
  and Laurence Chatterton 88
  and Christ 86, 107, 110–16
  Christmas in 95–7, 99, 115
  and Cicero 111
  and the Communion 84, 87, 98, 116
  and Crashaw 114
  on the Cross 111–15. *See also* Herrick,
    Robert, and the Passion
  and the Crucifixion. *See* Herrick, Robert, and
    the Passion
  and Simon D'Ewes 87, 88, 101
  and Donne 115
  and the Elizabethan church 85, 86
  and eyes 96, 111
  fairies in 97–8
  and John Field 98–9, 101
  and flesh-hooks 96–7
  and genuflection 87, 89–90, 101
  and gestures 84, 89–90, 98
  God in 107–10
  and Good Friday 110–12
  and Gosson 101, 115
  and Hall 12, 85–6, 88–9, 92, 93–5, 97, 105,
    116–17
  and Joan Herrick 87

  and William Herrick 87
  and Hooker 103, 116
  and idolatry 87, 98, 101
  idols in 98, 101
  and Jonson 105
  and the *King James Bible* 88
  and kneeling. *See* Herrick, Robert, and
    genuflection
  and Laud 81, 84, 97, 106
  and Laudianism 81–6, 91, 103
  and Laudian-Puritan controversy 83, 97, 103
  and Milton 202
  and Munday 101
  occasional meditation in 92, 93, 95, 97. *See
    also* Herrick, Robert, and Hall
  and Parliament 104
  and the Passion 99, 110–15
  and performance 86
  and Perkins 85, 86, 103, 116
  and players. *See* Herrick, Robert, and actors
  and priests 98–100
  and private ceremony 91, 95, 97, 115, 117–18
  and Prynne 95–6, 99–103, 108–9, 111, 115
  and puritanism 81–2, 87, 96, 101, 104
  and reading 115–16
  and redating of poems 12, 83–4
  and royalism 12, 102
  and sex 81, 91, 105
  and Shakespeare's *Sonnets* 115–16
  and Stubbes 98, 101
  and the theater 98–105, 107–16
  and Thomas Wilcox 98–9, 101
works:
Hesperides
  "The Argument of his Book" (H1) 94
  "The Rosarie" (H45) 91
  "To Anthea" (H74) 104–5
  "Corinna's going a-Maying" (H178) 91–2,
    94, 103
  "To the Lark" (H214) 92–3, 94
  "The Fairie Temple: or, Oberons Chappell"
    (H223) 97–8, 100, 103
  "Upon himself" (H285) 118
  "The Wake" (H761) 103–4, 110
  "Ceremonies for Christmasse" (H784) 95,
    96, 99
  "Christmasse-Eve, another Ceremonie"
    (H785) 95, 96, 99
  "Ceremonies for Candlemasse Eve"
    (H892) 95
  "Ceremonies for Candlemasse Day"
    (H893) 95
  "Upon Candlemasse day" (H894) 95

INDEX   247

"Ceremony Upon Candlemasse Eve"
 (H980) 95
"Upon Trap" (H1076) 99–100, 102, 103,
 108
"To Julia" (H1595) 81, 91
His Noble Numbers
 "God not to be comprehended"
  (N1138) 110
 "Affliction" (N1140) 107
 "Prayers must have Poise" (N1146) 117
 "God has a twofold part" (N1152) 108
 "Lip-labour" (N1164) 117
 "The Heart" (N1165) 117
 "Gods mirth, Mans mourning"
  (N1193) 108
 "Prayer" (N1288) 117
 "To God" (N1362) 107
 "God sparing in scourging" (N1372) 107
 "Good Friday: Rex Tragicus, or Christ
  going to His Crosse" (N1393) 110–12
 Untitled shape poem (N1398) 112–15,
  117–18
Herrick, William 87
Hieron, Samuel 10, 61–2, 63, 191, 199, 200–1
High Church Anglicanism 21–2, 81–6, 125. *See
 also* Anglicanism; Laudianism
homoeroticism 161, 175–6
Hooker, Richard
 adiaphora in 146
 and Anglicanism 20, 21
 authority of 21–2
 and the *Book of Common Prayer* 36–7, 48
 and Calvinism 21, 32–3
 on Christ 36
 on the Communion 33
 and conformity 17, 20, 21
 and Donne 146, 148, 155
 ecclesiology of 18
 and experientialism 30
 on externals in worship 37
 on grace 37–9, 71
 and Herrick 103, 116
 and Laudianism 21–2
 on the liturgy 37, 78–9
 and medieval piety 18
 and Milton 191, 217
 print history of 28
 and Prynne 22
 on the Real Presence 33–4
 on sacraments 37
 on salvation 37–8
 on set prayer 36–7
 and Shakespeare's *Sonnets* 48, 50, 65, 71, 78–9
 on signs 38–9

work:
 Lawes of Ecclesiastical Polity 11, 21, 48, 50,
  65, 71
Hooker, Thomas 25
Hunter, William B. 196
hypocrisy 11, 48, 55, 58, 61, 62

iconoclasm
 in Calvin 123
 in Donne 123–4, 127, 146, 157–8
 in Greville 13, 174, 175, 181
 of images 13, 19
 in Milton 188, 192–3, 197, 203, 216–17
 in Shakespeare's *Sonnets* 65, 75
iconoclasts 75, 187–9
icons. *See* idols; iconoclasm
idolatry
 and ceremony 39
 in Donne 121–2, 133–7, 141–2, 145–9, 151,
  153, 155–7
 in Greville 165, 166, 171
 in Herrick 87, 98, 101
 and idol worship 3, 19, 20
 in Jewel 134
 in Milton 185, 188, 189–90, 207–8, 213, 217
 in Perkins 124
 in Shakespeare's *Sonnets* 48, 64–5, 66, 101
idols
 in Donne 123, 127, 135–6, 145–6
 in Greville 175, 183
 in Herrick 98, 101
 in Milton 190
 in Perkins 41, 124, 157
 in Shakespeare's *Sonnets* 64, 66, 75
idol worship. *See* idolatry
Ignatius 149
images
 in the Church of England 127
 in Donne 12, 121–4, 127, 128, 131–5, 153–4
 of God 121–2, 128, 132–5, 153, 166
 in Greville 13, 176–7, 181, 182
 iconoclasm of 13, 19
 mental images 13, 122–4, 128, 155–6, 166
 in Milton 184, 186–7, 188, 189, 216
 in Perkins 124, 156, 165–6
 in Shakespeare's *Sonnets* 136
immaterialism 173–4
immortality (poetic) 75–6, 79
imputation 138
incarnation. *See* Christ, incarnation of
insincerity. *See* hypocrisy
Interregnum, the 28, 209

248 INDEX

inwardness
in Donne 152
in Hall 205
in Laud 185
in Milton 209, 217
in Perkins 157
in Shakespeare's *Sonnets* 54, 57, 71

Jacobean church 106, 126, 134, 149
James I 188
Jensen, Phebe 6
Jesus. *See* Christ
Jewel, John
and the *Book of Common Prayer* 134, 155
on the Communion 3, 5–6, 10, 14
and Donne 122–3, 134, 155
and experientialism 30
on gazers and lookers-on 3
on idolatry 134
on mental images 122–3, 155
and Shakespeare's *Sonnets* 11, 60, 69
and Shakespeare's *The Winter's Tale* 3–4, 14
Johnson, Kimberly 25, 126–7, 133
Johnson, Samuel 215
Jonson, Ben 105
Judgment Day. *See* Resurrection (Judgment Day)

Kendall, R. T. 9, 25
Kerrigan, John 64
King James Bible. See bible, the
Knapp, Jeffrey 25, 101
kneeling. *See* genuflection
knowledge. *See also* epistemology; proof
axiomatic knowledge 43
Calvinist experientialism as 21, 43–4
in Greville 172, 177
in Milton 214
science as 20, 43
Koener, Joseph 189
Kuchar, Gary 149

Lake, Peter 23–4
Latin 59
Laud, William. *See also* Laudianism
adiaphora in 185
ceremonialism of 31
and Charles I 185
and Donne 125
execution of 185
on externals 185
and Herrick 81, 84, 97, 106
and Hooker 22
and inwardness 185
and Milton 185

and puritanism 185
on uniformity 185, 186
Laudianism. *See also* Laud, William
and Donne 125, 153
and Herrick 81–6, 91, 103
and Hooker 21–2
Laudian-Puritan controversy 83, 97, 103
Leo, Russ 160
Lewalski, Barbara Kiefer 25, 136, 197–8
Lewis, C. S. 74, 77
Linaker, Robert 55–6, 57, 142, 143
liturgy
in the Catholic tradition 15–19, 30, 65, 81
in the Church of England 24. *See also Book of Common Prayer*
in Hooker 37
in Milton 13, 185–6, 191–3, 193–6, 197, 216, 217–18
public liturgy 5
in the Reformed tradition 10, 30, 39
in Shakespeare's *Sonnets* 54. *See also Book of Common Prayer*, Shakespeare's *Sonnets*
Loewenstein, David 188
lookers-on. *See* gazers and lookers-on
looking 121, 164, 165, 167, 168, 172–3, 174. *See also* gazers and lookers-on
Lupton, Julia Reinhard 6–7
lust 168
lyric, purposes of 50

magic 5, 7, 65 n.57
Maltby, Judith 48
Marcus, Leah S. 82, 102, 112, 196
Marlowe, Christopher 20
marriage
in the Church of England 139
of Donne 137–41
as idolatry 139
in Perkins 42–3
in Reformation culture 42, 199–201
as sacrament 42
as sign 42
Martin, Catherine Gimeli 141
Mass (Catholic) 59, 68, 191
Massachusetts Bay Colony 25, 143
materialism 174, 179
matrimony. *See* marriage
McCabe, Richard 93, 116
McCoy, Richard 52

INDEX 249

medieval culture
  devotion in 18
  performance in 18
  senses in 15–17
memory
  in Donne 144
  in Milton 198, 202, 213, 215
  in Perkins 124
  in Shakespeare's *Sonnets* 76
mental images. *See* images
Michael (archangel) 190, 202
Michaelmas 196–7
Milner, Matthew 15–18, 21, 22, 37, 40
Milton, John
  Adam and Eve in 13
    disobedience of 203, 208–9, 210, 216
    prayers of 193, 195, 197–8, 201–3, 206, 211
    and reason 209–10, 212
    sex between. *See* Milton, John, on sex
  altars in 202
  angels in 190, 194, 195, 202, 204, 205–6, 207,
      213–14, 215, 216
  and the bible
    biblical history 188
    King James Version of 194
    rewriting of 215
    chapters of:
    Matthew 18 196
    Psalms 185, 192, 193–4, 196, 197
    Psalm 140 196
    Psalm 141 196
    Psalm 148 198
    Ecclesiasticus 39 196
  birds in 194, 201
  blood in 205
  on the body 204, 205, 206, 218
  and the *Book of Common Prayer* 186, 189–90,
      192, 193–5, 196–7
  and Bullinger 199–200
  on Caesar 189
  and Calvin 205
  and Calvinism 206
  and Calvinist experientialism 203
  on Charles I 13, 184–91, 192, 203
    and Christ 187, 189
    image of 186–7, 189, 208
    prayers of 184–5, 186, 192
    work:
    Eikon Basilike 184–5, 186–7, 192
  Christmas in 195, 197
  on the Communion 196, 205–6
  on the Creation 213–15
  on David 192
  death in 203, 208–9, 212, 216

demons in 189–90
on devotional aids 202, 203, 205, 210
and devotional manuals 199–200
on devotional plagiarism 13, 184, 192–3
on the early church 188
on eating and digestion 13, 205–6, 215
and the English Civil War 188
eyes in 203, 211
on the Fall 13, 201–2, 203–4, 208–9, 217
on the flesh 208–9
on the Flood 190
genealogies in 188, 189, 213
and genuflection 186
on gestures 192
on God
  access to 202–3, 206–7
  appearance of 202–3
  on the Creation 214–15
  on prayer 210–11
and Gouge 200
on the Greeks 187–8
and Greville 163, 182, 184
and Hall 202, 205–6
Heaven in 194, 195, 202, 213, 214–15
Hell in 215
and Herrick 202
and Hieron 191, 199, 200–2
and Hooker 191, 217
iconoclasm of 188, 192–3, 197, 203, 216–17
on idolatry 185, 188, 189–90, 207–8, 213, 217
idols in 190
on images 184, 186–7, 188, 189, 216
inwardness in 209, 217
and James I 188
and Samuel Johnson 215
on knowledge 214
and Laud 185
on the liturgy 13, 185–6, 191–3, 193–6, 197,
    216, 217–18
on the Mass 191
and marriage 199–201
on memory 198, 202, 213, 215
Michael (archangel) in 190, 202
on Michaelmas 196–7
on the Nativity. *See* Milton, John, Christmas in
Nature in 208–9
on Nero 188
on Noah 190
and occasional meditation 202–3. *See also*
    Milton, John, and Hall
on Paradise 13, 193, 201–2, 205, 207, 213–14,
    216–17
and Parliament 185, 192
on the Passion 205–6

250 INDEX

Milton, John (*Continued*)
  and Perkins 191, 199, 205, 217
  on pleasure 206
  on prayer(s)
    of Adam and Eve. *See* Milton, John, Adam
      and Eve in
    of angels 207
    of Charles I. *See* Milton, John, and Charles I
    in the Church of England 185–6, 190–1,
      201, 217
    eating as 205–6
    in Eden 13, 185, 192–6, 217
    externals in 190, 192
    God on 210–11
    repetition in 206, 207, 215. *See also* Milton,
      John, repetition in
    set prayer 13, 185, 186, 189–90, 192–3,
      201–2
    sex as. *See* Milton, John, on sex
    spontaneous prayer 193, 194, 209, 210, 217
  and puritanism 185
  Raphael (archangel) in 205–6, 213–14
  and readers 184, 195
  on repentance 210–11
  repetition in 192, 206, 207, 209, 210–15
  on rites 190, 194, 198, 215
  on the Romans 188–9
  on the sacraments 185, 217–18
  Satan in 210, 213, 214–15
  on the senses 195, 206, 207, 210–11, 218
  on sex
    between Adam and Eve 198–9, 203
    between angels 204
    and the body 204, 206
    as devotional aid 201, 203, 205
    after the Fall 201, 203–4
    as prayer 13, 198–201, 205, 217
    as repetition 215. *See also* Milton, John,
      repetition in
    as rites 203
  and Sidney 184–5
  on sincerity 211
  and Smectymnuus [pseudonym] 191, 202
  suicide in 212
  on transubstantiation 205–6
  on the tree (of knowledge) 208, 210, 213–14,
    216
  on tyranny 188–9, 213
  works:
  Animadversions 191
  antiprelatical tracts 191
  Apology for Smectymnuus 191
  divorce tracts 200
  Eikonoklastes 184–5, 186–9, 192, 208, 211
  A Maske (*Comus*) 196–7

"On the Morning of Christs Nativity" 195–6,
  197
Paradise Lost 13, 189–90
polemical tracts 13, 184–5, 186, 189, 190, 194,
  200
mistresses
  in Donne 12, 133, 134, 137
  in Greville 161, 164, 167, 173–4
Mitchell, W. J. T. 146
Montagu, Richard 125
Montaigne, Michel de 162
Montrose, Louis 18
Moorman, Frederic W. 108
More, Anne 12, 137–9, 140
Morris, Brian 98
Mortimer, Anthony 196
Moshenska, Joe 33, 74
Munday, Anthony 101

Nativity, the. *See* Christmas
Nature
  in Greville 169, 175, 179
  in Milton 208–9
  in Sidney 176, 179
Nero 188
Netzley, Ryan 25
New Historicism 18
Newton, Thomas 193
Noah 190
nonconformity 23–4, 25–6, 28. *See also*
  puritanism

occasional meditation 92, 93, 95, 97, 154, 202–3.
  See also Hall, Joseph
Oliver, P. M. 22

Pacheco, Anita 166
pages (of book) 55, 59, 75, 76, 174. *See also*
  books; reading
Paradise
  and Edenic prayer 13, 185, 192–6, 217
  in Greville 13, 163–4, 168–70, 172, 181, 183
  in Milton 13, 193, 201–2, 205, 207, 213–14,
    216–17
paralysis 2, 147 n.72, 164
Parker, T. H. L. 9
Parliament 104, 185, 192
Passion, the
  in Charles I 187
  in Donne 129–30, 132, 133–4, 144, 153–4,
    156–7
  in Herrick 99, 110–15
  in Milton 205–6
  in Shakespeare's *Sonnets* 70

INDEX 251

Paul (apostle) 5, 59, 60
performance
  in devotion 32, 40, 42
  in Herrick 86
  in medieval culture 18
  in secular theater 18
  in Shakespeare's *Sonnets* 50, 86
Perkins, William
  on access to God 157
  on Adam and Eve 173
  on *adiaphora* 39
  on assurance 152
  on the body 35
  on ceremony 41
  on the Communion 35, 42
  on damnation 9–10
  on devotional aids 166
  devotional manuals of 10, 28, 30
  and Donne 12, 124, 126, 145, 151–4, 156–7
  on election 152
  on epistemology 23
  on experientialism 4, 9–10, 11, 20, 23, 25, 30
  on grace 157
  and Greville 159, 165–6, 170–1, 173
  and Herrick 85, 86, 103, 116
  on household management 23
  on idolatry 124
  on idols 41, 124, 157
  on images 124, 156, 165–6
  on inwardness 157
  marginal status of 27, 29
  on marriage 42–3
  on memory 124
  on mental images 124, 166. *See also* Perkins,
    William, on images
  and Milton 191, 199, 205, 217
  and nonconformity 28
  popular divinity of 10, 15, 17, 21, 25
  and predestination 22, 152
  print history of 27–9, 124
  on public prayer 39–40
  and puritanism 17, 18, 27, 28, 29
  on sacraments 23
  on salvation 39–40
  on senses 10, 124, 157
  on sex 23, 42
  and Shakespeare's *Sonnets* 77
  on sign hunting 10, 20, 23
  on signs 40, 41, 42, 140, 157
  works:
    A case of conscience 152
    Christian Oeconomie 42
    A Golden Chaine 86, 124, 153
    A graine of musterd-seede 151–2

Petrarch 63
Picciotto, Joanna 209
Plato 136, 165
Platt, Peter G. 14
players. *See* actors
pleasure
  in Greville 169, 172, 179–80
  in Milton 206
  in Sidney 179–80
Poole, Kristen 20–1, 22
popular divinity
  and Calvinist experientialism 10, 13, 24, 25
  and devotional manuals. *See* devotional
    manuals
  of Hall 12, 17, 116
  of Perkins 10, 15, 21
practical divinity. *See* popular divinity
prayer(s)
  of angels 207
  and the body 26, 31
  and the *Book of Common Prayer. See Book of
    Common Prayer*
  in the Church of England 185–6, 190–1, 201,
    217
  in Donne 144
  eating as 205–6
  in Eden 13, 185, 192–6, 217
  externals in 185, 190, 192
  gestures in 26, 42, 142
  in Hall 90–1
  and individual experience 26, 37
  in Milton 13, 185–6, 189–90, 190–6, 201–2,
    205–7, 209, 210–11, 215, 217
  of Milton's Adam and Eve 13, 193, 195, 197–8,
    201–3, 206, 211
  public prayer
    epistemological value of 40
    in Perkins 39–40
  repetition in 47–8, 57, 59–61, 64, 66, 76, 206,
    207, 215
  set prayer
    in Hooker 36–7
    in Milton 13, 185, 186, 189–90, 192–3,
      201–2
  sex as 13, 91, 198–201, 205, 217
  spontaneous prayer 36, 50, 55–6, 193, 194,
    209, 210, 217
  time for 90–1, 144
  variations in methods of 26, 90–1
  in the vernacular 56, 60–1
predestination
  and anxiety 22
  in Calvinism 9–10
  in Greville 170

252   INDEX

predestination (*Continued*)
  and paranoia 22
  in Perkins 22, 152
  and sign hunting 23
  signs in 40–1
priests 59, 98–100
proof. *See also* epistemology; knowledge
  body as 32
  in Calvin 32, 41
  in Donne 132
  in Greville 163, 166, 172
Prynne, William
  Christmas in 99
  and Herrick 95–6, 99–103, 108–9, 111, 115
  and Hooker 22
  work:
    Histrio-mastix 99–103
public prayer. *See* prayer(s)
puritanism
  and Anglicanism 23–4, 25–6
  and ceremony 81–2
  definitions of 25–6
  and Donne 139, 155
  and factionalism 23, 43
  and Hall 117
  and Herrick 81–2, 87, 96, 101, 104
  and Laud 185
  marginal status of 11, 24, 27
  and Milton 185
  and nonconformity 24, 25
  and Shakespeare's *Sonnets* 49, 54
  stereotypes about 10
Puritans. *See* puritanism

Questier, Michael 24, 26

Raphael (archangel) 205–6, 213–14
readers. *See* reading
reading
  in Donne 149, 154
  in Greville 177–8
  in Herrick 115–16
  in Milton 184, 195
  of plays 115–16, 177–8
  in Shakespeare's *Sonnets* 53–4, 57, 72, 76, 77, 79
Real Presence, the
  and Calvinism experientialism 5, 14
  in Catholicism 5, 6, 14
  in the Communion 33–4
  in Cranmer 33–4
  in Hooker 33–4
  in Shakespeare's *Sonnets* 74
  in Shakespeare's *The Winter's Tale* 5, 6–7, 14

reason 209–10, 212
religious identity. *See also* Anglicanism, and
    puritanism
  challenges of categorizing 25–6, 49, 87, 149,
    186
  and Donne 125, 149–50
repentance
  in Donne 129–30, 141, 148
  in Greville 171–2
  in Milton 210–11
repetition (poetic)
  in Milton's *Paradise Lost* 192, 206, 207, 209,
    210–15
  in Shakespeare's *Sonnets* 47–8, 57, 59–61, 64,
    66, 76
Resurrection (Judgment Day) 128, 131
Reynolds, John 139
ritual
  in the Church of England 19
  in Donne 31
  in Milton 190, 194, 198, 203, 215
  in Shakespeare's *Sonnets* 47
rival poets 67, 72, 73, 80
Röder, Katrin 160
Rollin, Roger B. 112
Romans, the 188–9
rosary, the. *See* beads (of the rosary)
Rosendale, Timothy 25, 37, 40
royalism 12, 102. *See also* Charles I
Russia 28
Rust, Jennifer R. 16, 18
Ryrie, Alec 26, 49, 55, 58, 87, 142, 186

sacrament(s)
  of baptism 5, 139
  in Calvin 140
  in the Catholic tradition 15–19
  in the Church of England 24
  of Communion. *See* Communion (sacrament)
  in Donne 139–40
  in Hooker 37
  marriage as 42, 199–201
  in Milton 185, 217–18
  in the Reformed tradition 10, 39
  and Shakespeare's *Sonnets* 51
  as signs 51
salvation
  in Calvin 35
  in Donne 128–30, 144, 151
  in Hooker 37–8
  in Perkins 39–40
  signs of 10

INDEX 253

Sanchez, Michelle Chaplin 8
Satan
  in Donne 138
  in Greville 168, 170
  in Milton 210, 213, 214–15
  and the serpent 153, 168
Schalkwyk, David 63, 64
Schoenfeldt, Michael 24
Schreiner, Susan 7–8, 10, 36
Schwartz, Regina 25
Selleck, Nancy 73
senses
  and the body 18
  and confusion 1, 15
  in Donne 30, 127
  in Greville 174
  and interpretation 1–2
  in Milton 195, 206, 207, 210–11, 218
  and paralysis 2
  in Perkins 124, 157
  in Shakespeare's *Sonnets* 63
serpent, the 153, 168. *See also* Satan
set prayer (unofficial) 55, 61–2, 64, 201. *See also* prayer(s), and the *Book of Common Prayer*
sex
  between Adam and Eve 198–9, 203
  between angels 204
  and the body 204
  as devotional aid 13, 201, 203, 205
  after the Fall 201, 203–4
  in Herrick 81, 91, 105
  in Milton 13, 198–9, 201, 203–6
  in Perkins 23, 42
  as prayer 13, 91, 198–201, 205, 217
  as repetition 215
  as rites 203
Shakespeare, William
  and audiences 1
  print history of 28
  and theater 1, 51, 54, 69
  works:
  Cymbeline 14
  King Lear 57–8
  Pericles 14
  Sonnets, the
    actors in 52, 53, 107, 144
    adiaphora in 59
    amens in 59, 61, 62, 74, 78, 93
    anachronistic readings of 48, 68
    and Anglicanism 48
    and antitheatricalism 54
    audiences in 63, 68, 69, 71, 72
    blasphemy in 62, 64–5

    and the *Book of Common Prayer* 12, 48, 54, 60, 61–2, 64, 67, 68–70, 73–4
    books in 53, 55, 57
    and Caroline church 48, 68
    and Catholic tradition 65
    and ceremonialism 12
    Christ in 48, 64–5, 70, 72, 74, 78
    and the Communion 67–8, 69, 70, 73–4, 84
    and Cranmer 11, 48, 60, 73–4, 75, 80, 98
    devotional access in 51, 71
    eyes in 53–4, 57, 76, 77, 79
    gazers and lookers-on in 66–8, 69
    gestures in 47, 55, 63, 64, 66, 72
    glossolalia in 59, 60–1
    and grace 71
    and Greville 63, 161, 163
    and Herrick 115–16
    hypocrisy in 11, 48, 55, 58, 61, 62
    and Christopher Harvey 62
    and Hieron 61–2, 63
    and Hooker 48, 50, 65, 71, 78–9
    and iconoclasm 65, 75
    idolatry in 48, 64–5, 66, 101
    idols in 64, 66, 75
    images in 136
    immortality in 75–6, 79
    and insincerity. *See* hypocrisy
    and inwardness 54, 57, 71
    and Jewel 11, 60, 69
    Latin in 59
    liturgy in 54
    and the Mass 59, 68
    and memory 76
    pages (of book) in 55, 59, 75, 76. *See also* Shakespeare, William, *Sonnets*, the, books in
    and the Passion 70
    Paul in 59, 60
    performance in 50, 86
    and Perkins 77
    priests in 59
    and Puritans 49, 54
    reading in 53–4, 57, 72, 76, 77, 79
    and the Real Presence 74
    repetition in 47–8, 57, 59–61, 64, 66, 76
    ritual in 47
    rival poets in 67, 72, 73, 80
    and sacraments 51
    and the senses 63
    and set prayer 55, 64
    sincerity in 57, 63
    spontaneity in 50, 55
    and stage fright 52, 107
    and superstition 65–6

254 INDEX

Shakespeare, William (*Continued*)
  and theater 51, 54, 69, 86
  tongues (speaking in) in. *See* Shakespeare, William, *Sonnets*, the, *glossolalia* in
  tongue-tied in 56, 57, 80
  and transubstantiation 69
  and Tyndale 59, 78–9
  and vernacular language 56, 59–60
  and *The Winter's Tale* 67
  young man in 47, 53, 57, 58, 63, 64, 66, 71, 72–3, 75–7, 79
  sonnets in:
  Sonnet 15 76–7
  Sonnet 16 77
  Sonnet 23 52–4, 55, 58
  Sonnet 31 136
  Sonnet 51 79
  Sonnet 55 75–6, 77
  Sonnet 77 76
  Sonnet 81 76, 77, 79
  Sonnet 85 59, 60–1, 63–4
  Sonnet 105 64, 66
  Sonnet 108 47, 57–9
  Sonnet 125 66–7, 70, 71, 72, 73, 74, 75, 77
  The Tempest 14
  Troilus and Cressida 73
  The Winter's Tale
    and Calvinist experientialism 11, 13–14, 15
    and certitude 1–4, 8, 42
    and confusion 1–4, 15
    and Cranmer 14
    and eating 5
    and gazers and lookers-on 2, 3–4, 6, 14, 31
    and magic 5, 7, 65 n.57
    and the Real Presence 5
    and the senses 14
    and the *Sonnets* 65 n.57, 67
Shore, Daniel 192
Shuger, Debora Kuller 126
Sibbes, Richard 25, 56, 57
Sidney, Philip
  on the body 180
  God in 180
  and Greville 13, 162–4, 176–83, 184
  and Milton 184–5
  Nature in 176, 179
  pleasure in 179–80
  and Shakespeare's *Sonnets* 63
  works:
    Arcadia 178–9, 181, 184
    Astrophil and Stella 163
    Certain Sonets 179–80
    Denfense of Poesy 163, 175
Sierhuis, Freya 160, 162–3

sighs 56, 141–3, 145, 148, 149, 151–2
sign hunting 10, 20, 23, 132
signs. *See also* grace; salvation
  the body as 43
  in Calvin 32, 104
  in Calvinist predestinarianism 40–1
  ceremony as 41
  in Donne 126, 128–9, 132, 133, 139–40, 149, 150–1
  as epistemology 43
  in Hooker 38–9
  marriage as 42
  in Perkins 40, 41, 140, 157
  sacraments as 51
sin
  in Donne 141, 145, 147–8
  in Greville 168–9, 170, 171
sincerity 57, 63, 211
Smectymnuus [pseudonym] 86 n.11, 191, 202
soul, the
  in Donne 128–9, 137, 150–1
  in Greville 170
Spinks, Brian D. 51
Stachniewski, John 22–3, 166
stage fright 52, 107, 167
state church. *See* Church of England
Stewart, Susan 50
St. Paul's Cross 30, 121, 135
Strier, Richard 5, 8, 25, 126, 133
Stroup, Thomas 195
Stubbes, Philip 98, 101
Stuermann, Walter 43–4
suicide 128, 212
Summers, Joseph 197–8
superstition 65–6
Symposium, the. *See* Plato

Taaffe, James 196
Targoff, Ramie 24, 36–7, 40, 50
tears 141, 143, 145, 148, 149
Teskey, Gordon 204
theater
  and audiences 1
  and Donne 138
  and Greville 167, 177
  and Herrick 98–105, 107–16
  and secular performance 18
  and sensory confusion 1, 15
  and Shakespeare 1, 51, 54, 69, 86
Thomism. *See* Aquinas, Thomas
tongues (speaking in). *See glossolalia*
tongue-tiedness 56, 57, 80
transubstantiation 69, 205–6
tree (of knowledge) 170, 208, 210, 213–14, 216

Turner, James Grantham 205
Tyndale, William 59, 78–9
tyranny 188–9, 213

Vendler, Helen 58
vernacular language 56, 59–60

Waldron, Jennifer 18–20, 21, 22, 32–3
Walsham, Alexandra 26, 49, 87, 149, 186

Whalen, Robert 25
Wilcox, Thomas 54–5, 98–9, 101
Williamson, Elizabeth 6
Winthrop, John 143
worship
    official. *See* Church of England
    popular. *See* popular divinity

Zysk, Jay 6, 16, 18